D1871589

# ON YUAN CHWANG'S
## TRAVELS IN INDIA
## 629—645 A. D.

# ON YUAN CHWANG'S

## TRAVELS IN INDIA

629—645 A. D.

by

THOMAS WATTERS M.R.A.S.

Edited, After His Death,

by

T. W. RHYS DAVIDS, F.B.A.

and

S. W. BUSHELL, M.D.; C.M.G.

GYAN

*Published by*

GYAN

Gyan Publishing House
5, Ansari Road
Daryaganj, New Delhi-110002
Phone: 011-47034999, 9811692060
E-mail: books@gyanbooks.com

*Distribution Network*
gyanbooks.com
India, USA, Canada, UK, Australia, France

**© Publisher**

All rights reserved. No part of this work may be reproduced, stored, adapted, or transmitted in any form or by any means, electronic, mechanical, photocopying, micro-filming, recording or otherwise, or translated in any language, without the prior written permission of the copyright owner and the publisher.

ISBN : 978-81-212-2645-5 (PB)
First Published, 1904

2nd Impression 2021

*Printed at:* Gyan Press, Delhi.

The book is sold subject to the condition that it shall not, by way of trade or otherwise, be lent, resold, hired out, or otherwise circulated without the prior publisher's written consent.

**On Yuan Chwang's**
**Travels in India**
**629—645 A. D.**
Author: Thomas Watters

ORIENTAL TRANSLATION FUND
NEW SERIES.
VOL. XIV.

# ON YUAN CHWANG'S

## TRAVELS IN INDIA

629—645 A.D.

BY

THOMAS WATTERS M.R.A.S.

EDITED, AFTER HIS DEATH,
BY

T. W. RHYS DAVIDS, F.B.A.
AND
S. W. BUSHELL, M.D.; C.M.G.

LONDON
ROYAL ASIATIC SOCIETY
22 ALBEMARLE STREET
1904.

# CONTENTS.


| | | |
|---|---|---|
| PREFACE | | V |
| THOMAS WATTERS | | VIII |
| TRANSLITERATION OF THE PILGRIM'S NAME | | XI |
| CHAP. 1. | TITLE AND TEXT | 1 |
| „ 2. | THE INTRODUCTION | 22 |
| „ 3. | FROM KAO CHANG TO THE THOUSAND SPRINGS | 44 |
| „ 4. | TARAS TO KAPIS | 82 |
| „ 5. | GENERAL DESCRIPTION OF INDIA | 131 |
| „ 6. | LAMPA TO GANDHĀRA | 180 |
| „ 7. | UDYĀNA TO KASHMIR | 225 |
| „ 8. | KASHMIR TO RAJAPUR | 258 |
| „ 9. | CHEH-KA TO MATHURĀ | 286 |
| „ 10. | STHANEŚVARA TO KAPITHA | 315 |
| „ 11. | KANYĀKUBJA TO VIŚOKA | 340 |
| „ 12. | SRĀVASTI TO KUSINĀRĀ | 377 |

# PREFACE.

As will be seen from Dr. Bushell's obituary notice of Thomas Watters, republished from the *Journal of the Royal Asiatic Society* for 1901 at the end of those few words of preface, Mr. Watters left behind him a work, ready for the press, on the travels of Yüan-Chwāng in India in the 7th Century A. D. The only translation into English of the *Travels* and the *Life* of Yüan-Chwāng, the one made by the late Mr. Beal, contains many mistakes. As Mr. Watters probably knew more about Chinese Buddhist Literature than any other European scholar, and had, at the same time, a very fair knowledge both of Pali and Sanskrit, he was the very person most qualified to correct those mistakes, and to write an authoritative work on the interpretation of Yüan-Chwāng's most interesting and valuable records. The news that he had left such a work was therefore received with eager pleasure by all those interested in the history of India. And Mr. F. F. Arbuthnot, who had so generously revived our Oriental Translation Fund, was kind enough to undertake to pay for the cost of publishing the work in that series. I was asked by the Council to be the editor, and was fortunate enough to be able to receive the cooperation of Dr. S. W. Bushell C. M. G., late medical officer attached to our embassy at Peking.

We have thought it best to leave Mr. Watters's Ms. untouched, and to print the work as it stands. The reader is requested therefore never to lose sight of the fact that, as printed, it has not had the advantage of any such corrections or improvements as the author might have made, had it passed through the press under his supervision.

As a rule the author gives the Indian equivalents for the Chinese names of persons and places in their Sanskrit form. But occasionally he uses the Pali form, and there are cases where we find both Pali and Sanskrit forms used even on the same page. I gathered from many conversations with the author, that this apparent inconsistency was intentional. At the time when Yüan-Chwāng travelled in India, not only all the most famous Buddhist teachers, but all the teachers of the school of thought especially favoured by the famous pilgrim, the school of Vasubandhu, wrote in Sanskrit. But Pali was still understood; and the names of places that the pilgrim heard in conversation were heard in local dialects. In his transcription the pilgrim would naturally therefore reproduce, as a rule, the Sanskrit forms, but he knew the Pali forms of ancient names, and the local forms of modern ones. It is not therefore improper, in an English work on Yüan-Chwāng, to use occasionally the Pali or vernacular forms of Indian names.

As regards the author's method of transliterating the name of the pilgrim I annex the copy of a letter by myself in the Journal of our society. Yüan-Chwāng is the correct presentation of the present Pekinese pronunciation. What would be the correct presentation, in English letters, of the way in which the pilgrim himself pronounced it, is not known.

Full indices, by the author and ourselves, and two maps which Mr. Vincent Smith has been kind enough to undertake, will be included in the second volume, which is in the press, and which we hope to bring out in the course of next year.

With these few remarks I venture to ask for a generous and sympathetic reception of this posthumous work by an author whose untimely death was an irreparable loss to historical science, whose rare qualities of mind and the breadth of whose knowledge earned the admiration of those most qualified to judge, and whose personal qualities endeared him to all who knew him.

T. W. Rhys Davids

Nālanda, May 1904.

---

# THOMAS WATTERS,

## 1840—1901.

With very much regret for the loss of an old friend, I have to notice the death of Mr. Watters, at Ealing, on January 10th. He was a member of the Council of the Society from 1897 to 1900, and a valued contributor to the Journal. The loss of a scholar who had such a wide knowledge of the vast literature of Chinese Buddhism will be deeply felt by those interested in the subject, as was amply acknowledged by Professor Rhys Davids in a few well-chosen, appreciative words addressed to the last meeting of the Society.

He was born on the 9th of February, 1840, the eldest son of the Rev. Thomas Watters, Presbyterian Minister of Newtownards, co. Down. His father died some ten years ago, after having ministered to the same congregation for fifty-six years; his mother is still living at Newtownards. It was from his father that he inherited his great love of books, and he was educated by him at home until he entered Queen's College, Belfast, in 1857. His college career was most distinguished, and he gained many prizes and scholarships during the three years. In 1861 he graduated B.A. in the Queen's University of Ireland, with first-class honours in Logic, English Literature, and Metaphysics; and in 1862 took his M. A. degree, with first-class honours, again, in the same subjects and second-class in Classics.

In 1863 he was appointed to a post in the Consular Service of China, after a competitive examination, with an honorary certificate. He proceeded at once to Peking, and subsequently served in rotation at many responsible spots in all parts of the Chinese empire. He was Acting Consul General in Corea 1887—1888, in Canton 1891—1893, and afterwards Consul in Foochow until April, 1895, when impaired health compelled him to retire finally from the Far East, after over thirty-two years' service.

But this is hardly the place to refer to Mr. Watters's official work, or to the blue-books in which it is bound up. In his private life he was always courteous, unselfish, and unassuming, a special favourite with his friends, to whose service he would devote infinite pains, whether in small matters or grave.

His early philosophical training fitted him for the study of Oriental religions and metaphysics, which always remained his chief attraction. The character of his work may be summarized in the words of an eminent French critic, who says of Mr. Watters: "A ses moindres notices sur n'importe quoi, on sentait si bien qu'elles étaient puisées en pleine source; et sur chaque chose il disait si bien juste ce qu'il voulait et ce qu'il fallait dire."

Much of his best works is, unfortunately, buried in the columns of periodicals of the Far East, such as the *China Review* and the *Chinese Recorder*, his first published book being a reprint of articles in the *Chinese Recorder*. The list of his books is —

"Lao-tzŭ. A Study in Chinese Philosophy." Hongkong, London, 1870.
"A Guide to the Tablets in the Temple of Confucius." Shanghai, 1879.
"Essays on the Chinese Language." Shanghai, 1889.
"Stories of Everyday Life in Modern China. Told in Chinese and done into English by T. Watters." London, 1896.

In our own Journal two interesting articles were contributed by him in 1898, on "The Eighteen Lohan of Chinese Buddhist Temples" and on "Kapilavastu in the Buddhist Books."

A far more important and extensive work remains in manuscript, being a collection of critical notes on the well-known travels throughout India, in the seventh century of our era, of the celebrated Buddhist pilgrim Yüan-Chuāng (Hiouen - Thsang). In this Mr. Watters discusses and identifies all the Sanskrit names of places, etc., transliterated in the original Chinese text, and adds an elaborate index of the persons mentioned in the course of the travels. The work appears to be quite ready for publication. Should means be forthcoming, its appearance in print will be eagerly looked for by all interested in Buddhist lore and in the ancient geography of India.

Mr. Watters has given his library of Chinese books, I am informed, to his friend Mr. E. H. Fraser, C.M.G., a Sinologue of light and learning and a Member of our Society, who may be trusted, I am sure, to make good use of the valuable bequest.

S. W. Bushell.

# YÜAN CHWĀNG OR HIOUEN THSANG?

The name of the celebrated Chinese pilgrim and translator is spelt in English in the following ways (among others): —

1. M. Stanislas Julien . . . . . . . Hiouen Thsang.
2. Mr. Mayers[1]. . . . . . . . . . . . Huan Chwang.
3. Mr. Wylie . . . . . . . . . . . . . . Yuén Chwàng.
4. Mr. Beal . . . . . . . . . . . . . . . Hiuen Tsiang.
5. Prof. Legge[2]. . . . . . . . . . . . Hsüan Chwang.
6. Prof. Bunyiu Nanjio[3] . . . . . . Hhüen Kwân.

Sir Thomas Wade has been kind enough to explain this diversity in the following note :—

"The pilgrim's family name was 陳, now pronounced *ch'ên*, but more anciently *ch'in*. His 'style' (official or honorary title) appears to have been both written

玄奘 1 and 元奘 2.

In modern Pekinese these would read in my transliteration (which is that here adopted by Dr. Legge)—

1 hsüan chuang.
2 yüan chuang.

The French still write for these two characters—

1 *hiouen thsang,*
2 *youan thsang,*

following the orthography of the Romish Missionaries, Premare and others, which was the one adapted to English usage by Dr. Morrison I doubt, *pace* Dr. Edkins, that we are quite sure of the contemporary pronunciation, and should prefer, therefore, myself, to adhere to the French

[1] Readers Manual, p. 290. [2] Fa Hien, p. 83, etc. [3] Catalogue, p. 435.

Hiouen, seeing that this has received the sanctification of Julien's well-known translation of the pilgrim's travels."

It is quite clear from the above that in the Chinese pronunciation of the first part of the name there is now nothing approaching to an English H. And of course Julien never intended to represent that sound by his transliteration. Initial H being practically silent in French, his Hiouen is really equal to Iouen, that is, to what *would be expressed by Yuan* in the scientific system of transliteration now being adopted for all Oriental languages. But the vowel following the initial letter is like the German ü, or the French u, so that *Yüan* would, for Indianists, express the right pronunciation of this form of the word. It is particularly encouraging to the important cause of a generally intelligible system of transliteration to find that this is precisely the spelling adopted by Sir Thomas Wade.

This is, however, only one of two apparently equally correct Chinese forms of writing the first half of the name. The initial sound in the other form of the word is unknown in India and England. Sir Thomas Wade was kind enough to pronounce it for me; and it seems to be nearly the German ch (the palatal, not the guttural,—as in Mädchen) or the Spanish x, only more sibilant. It is really first cousin to the Y sound of the other form, being pronounced by a very similar position of the mouth and tongue. If it were represented by the symbol HS (though there is neither a simple h sound nor a simple s sound in it), then a lazy, careless, easy-going HS would tend to fade away into a Y.

The latter half of the name is quite simple for Indianists. Using c for our English ch and ŋ for our English ng (ṅ or ṁ or ṃ), it would be simply cwāŋ.

Part of the confusion has arisen from the fact that some authors have taken one, and some the other, of the two Chinese forms of the name. The first four of the transliterations given above are based on Sir Thomas Wade's No. 2, the other two on his No. 1. All, except only that of Mr. Beal, appear to be in harmony with different complete systems of representing Chinese characters in English letters, each of which is capable of defence. The French, not having the sound of our English CH, for instance, have endeavoured to reproduce it by THS. This may no longer be used even by scholars; but in Julien's time reasons could be adduced in support of it.

It appears, therefore, that the apparently quite contradictory, and in some parts unprononceable, transliterations of this name, so interesting to students of Indian history, are capable of a complete and satisfactory explanation, and that the name, or rather title, is now in Pekinese—whatever it may have been elsewhere, and in the pilgrim's time—YÜAN CHWĀNG.

T. W. RHYS DAVIDS.

# ORIENTAL TRANSLATION FUND.

## NEW SERIES.

THE following works of this series are now for sale at the rooms of the Royal Asiatic Society, 22, Albemarle Street, London, W. Price 10*s*. a volume, except vols. 9, 10.

1, 2. REHATSEK (Mr. E.) Mīr Khwānd's 'Rauẓat-us-Safā', or 'Garden of Purity', translated from Persian. Part I (Vols. I and II) containing the lives of the prophets from Adam to Jesus, and other historical matter. 1891 and 1892.

3, 4. Part II (Vols. I and II) of the above, containing a life of Muhammad. 1893.

5. Part II (Vol. III) of the above, containing the lives of Abu Baḳr, 'Umar, 'Uthmân, and 'Alī, the immediate successors of Muhammad. 1894.

6. TAWNEY (Mr. C. H.) The Kathā Koṣa, a collection of Jain stories, translated from Sanscrit. 1895.

7. RIDDING (Miss C. M.). Bāṇa's Kādambarī. 1896.

8. COWELL (Professor E. B.) and Mr. THOMAS (of Trinity College, Cambridge). Bāṇa's Harṣa Carita. 1897.

9, 10. STEINGASS (Dr. F.). The last twenty-four Maāḳmāts of Abu Muhammad al Ḳasim al Ḥarīrī, forming Vol. II; Chenery's translation of the first twenty-four Maḳāmāts sold with it as Vol. I. 1898. Price 15*s*. a volume.

11. GASTER (Dr. M.). The Chronicles of Jerahmeel, or the Hebrew Bible Historiale. A collection of Jewish legends and traditions translated from the Hebrew. 1899.

12. DAVIDS (Mrs. Rhys). A Buddhist manual of psychological ethics of the fourth century B.C., being a translation of the Dhamma Sangaṇi from the Abhidhamma Pitaka of the Buddhist Canon. 1900.

13. BEVERIDGE (Mrs. H.). Life and Memoirs of Gulbadan Begum, aunt of Akbar the Great, translated from the Persian. 1902. With illustrations.

*In preparation—*

14, 15. WATTERS (T.). On Yuan Chwang's Travels. (Vol. XIV ready. Vol. XV in the press.)

16. DAVIDS (Professor Rhys). The Kathā Vatthu.

17. ROSS (Principal E. D.). History of the Seljuks.

# ASIATIC SOCIETY MONOGRAPHS.

Arrangements have been madefor the publication of the following:

(1) GERINI (Lieut.-Col. G. E.). Researches on Ptolemy's Geography. (*In the Press.*)

(2) WINTERNITZ (Dr. M.). Catalogue of Sanskrit MSS. in the Royal Asiatic Society's Library, with an Appendix by Mr. F. W. Thomas. 8vo; pp. xvi, 340. (Price 5*s.*, or 3*s.* 6*d.* to members.)

(3) HIRSCHFELD (Dr. H.). New Researches into the Composition and Exegesis of the Qoran. 4to; pp. 155. (Price 5*s.*, or 3s. 6*d.* to members.)

(4) DAMES (M. Longworth). The Baloch Race. A Historical and Ethnological Sketch. (Price 5*s.*, or 3*s.* 6*d.* to members.)

(5) LE STRANGE (Guy). Description of Persia and Mesopotamia in the year 1340 A.D., from the Nuzhat-al-Ḳulūb of Ḥamd-Allah Mustawfi, with a summary of the contents of that work. (Price 5*s.*, or 3*s.* 6*d.* to members.)

(6) BROWNE (Professor E. G.). Chahár Maqála ("Four Discourses") of Niḏẖámí-i-'Arúḍí-i-Samarqandí. (Price 3*s.*)

(7) CODRINGTON (O.), M.D., F.S.A. A Manual of Musalman Numismatics. (Price 7*s.* 6*d.*)

The above works, so far as ready, are for sale at the Office of the Society:

22, ALBEMARLE STREET, LONDON, W.

## CHAPTER I.

### THE TITLE AND TEXT.

THE Chinese treatise known as the *Hsi-yü-chi* (or Si-yü-ki) is one of the classical Buddhist books of China, Korea, and Japan. It is preserved in the libraries attached to many of the large monasteries of these countries and it is occasionally found for sale in bookshops. The copies offered for sale are reprints of the work as it exists in some monastery, and they are generally made to the order of patrons of learning or Buddhism. These reprints are more or less inaccurate or imperfect, and one of them gives as the complete work only two of the twelve *chüan* which constitute the treatise.

The full title of the book is Ta-T'ang-Hsi-yü-chi (大唐西域記), that is, "Records of Western Lands of the Great T'ang period". By the use of the qualifying term "Great T'ang" the dynasty within which the treatise was composed is indicated and this particular work is distinguished from others bearing the same general name. In some native writings we find the treatise quoted or designated by the title *Hsi-yü-chuan* (傳) which also means "Records of Western Lands". But it does not appear that the work was ever published or circulated with this name. In its original state and as it exists at present the treatise is divided into twelve *chüan*, but we find mention of an edition brought out in the north of China in which there are only ten *chüan*.[1]

---

[1] Hsiao-yueh-tsang-chih-chin (小閱藏知津) *ch.* 4.

On the title-page of the Hsi-yü-chi it is represented as having been "translated" by Yuan-chuang and "redacted" or "compiled" by *Pien-chi* (辯機). But we are not to take the word for *translate* here in its literal sense, and all that it can be understood to convey is that the information given in the book was obtained by Yuan-chuang from foreign sources. One writer tells us that Yuan-chuang supplied the materials to Pien-chi who wrought these up into a literary treatise. Another states that Yuan-chuang communicated at intervals the facts to be recorded to Pien-chi who afterwards wove these into a connected narrative.

This Pien-chi was one of the learned Brethren appointed by T'ai Tsung to assist Yuan-chuang in the work of translating the Indian books which Yuan-chuang had brought with him. It was the special duty of Pien-chi to give literary form to the translations. He was a monk of the Hui-chang (會昌) Monastery and apparently in favour at the court of the Emperor. But he became mixed up in an intrigue with one of T'ai Tsung's daughters and we cannot imagine a man of his bad character being on very intimate terms with the pilgrim. As to the Hsi-yü-chi we may doubt whether he really had much to do with its formation, and perhaps the utmost that can be claimed for him is that he may have strung together Yuan-chuang's descriptions into a connected narrative. The literary compositions of Yuan-chuang to be found in other places seem to justify us in regarding him as fully competent to write the treatise before us without any help from others. Moreover in an old catalogue of books we find the composition of a "Ta-T'ang-Hsi-yü-chi" ascribed to Yuan-chuang and a "Hsi-yü-chi" ascribed to Pien-chi in similar terms.[1] Further in Buddhist books of the T'ang and Sung periods we frequently find a statement to the effect that Yuan-chuang *composed* the Hsi-yü-chi, the word used being that which has been here rendered for the moment "redacted" or "compiled" (撰).[2] It is possible that the text as we have it now

[1] T'ung-chih-liao, the Yi-wên-liao, *ch.* 4 (通志略 the 藝文略).

[2] K'ai-yuan-lu (No. 1485) *ch.* 8: Su-kao-sêng-chuan (No. 1493), *ch.* 4. See also Y.'s Memorial to the Emperor in *Ch.* 6 of the Life

is for at least nine out of the twelve *chüan* practically that of the treatise drawn up by Yuan-chuang and presented to his sovereign. Some of the notes and comments may have been added by Pien-chi but several are evidently by a later hand. In some of the early editions these notes seem to have been incorporated in the text and there is reason for supposing that a few passages now in the text should be printed as interpolated comments.

The Hsi-yü-chi exists in several editions which present considerable variations both in the text and in the supplementary notes and explanations. For the purposes of the present Commentary copies of four editions have been used. The first of these editions is that known to scholars as the *Han-shan* (寒山) *Hsi-yü-chi*, which was brought out at private expense. This is substantially a modern Soochow reprint of the copy in one of the collections of Buddhist books appointed and decreed for Buddhist monasteries in the time of the Ming dynasty. It agrees generally with the copy in the Japanese collection of Buddhist books in the Library of the India Office, and it or a similar Ming copy seems to be the only edition of the work hitherto known to western students. The second is the edition of which a copy is preserved in the library of a large Buddhist monastery near Foochow. This represents an older form of the work, perhaps that of the Sung collection made in A. D. 1103, and it is in all respects superior to the common Ming text. The third is an old Japanese edition which has many typographical and other errors and also presents a text differing much from other editions. It is apparently a reprint of a Sung text, and is interesting in several respects, but it seems to have many faults and it is badly printed. The fourth is the edition given in the critical reprint which was recently produced in the revised collection of Buddhist books brought out in Japan. This edition

---

on the completion of the Records which does not contain any mention or hint of assistance. Instead of the B reading 僎 the other texts have 撰 which is the correct form.

is based on the text recognized in Korea and it supplies the various readings of the Sung, Yuan, and Ming editions. Some of these variations are merely different ways of writing a character but many of them give valuable corrections for the Korean text which is often at fault.

## THE TRANSLATORS.

In 1857 M. Julien published his long promised translation of the "Ta-T'ang-Hsi-yü-chi" with the title "Mémoires sur les Contrées occidentales traduits du Sanscrit en Chinois, en l'an 648, par Hiouen-Thsang, et du Chinois en Français." This work was regarded by the learned translator as supplementary to his "Histoire de la Vie de Hiouen-Thsang et de ses voyages dans l'Inde, depuis l'an 629 jusqu'en 645" translated by him from the Chinese and published in 1853. He had already supplemented the latter treatise by an interesting series of "Documents Géographiques" on the countries of which the book makes mention. Julien's "Mémoires sur les Contrées occidentales" is a work of great merit, and it shows a wonderful knowledge of the Chinese language. Much use has been made of it by students of the history, geography, antiquities, and religions of India and Central Asia and on all these subjects it has been regarded as an authority. And although it is not wise to accept with unquestioning faith all the renderings and identifications of the translator yet it is not without diffidence that one dissents from or condemns his interpretation of a difficult phrase or passage either in the Life or the Records.

The only other translation of the "Hsi-yü-chi" into a western language is the English version by the late Rev^d^ S. Beal. This was published in 1884 with the title "Buddhist Records of the Western World, Translated from the Chinese of Hiuen Tsiang (A. D. 629)". The title is characteristic of the translator, and the reader may compare it with that given by Julien to his translation. M^r^ Beal's work is a translation partly "from the Chinese" and partly from the French. In it many of the careless mistakes which disfigure Julien's treatise are corrected and its notes supply the student with numerous references to old and recent western authorities.

Within the last few years the Preface to the Hsi-yü-chi attributed to Chang yueh, to be noticed presently, has attracted the attention of some western students of Chinese. In the "Muséon" for November 1894 there appeared an article by M. A. Gueluy entitled "A propos d'une Préface. Aperçu critique sur le Bouddhisme en Chine au 7ᵉ siècle." This article gives M. Gueluy's criticism on Julien's translation of the Preface and a new rendering by the critic. One can scarcely treat M. Gueluy's production seriously, it is so full of fancies and fictions and shows such a slight acquaintance with Buddhism and the Chinese language.

Professor Schlegel, however, took the "A propos d'une Preface" seriously and has given us a criticism of it together with a new translation of this Préface to the Hsi-yü-chi. The Professor's treatise, which shows much industry and ingenuity, is entitled „La Loi du Parallélisme en style Chinois demontrée par la Préface du Si-yü-ki." In this he defends some of Julien's translations against the criticism of M. Gueluy and shows how absurdly wrong is the latter's version. M. Schlegel brings numerous quotations from Chinese books to support his own renderings of the difficult passages in the Preface. Many of these renderings are apparently correct and an improvement on those by Julien, but in several instances the learned Professor seems to have missed the author's meaning. His criticisms on M. Gueluy's "A propos d'une Préface" drew from M. Gueluy a reply which is not convincing: it is entitled "L'Insuffisance du Parallélisme prouvée sur la Préface du Si-iu-ki contre la traduction de M. G. Schlegel."

## THE PILGRIM.

The life of Yuan-chuang is narrated at length in the book entitled "Ta T'ang Ta Tzŭ-ên-ssŭ San-tsang-fa-shih-chuan", that is "Record of the Tripiṭaka Master of the Great Compassion Monastery". It is this work of which Julien's "Histoire de la Vie de Hiouen Thsang" is an abstract, and of which Mr Beal has given us a similar abstract in English. It is also the work usually cited in the following pages by the short title "the Life". From this and a few other Chinese treatises the following short summary of the ancestry and life of the pilgrim has been compiled.

The surname of the family to which he belonged was *Ch'ên* (陳) and his personal name was *I* (禕).[1] But he seems never to have been known in history, literature, or religion, or among his contemporaries by any other name than that written 玄 (or 元) 奘 and read *Hsüan* (or *Yuan*)-*chuang* (or *ts'ang*). In modern literature the character for *Yuan* is commonly used in writing the pilgrim's name, and this is said to be due to the character for *Hsüan* entering into the personal name of the Emperor Kanghsi. But we find Yuan in the pilgrim's name before the reign of Kanghsi and we find Hsüan in it during that reign and since. This interchange of the two characters is very common and is recognized. The personal name of the Chinese envoy Wang who went to India in Yuan-chuang's time is given as *Hsüan* (and *Yuan*)-*tsê* (王玄 or 元策) and the name of another great contemporary of the pilgrim is written Fang Hsüan-ling and Fang Yuan-ling (房玄 or 元齡). The two characters at the T'ang period may have had the same sound, something like Yun, and our pilgrim's name was probably then pronounced *Yun-ts'ang*.[2] This was his *hui* (諱) or "appellation", called in the Life also his *tzŭ* (字). This word *hui* is often used to denote the *Fa-hao* or "name in religion" of a Buddhist monk, and it is sometimes replaced by *tu*(度)-*hui* or "ordination name". It commonly means simply "the name of the deceased" that is, the name given to him when capped,

---

[1] Su-kao-sêng-chuan, l. C.: Shên-sêng-chuan (No. 1620) *ch.* 6.

[2] The Japanese write the name *Hsüan-ts'ang* but call the pilgrim Gen-jo corresponding to the Chinese *Yuan-ts'ang*. In Tibetan books the name is given as T'ang Ssen-tsang or T'ang Sin (or Sang), and Ssen-ts'ang is, I think, for Hsüan-ts'ang and not for San-tsang.

and I do not know of any authority for Julien's rendering "nom d'enfance".

The family from which Yuan-chuang sprang is said to have been descended from the semi-mythical Huang-Ti through the great Emperor Shun, and to have originally borne the territorial designation of Shun, viz. *Kuei* (媯). In very early times the seat of the family was in the district now bearing the name Kuei-tê (歸德)-foo in the east of Honan, and it was afterwards removed for a time to the neighbourhood of the present Ts'ao-chou in Shantung. At the time of Wu Wang, the first king of the Chow dynasty, a man known as *Hu-kung-kuei-man* (胡公媯滿) was regarded as the lineal representative of the Shun family. This man was the son of *O-fu* (閼父) of *Yü* (虞) who had served Wu Wang as his *T'ao-chêng* (陶正), an officer variously explained as Director of Potteries and as Superintendent of Schools. The office was apparently hereditary and Wu-Wang rewarded Man by giving him his eldest daughter in marriage while at the same time he ennobled him as *How* or Marquis, and endowed him with the fief of *Ch'ên* (陳) that he might be able to continue the services of worship to his ancestor Shun. These honours made Man one of the *San-k'ê* (三恪) or "Three Reverends", that is, three who were faithfully diligent in the discharge of their public duties. The other *K'ê*s were according to some accounts the representatives of the ancient emperors Huang Ti and Yao, and according to other accounts the representatives of the founders of the Hsia and Yin dynasties.[1] Man's fief comprised the modern prefecture of Ch'ên-chow in Honan together with the adjacent territory. It existed as a separate principality down to B. C. 478 when it was extinguished. The members of the reigning family were then dispersed but they retained Ch'ên as their surname.

---

[1] T'ung-chih-liao, the Li (禮)-liao, *ch.* 3. These circumstances about Yuan-chuang's reputed ancestors are mentioned here because they are alluded to in the Preface.

We have to come down to the end of the third century B. C. before we find a Ch'ên of historical celebrity. We then meet with the famous Ch'ên P'ing (陳平) a native of Yang-wu (陽武) in the present Prefecture of K'ai-fêng (開封) of Honan. In the time of the Han dynasty this Prefecture bore the name Ch'ên-liu (陳留) and this explains why Yuan-chuang is sometimes described as a Ch'ên-liu man. His ancestor P'ing was an eccentric genius who, rising from extreme poverty to wealth and power, founded a great family and made himself immortal in history. His success in life and his posthumous fame were mainly due to his ready wit which never left him without an answer, and to his ingenuity in devising expedients in desperate circumstances. Of these expedients six were counted extraordinary and successful above the others, and hence came the saying in his time *liu-ch'u-ch'i-chi* (六出奇計) that is, "six times he brought out extraordinary plans". These were all employed on behalf of Liu Pang, the Han Kao Tsu of history. They were stratagems or expedients devised to meet special occasions, they were kept very secret and were all successful.

In the second century of our era we have another great man claimed as an ancestor of Yuan-chuang. This is Ch'ên Shih (陳寔) better known by his other name Chung-Kung (仲弓), a native of Hsü (許) a district corresponding to the present Hsü-chow-foo in Honan. At the time of the Han dynasty Hsü was in the political division called Ying-ch'uan (穎川) and hence we find Yuan-chuang often described as a Ying-ch'uan man. This man Ch'ên-Shih was called to office and served in the reign of Han Huan Ti (A. D. 147 to 167). As an official Shih was pure and upright. attentive to business and zealous for the welfare of his people. Gentle but firm and kind but strict he won the affection, confidence and esteem of the people. His fame is chiefly associated with his administration of T'ai-Ch'iu (太丘), now the Yung-ch'êng (永城) District in the Kuei-tê Prefecture of Honan. Here his personal influence was great and he made the people ashamed to do wrong. The effects of his just decisions and benevolent government spread over all the country, and people flocked to him from surrounding districts. Resigning office, however, after a few years he retired to his native place. He was happy and successful also in his family, and sons and grandsons grew up before him to virtue and honour. His family was recognized to be a cluster of *Tê-shing* (德星) Stars of virtuous merit, and Heaven took notice of the fact and visibly responded. In later life Chung-kung refused to return to office and died at home in the year A. D. 187 in the 84th year of his age.[1]

The next one that we have to notice in the line of descent is Ch'ên Ta (達) the sixth from Shih. Ta lived in the 4th century A. D. in the time of the Chin (晉) dynasty. He also was a learned man and an official of some distinction. Being appointed Magistrate of Ch'ang-ch'êng (長城) in the present Hu-chow (湖州) Foo of Chekiang he prophesied that his posterity would sit on the throne. This prediction was fulfilled in the year 556 when the tenth from Ta the illustrious Ch'ên Pa-hsien (霸先) established the Ch'ên dynasty. This branch of the family was settled in Hu-chow for more than 200 years, and it was not from it, apparently, that the immediate ancestors of our pilgrim were derived.

We now come to Yuan-chuang's great-grandfather whose name was Ch'in (欽). He was an official of the After Wei dynasty and served as Prefect of Shang-t'ang (上黨) in Shansi. The grand-father of our pilgrim, by name K'ang (康), being a man of distinguished learning in the Ch'i dynasty obtained the envied appointment of Professor in the National College at the capital. To this post were attached the revenues of the city of Chou-nan corresponding to the modern Lo-yang-hsien in Honan. The father of our pilgrim, by name Hui (慧), was a man of high character. He was a handsome tall man of stately manners, learned and intelligent, and a Confucianist of the strict

---

[1] Hou Han-shu, *ch.* 62.

old-fashioned kind. True to his principles he took office at the proper time, and still true to them he gave up office and withdrew into seclusion when anarchy supplanted order. He then retired to the village Ch'ên-pao-ku (陳堡谷) at a short distance south-east from the town of Kou-shih (緱氏). This town was in the Lo-chow, now Ho-nan, Prefecture of Honan, and not far from the site of the modern Yen-shih (偃師) Hsien. Yuan-chuang is sometimes called a Kou-shih man and it was probably in his father's home near this town that he was born in the year 600.

The family of Ch'ên Hui was apparently a large one and Yuan-chuang was the youngest of four sons. Together with his brothers he received his early education from his father, not, of course, without the help of other teachers. We find Yuan-chuang described as a rather precocious child shewing cleverness and wisdom in his very early years. He became a boy of quick wit and good memory, a lover of learning with intelligence to make a practical use of his learning. It was noted that he cared little for the sports and gaieties which had over-powering charms for other lads and that he liked to dwell much apart. As a Confucianist he learned the Classical work on Filial Piety and the other canonical treatises of the orthodox system.

But the second son of the family entered the Buddhist church and Yuan-chuang, smitten with the love of the strange religion, followed his brother to the various monasteries at which the latter sojourned. Then he resolved also to become a Buddhist monk, and proceeded to study the sacred books of the religion with all the fervour of a youthful proselyte. When he arrived at the age of twenty he was ordained, but he continued to wander about visiting various monasteries in different parts of the country. Under the guidance of the learned Doctors in Buddhism in these establishments he studied some of the great works of their religion, and soon became famous in China as a very learned and eloquent young monk. But he could not remain in China for he longed vehemently to visit the holy land of his religion, to see its far-famed shrines, and all the visible evidences of the Buddha's ministrations. He had learned, moreover, to be dissatisfied with the Chinese translations of the sacred books, and he was desirous to procure these books in their original language, and to learn the true meaning of their abstruse doctrines from orthodox pundits in India. After making enquiries and preparations he left the capital Ch'ang-an (長安), the modern Hsi-an (西安)-foo, in the year 629, and set out secretly on his long pilgrimage. The course of his wanderings and what he saw and heard and did are set forth in the Life and Records.

After sixteen year's absence Yuan-chuang returned to China and arrived at Ch'ang-an in the beginning of 645, the nineteenth year of the reign of T'ang T'ai Tsung. And never in the history of China did Buddhist monk receive such a joyous ovation as that with which our pilgrim was welcomed. The Emperor and his Court, the officials and merchants, and all the people made holiday. The streets were crowded with eager men and women who expressed their joy by gay banners and festive music. Nature, too, at least so it was fondly deemed, sympathised with her children that day and bade the pilgrim welcome. Not with thunders and lightnings did she greet him, but a solemn gladness filled the air and a happy flush was on the face of the sky. The pilgrim's old pine tree also by nods and waves whispered its glad recognition. This tree, on which Yuan-chuang patted a sad adieu when setting out, had, obedient to his request, bent its head westward and kept it so while the pilgrim travelled in that direction. But when his face was turned to the east and the homeward journey was begun the old pine true to its friend also turned and bowed with all its weight of leaves and branches towards the east.[1] This was at once the first sign of welcome and the first intimation of the pilgrim having set out on his journey home. Now he had arrived whole and well, and had become a many days' wonder. He had been

[1] Fo-tsu-t'ung-chi (No. 1661), *ch.* 29.

where no other had ever been, he had seen and heard what no other had ever seen and heard. Alone he had crossed trackless wastes tenanted only by fierce ghost-demons. Bravely he had climbed fabled mountains high beyond conjecture, rugged and barren, ever chilled by icy wind and cold with eternal snow. He had been to the edge of the world and had seen where all things end. Now he was safely back to his native land, and with so great a quantity of precious treasures. There were 657 sacred books of Buddhism, some of which were full of mystical charms able to put to flight the invisible powers of mischief. All these books were in strange Indian language and writing, and were made of trimmed leaves of palm or of birch-bark strung together in layers. Then there were lovely images of the Buddha and his saints in gold, and silver, and crystal, and sandalwood. There were also many curious pictures and, above all, 150 relics, true relics of the Buddha. All these relics were borne on twenty horses and escorted into tne city with great pomp and ceremony.

The Emperor T'ai Tsung forgave the pilgrim for going abroad without permission, made his acquaintance and became his intimate friend. He received Yuan-chuang in an inner chamber of the palace, and there listened with unwearied interest from day to day to his stories about unknown lands and the wonders Buddha and his great disciples had wrought in them. The Emperor tried to persuade Yuan-chuang that it was his duty to give up the religious life and to take office. But the heart of the pilgrim was fixed, and as soon as he could he withdrew to a monastery and addressed himself to the work of translating into Chinese his Indian books. On his petition the Emperor appointed several distinguished lay scholars and several learned monks to assist in the labour of translating, editing, and copying. In the meantime at the request of his Sovereign Yuan-chuang compiled the Records of his travels, the Hsi-yü-chi. The first draft of this work was presented to the Emperor in 646, but the book as we have it now was not actually completed until 648. It was apparently copied and circulated in Ms in its early form during the author's life and for some time after. When the Hsi-yü-chi was finished Yüan-chuang gave himself up to the task of translating, a task which was to him one of love and duty combined. In his intervals of leisure he gave advice and instruction to the young brethren and did various kinds of acts of merit, leading a life calm and peaceful but far from idle. In the year 664 on the 6th day of the second month he underwent the great change. He had known that the change was coming, and had made ready for his departure. He had no fears and no regrets: content with the work of his life and joyous in the hope of hereafter he passed hence into Paradise. There he waits with Maitreya until in the fullness of time the latter comes into this world. With him Yuan-chuang hoped to come back to a new life here and to do again the Buddha's work for the good of others.

In personal appearance Yuan-chuang, like his father, was a tall handsome man with beautiful eyes and a good complexion. He had a serious but benevolent expression and a sedate and rather stately manner. His character as revealed to us in his Life and other books is interesting and attractive. He had a rare combination of moral and intellectual qualities and traits common to Chinese set off by a strongly marked individuality. We find him tender and affectionate to his parents and brothers, clinging to them in his youth and lovingly mindful of them in his old age. He was zealous and enthusiastic, painstaking and persevering, but without any sense of humour and without any inventive genius. His capacity for work was very great and his craving for knowledge and love of learning were an absorbing passion. Too prone at times to follow authority and accept ready-made conclusions he was yet self possessed and independent. A Confucianist by inheritance and early training, far seen in native lore and possessing good abilities, he became an uncompromising Buddhist. Yet he never broke wholly with the native system which he learned from his father and early teachers. The splendours of India and the glories of its religion did not weaken or shake his love for China and his admiration for its old ways of domestic, social, and political life. When he was more than sixty years of age he wished to pay the duty of filial piety at his parents' tombs. Unable to discover these he sought out his married sister M[rs] Chang, and by her help he found them. Then, distressed at the bad state in which the tombs were at the time, he obtained leave from the Emperor to have the remains of his parents transferred to a happy ground and reinterred with honourable burial. Though the man had long ago become a devoted son of Sākyamuni he still owned a loving duty to his earthly parents.

As a Buddhist monk Yuan-chuang was very rigorous in keeping the rules of his order and strict in all the observances of his religion. But his creed was broad, his piety never became ascetic, and he was by nature tolerant. There were lengths, however, to which he could not go, and even his powerful friend the Emperor T'ai Tsung could not induce him to translate Lao-tzŭ's "Tao-Tê-Ching" into Sanskrit or recognize Lao-tzŭ as in rank above the Buddha. Modest and self-denying for himself Yuan-chuang was always zealous for the dignity of his order and bold for the honour of its founder. He was brave to a marvel, and faced without fear the unknown perils of the visible world and the unimagined terrors of unseen beings. Strong of will and resolute of purpose, confident in himself and the mission on which he was engaged, he also owned dependence on other and higher beings. He bowed in prayer and adoration to these and sued to them for help and protection in all times of despair and distress. His faith was simple and almost unquestioning, and he had an aptitude for belief which has been called credulity. But his was not that credulity which lightly believes the impossible and accepts any statement merely because it is on record and suits the convictions or prejudices of the individual. Yuan-chuang always wanted to have his own personal testimony, the witness of his own senses or at least his personal experience. It is true his faith helped his unbelief, and it was too easy to convince him where a Buddhist miracle was concerned. A hole in the ground without any natural history, a stain on a rock without any explanation apparent, any object held sacred by the old religion of the fathers, and any marvel professing to be substantiated by the narrator, was generally sufficient to drive away his doubts and bring comforting belief. But partly because our pilgrim was thus too ready to believe, though partly also for other reasons, he did not make the best use of his opportunities. He was not a good observer, a careful investigator, or a satisfactory recorder, and consequently he left very much untold which he would have done well to tell.

We must remember, however, that Yuan-chuang in his travels cared little for other things and wanted to know only Buddha and Buddhism. His perfect faith in these, his devotion to them and his enthusiasm for them were remarkable to his contemporaries, but to us they are still more extraordinary. For the Buddhism to which Yuan-chuang adhered, the system which he studied, revered, and propagated, differed very much from the religion taught by Gautama Buddha. That knew little or nothing of Yoga and powerful magical formulæ used with solemn invocations. It was not on Prajñapāramita and the abstract subtleties of a vague and fruitless philosophy, nor on dream-lands of delight beyond the tomb, nor on P'usas like Kuan-shi-yin who supplant the Buddhas, that the great founder of the religion preached and discoursed to his disciples. But Yuan-chuang apparently saw no inconsistency in believing in these while holding to the simple original system. Yet he regarded those monks who adhered entirely to the "Small Vehicle" as wrong in doctrine and practice, and he tried to convert such to his own belief wherever he met them or came into correspondence with them.

After Yuan-chuang's death great and marvellous things were said of him. His body, it was believed, did not see corruption and he appeared to some of his disciples in visions of the night. In his lifetime he had been called a "Present

Sākyamuni", and when he was gone his followers raised him to the rank of a founder of Schools or Sects in Buddhism. In one treatise we find the establishment of three of these schools ascribed to him, and in another work he is given as the founder in China of a fourth school. This last is said to have been originated in India at Nālanda by Sīlabhadra one of the great Buddhist monks there with whom Yuan-chuang studied.[1]

In some Buddhist temples we find images of our pilgrim to which a minor degree of worship is occasionally offered. These images usually represent the pilgrim seated clothed in his monk's robes and capped, with his right hand raised and holding his alms-bowl in his left.

## THE PREFACES TO THE HSI-YÜ-CHI.

There is only one Preface in the A, B, and C editions of the "Hsi-yü-chi", but the D edition gives two Prefaces. The second of these is common to all, while the first is apparently only in D and the Corean edition. This latter was apparently unknown to native editors and it was unknown to the foreign translators. This Preface is the work of Ching Po (敬播), a scholar, author, and official of the reigns of T'ang Kao Tsu and T'ai Tsung. Ching Po was well read in the history of his country and was in his lifetime an authority on subjects connected therewith. He was the chief compiler and redactor of the "Chin Shu (晉書), an important treatise which bears on its title-page the name of T'ang T'ai Tsung as author. Ching Po's name is also associated with other historical works, and notably with two which give an official account of the rise of the T'ang dynasty and of the great events which marked the early years of T'ai Tsung. It is plain from this Preface that its author was an intimate friend

---

[1] Chên-ming-mu-t'u (眞名目圖) last page: Fo-tsu-t'ung-chi, l. c. where Yuan-chuang is the founder of the Tzŭ-ên-tsung (慈恩宗) in China, and this is the Fa-hsiang (法相)-tsung of the San-kuo-fa-chuan (三國法傳) and other works: See also Mr Bunyiu Nanjio's "Short History of the Twelve Buddhist Sects" p. 33.

of Yuan-chuang whose name he does not think it necessary to mention. He seems to have known or regarded Yuan-chuang as the sole author of the "Hsi-yü-chi", writing of him thus:—"he thought it no toil to reduce to order the notes which he had written down". Ching Po must have written this Preface before 649, as in that year he was sent away from the capital to a provincial appointment and died on the way. The praises which he gives Yuan-chuang and their common master, the Emperor, are very liberal, and he knew them both well.

The second Preface, which is in all editions except the Corean, is generally represented as having been written by one Chang Yüeh (張 說). It has been translated fairly well by Julien, who has added numerous notes to explain the text and justify his renderings. He must have studied the Preface with great care and spent very many hours in his attempt to elucidate its obscurities. Yet it does not seem to have occurred to him to learn who Chang Yüeh was and when he lived.

Now the Chang Yüeh who bore the titles found at the head of the Preface above the name was born in 667 and died in 730, thus living in the reigns of Kao Tsung, Chung Tsung, Jui Tsung, and Hsüan Tsung. He is known in Chinese literature and history as a scholar, author, and official of good character and abilities. His Poems and Essays, especially the latter, have always been regarded as models of style, but they are not well known at present. In 689 Chang Yüeh became qualified for the public service, and soon afterwards he obtained an appointment at the court of the Empress Wu Hou. But he did not prove acceptable to that ambitious, cruel and vindictive sovereign, and in 703 he was sent away to the Ling-nan Tao (the modern Kuangtung). Soon afterwards, however, he was recalled and again appointed to office at the capital. He served Hsüan Huang (Ming Huang) with acceptance, rising to high position and being ennobled as Yen kuo kung (燕 國 公).

Now if, bearing in mind the facts of Chang Yüeh's

birth and career, we read with attention the Preface which bears his name we cannot fail to see that it could not have been composed by that official. Passing by other arguments, let us take the following statement in the Preface—"the reigning sovereign when heir-apparent composed the "Shu-shêng-chi" (述聖記), or Memoir on the transmission of Buddhism, in 579 words." Now the sovereign who wrote the "Shu-shêng-chi" was, as we know from the Seventh Book of the Life and other sources, Kao Tsung. That Emperor died in 683 when Chang Yüeh was only sixteen years of age and the Preface must have been written before that date. So, according to the Chinese authorities and their translators Julien and Professor G. Schlegel, it was a schoolboy who composed this wonderful Preface, this "morceau qui offre un spécimen bien caractérisé de ces éloges pompeux et vides, et présente, par conséquent les plus grandes difficultés, non-seulement à un traducteur de l'Occident, mais encore à tout lettré Chinois qui ne connaitrait que les idées et la langue de l'école de Confucius." We may pronounce this impossible as the *morceau* is evidently the work of a ripe scholar well read not only in Confucianism but also in Buddhism. Moreover the writer was apparently not only a contemporary but also a very intimate friend of Yuan-chuang. Who then was the author?

In the A and C editions and in the old texts Chang Yüeh's name does not appear on the title-page to this Preface. It is said to have been added by the editors of the Ming period when revising the Canon. Formerly there stood at the head of the Preface only the titles and rank of its author. We must now find a man who bore these titles in the Kao Tsung period, 650 to 683, and who was at the same time a scholar and author of distinction and a friend of the pilgrim. And precisely such a man we find in Yü Chih-ning (于志寧), one of the brilliant scholars and statesmen who shed a glory on the reigns of the early T'ang sovereigns. Yü was a good and faithful servant to T'ai Tsung who held him in high esteem and took his counsel even when it was not very palatable. On the death of T'ai Tsung his son and successor Kao Tsung retained Yü in favour at Court and rewarded him with well-earned honours. In 656 the Emperor appointed Yü along with some other high officials to help in the redaction of the translations which Yuan-chuang was then making from the Sanskrit books. Now about this time Yü, as we know from a letter addressed to him by Hui-li and from other sources, bore the titles which appear at the head of the Preface. He was also an Immortal of the Academy, a Wên-kuan Hsüo-shĭ (文館學士). He was one of the scholars who had been appointed to compile the "Sui Shu" or Records of the Sui dynasty and his miscellaneous writings from forty *chüan.* Yü was probably a fellow-labourer with Yuan-chuang until the year 660. At that date the concubine of many charms had become all-powerful in the palace and she was the unscrupulous foe of all who even seemed to block her progress. Among these was Yü, who, accordingly, was this year sent away into official exile and apparently never returned.

We need have little hesitation then in setting down Yü Chih-ning as the author of this Preface. It was undoubtedly written while Yuan-chuang was alive, and no one except an intimate friend of Yuan-chuang could have learned all the circumstances about him, his genealogy and his intimacy with the sovereign mentioned or alluded to in the Preface. We need not suppose that this elegant composition was designed by its author to serve as a Preface to the Hsi-yü-chi. It was probably written as an independent eulogy of Yuan-chuang setting forth his praises as a man of old family, a record-beating traveller, a zealous Buddhist monk of great learning and extraordinary abilities, and a propagator of Buddhism by translations from the Sanskrit.[1]

This Preface, according to all the translators, tells us

[1] Life, *ch.* 8: Ku-chin-i-ching-t'u-chi (No. 1487) last page: Postscript to Y.'s "Ch'êng-wei-chih-lun" (No. 1197) where Yü Chih-ning is styled as in the heading to the Preface.

that the pilgrim acting under Imperial orders translated 657 Sanskrit books, that is, all the Sanskrit books which he had brought home with him from the Western Lands. No one seems to have pointed out that this was an utterly impossible feat, and that Yuan-chuang did not attempt to do anything of the kind. The number of Sanskrit texts which he translated was seventy four, and these seventy four treatises (*pu*) made in all 1335 *chüan*. To accomplish this within seventeen years was a very great work for a delicate man with various calls on his time.[1]

The translations made by Yuan-chuang are generally represented on the title-page as having been made by Imperial order and the title-page of the Hsi-yü-chi has the same intimation. We know also from the Life that it was at the special request of the Emperor T'ai Tsung that Yuan-chuang composed the latter treatise. So we should probably understand the passage in the Preface with which we are now concerned as intended to convey the following information. The pilgrim received Imperial orders to translate the 657 Sanskrit treatises, and to make the Ta-T'ang-Hsi-yü-chi in twelve *chüan*, giving his personal observation of the strange manners and customs of remote and isolated regions, their products and social arrangements, and the places to which the Chinese Calendar and the civilising influences of China reached.[2]

Then the number 657 given here and in other places as the total of the Sanskrit treatises (*pu*) does not agree with the items detailed in the various editions of the Life and the A, B, and D texts of the Records. In the C text of the Records, however the items make up this total They are as follows:—

---

[1] See Life *ch.* 10. Julien's translation of this passage cannot be used. B. Nanjio's Catalogue p. 435. Mr Nanjio makes the total 75, but he counts the *Chin-kang-ching* twice.

[2] See Life *ch.* 6. The term here rendered "civilizing influences of China" is *shêng-chiao* (聲教). This term is often used by Buddhist writers as a synonym for "Buddhist religion".

| | |
|---|---|
| Mahāyānist sūtras | 224 pu |
| Mahāyānist śāstras | 192 „ |
| Sthavira sutras, śāstras and Vinaya | 14 „ |
| Mahāsañgika „ „ „ | 15 „ |
| Mahīśāśaka „ „ „ | 22 „ |
| Saṃmitiya „ „ „ | 15 „ |
| Kāśyapiya „ „ „ | 17 „ |
| Dharmagupta sūtras, Vinaya, śāstras | 42 „ |
| Sarvāstivādin „ „ „ | 67 „ |
| Yin-lun (Treatises on the science of Inference) | 36 „ |
| Shêng-lun (Etymological treatises) | 13 „ |
| | 657 *pu* |

## CHAPTER II.

### THE INTRODUCTION.

At the beginning of *Chüan* I of the Records we have a long passage which, following Julien, we may call the Introduction. In a note Julien tells us that "suivant les éditeurs du *Pien-i-tien*, cette Introduction a été composé par *Tschang-choue* (i. e. Chang Yue), auteur de la préface du *Si-yu-kï*". Another native writer ascribes the composition of this Introduction to Pien-chi. But a careful reading of the text shews us that it could not have been written by either of these and that it must be regarded as the work of the pilgrim himself. This Introduction may possibly be the missing Preface written by Yuan-chuang according to a native authority.

> The Introduction begins—"By going back over the measures of the [Three] *Huang* and examining from this distance of timo the records of the [Five] *Ti* we learn the beginnings of the reigns of Pao-hsi (Fu-hsi) and Hsien-Yuan (Huang Ti) by whom the people were brought under civil government and the country was marked off into natural divisions. And [we learn how] Yao of T'ang receiving astronomical knowledge (lit. "Celestial revolutions") his light spread everywhere, and how Shun of Yü being entrusted with the earthly arrangements his excellent influences extended to all the empire. From these down only the archives of recorded events have been transmitted. To hear of the virtuous in a far off past, to merely learn from word-recording historians—what are these compared with the seasonable meeting with a time of ideal government and the good fortuna living under a sovereign who reigns without ruling?"

The original of the last two sentences of this passage is rendered by Julien thus. "Depuis cette époque (i. e., the time of Yao and Shun) jusqu'à nos jours c'est en vain qu'on consulte les annales où sont consignés les événements, que l'on écoute les opinions émanées des anciens sages, que l'on interroge les historiens qui recueillaient les paroles mémorables. Il en est bien autrement lorsqu'on vit sous une dynastie vertueuse et qu'on est soumis à un prince qui pratique le *non-agir*." The text is here given, 自玆已降空傳書事之冊逖聽前修徒聞記言之史豈若時逢有道運屬無爲者歟 and it will be seen that Julien's translation is hasty and inaccurate and that it does an injustice to the author. No Chinese scholar, Buddhist or Confucianist, would ever write in this disparaging way of the books of national history including the "Springs and Autumns" of Confucius, the commentaries on that treatise, and later works. What our author here states to his reader is to this effect. In the records of the very early times we find the institution of government officials to guide and teach the people (司牧黎元), the first mapping out of the empire into natural divisions with corresponding star-clusters (疆畫分星子), the adaptation of astronomical learning to practical uses, and the first systematic reclamation of land and distribution of the country into political divisions. These great and beneficial achievments of the early sovereigns are mentioned only with the view of comparing the Emperor on the throne with these glorified remote predecessors. From the time of Yao and Shun down, according to our author, the annals of the empire contained only dry records of ordinary events.

All this is only the prelude to the generous panegyric which our author proceeds to lavish on the T'ang dynasty or rather on the sovereign reigning at the time, viz. T'ai Tsung. A rough and tentative translation of this eulogy is now given and the reader can compare it with Julien's version.

"As to our great T'ang dynasty, it assumed empire[1] in accor-

[1] The term here rendered "assumed empire" is *yü-chi* (御極) which J. translates by "gouverne". But the context seems to show

dance with Heaven, and taking advantage of the times it concentrated power to itself. [His Majesty] has made the six units of countries into one empire and this his glory fills; he is a fourth to the Three *Huang* and his light illumines the world. His subtle influence permeates widely and his auspicious example has a far-reaching stimulus. Combining Heaven's covering with Earth's containing powers he unites in himself the rousing force of wind and the refreshing action of rain. As to Eastern barbarians bringing tribute and "Western barbarians submitting themselves"[1] in founding an imperial inheritance for his posterity,[2] in bringing order out of chaos and restoring settled government,[3] he certainly surpasses former kings and sums up in himself all that previous dynasties had attained. That there is a uniformity of culture[4] over all the empire is the marvellous

---

that the term is to be taken here, as commonly, in the sense of "begin to reign", "accede to empire". Thus the phrase *shêng-t'ien-tzŭ-yü-chi-yi-lai* means "since His Majesty ascended the throne".

[1] This is a quotation from the Yü-Kung of the Shu-Ching where it is used of the western tribes submitting to the regulations of the emperor Yü. The Hsi Jung or "western barbarians" of this passage are described as Tibetan tribes living in the neighbourhood of the Koko Nor.

[2] The text is Chuang-ye-ch'ui-t'ung (創業垂統). This is a stock phrase of Chinese literature and occurs, for example, in the 17th *ch.* of the Shih-Chi as a popular quotation. It or a part of it is often used of T'ang Kao Tsu and his successor although properly it applies only to the former. One writer amplifies the meaning of the expression thus—"Kao Tsu laid the foundation (創基) and established the patrimony (定業) and T'ai Tsung enlarged and gave peace to the empire". (Ta T'ang-nei-tien-lu *ch.* 5. Bun. No. 1485).

[3] The original is *poh-luan-fan-chêng* (撥亂反正). Here the word *poh*, we are told, is to be taken in the sense of *regulate* or *reduce to order*, and *chêng* denotes *settled government.* The phrase is applied to the Ch'ün-Ch'iu of Confucius by Kung-yang at the end of his commentary on that classic. It occurs also in the Han-Shu (*ch.* 22) where the commentator explains it as meaning "to exterminate disorder and restore a right state of affairs". One of T'ai Tsung's Ministers is represented as applying the phrase to that emperor in a conversation with him, saying to His Majesty that "in bringing order out of anarchy and restoring good government (poh-luan-fan-chêng) and in raising men from mud and ashes" he had far transcended the achievments of the founders of the Chow and Han dynasties.

[4] The Chinese is *t'ung-wên-kung-kuei* (同文共軌) which means to "have the same writing and go in the same rut". There is

result of his perfect government. If I did not mention them in these Records I should not have wherewith to praise his great institutions and if I did not publish them abroad I could not shed light on his abundant merits.

In my mention of the natural characteristics of the people in any place which I visited though I did not investigate local peculiarities of custom yet I am to be believed. Beyond the Five [*Ti*] and the Three [*Huang*] (or, according to another interpretation, "In more than three-fifths of the places I traversed") all living creatures feel the genial influence [of H. M$^{s}$. reign] and every human being extols his merit. From Ch'ang-an to India the strange tribes of the sombre wastes, isolated lands and odd states, all accept the Chinese calendar and enjoy the benefits of H. M$^{s}$. fame and teaching. The praise of his great achievments in war is in everybody's mouth and the commendation of his abundant civil virtues has grown to be the highest theme.[1] Examine the public records and they have no mention of anything like this, and I am of opinion that there is no similar instance in private genealogies. Were there not the facts here set forth I could not record the beneficial influences of His Majesty. The narrative which I have now composed is based on what I saw and heard."

大唐御極則天椉時握紀一六合而光宅四三皇而照臨玄化滂流祥風遐扇同乾坤之覆載齊風雨之鼓潤與夫東夷八貢西戎即敘創業垂統撥亂反正固以跨越前王囊括先代同文共軌至治神功非載記無以贊大猷非昭宣何以光盛業玄奘輒隨遊至舉其風土雖未考方辨俗信已越五踰三含生之儔咸被凱澤能言之類莫不稱功越自天府暨諸天竺幽荒異俗絕域殊邦咸承正朔俱霑聲教&c.

This is an address well spiced with flattery in good oriental fashion. We may perhaps regard it as a sort of Dedication to the pilgrim's great friend and patron, the

---

apparently a reference to Ch. 6 of the "Chung-yung" where we read, in Legge's translation.—"Now, over the empire, carriages have all wheels of the same size: all writing is with the same characters; and for conduct there are the same rules." (Life and Teachings of Confucius p. 312.) So also of the uniformity which Ch'in Shih Huang Ti produced it was said *Ch'ê-t'ung-kuei-shu-t'ung-wên-tzŭ* (車同軌書同文字), "carriages went in the same ruts and books were in one writing" (Shih-chi *ch.* 6).

[1] The pilgrim's report of his Imperial Master's fame in India will be illustrated when we come to *chüan* 5 and 10 of the Records.

second Emperor of the T'ang dynasty. For though, as has been seen, the writer uses the term Ta T'ang, yet the context shews he had in his mind only, or chiefly, T'ai Tsung. The founder of the T'ang dynasty, it should be remembered, was neither a hero nor a man of extraordinary genius, and he came near being a prig and a hypocrite. His loyalty and honour were questioned in his lifetime, and history has given him several black marks. While sick of ambition, he was infirm of purpose, and wishing to do right he was easily swayed to do what was wrong. He had undoubted abilities, a happy knack of turning events to his advantage, and a plausible manner with friends and foes. But all his success in later life, and the fame of his reign were largely due to the son who succeeded him on the throne. This son, T'ai Tsung, meets us several times in the pilgrim's wanderings, and it will help us to understand and appreciate the passage now before us and the references to him in other parts of the work, if we recall some particulars of his life and character.

The Li family, from which the founder of the T'ang dynasty sprang, claimed to have a long and illustrious line of ancestors, many of whom had deserved well of the State. The founder himself, whose name was Yuan (李淵), was born at Ch'ang-an, and was related to the family of the reigning dynasty, the Sui. He was a hereditary nobleman with the title T'ang Kung, and he served with distinction under Sui Yang Ti (601 to 616). But that despot could not brook Yuan, who was gaining favour with army and people, and he tried to get rid of him.

At this time the two eldest sons of Li Yuan were also in the public service, and it is with the younger of these that we are now concerned. This boy, who seems to have been extraordinary from a very early stage of his life, was born in the year 597. When he was four years of age a mysterious stranger, dressed like a professional scholar, came one day to Li Yuan's house. Professing to be able to read fortunes, this stranger recognised Yuan as destined to greatness. Then taking the little child, he read fate's characters in his face, and predicted that the child would rise to power and that he would "save the age and give peace to the people"—*Chi-shih-an-min* (濟世安民). The father, perhaps finding the prophecy jump with his thoughts, and wishing to prick lagging destiny, gave to his son a name, Shih-min, which recalled the prediction.

But fate made no delay, and Li Shih-min while only a boy, on the summons of Sui Yang Ti, entered the public service as a military officer. He soon found, however, that to propagate a tottering dynasty was not his destined work. The whole country, moreover, was now in a dreadful state of violence and disorder. Hydra-headed rebellion wasted the land, and the monster who sat on the throne was hated and rejected even by his own kindred. The districts of the Empire which marched with the lands of the barbarians were the prey of these ruthless savages who again and again, swooping with harpy-flight on town and country, made life in such places impossible. But when the people fled thence into the central parts of the Empire, they found neither peace nor safety, for the line of confusion and the plummet of stones were stretched out in the land. Over all the country, life and property were at the mercy of powerful rebels and bands of marauders and murderers. The good found safety in flight or concealment, and only the lawless and violent prevailed. So Li Shih-min, like others, saw that the Decree had passed and that the collapse of the Sui dynasty was imminent. He now resolved to help those who wished to hasten that event, and joined the conspiracy which succeeded in effecting the dethronement of Yang Ti. Then Shih-min's father, Li Yuan, became Emperor in 618 to the satisfaction of most, and the Empire began to have peace again. It was Shih-min who placed his father on the throne and won the Empire for him. During all Kao Tsu's reign, also, Shih-min took a very active and prominent part in public affairs. He fought many hard battles, and won great and splendid victories, thereby extending and consolidating the newly-won Empire. For he was wise and daring in counsel and brave and skilful in battle. He was much beloved by his father who rewarded his services with many honours. Among these was the title *Ch'in* (秦) Wang, Prince of Ch'in, a title by which he is still remembered. In 626 Kao Tsu resigned, appointing Shih-min his successor. The latter, the T'ang T'ai Tsung of history, mounted the throne with apparent reluctance, but with eager delight and earnest purpose, and he reigned "with unrivalled splendour" until his death in 649.

This reign is perhaps the most celebrated in all the history of China, and T'ai Tsung is still regarded as one of her greatest and wisest rulers. From the moment he mounted the throne, he set himself to govern the people for their welfare, and began by enabling them to live in confidence and security. No ruler before ever wove so quickly and deftly into a fair web of peace and order such tangled threads of wild lawlessness. Only four years had he been in power, when over all the country the people had returned to settled lives, and the fame of his greatness and goodness had brought back hope and happiness. He crushed internal rebellion and reduced all parts of the Empire to his sway. He broke the power of the hereditary foes of China on her frontiers and made them willing and appreciative vassals. He introduced a new and improved distribution of the Empire into Provinces, each of these again divided and sub-divided to suit natural or artificial requirements. In the civil list he inaugurated great reforms, and he succeeded in calling into active service for the State some of the best men China has produced. His ministers, native historians tell us, administered the government with combined ability and honesty, such as had never been known before. In the military organisation also he made improvements, and above all he reformed the penal code and the administration of justice, tempering its severity. Learning of all kinds was fostered and promoted by him with an intelligent earnestness and a personal sympathy. He knew himself how to write and he made some permanent contributions to the native literature. In astronomy he made reforms and he tried to restore that science and astrology to their high estate, that is, as branches of practical learning. Solicitous above all things for the welfare of his people, he set them an example of plain living and frugality. His influence was immense, and his fame and character were known not only over all the Empire but also in countries far beyond its limits. He had an impulsive affectionate disposition, and his loving services to his father and mother are household stories. He was also social and genial in his intercourse with his statesmen, whose criticism he invited and whose censures he accepted.

The splendour of T'ai Tsung's great achievements, the conspicuous merits of his administration, and the charm of his sociable affable manner made the people of his time forget his faults. Even long after his death, when the story of his life came to be told, the spell was in the dull dry records, and passed over him who wrought those into history. So it came that the historian, dazed by the spell and not seeing clearly, left untold some of the Emperor's misdeeds and told others without adding their due meed of blame. For this great ruler smutched his fair record by such crimes as murder and adultery. The shooting of his brothers was excusable and even justifiable, but his other murders admit of little palliation and cannot plead necessity. Though he yielded to his good impulses, again, in releasing thousands of women who had been forced into and kept in the harem of Sui Yang Ti, yet he also yielded to his bad impulses when he took his brother's widow and afterwards that maid of fourteen, Wu Chao, into his own harem. His love of wine and women in early life, his passion for war and his love of glory and empire, which possessed him to the end, were failings of which the eyes of contemporaries dazzled by the "fierce light" could not take notice.

But when the crimes and failings of T'ai Tsung are all told, they still leave him a great man and a ruler of rare excellence. His genius gave life to all his laws and institutions, and his personal influence was felt in every department of government. Nor was it until long after his death that it was found how much the good reforms he made owed to his personal presence and action. Happy in the character he bore among contemporaries, he became still greater with their successors, and there is almost a perfect unanimity of consent to count him great and good. Indeed the native panegyrists generally write of him as above all who preceded him, except those semi-mythical sovereigns who moulded man from the brute. The Chinese youth and patriots love and praise T'ai Tsung for the great feats he achieved in battle and his hard won victories which restored the country to its old splendour and supremacy. The native student praises him for the success he had in preserving the valuable literature then extant but in danger of being lost, and for the great encouragement he gave to learning. The Buddhist praises him for the patronage he extended to his religion, and the friendly interest he took in its affairs. The Taoist praises him for his exaltation of that dim personage, a reputed ancestor of the Emperor, the fore-father of Taoism. Even the western Christian joins the chorus of praise, and to him the "virtuous T'ai Tsung" is a prince nearly perfect ("Princeps omnibus fere numeris absolutus"). It was during the reign of this sovereign, in the year 636, that Christianity was first introduced into China. The Nestorian missionaries, who brought it, were allowed to settle in peace and safety at the capital. This was the boon which called forth the gratitude of the Christian historian and enhanced in his view the merits of the heathen sovereign.

The author next proceeds to give a short summary of the Buddhistic teachings about this world and the system of which it forms a constituent. He begins—

"Now the Sahā world, the Three Thousand Great Chiliocosm, is the sphere of the spiritual influence of one Buddha. It is in the four continents (lit. "Under heavens") now illuminated by one sun and moon and within the Three Thousand Great Chiliocosm that the Buddhas, the World-honoured ones, produce their spiritual effects, *are visibly born and visibly enter Nirrvāna*, teach the way to saint and sinner."

For the words in italics the original is *hsien-shêng-hsien-mie* (現生現滅) which Julien renders "tantôt ils apparaissent, tantôt ils s'éteignent". This does not seem to express the author's meaning and is not quite correct. All the Buddhas, the writer tells us, exercise their spiritual sovereignty ("send down their transforming influence") in one or other of the four great divisions of the habitable world; in one of these each Buddha becomes incarnate as a man, teaches saints and common people, and passes into Nirvana.

Our author proceeds—

"In the ocean, resting on a gold disk, is the mountain Sumeru composed of four precious substances: along its middle the sun and moon revolve and on it the Devas sojourn."

The phrase for "revolve along its middle" is *hui-po* (回 (or 迴) 薄 (or 泊)). Here the word *po* in the first form does not seem to have any appropriate meaning, and the second form which means "to stop" or "anchor" is also unsatisfactory. From a paraphrase of the passage, however, we learn the meaning of the phrase, the words of the paraphrase being "the sun and moon revolve along its waist" (日月迴薄於其腰). The word *po* in this sense of "waisting" a hill is still used in the colloquial of some parts of China, but there does not seem to be any certain character to represent it in writing. In some books we find the word written 博 *po*, as by Fa-hsien, for example. Instead of *hui-po* in the above passage the D text has *Chao-hui* (照回), "to illuminate in revolving", a reading which agrees with statements about Sumeru in other Buddhist writings.[1]

Around the Sumeru Mountain, our author continues, are seven mountains and seven seas and the water of the seas between the mountains has the "eight virtues": outside the seven Gold

[1] In the Fo-shuo-li-shih-a-p'i-tan-lun *ch.* 1 (No. 1297) the sun and moon are described as making their revolutions at a height of 40000 Yojanas above the earth and half-way up Mount Sumeru, and a similar statement is made in the Yu-ka-shih-ti-lun *ch.* 2 (No. 1170).

Mountains is the Salt Sea. In the sea (or ocean) there are, speaking summarily, four habitable Islands, viz-*P'i-t'i-ha* Island in the east, *Chan-pu* Island in the south, *Ku-t'o-ni* in the west, and *Kou-lo* Island in the north. The influence of a Gold-wheel king extends over these four Islands, a Silver-wheel king rules over all except the north one, a Copper-wheel king rules over the South and East Islands, and an Iron-wheel king bears sway only over *Chan-pu* Island. When a "Wheel-king" is about to arise a gold, silver, copper, or iron wheel, according to the Karma of the man, appears for him in the air and gives him his title while indicating the extent of his dominion.

In the centre of Chan-pu Island (Jambudvīpa), south of the Perfume Mountain and north of the Great Snow Mountain is the *A-na-p'o-ta-to* (Anavatapta) Lake above 800 *li* in circuit. Its banks are adorned with gold, silver, lapis-lazuli, and crystal: all its sand are golden and it is pure and clear. The p'usa *Ta-ti* (Great-land) having by the force of his prayer become a dragon-king lives in the depths of the Lake and sends forth its pure cold water for Jambudvīpa. Thus from the silver east side through the Ox Mouth flows the Ganges which after going once round the Lake flows into the south-east sea: from its gold south side through the Elephant Mouth flows the *Sin-tu* (Indus) which after flowing round the Lake enters the south-west sea: from the lapis-lazuli west side through the Horse Mouth the Fo-chu (Oxus) flows passing round the Lake and then on into the north-west sea: from the crystal north side through the Lion Mouth flows the Si-to (Sītā) river which goes round the Lake and then on the north-east sea. Another theory is that the Sītā flows underground until it emerges at the *Chi-shih* ("Heaped up stones") Mountain and that it is the source of the [Yellow] River of China.

The seven mountains here represented as surrounding Sumeru are supposed to form seven concentric circles with seas separating them. These seven rows of mountains are golden, and we read in other accounts of the Buddhist cosmogony of seven circles of iron mountains surrounding the habitable world.

The names of the four great Islands of this passage are not all known as divisions of the world to orthodox Indian writers, but they are found in Buddhist treatises. Our pilgrim calls the first *chou* or Dvīpa (Island) *P'i-t'i-ha* restored as Videha. This name is properly used to designate a particular district in India corresponding to the modern Tirhut in Behar. But here it is the Pūrva-Videha, (in Pali Pubbavideho), the Eastern Continent or great Island of Buddhist cosmogony. Our pilgrim in his translation of a śāstra renders the word Videha by *Shêng-shên* (勝身) or "Superior body", and the Tibetan rendering is *Lus-hp'ags* with a similar meaning. But the old transcriptions for the name of the East Island as given in a note to our text are *Fu-p'o-t'i* (弗婆提) and *Fu-yü-ti* (弗于逮) which seem to point to an original like Pubbadik or "East Region". It is the *Fu-p'o-t'i* of this note which is given as the name in the "Fo-shuo-ch'u-chia-kung-tê-ching" translated in the 4th century A. D. (No. 776).

The second dvīpa is *Chan-pu*, Jambu, as in most other works. But the character read *Chan* should perhaps be read *Yen*, and this would agree with the other transcriptions given in the note, viz.-Yen-fou-t'i (閻浮提) and *Yen*(剡)-*fou*, the former appearing in the sūtra just quoted.

Our pilgrim in the śāstra referred to translates his *Ku-t'o-ni*, the name of the West Island, by *Niu-huo* or "Cattle goods", that is, cattle used as a medium of exchange. The name has been restored as Godhāna or Godhanya, the Gauḍana of the Lalitavistara, but Godhāni or Godāni would be nearer the transcription. Other names given by the annotator are *Ku-yi(ya)-ni* and *Kou-ka-ni*, the former of these appears in the old sūtra already quoted, and it agrees with the Pali form Apara-goyānam.

The North Island is the Kurudvīpa, the Uttara-Kuru of other writers: it is also the *Yü-tan-yueh* (*viet*) of the sūtra already quoted and of many other Buddhist texts. This *Yü-tan-viet* may perhaps represent a word like Uttamavat.[1]

The *A-na-p'o-ta-to* (Anavatapta) Lake is here, we have seen, described as being in the middle of Jambudvipa to the south of the Perfume (that is Fragrance-intoxicating or Gandhamādana) Mountain, and north of the Great

[1] See Yuan-chuang's A-pi-ta-mo-tsang-hsien-lun *ch.* 16 (Bun. No. 1266) and his A-pi-ta-mo-ku-she-lun *ch.* 11 (No. 1267): Chang-a-han-ching *ch.* 18 (No. 545). For the four Wheel-kings see Yuan-chuang's A-pi-ta-mo-shun-chêng-li-lun *ch.* 32 (No. 1265).

Snow (Himavat) Mountain. This is the situation ascribed to the Lake in certain śāstras, but in the Chang-a-han-ching and some other authorities it is on the summit of the Great Snow Mountain. In a note to our text we are told that the Chinese translation of the name is *Wu-jê-nao* (無 熱 惱) or "Without heat-trouble". This is the rendering used by Yuan-chuang in his translations and it is the term commonly employed by Chinese writers and translators, but the word Anavatapta means simply "unheated". It is said to have been the name of the Dragon-king of the Lake and to have been given to him because he was exempt from the fiery heat, the violent storms, and the fear of the garuḍas which plagued other dragons.[1] Our pilgrim's statement that the Ganges, Indus, Oxus, and Sitā (or Śitā) all have their origin in this Lake is found in several Buddhist scriptures: one of these as translated by Yuan-chuang used the very words of our passage,[2] but in two of them there are differences as to the directions in which the rivers proceed.[3] Nāgasena speaks of the water of this Lake, which he calls *Anotatta daha*, as flowing into the Ganges.[4] In the early Chinese versions of Buddhist works the name is given, as in the note to our text, A-nu-ta (阿 耨 達) which evidently represents the Pali form Anotatta. Then the pilgrim mentions a supposition that the Sitā had a subterranean course for a distance and that where it emerged, at the *Chi-shih* (積 石) "Accumulated-rocks" Mountain, it was the source of the Yellow River. The *Chi-shih-shan* of this theory is the Chi-shih of the Yü-kung chapter of the Shu-Ching. This Chi-shih was the place at which, according to some, the Yellow River had its source and it was a district in what is now the western part of Kansuh Province. But the term Chi-shih is also used in the sense of "mountain" as a synonym of *shan*.

---

1 Chang-a-han-ching l. c.

2 Abhi-ta-vib. *ch.* 5 (No. 1263). See also Nos. 1266, 1267 l. c.

3 Chang-a-han-ching l. c.: Hsin-ti-kuan-ching *ch.* 4 (No. 955): Abhi. vib-lun *ch.* 2 (No. 1264).

4 Milindapañho ed. Trenckner p. 286.

It has been stated by some western writers that our pilgrim confuses the Anavatapta Lake with the Sarikul of the Pamirs, but this is not correct. Some other Chinese writers seem to make this mistake but Yuan-chuang does not. Then the Anavatapta Lake has been identified with the Manasarowar Lake of Tibet, but this cannot be accepted. We must regard the "Unheated" Lake as a thing of fairy-land, as in the Earthly Paradise or Garden of Eden. It is expressly stated that the Lake could be reached only by those who had supernatural powers, the faculty of transporting themselves at will by magic.[1] The Buddha and his arhats visited it on several occasions passing through the air from India to it in the twinkling of an eye or the raising of an arm, and down to the time of Asoka great Buddhist saints came to lodge on its banks.[2] Here was that wonderful incense the burning of which yielded a wide-spreading perfume which released all the world from the consequences of sin.[3] Here too was a goodly palace, and all about were strange trees and flowers through which breathed fragrant airs and birds with plaintive songs made harmony.[4]

I have not discovered the source from which the pilgrim obtained his information that the dragon-king of the Anavatapta Lake was the *Ta-ti* or "Great-land" p'usa. As the words of the text show, this p'usa was not the Buddha in one of his preparatory births, but a p'usa still living as the Nāga-rāja of the Lake. In the D text instead of *Ta-ti* we have *Pa-Ti* or "Eight-lands". This reading seems to point to some Mahāyānist p'usa who had attained to *eight-lands*, that is eight of the ten stages to perfection.

The pilgrim next goes on to tell of the Four Lords (or Sovereigns) who divide Jambudvīpa when no one has the fate to be universal sovereign over that Island, and of the lands and peoples over which these Lords rule. In the south is the Ele-

---

1 Nos. 1266, 1267 l. c.

2 Divyāv. p. 399.

3 Hua-yen-ching *ch.* 67 (No. 88).

4 Chang-a-han-ching l. c.

phant-Lord whose territory has a hot moist climate with people energetic, devoted to study and addicted to magical arts, wearing garments which cross the body and leave the right shoulder bare: their hair is made into a topknot in the middle and hangs down on the sides: they associate in towns and live in houses of several storeys. In the west is the Lord of Precious Substances who rules over the sea abounding in pearls, whose subjects are rude and covetous, wear short coats fastened to the left, cut their hair short and have long mustachios; they live in towns also and are traders. The Horse-Lord rules in the north: his country is very cold, yielding horses, and with inhabitants of a wild fierce nature who commit murder without remorse, they live in felt tents and are migratory herdsmen. In the East (that is, in China) is the Man-Lord, who has a well-peopled territory with a genial climate where all good manners and social virtues prevail, and the people are attached to the soil. Of these four territories it is only the East country that holds the south direction in respect, the other three regions making the east their quarter of reverence. The East country (China) excels the other regions in its political organization. The system of religion which teaches purification of the heart and release from the bonds [of folly] and which instructs how to escape from birth and death flourishes in the country of the Elephant-Lord (India).

All these matters are set forth in authoritative writings (lit.- canonical treatises and official declarations) and are learned from local hearsay. From a wide study of the modern and the old and a minute examination of what is seen and heard we learn that Buddha arose in the west region and his religion spread to the east country (China), and that in the translation [from Sanskrit into Chinese] words have been wrongly used and idioms misapplied. By a misuse of words the meaning is lost and by wrong phrases the doctrine is perverted. Hence it is said— "What is necessary is to have correct terms" and to set value on the absence of faulty expressions.

Now mankind differ in the quality of their natural dispositions and in their speech, the difference being partly due to local climatic circumstances and partly caused by continued use. As to varieties of physical scenery and natural products in the country of the Man-Lord (China), and as to the differences in the customs and dispositions of its people, these are all described in our national records. The peoples of the Horse-Lord and the districts of the Lord of Precious Substances are detailed in our historical teachings, and a general account of them can be given. But as to the country of the Elephant-Lord (India) our ancient literature is without a description of it. We have the statement (made by Chang-Ch'ien) that "the land has much heat and moisture", and this other "the people are fond of benevolence and compassion"; such mention may occur in topographies but we cannot have thorough information. Whether caused by the alternate flourishing and depression of good government, or as the natural result of secular changes, the fact is that with reference to those who, knowing the due season for giving in allegiance and enjoying the benefits of [Chinese] civilisation, came to the Emperor's Court, who passing danger after danger sought admittance at the *Yü-mên* [Pass], and bearing tribute of native rarities bowed before the Palace Gate, we cannot relate their experiences. For this reason as I travelled far in quest of truth (that is, the Buddhist religion) in the intervals of my studies I kept notes of natural characteristics.

Julien in his translation of this passage gives the Sanskrit equivalents for Horse-Lord, Elephant-Lord, and Man-Lord; and tells us that a word meaning "Parasol-Lord" is found in a certain authority instead of the Precious-substances-Lord of our text. Throughout the passage, however, the pilgrim seems to be writing as a Chinese Buddhist scholar not drawing from Indian sources but from his own knowledge and experience. His information was acquired partly from Chinese books, and he perhaps learned something from the Brethren in Kashmir and other places outside of India. To him as a Chinese the people of China were *men* (*jen*), all outlying countries being peopled by *Man* and *Yi* and *Hu* and *Jung*, although as a good Buddhist he admitted the extension of the term *jen* to the inhabitants of other lands.

Our author, in writing the paragraph of this passage about Buddhism, evidently had in his memory certain observations which are to be found in the 88th Chapter of the "Hou Han Shu". These observations with the notes appended give us some help in finding out the meaning of several of the expressions in the text. For his statement here about the faults of previous translators the author has been blamed by native critics. These maintain that the transcriptions of Indian words given by Yuan-chuang's predecessors are not necessarily wrong merely because they differ from those given by him. The foreign sounds, they say, which the previous translators heard may not have been those which our pilgrim heard, and, moreover, Chinese characters under the influence of time and place, may have changed both meaning and pronunciation. As to mistakes of interpretation, there are doubtless many to be found in the early translations, but in this matter Yuan-chuang also is far from perfect.

In the next paragraph Julien apparently understood his author to state that there existed documents in their own countries on the peoples of the Horse Lord (i. e., the northern tribes) and those of the Lord of Precious substances (i. e., the nations to the south-west of China). But the writer has in his mind here only Chinese literature. So also his *fang-chih* (方志) are not "des descriptions locales" of India. They are the *books of travel* or *topographies* of Chinese literature. The term is applied to such treatises as the "Hsi-yü-chi" which in fact is called a *fang-chih*. Our author states that Chinese topographies have little about India, and that consequently he had no native authorities to quote or refer to. Other writers of the same period make similar complaints; and there was some reason for the complaint. Even the information communicated by the pilgrims who had preceded Yuan-chuang had not been incorporated in the national histories.

The word here rendered by "good government" is *tao* (道) which Julien translated "la droite voie". We might also render it by "the Buddhist religion", an interpretation which seems to be favoured by other passages on this subject. But the terms applied to the word here, viz. *hsing tsang* (行藏), seem to require that we should render it by some such Confucian expression as "true principles" or "good government". In the last sentences of this passage Julien seems to have misunderstood his author whom he makes write about "peoples" and "all the nations". There is nothing in the text which corresponds to or requires these expressions, and the writer evidently still refers to Indian countries, the envoys from which to China had been few and little known. In the Later Ḥan period there was one, in the reign of Ho Ti (A. D. 89 to 105);

during the Liu Sung period there were two, one in 428 and one in 466; and there were none, apparently, after this last date down to the Sui period. Now of the travels of these envoys the Chinese records had not preserved any particulars; and the references to India and the neighbouring countries in the histories of the Han and other dynasties down to the T'ang period are very meagre. It was because the records were thus imperfect, and information was unobtainable, that the pilgrim took notes of the topography and ethnology of the districts which he visited in the course of his pilgrimage.

The author next proceeds to make a few summary observations the text of which is here reproduced for the purpose of comparison. 黑嶺已來莫非胡俗雖戎人同貫而族類群分畫界封疆. In Julien's rendering the beginning of the passage runs thus—"A partir des montagnes noires, on ne rencontre que des mœurs sauvages. Quoique les peuples barbares aient été réunis ensemble, cependant leurs différentes races ont été tracées avec soin." But this does not seem to give the author's meaning which is rather something like this—

> "From the Black Range on this side (i. e. to China) all the people are Hu: and though Jungs are counted with these, yet the hordes and clans are distinct, and the boundaries of territories are defined."

Now if we turn to the last section of *Chuan* I we learn what is meant by the "Black Range". We find that the frontier country on the route to India was Kapisa, which was surrounded on all sides by lofty mountains. One great range bounded it on the east, west, and south sides, separating it from "North India". This was called the Hei Ling, or Black Range, a name which translates the native term Siah-kōh, though it is also used to render another native term, Kara Tagh, with the same meaning. From China to the mountains of Kapisa along the pilgrim's route the inhabitants, he tells us, were all Hu. These Hu are described by some writers as the descendants of early Jung settlers. But Yuan-chuang, who uses Hu as a collective designation for all the settled nations and tribes through which he passed on his way to and from India, seems to consider the Jung as a race distinct from the Hu proper. Other writers also make this distinction, regarding the Jung as of the Tibetan stock and the Hu as of Turkic kindred. But the distinction is not generally observed, and we can only say that the Hu include the Jung, who were not supposed, however, to be found beyond the Ts'ung Ling westward. In early Chinese history, e. g. in the Yü kung of the "Shu Ching" we find Jung occupying the country about the Koko Nor. They were then pastoral tribes, rearing cattle and wearing clothing prepared from the skins of their animals. Afterwards they spread to Hami and to Turfan and the Ts'ung Ling, becoming mainly agricultural peoples.

Instead of *Jung* (戎) in the text here the C text has Shu (戍) which the editors explain as *soldier*, the *Shu jên* being the Chinese troops stationed in the Hu Countries. But this reading, which does not seem to be a good one, was perhaps originally due to a copyist's error.

> The pilgrim's description proceeds—"For the most part [these tribes] are settled peoples with walled cities, practising agriculture and rearing cattle. They prize the possession of property and slight humanity and public duty (lit. benevolence and righteousness). Their marriages are without ceremonies and there are no distinctions as to social position: the wife's word prevails and the husband has a subordinate position. They burn their corpses and have no fixed period of mourning. *They flay (?) the face and cut off the ears: they clip their hair short and rend their garments. They slaughter the domestic animals and offer sacrifice to the manes of their dead.* They wear white clothing on occasions of good luck and black clothing on unlucky occasions. This is a general summary of the manners and customs common to the tribes, but each state has its own political organization which will be described separately, and the manners and customs of India will be told in the subsequent Records."

This brief and terse account of the social characteristics common to the tribes and districts between China and India presents some rather puzzling difficulties. It is too summary, and is apparently to a large extent secondhand information obtained from rather superficial observers, not derived from the author's personal experience, and it does not quite agree with the accounts given by previous writers and travellers. Thus the pilgrim states that the tribes in question had no fixed period of mourning, that is, for deceased parents, but we learn that the people of Yenk'i observed a mourning of seven days for their parents. Nor was it the universal custom to burn the dead; for the T'ufan people, for example, buried their dead.[1]

All the part of the passage which I have put in italics is taken by Julien to refer to the mourning customs of the tribes, and this seems to be the natural and proper interpretation. But it is beset with difficulties. The original for "they flay the face and cut off the ears" is rendered by Julien—"Ils se font des incisions sur la figure et se mutilent les oreilles." The word for "flay" or "make cuts in" is in the D text *li* (釐) which does not seem to give any sense, and in the other texts it is *li* (剺) which is an unknown character but is explained as meaning to "flay". Julien evidently regarded the latter character as identical with *li* (剺) which is the word used in the T'ang-Shu.[2] This last character means originally to *inscribe* or *delineate* and also to *blacken* and to *flay*. As an act of filial mourning for a dead parent the T'ufan people, we are told, blackened (*tai* 黛) their faces, and among some tribes it apparently was the custom to tear or gash the face at the funeral of a parent or chief. But to flay or brand the face and to cut off an ear were acts of punishment which were perhaps common to all the tribes in question.

Then "to cut the hair short" was an act of filial mourning in T'ufan, but in the first foreign countries which the pilgrim reached it was the universal custom for the men, and it was done, we learn elsewhere, to set off the head.[3] In Khoten, however, the hair was cut off and the face disfigured as acts

---

1 Wei-Shu *ch.* 102: T'ang-shu *ch.* 216: Ma T. l. *ch.* 334.

2 *Ch.* 217.

3 Wei-Shu l. C.

of mourning at a funeral.[1] We find it recorded moreover that when the death of T'ang T'ai Tsung was announced, the barbarians sojourning at the capital expressed their sorrow by wailing, cutting off their hair, gashing? (*li* 剺) their faces, and cutting their ears, until the blood washed the ground.[2]

Then as to the phrase "rend their garments", the words *lie-ch'ang* (裂裳) would seem to be susceptible of no other interpretation, and the pilgrim tells us afterwards that the people of India "rent their garments and tore out their hair" as expressions of mourning. The rending of the garments, however, was not a custom common to the tribes between India and China, and it could not have been practised by them generally on account of the material which was in general use for their clothing. Some native scholars explain the words *lie-ch'ang* here as meaning "they wear clothes without folds and seams", that is, their garments are strips or single pieces. Something like this was the style of the outer articles of a Chinaman's dress in the T'ang period and it was probably adopted by some of the foreign tribes to which Chinese influence reached. We still see survivals of it on the streets in Korea.

As to the slaughter of domestic animals, this was practised at funerals by the T'ufan people but not by all the other tribes. The Turks, who also gashed their faces in mourning, slew sheep and horses in front of the tent in which the body of a deceased parent was placed pending the completion of arrangements for burial. It is to be noted, however, that the T'ufan people and the Turks are not said to have slain their domestic animals in sacrifice to the *manes* of their deceased parents.[3] These animals were killed, we are expressly told in the case of the T'ufan people, that they might be at the service of the departed one, as the human beings who were slain, or killed themselves, on the death

---

[1] Ka-lan-chi *ch.* 5.

[2] T'ung-chien-kang-mu *ch.* 40.

[3] See Ma T. l. *ch.* 334, 343.

of a relative or chief went to serve the deceased in the other world. Julien makes our pilgrim here state that the tribes slew their domestic animals to make offerings to their dead. This is perhaps more than is in the text which is simply that they "slaughter their domestic animals, and offer sacrifice to the *manes*".

# CHAPTER III.

## FROM KAO-CH'ANG TO THE THOUSAND SPRINGS.

### A-K'I-NI (YENK'I).

The narrative in the Records now begins with this account,

> Going from what was formerly the land of *Kao-ch'ang* we begin with the country nearest to it and called *A-k'i-ni*: this is above 600 *li* from east to west and 400 *li* from north to south, its capital being six or seven *li* in circuit.

In the Life we have a detailed account of the unpleasant and adventurous journey from the Chinese capital to the chief city of Kao-ch'ang. This city, we know, was in the district which is now called Turfan and it is said to be represented by the modern *Huo-chow* (火 州) otherwise Karakhojo. At the time of our pilgrim's visit Kao-ch'ang was a thriving kingdom, and its king, though a vassal of China, was a powerful despot feared by the surrounding states. This king, whose name was *Kü-wên-tai* (麴 文 泰) or as it is also given, *Kü-ka* (嘉), had received Yuan-chuang on his arrival with great ceremony and kindness, had tried entreaty and flattery and even force to retain him, and had at last sent the pilgrim on his way with great honour, giving him presents and provisions and also letters of introduction to other sovereigns. Then why does Yuan-chuang here write of Kao-ch'ang as a state which had ceased to exist? The explanation is to be found in the great change which that kingdom had experienced between the years 630 and 646. We learn from history that in the year A. D. 639 the Chinese emperor T'ai Tsung sent an army to invade Kao-ch'ang and punish its ruler, who had dared to defy the imperial power. This ruler was the Kü-wên-t'ai who had been Yuan-chuang's host. He thought himself safe from Chinese invasion and boasted and swaggered at the threat of a Chinese army coming into his country until the invading force was actually within his borders. When he learned, however, that the hostile army was fast approaching his capital, he became so utterly possessed by abject fear that he became helpless. And his death soon followed. Hereupon his wise son and successor at once submitted to the Chinese general who, however, "extinguished Kaoch'ang"; whereupon T'ai Tsung made its territory a Prefecture of the Empire. This procedure called forth a generous protest from one of the Emperor's wise and faithful ministers, but the remonstrance was in vain and in 640 Kaoch'ang became the Chinese *Hsi-chow* (西州). Thus Yuan-chuang, writing under imperial orders and for the Emperor's reading, must needs take notice of the great political change which had taken place in the Kaoch'ang country since the date of his visit. The change proved bad for China and the new state of affairs did not last very long. For the present, however, our author has to describe the "Western Lands", that is, the countries which were outside of the western border of the Chinese empire. Up to 640 Kaoch'ang was one of these countries, but from that year the empire reached on the east to the ocean, and on the west to the kingdom which was the first to the west of Kaoch'ang, viz. the *A-k'i-ni* of this narrative.

There cannot be any doubt that the country which Yuan-chuang here calls *A-k'i-ni* (阿耆尼) was, as has been stated by others, that which is known in Chinese history as *Yenk'i* (焉耆). This state rose to power in the Han period, and from that time down to the T'ang dynasty it bore in Chinese treatises this name Yenk'i which is still its classical and literary designation in Chinese literature.

Then why did Yuan-chuang use the name A-k'i-ni, a name for which he seems to be the sole authority?

The explanation is simple. There was, we learn from an "interpolated comment" to the text, an old name for this country which is given as *Wu-k'i* (烏 or 隝耆). This seems to have been the name used by the translators of the sacred books and by Buddhist writers generally. Thus in the translation of the "Ta-pao-chi-ching" by Fa-hu of the Western Ch'in dynasty we find mention of Wuk'i along with Khoten and other countries. So also Tao-hsüan in his "Su-kao-sêng-chuan" mentions Wuk'i as the country between Kutzŭ (Kuchih) and Kaoch'ang. In the Fang-chih also we find the name given as Wuk'i, and Fa-hsien's *Wu-i* (傷夷) is apparently the country under consideration. The first character, *wu*, in each of these varieties of the name was probably pronounced *a* or *o*, and the second character represented a sound like *k'i* or *gi*, the whole giving us a name like *akhi* or *agi*. Thus we have at Yuan-chuang's time three different designations for this country:—the *Yenk'i* of Chinese historians, the *Wuk'i* of the Buddhist writers, and Y.'s own name for it, *A-k'i-ni*. The explanation of this variety is instructive, as the theory which underlies it applies to several other districts. In Yenk'i we have the local or Hu name. This apparently was (or was understood to be) Yanghi, a Turkish word for *fire*, the full name being perhaps something like Yanghi-shaher or "Fire-city". Now in all the Hu countries the Buddhist monks, we are told, used among themselves the language of India. In this language the correct Sanskrit name for *fire* is *agni*, the *a-k'i-ni* of our author. We find the three characters of the text used by Yuan-chuang in a translation of a sacred book to transcribe *agni* as the Sanskrit name for *fire*, and by Guṇabhadra in one of his translations to transcribe this word in the proper name Agnidatta.[1] But the monks of the Hu

---

[1] A-pi-t'a-mo-ta-p'i-p'o-sha-lun, *ch.* 15 (Bun. No. 1263): Tsa-a-han-ching, *ch.* 25 (No. 544).

countries did not all come from "Central India" and they did not talk Sanskrit. They spoke and wrote dialectic varieties with vernacular forms of Indian words, and they often used words which were foreign but were made to assume a Sanskrit garb. So the Brethren of the country with which we are now concerned had apparently used the Pali form Agi instead of Agni, and this had been used by others, but Yuan-chuang being a purist preferred to write the Sanskrit form.

In the periods of the Yuan and Ming dynasties the city and district called Yenk'i, still retaining this name, were grouped with four others in the political aggregate called Bish-balik or Pentapolis. Hence we sometimes find it stated that Yenk'i is Bishbalik, but this latter name is more frequently applied to Urumtsi.[1] At the present time the city called Kara- (or Khara-)shahr is generally taken to be the representative of the ancient capital of Yenk'i. But the site of the latter was apparently somewhat to the west of the modern Kharashahr at a place which has several ancient ruins. This modern city is said to have received its name from the grimy appearance of its walls and houses, Karashahr in Turkic meaning "Black city", an etymology which is confirmed by Dr. Sven Hedin's account.[2]

Like many other states in this part of Asia Yen-k'i has had many ups and downs, passing several times from power and preeminence to subjection and vassalage. One of these

---

[1] Li-tai-yen-ko-piao (歷代沿革表) *ch.* 3: Med. Res. Vol. II, p. 229. But the name Bishbalik seems to have been applied to *six* cities regarded as forming a political unit.

[2] Dr. Sven Hedin writes—"Kara-shahr (the Black Town) fully deserves its name: for it is without comparison the dirtiest zown in all Central Asia. It stands on the left bank of the river (the Hädick- or Khaidik-gol), on a level, barren plain, totally destitute of any feature of interest. Nevertheless it is a large town, very much larger than Korla, consisting of a countless number of miserable hovels, courtyards, bazaars, and Mongol tents, surrounded by a wall, and is the chief commercial emporium in that part of Chinese Turkestan." 'Through Asia', p. 859.

vicissitudes was experienced by it in A. D. 643—644, when the Chinese emperor T'ai Tsung sent an army which invaded the country, conquered it, and made its king a prisoner for a time. A similar disaster befell it in A. D. 648, when its king was beheaded by the Turkish invader.[1] The country under the official designation *Kharashahr* (喀喇沙爾) is now a military station, and an important Sub-Prefecture of the Chinese empire.

It is remarkable that neither in the Records, nor in the Life of our pilgrim, nor in the itinerary of Wu-k'ung, is the distance of Yen-k'i from Kao-ch'ang given, but we learn from other sources that it was 900 *li*.[2] In another account of the country the capital is described as being 30 *li* in circuit which is a much larger area than that given in our text, but another account makes it to be only two *li* square. The name of the capital also is given as *Nan-ho-ch'êng* (南河城) and also as *Yun-k'ü* (員渠) which is perhaps only another form of Yen-k'i.[3] The city was situated 70 *li* south of the White Mountain and a few *li* from a lake.[4] This lake, which is described as having salt and fish and as abounding in reeds, has many names. It is sometimes simply the "sea" or Dengir, and it is the Bostang, or Barashahr, or Bagrash Lake. The description in our text, proceeding, states that

> [the country] on four sides adjoins hills, with roads hazardous and easily defended. The various streams join in zones, and their water is led in for the cultivated land. The soil grows millet, spring wheat, scented jujubes, grapes, pears, and prunes. The climate is genial and the people have honest ways. Their writing is taken from that of India with slight modifications. Their garments are of fine and coarse woollen stuffs. The men cut their hair short and do not wear any head-dress. They use gold silver and small copper coins. Their king is a native of the country, who is brave, but without practical ability and conceited. The country

---

1 T'ung-chien-kang-mu *ch.* 40 (18th year of T'ang T'ai Tsung by the Chinese, and 22d year by the Turks): Ma T. l. *ch.* 336.

2 Ma T. l. l. c.: T ung-chih-liao, the 邑 畧 *ch.* 1.

3 Ch'ien Han shu *ch.* 96: Wei shu *ch.* 102.

4 Wei Shu l. c.: Ma T. l. l. c.: Ch'ien Han shu l. c.

is without a political constitution, and its laws are not reduced to order.

The first sentence of this passage is not very clear as to whether the description is meant for the whole country or only for the district of the capital. Our pilgrim seems to have drawn his information partly from the source which supplied the author of the "Hou Han-Shu".[1] In that work, and in Ma Tuan-lin's treatise which follows it, it is the Yenk'i country which is described as being surrounded by hills or mountains. But there were apparently no mountains on the east side of Yenk'i, and the Life tells only of two cities which the pilgrim passed on his way from the capital of Kao-ch'ang, without any mention of a mountain. That the roads were dangerous and easily guarded is also stated in the Hou Han-Shu almost in the words used in our text, and this also seems to indicate that it is the country which is described. But the expression "on four sides adjoins (or abuts on) hills" (四面據山) is apparently more appropriate to a city than to a country. Then we have the statement that "the various streams join in zones" that is, unite to form belts or lines of water. For this the original is "ch'üan (in the B text *chung-liu-chiao-tai* (泉 in B 衆流交帶), and Julien translates „une multitude des courants qui viennent se joindre ensemble, l'entourent comme une ceinture." The term *chiao-tai* seems to have in some places the meaning here given to it by Julien, but it commonly means to *join in forming a continuous line.* Thus it is used of a series of tanks formed or connected by a river and of tears uniting to form streams on the cheeks. This sense of "joining and carrying on" the stream seems to suit our passage, and the circumstances of the district. In Yenk'i the becks of the mountains joined in forming the various rivers by which the country was watered. Thus the Khaidu, the principal river, was formed by the junction of a large number of tributary streams from the Northern or White mountain.

---

[1] *Ch.* 88.

In the passage of the Han-Shu already referred to we find the statement that the "water of the sea (that is the Bostang Lake to the south-east of the capital) was deflected into the four mountains and flowed all about the capital (其城) for above thirty li", a statement which is repeated by Ma Tuan-lin. And although the kingdom contained several (according to one account, ten) other towns, it was doubtless of the capital and the surrounding districts that the words of our text were written. The water from the various rivers was led in channels from the lines of current to irrigate the land devoted to the cultivation of crops and fruit-trees. This artificial irrigation mentioned by our pilgrim is not noticed in the Han-Shu, but it was known to the author of the "Shui-ching-chu" (水經注), and it is referred to in recent works such as the Travels of Timkowski.[1]

In the list of products here given the term translated "millet" is *mi-shu* (糜黍) which Julien renders "millet rouge", the same rendering being given for the one character *mi* in the next page. Instead of this character the D text has in both places the word *mei* (or *meh* 穈) the name of a kind of millet "with reddish culms". The texts may be corrupt and Yuan-chuang may have written *mei* (穈) which, we learn from the "Yü-pien" was a synonym for *Chi* (禾祭) a kind of panicled millet much cultivated in the north and northwest of China. By "spring wheat" (宿麥) is meant the wheat which is sown in autumn and ripens in the following spring. This spends the winter in the ground; and in this way it passes from one year into the next, and hence its distinctive name.

The sentence 'Their writing is taken from that of India with slight modifications: their garments are of fine and coarse woollen stuffs' is in the original *wên-tzŭ-chü-tsê-yin-tu-wei-yu-tsêng-chüan-fu-shih-tieh-ho* (文字取則印度微有增損服飾氎褐) in the A, B, and C texts. The D

[1] Hsin-chiang *ch.* 3: Timkowski's Travels Vol. I, pp. 398, 410. The artificial irrigation is mentioned in the T'ang Shu *ch.* 221.

text has differences and it reads—'The writing is modeled after that of India. There is little of silk stuffs, the dress is of felt and serge.' Here we have *tsêng-chüan* (繒絹) "silk stuffs" instead of the other *tsêng-chüan* meaning "addings to and takings from" or "modifications", and we have *chan* (氈) "felt" or "coarse woollen stuff" instead of the *tieh* of the other texts. All the texts, we see, agree in the statement that the writing of this country was taken from that of India, and the Wei-Shu makes the same statement. If we are to take the author as adding that slight changes had been made in the Indian writing in Yenk'i the information may be regarded as correct.

So also if the D text is genuine and we are to substitute for "there are slight modifications" the words "there are few silks" we have a statement which is confirmed by other accounts. The people of Yenk'i had the silkworms, but they did not know how to make silk, and the only silk-stuffs they used were imported. So they did not wear silk, and their dress was of woollen material. Julien translates the four words *fu-shih-tieh-ho* by "Les vêtements sont faits de coton ou de laine". But the reading should probably be *chan* as in the D text. This reading of *chan* instead of *tieh* is supported by the epithet "Wearers of felt and serge" which the Chinese applied to the Hu and Jung in contrast to themselves as "silk-wearers". Then we have also the testimony of I-ching that the inhabitants of the countries with which we are concerned used mainly felt and fur as clothing, and that they had little cotton cloth (少有刧貝). But even if we take *tieh* to be the reading in the passage before us, it is at least doubtful whether it should be translated here by *cotton*. The word did come to be used as a name for cotton; and Yuan-chuang seems to employ it, in other passages, to denote something like fine cotton or muslin. In the T'ang-Shu we find *pai-tieh* described as the name of a plant of Kao-ch'ang from the flowers of which a cloth was made, and in this treatise *tieh* is cotton. But on the other hand the word is explained in old glossaries and dictionaries as denoting a "cloth made of

D*

hair (or wool)", and the formation of the character seems to point to such material. Then we find such expressions as *pai-chan-tieh*, "white felt-cloth", and *tieh* alone, mentioned along with the *kieh-pei* or Kibat (Karpura) "cotton-cloth" as different materials. Moreover the modern equivalent for *tieh* in Chinese books about the Mongols, Tibetans, and peoples of Turkestan is *p'u-lu*, which is the name of a woollen fabric manufactured in the "west countries".[1] There is great confusion in the use of *chan* and *tieh* (not only in these Records, and the Life, but also in many other works,) and we have often to make the Context decide whether the author meant *cotton* or *woollen*.

The king of Yenk'i whose character is briefly described in the passage before us was *Lung-T'uk'ichi* (龍突騎支) of which Lung was the surname and T'uk'ichi (Dughitsi?) the name. This prince secretly renounced his duty and allegiance to China, and entered into an engagement with the West Turks to harass China. So the emperor T'ai Tsung in 643 sent an army to invade Yenk'i and punish its perfidious ruler. The latter was dethroned and taken prisoner in 644, but in the course of a few years the Chinese found it necessary to restore him to the throne.[2]

For the words—'The country is without a political constitution, its laws are not reduced to order' the text is *Kuo-wu-kang-chi-fa-pu-chêng-su* (國無綱紀法不整肅) Julien translates this—"Ce royaume ne possède point de code, l'ordre et la paix se maintiennent sans le secours des lois." The latter clause of this sentence does not seem to be possible as a rendering of the Chinese. Moreover in the term *Kang-chi* are included not merely a code, but also the ethical and political maxims which form the basis of the political system, and give the state enactments their sanction. Then *Kang-chi* comes to denote the general principles or essentials of goverment, and the particular rules or institutions of a State or Empire. Thence the

---

[1] Nan-hai-ch'i-kuei *ch.* 2: Yü-pien s. v. *Tieh*: Sung Shih *ch.* 489.

[2] T'ung-chien-kang-mu l. c.

term was extended to the constitution and laws of any system political or religious, and Yuan-chuang, for example, uses it with reference to Buddhism. As to Yenk'i, the author states, it had no fundamental statutes or national political regulations, and it was also without any system of definite laws in force among the people. This is a reproach which we find brought against the Country also in the Wei-Shu which writes of it as "without a political system and laws (無綱紀法令)".[1]

The pilgrim's description proceeds—

> "There are above ten Buddhist monasteries with above 2000 ecclesiastics of all degrees, all adherents of the Sarvāstivādin school of the "Small Vehicle" system. Since as to the sūtra teachings and vinaya regulations they follow India, it is in its literature that students of these subjects study them thoroughly. They are very strict in the observance of the rules of their order but in food they mix (take in a miscellaneous way) the three pure [kinds of flesh] embarrassed by the 'gradual teaching.'

One of the large monasteries in this country was that known as the Araṇya-vihāra: here Dharmagupta lodged in the year A. D. 585 when on his way to China. The Sarvāstivādin school to which the Brethren in Yenk'i belonged was a branch from the ancient Sthavira school It had its name from its *assertion* that *all were real*, viz. past, present, future, and intermediate states. Its adherents claimed to represent the original teaching of the Master, as it was delivered, and as settled in Council by the "Elders" (Sthaviras) who had heard it from his lips. So they considered themselves strictly orthodox, and they were zealous enthusiastic adherents of what they regarded as the simple primitive religion. The Brethren in Yenk'i followed the teachings of the Buddha as recorded in the Indian scriptures. of which they were diligent students.

---

[1] The *kang* of *kang-chi* is originally the large thick rope of a fisherman's casting-net and the *chi* are the small cords of the same. Then *kang-chi* (or *chi-kang*) came to be applied to the established controlling principles of government, the codified means of preserving order in a state. From this use the term came to be extended to social institutions and to systems of religion and philosophy.

The next part of this paragraph has received bad treatment at the hands of the translators. Julien's version of it is—"Les religieux s'acquittent de leurs devoirs et observent les règles de la discipline avec un pureté sévère et un zèle persévérant. Ils se nourrissent de trois sortes d'aliments purs, et s'attachent à la doctrine graduelle." The words of the original are Chie-hsing-lü-i-chie-ch'ing-chin-li-jan-shih-tsa-san-ching-chih-yü-chien-chiao-i (戒行律儀潔清勤勵然食雜三淨滯于漸教矣). It is not easy to conjecture why *chie-hsing* should be here rendered "s'acquittent de leurs devoirs". The term is part of the clause which tells us that the Brethren were careful observers of the Vinaya commands to do and abstain from doing. Then the translation leaves out the important words *jan* meaning "but" and *tsa* meaning "to mix", and it renders *chih-yü*, "to stick in" or "be detained in" by "s'attachent surtout à". Then Julien did not know what was meant by the "trois sortes d'aliments purs", so he gives us in a note an account of certain five "aliments purs" derived from another treatise. What the pilgrim tells us here is plain and simple. The Buddhist Brethren in the monasteries of Yenk'i were pure and strict in keeping all the laws and regulations of their order according to their own Vinaya. But in food they took, along with what was orthodox, the three kinds of pure flesh, being still held in the "gradual teaching". The student will be helped in understanding this passage if he turns to the account of the next country, Kuchih, and to the pilgrim's experience in that country as set forth in the Life, and to the account of the Swan Monastery in *Chuan* IX of the Records (Julien III. p. 60) and *Chuan* III of the Life (*ib.* I. p. 162).

The explanation of the *san-ching* or "three pure kinds of flesh" is briefly as follows. In the time of Buddha there was in Vaiśāli a wealthy general named Sīha who was a convert to Buddhism. He became a liberal supporter of the Brethren and kept them constantly supplied with good flesh food. When it was noised abroad that the bhikshus were in the habit of eating such food specially provided for them the Tirthikas made the practice a matter of angry reproach. Then the abstemious ascetic Brethren, learning this, reported the circumstances to the Master, who thereupon called the Brethren together. When they were assembled, he announced to them the law that they were not to eat the flesh of any animal which they had seen put to death for them, or about which they had been told that it had been killed for them, or about which they had reason to suspect that it had been slain for them. But he permitted to the Brethren as "pure" (that is, lawful) food the flesh of animals the slaughter of which had not been seen by the bhikshus, not heard of by them, and not suspected by them to have been on their account.[1] In the Pali and Ssŭ-fên Vinaya it was after a breakfast given by Sīha to the Buddha and some of the Brethren, for which the carcase of a large ox was procured, that the Nirgranthas reviled the bhikshus and Buddha instituted this new rule declaring fish and flesh "pure" in the three conditions.[2] The animal food now permitted to the bhikshus came to be known as the "three pures" or "three pure kinds of flesh", and it was tersely described as "unseen, unheard, unsuspected", or as the Chinese translations sometimes have it "not seen not heard not suspected to be on my account (不見不聞不疑爲我)". Then two more kinds of animal food were declared lawful for the Brethren, viz. the flesh of animals which had died a natural death, and that of animals which had been killed by a bird of prey or other savage creature. So there came to be five classes or descriptions of flesh which the professed Buddhist was at liberty to use as food.[3] Then the "unseen, unheard, unsuspected" came to be treated as one class, and this together with the "natural death (自死)" and

---

[1] Shih-sung-lu *ch.* 26 (No. 1115): Sêng-ki-lü *ch.* 32 (No. 1119).

[2] Vin. Mah. V. 31: Ssŭ-fên-lü *ch.* 42 (No. 1117).

[3] Shou-lêng-yen-ching-hui-chie *ch.* 12 (Nos. 446 and 1624): Lung-shu-ching-t'u-wên (龍舒淨土文) *ch.* 9. The number of kinds of "pure flesh" was afterwards increased to nine, these five being included.

"bird killed (鳥殘)" made a *san-ching*. It is evidently in this latter sense that the term is used in these Records.

Then we have the "gradual teaching" which to Yuan-chuang's mind was intimately connected with the heresy of sanctioning flesh-food. Here we have a reference to an old division of the Buddha's personal teachings into "gradual (or progressive)", *chien* (漸) and "instantaneous", *tun* (頓).[1] Of these the former, according to the Mahāyānists, contained all those scriptures which gave the Buddha's early teaching, and also the rules and regulations which formed the Vinaya. The Buddha suited his sermons and precepts to the moral and spiritual attainments and requirements of his audience. Those who were low in the scale he led on gradually by the setting forth of simple truths, by parable and lesson, and by mild restrictions as to life and conduct. At a later period of his ministry he taught higher truths, and inculcated a stricter purity and more thorough self-denial. Thus in the matter of flesh-food he sanctioned the use of it as an ordinary article of food by his own example and implied permission. Afterwards when he found that some of his disciples gave offence by begging for beef and mutton, and asking to have animals killed for them, and eating as daily food flesh which should only be taken in exceptional circumstances he introduced restrictions and prohibitions. But the "Instantaneous Teaching", which took no note of circumstances and environments, revealed sublime spiritual truths to be comprehended and accepted at once by higher minds, taught for these a morality absolute and universal, and instituted rules for his professed disciples to be of eternal, unchanging obligation.

The "Gradual Teaching" is practically coextensive with the Hīnayāna system, and the Buddha describes his teaching and Vinaya as *gradual*, growing and developing like the mango fruit according to some

---

[1] Hua-yen-yi-shêng-chiao-yi-fên-chi-chang (No. 1591): Ssŭ-chiao-yi (No. 1569). In the Chung-a-han-ching (No. 542) *ch.* 9 Buddha's dharma and vinaya are described as *gradual.*

scriptures. The "Instantaneous Teaching" is the Mahāyāna system as found in those scriptures of the Buddhists which are outside of the Hīnayānist Tripiṭaka. This distinction, derived from a passage in the Laṇkāvatāra sūtra, is ascribed to Dharmapāla (*Hu-fa* 護法). The Nirvāṇa sūtras are quoted as specimens of the Gradual Teaching and the Avatamsaka sūtras are given as examples of the *Tun-chiao* or "Instantaneous Teaching".

Our pilgrim being an adherent of the Mahāyānist system refused to admit the validity of the "three-fold pure" flesh-food indulgence which the excellent Hinayānist Brethren of Yenk'i followed. The Buddhist Scriptures to which Yuan-chuang adhered prohibit absolutely the use of flesh of any kind as food by the "sons of Buddha".[1] This prohibition is based on the grounds of universal compassion, and the doctrine of karma. Mahāyānism teaches that the eating of an animal's flesh retards the spiritual growth of the Brother who eats it, and entails evil consequences in future existences. Some Mahāyānists were strict in abstaining, not only from all kinds of flesh food, but also from milk and its products. In this they agreed, as we shall see, with the sectarians who were followers of Devadatta. There have also, however, been Mahāyānists who allowed the use of animal food of certain kinds, and we find wild geese, calves, and deer called *san-ching-shih* or "Three pure (lawful) articles of food". It was a common occurrence for a Hīnayānist to be converted and "advance" to Mahāyānism, but the Yenk'i Brethren were still *detained* or *embarrassed* in the "Gradual Teaching" of the Hīnayāna. The word for *detained* is *chih* (滯) which means to be fretted, or delayed, as a stream by an obstacle in its course.. Then it denotes the mental suspense caused by doubts and difficulties, and the check given by these to spiritual progress; it is often associated with the word for *doubt*.

---

[1] Fan-wang-ching *ch.* 2 (No. 1087): Ta-pan-nie-p'an-ching *ch.* 4 (No. 114): Ju-lêng-ka-ching *ch.* 8 (No. 176): Shou-lêng-yen-ching-hui-chie, l. c.

## KUCHIH.

The pilgrim now goes on to tell us that from Yenk'i he went south-west above 200 *li*, crossed a hill and two large rivers west to a plain, and after travelling above 700 *li* from that he came to the *Ku-chih* country. This country was above 1000 *li* from east to west and 600 *li* from north to south: its capital being 17 or 18 *li* in circuit.

According to the account in the Life the pilgrim passed only one large river in the journey from Yenk'i to Kuchih. In other works the distance between these two places is somewhat greater, and the area of the capital of Kuchih is much less than in our text.

The Chinese annotator here tells us that the old name of Ku-chih (屈支) was *Ku-tse* (龜茲), as we are told to pronounce these characters. This is not only the old name but also the only one by which the country was known to the Chinese until a comparatively modern time.[1] A Sanskrit-Chinese Vocabulary gives Kuchina (俱支曩) as its Sanskrit designation; but the word does not seem to be otherwise known. There are various transcriptions of the sound Ku-tse, but Wu-k'ung tells us that Ku-chih is the correct form of the name.[2] The modern Chinese official name of the district and its capital is *K'u-ch'ê* (庫車), the Kuchah and Kocha of our maps. This term is explained as meaning the "Dry well of K'u", but the etymology cannot be accepted.[3] In modern Tibetan books the name is given as Khu-chhu or Khu-the. This country was known to the Chinese from the early Han time, and in

---

[1] An old variety of the name is *K'ucha* (苦叉). As Goez calls the country *Cucia* the modern official name was apparently in use before the Manchu conquest of China (See Yule's Cathay p. 573). Ku-tsang (姑藏), which is sometimes identified with Kutse, was the name of an old district in what is now the Province of Kansu.

[2] The first syllable is found written also 丘 邱, and 屈, and the second syllable is sometimes 慈. See Shih-li-ching, and J. A. T. VI. p. 363 and note.

[3] Hsin-chiang *ch.* 3. Here it is stated that the country got its name from the "dry wells" in it.

A. D. 435 it became a vassal to China.[1] The old Kutse embraced, not only the district now called K'u-ch'ê, but also that of the present Sairam and other territory. It was an ancient state, and its extent varied at different periods. In a translation of a Buddhist book we find it mentioned as one of the parts of his great empire which Asoka proposed to give over to his son Kunāla.[2] The capital of Kutse was at one time (in the 1th cent. A. D.) the Yen (延) city, and afterwards it was *Yi-lo-lu* (伊羅盧).[3] In the Yuan period it was a constituent part of the Bishbalik territory, and it was also called *I-li-pa-li* or Il-balik.[4] We find it described as being 200 or 170 *li* south of the Ak-tagh or White Mountains which emitted fire and smoke and yielded sal-ammoniac.[5]

> This country, the pilgrim continues, yielded millet, wheat, rice, grapes, pomegranates, and plenty of pears, plums, peaches, and apricots. It produced also gold, copper, iron, lead, and tin: its climate was temperate and the people had honest ways: their writing was taken from that of India but had been much altered; they had great skill with wind- and stringed-musical instruments; they dressed in variegated woollen cloth, cut their hair short, wore turbans, used coins of gold and silver and small copper ones, and they flattened the heads of their babies. Their king was a Kuchih man, he had few intellectual resources, and was under the sway of powerful statesmen.

The word here rendered "millet" is the *mi* (糜) of the previous section. But instead of this character the C text has *ma* (麻), "hemp", and the D text has *mei* as before. The word *hsing* (杏) here rendered by "apricots" is translated "almonds" by Julien although in his "Documents Geographiques" he has given the correct rendering "abricots". The skill of the Kuchih people in music is mentioned by

---

1 T'ung-chien-kang-mu *ch.* 25 (Sung Wên Huang Ti Yuan-chia 12th year.

2 A-yü-wang-hsi-huai-mu-yin-yuan-ching (No. 1367).

3 Ch'ien Han Shu *ch.* 96: Wei-Shu *ch.* 102: Ma T. l. *ch.* 336. It was in the T'ang period that the capital was *Yi-lo-lu.*

4 Li-tai-yen-ko-piao, l. c.: T'ung-chien-kang-mu. *ch.* 25.

5 Sui Shu *ch.* 83: Ta-ch'ing-yi-t'ung-chih *ch.* 351: See also Timkowski's Voyage Vol. I. p. 398.

other writers, and their music and musical instruments became well known to the Chinese. So also the woollen cloths and good rugs of this country were known to the Chinese before the time of our pilgrim, as were also its iron and copper products. We learn also that its king had a golden throne, and wore a magnificent turban with a long streamer hanging down behind. The reigning sovereign at the time of Yuan-chuang's visit had the surname Pai (白) and was a lineal descendant of the man whom Lü kuang (呂光) had put on the throne more than 200 years before Yuan-chuang's time. This king showed his want of political wisdom in renouncing Chinese suzerainty in favour of an alliance with the Turks, who in A. D. 648 invaded his country and took him prisoner.[1]

The pilgrim's description proceeds to relate that there were in this country more than 100 Buddhist monasteries with above 5000 Brethren who were adherents of the Sarvāstivādin branch of the "Little Vehicle" and studied the books of their religion in the language of India. These Brethren also were held in the "gradual teaching", and took along with other food the "three pure" kinds of flesh, but they were extremely punctilous in observing the rules of their code of discipline.

As we learn from other sources the people of this country were good Buddhists, and the number of Buddhist images and buildings throughout the land was very great.[2] Our pilgrim passed more than one monastery in it on his way to the capital, and he spent his first night there with the Kao-ch'ang Brethren in their monastery. That the lay people, or at least the king, kept the vows of lay disciples we may infer from the Life's account of the king's breakfast to the pilgrim. It is specially mentioned that among the food served at this entertainment were the "three pure" kinds of meat; Yuan-chuang partook of the rest of the food but declined these, explaining that although they were allowed by the "gradual teaching" they were for-

---

[1] Wei Shu, l. c.: Sui shu l. C.: T'ung-chien-kang-mu *ch.* 40.

[2] Fang-chih *ch.* 1: Chin (晉) Shu *ch.* 97: Tarikh-i-Rashid by Elias and Ross p. 124, note.

bidden by the "Great Vehicle" of which he was an adherent. The Brethren, who were all Hīnayānists, gave the pilgrim in their several monasteries as light refreshment grape-syrup which was a strictly orthodox beverage for all. Ku-chih had long been converted to Buddhism but it had not always been Hīnayānist as we read of one of its former kings being a devoted Mahāyānist.

The pilgrim's description proceeds to relate that in the eastern part of Kuchih was a large Dragon-Tank in front of a Deva-Temple to the north of a city. The dragons of this tank changed themselves into horses, and then coupled with mares: the offspring of this union was a fierce intractable breed, but the next generation formed fine horses patient of harness, and of these there were very many. Local tradition told of a king in recent times named Gold-Flower who by his regal ordinances and judicial impartiality moved the dragons to become his vehicles, and when he wanted to die he touched the dragon's ears with a whip, whereupon he sank out of sight with them to the present time. There were no wells in the city and the people drew water from the Tank: the dragons now changed themselves into men and had intercourse with the women: the offspring of this union became daring and fleet as horses, and all the inhabitants gradually came to have a mixture of the dragon in them; trusting to their might they made themselves feared, and came to slight the king's commands, whereupon the king brought in the Turks who slew all the living creatures in the city, and this was now a jungle without human inhabitants.

This interpretation of the story about king Gold-Flower differs from the translation of the passage given by Julien which does not seem to be correct. It reads—"Le roi montrait, dans ses lois, une rare pénétration. Il sut toucher les dragons et les atteler à son char. Quand il voulait se rendre invisible, il frappait leurs oreilles avec son fouet et disparaissait subitement. Depuis cette époque, jusqu'à ce jour, la ville ne possède point de puits, de sorte que les habitants vont prendre dans le lac l'eau dont ils ont besoin." By a comparison of this with the original[1] we

[1] The original of the passage quoted from Julien is:—政教明察感龍馭乘王欲終沒鞭觸其耳因卽潛隱以至于今城中無井取汲池水.

see that Julien did not notice that it was the secret influence of the king's wise and impartial government which moved the dragons to become his vehicles, and *Kan-lung-yü-shêng* cannot be made to mean "Il sut toucher les dragons et les atteler à son char." Then "se rendre invisible" is not right for *chung-mê* which means "to die"; the word *yin*, "hereupon" is omitted, and the words *yi-chi-yü-chin*, "down to the present" are divorced from their proper connection. This version also makes the author state that the inhabitants still "vont prendre" water and yet a few lines after we learn that the city was utterly uninhabited.

Our narrative proceeds to relate that above forty *li* north of the depopulated city at the slopes of the hills, and separated by a river, were two monasteries which bore the common name *Chao-hu-li* distinguished respectively as Eastern and Western. The images of the Buddha in these monasteries were beautiful almost beyond human skill; and the Brethren were punctilious in discipline and devoted enthusiasts. In the Buddha-Hall of the East *Chao-hu-li* monastery was a slab of Jade-stone above two feet wide, of a pale yellow colour, and like a clam, and on it was an impress of Buddha's foot; this was one foot eight inches long by above eight (in the D text, six) inches wide, and on fast days it sent forth a brilliant light.

The *Chao-hu-li* (昭 or 照 怙 釐) of this passage is apparently a foreign, perhaps an Indian word, but we have no hint as to its meaning. In other works we read of a great *Chio-li* Buddhist monastery in this[1] country, but we also find *Chio-li* Buddhist buildings in other places. This *Chio-li* is perhaps another form of the word transcribed *Chao-hu-li*, although I-ching tells us it is Chinese.[2] As a Chinese term transcribed 雀 離 *Chio-li* would mean "small birds such as sparrows and finches", but it is also written *Chio-li* (亅 梨) and this seems to be a foreign word. Our pilgrim's *Chao-hu-li* and the *Chio-li* of other writers may perhaps represent the Indian word *Chūri* which denotes a small bird like the sparrow. But the tope at the place where the brahmin carrying a sparrow

---

[1] Shui-ching-chu: Kao-sêng-chuan *ch.* 2 (No. 1490).

[2] Shih-li-ching and J. A. T. VI. p. 363.

interrogated the Buddha is the only one of the Buddhist buildings called *Chio-li* to which this interpretation can be applied with any probability. Another suggestion is that *Chio-li* and *Chao-hu-li* may be the foreign term represented by the common transcription *Chu-li* (侏離) which means *motley* or *particoloured*, of mixed bright and dark colours. This interpretation would evidently suit some, and perhaps would apply to all, of the buildings to which the terms in question are applied.

Outside of the west gate of the capital, the narrative relates, were two standing images of the Buddha, above ninety feet high, one on each side of the highway. These images marked the place where the great quinquennial Buddhist assemblies were held, and at which the annual autumn religious meetings of clergy and laity occurred. The latter meetings lasted for some tens of days, and were attended by ecclesiastics from all parts of the country. While these convocations were sitting the king and all his subjects made holiday, abstaining from work, keeping fast, and hearing religious discourses. All the monasteries made processions with their images of Buddha, adorning these with pearls and silk embroideries. The images were borne on vehicles, and beginning with a thousand, they became a great multitude at the place of meeting. North-west from this place of assembly and on the other side of a river was the *A-shê-li-yi* (阿奢理貳 or 兒) Monastery. This had spacious halls and artistic images of the Buddha: its Brethren were grave seniors of long perseverance in seeking for moral perfection and of great learning and intellectual abilities: the monastery was a place of resort for men of eminence from distant lands who were hospitably entertained by the king and officials and people. The pilgrim then gives the curious legend about the origin of the monastery.

We know from the Life that our pilgrim's account of the Buddhist procession of images here was derived from his own experience as he reached the country in time to witness one of these processions. The native annotator explains the *A-shê-li-yi* here by "marvellous" and it is evidently a transcription of the Sanskrit word *āścharya*, meaning a *marvel* or *miracle*.[1] According to the legend

[1] The character here read *yi* is 貳 and Julien transliterates it *ni*, but the old and correct sound of the character is *yi*, and in the Life

related by the pilgrim the monastery was erected by a king to commemorate the miracle which was wrought on his pure and noble-minded brother. One of its chief monks at this time, we learn from the Life, was the Brother known in religion by the name Mokshagupta, a Hīnayānist who had studied above twenty years in India, and had acquired a great reputation in Kuchih, especially for his knowledge of the commentaries and etymology. When Yuan-chuang arrived Mokshagupta treated him merely with the ordinary courtesy due to any guest, but when the pilgrim exposed the ignorance of his host the latter came to treat him as his master in religion. This monastery is mentioned in Wu-k'ung's itinerary by the name *A-shê-li-yi.* It is also perhaps the Wang-Ssŭ or Royal Vihāra of other writers, and we find Dharmagupta lodged in the Royal Vihāra about A. D. 585 while he stayed in this country. The Miracle Monastery, Yuan-chuang tells us, drew learned Brethren from distant places to it, and it seems that these men came chiefly to study the Vinaya. One of these great students was Vimalāksha, popularly known as the "Dark-eyed Vinaya-Master", a contemporary of Kumārajīva.[2]

## Poh-lu-ka.

Our pilgrim continuing his narrative tells us that

> from this (viz. Kuchih city) a journey of above 600 li west across a small desert brought him to the *Poh-lu-ka* country. This was above 600 *li* from east to west by more than 300 *li* from north to south, and its capital was five or six *li* in circuit. In general characteristics this country and its people resembled Kuchih and its people, but the spoken language differed a little. The fine cloth and serge of the district were esteemed by the neighbouring countries. There were some some tens of monasteries with above 1000 Brethren all adherents of the Sarvāstivādin school.

A Chinese note to our text tells us that old names for *Poh-lu-ka* were *Ki-mê* and *Ku-mê* in some

---

we have instead of this character another also read *yi*, viz. 兒. Wu-k'ung's transcription of the name is 阿遮哩貳.

1 Su-kao-sêng-chuan *ch.* 2 (No. 1493).

2 K'ai-yuan-lu *ch.* 3 (No. 1485).

copies 姑 by mistake). This Ku-mê is found in the Han-Shu and is subsequent histories as the name of a state to the west of Kuchih. It had a capital called Nan-ch'êng or "South city", and it yielded copper, iron, and orpiment.[1] M. V. de St. Martin makes Ku-mê or Poh-lu-ka correspond to the modern district of Aksu and this identification has been adopted by others. Some Chinese writers identify it with the modern Bai city (拜 城), while others more correctly regard it as represented by the present Yurgun or Khara-yurgun (哈 拉 玉 爾 滾), the Karayalghan or Khara-yurgun of our maps, which is within the political district of Aksu.[2] It seems that Yuan chuang was the first to use this name Poh-lu-ka, and it is known only through these Records and the Life, for the "T'ang-Shu" evidently derived its information direct from the Records.[3] The explanation of its use is apparently simple. The *Ku-mê* of the Histories transcribes the Turkish word Kum (or Qum) which means "sand" or "a desert", a word of frequent occurrence in names of places in Central Asia. Then the Buddhist Brethren from India substituted for Kum its Sanskrit equivalent Bālukā which in our pilgrim's transcription became *Poh-lu-ka.*

The word translated in the above passage by "cloth" is *tieh* in the B text and *chan* or "felt" in the C and D texts. The latter in the sense of "woollen cloth" is probably here, as in other passages, the correct reading, and it was the reading in the text of the Record used by the compiler of the T'ang-Shu". It was the fine woollen fabrics of this district which were held in esteem by the surrounding countries.

---

[1] Ch'ien Han-Shu, *ch.* 96: Wei-Shu, *ch.* 102 where Ku-mê is a dependency of Ku-tse.

[2] Hsin-ch'iang, ch. 1, 3. According to this treatise the "small desert" is the modern *Ch'a-êrh-chih-ko,* the Charchik of our maps. See Proceedings of R. G. S. Vol. XII, No. 2, p. 86.

[3] T'ang-Shu, *ch.* 221. But the P'o-lu-ka (婆 樓 迦) or Bāluka of the Tà-fang-têng-ta-chi-ching *ch.* 55 (No. 62) is evidently the Bāluka of our text.

## THE ICE MOUNTAIN AND CLEAR LAKE.

The pilgrim goes on to relate that

> going north-west from Poh-lu-ka above 300 *li* passing along (or crossing) a stony desert he came to the *Ling-shan* (Ice Mountain). This was the north beginning of the Ts'ung-Ling and most of the streams from it flowed east. The gorges of the mountain accumulated snow and retained their coldness spring and summer, and although there was the periodical melting the freezing set in immediately; the path was dangerous, cold winds blew fiercely. There were many troubles from savage dragons who molested travellers: those going by this road could not wear red clothes or carry calabashes or make a loud noise; a slight provocation caused immediate disaster; fierce winds burst forth and there were flying sand and showers of stones, those who encountered these died, life could not be saved. A journey of over 400 *li* brought the pilgrim to a great clear lake above 1000 *li* in circuit, longer from east to west than from north to south. The lake had hills on all sides and was the meeting-place for various streams; its waters were of a deep azure hue and had a sharp brackish taste; it was a vast expanse with tumultuous billows. Fish and dragons lived in it pell-mell, and supernatural prodigies appeared in it occasionally. So travellers prayed for good luck, and although fish abounded no one would venture to catch them.

From the Life we learn that Yuan-chuang was seven days in crossing the Ice Mountain, and from the Fang-chih we learn that he travelled in a western direction across it. The term which he uses for the Ice Mountain is *Ling-shan* (淩 山), *ling* being the classical word for "ice". The modern Chinese name is *Ping-shan* with the same meaning, the Turkish designation being Musur-dabghan. According to the Life the mountain was high as the heavens and covered with eternal snow, and the Pass was extremely difficult and hazardous on account of its blocks of ice and masses of rock. Our pilgrim's Ling-shan regarded as a Pass has been identified with the present Muzart or Ice-Pass, and there is much in favour of this identification although there are also difficulties in the way of its acceptance. Thus our pilgrim says he went north-west from the Kum or Kharayurgun district, but the Muzart is due north of that. M. St. Martin, accordingly, has to change the direction of the pilgrim's route and he tells us that "Hiouen-thsang, en quittant Po-lou-kia (Aksou), se porte au nord vers de grandes montagnes, qui forment, dit-il, l'angle (l'extrémité) septentrionale des monts Tsong-ling." [1] Some Chinese writers on the subject also describe the great mountain range south of Ili as the north "corner" (or "beginning") of the Ts'ung-Ling. But the Musur-dabghan is said to belong to a different range, not to the Ts'ung-Ling. The Muzart was and perhaps still is used by the traders passing between Kulja (Ili) and the districts of Kashgar, Yarkhand, and Khoten.[2] It is still very difficult and hazardous to cross the Muzart from the south side, aud the trading caravans go from Kashgar to Kulja by other Passes, and take this one only on the return journey. Moreover our pilgrim's account of his journey over the *Ling-shan* Pass agrees well with the descriptions we have of the Muzart. But the Pass by which he crossed the great mountain may have been the Bedal, or one between that and the Muzart, or he may have gone north to the last and then in a westerly direction over the mountain to the "great clear lake".

A note to the text here tells us that this lake was the Hot Sea (熱海) and Salt Sea (鹹海) of others. It is the Issik-kül or Hot Lake of the Turkic-speaking people and the Temurtu-nor or Ferruginous Lake of the Mongols. It is explained that the water of the Lake is not actually hot, but that the Lake was called "Hot Sea" because although girt by snow-clad mountains its waters never froze. It was called Temurtu-nor on account of the abundant presence of flakes of iron brought down by the tributary streams.[3]

---

[1] Julien III. p. 266.

[2] Hsin-ch'iang, *chs.* 1. 3. 4.

[3] See Reclus L'Asie-Russe p. 350: Proc$^{s}$. R. G. S. Vol. XVIII, p. 249: Hsin-ch'iang, *chs.* 1. 4: T'ung-chien-kang-mu, *ch.* 41: Sven Hedin's Through Asia, Vol. II, p. 858. Description of Issik Kul in Schuyler's Turkestan, Vol. II, p. 128.

It will be noticed that the information which our pilgrim gives about this "great clear lake" is such as might have been acquired without a personal visit. Comparing the combined accounts of the Records and the Life with the descriptions given by later travellers, we are perhaps justified in at least doubting whether the pilgrim actually reached the Issik-kül. Other travellers, Chinese and western, agree in describing this lake as being actually hot, at least near the banks, the only parts accessible until lately. No mention, however, is made either in the Records or the Life of the nature of the banks, of the tribes who lived on them, or of the vestiges of a former state of affairs. In connection with the statement that no one dared to fish in the lake we may recall the fact that the Syrians forbade any interference with the large tame fish in the river Chalos, regarding the fish as divine.[1] Our pilgrim was evidently told that the Lake was the abode of mysterious powerful supernatural beings easily excited and supposed to be malevolent. It was by these creatures that the waters, even when there was no wind, were agitated, and monstrous billows put in motion. Through fear of these unseen beings also, apparently, the people of the district did not dare to fish in the Lake.

Yuan-chuang here makes the Issik-kül to be above 1000 *li* in circuit, and the Life makes it 1400 or 1500 *li* in circuit, but some other Chinese authorities represent it as only a few hundred *li* in circuit.

The pilgrim goes on the relate that

> [from] Issik-kül going north-west he travelled above 500 *li* to the city of the *Su-she* water which was six or seven *li* in circuit. It was inhabited by traders and Tartars (*Hu*) from various districts; the country yielded millet, wheat, grapes, but trees were sparse; its climate was regular and its winds cold; the people wore woollen (felt and serge) clothing. To the west of *Su-she* were some tens of isolated cities each with its own governor but all under the rule of the Turks.

---

[1] Xenophon Anab. A. IV. 9.

The translators seem to have understood the first words of the text of this passage as meaning that the pilgrim following the north side of Issik-kül went north-west 500 *li* from it. But the Life gives the direction as "north-west following the Lake". Then Ma Tuan-lin, whose inspiration was derived from the Records, does not mention the "Clear lake" and places the "Su-she water City" 500 *li* north-west from the Ling-shan.[1] It seems to me that we must regard the pilgrim as coming out from the Ice Mountain on the south side of the Lake and going on keeping the Lake on his right hand travelling north-west 500 *li* to the city of the *Su-she* water. The name of this "water" or river is written 素葉 but we are told that the second character is to be read *she* and not *ye*, and Julien corrected his "Su-ye" to "Su-che", that is Sushe or Susa. We do not seem to know of this city, at least by this name, except through our pilgrim's narrative, although we find mention of another *Su-she* river. We read in the history of the T'ang dynasty of a city to the east of the *Hot Lake* called Sui-ye (or -she) (碎葉) and this is taken by Dr. Bretschneider and others, Chinese included, to be the *Su-she* of the present passage.[2] But this Sui-she city did not come into existence until A. D. 679 when it was built by the Chinese.[3] The expression used is chu-Sui-she-ch'êng (築碎葉城) "build the Sui-she city, but the words have been taken to mean that the Chinese built a fort at Sui-she. This city was apparently substituted for Yenk'i as one of the Four Stations under the Chief Resident of An-hsi: we have mention of it being restored to that position in the year A. D. 692, and in 748 it was destroyed. The T'ang-Shu mentions the *Sui-she* valley (川), 80 *li* from the mouth of which was the city of General P'ei Lo (裴羅), and 40 *li* west from it was the *Sui-she* city; on the north of this was the river with the same name, and 40 *li* north of it

---

[1] *Ch.* 336.

[2] Med. Res. Vol. i. p. 227.

[3] T'ung-chien-kang-mu, *ch.* 41 (T'ang Kao Tsung Tiao-li 1st year).

was the *Ku-tan* (羯丹) hill, the spot at which the Khans of the Ten surnames were crowned.[1] This city seems to have disappeared ever since the T'ang period. Its remains are supposed by some to exist at a place on the north side of the Issik-kül, but this does not suit the position of the city with reference to the Lake. The Su-she for our text was apparently situated to the west of Issik-kül, south of Tokmak, and not very far to the north-west of the Son-kül. Modern Chinese maps place in that neighbourhood a river called *Su-sa-ma-êrh* (蘇薩瑪爾), that is perhaps, "Susa water". In some of our maps this river appears as "Susamir", a name also given to a range of mountains in the neighbourhood. In some old maps of the Persian empire at the height of its greatness we find to the north of Samarkand a town called "Teras" and north-east from it a river "Sosechi". Further it is to be observed that some Chinese geographers understand *Sui-she-shui* to be an old name for the Issik-kül.[2] At the time of our pilgrim's visit the Su-she river and its city had been a part of the great Persian empire; and we may with some probability take the name Su-she to be for Susa, transferred from the old Susa "by Choaspes' amber stream, the drink of none but kings". Professor Hirth, who considers the Su-she of our text to be the Sui-she of the T'ang History, restores the name Sui-she as Sūj-āb.[3] He writes *Su-ye* and *Sui-ye*, and if the latter term is regarded as a Chinese name his transcription of the characters may be correct. But the former is a foreign word read *Su-she*, and our pilgrim's *Su-she-shui* may possibly correspond to the Sūj-āb of Tabari quoted by Dr. Hirth.

---

[1] *Ch.* 43. The "General Pei Lo" of this passage is perhaps the civil official Pei Hing-chien (裴行儉) who caused a general to build the city.

[2] Hsin-ch'iang, *ch.* 1 where the expression is *Sui-sheh-chuan* (川).

[3] Nachworte z. Inschrift d. Tonjukuk S. 71 and cf. S. 73. 75. (Die Alt-Türkischen Inschriften d. Mongolen. Radloff).

## SU-LI.

The pilgrim adds—

From the city of the Su-she water to the Kasanna country the territory and its inhabitants are called *Su-li.* This name is applied also to the language and the writing of the people. The letters of their language are only 20 (in the B text 30) odd which have come to produce a vast vocabulary: they read their writing vertically: teacher transmits instruction to his successor in unbroken continuity. Their garments, which are tight-fitting, are felt (in B *tieh*) and serge for inside and skins and wool (or Cotton *tieh*) outside. They cut the hair even leaving the top of the head exposed, some shave off all the hair, and they bind the forehead with a silk band. They are of large stature but of a cowardly disposition: they are treacherous and deceitful in their ways and very avaricions. Father and son scheme for gain: wealth gives eminence: there is no distinction between the well-born and the low-born: one who is extremely rich may live on poor food and wear coarse clothing. The people are half-and-half traders and farmers.

The country and people here called *Su-li* (窣利) are apparently almost unknown, at least by this name. I-ching several times mentions a region and people which he calls *Su-li* (速利) and this word is probably the Su-li of our passage. But whereas Yuan-chuang restricts his name to a small defined district, I-ching seems to use his Su-li as a general name for the northern extra-India people called Hu (胡) or at least for a main division of the Hu.[1] So also in his Sanskrit-Chinese Vocabulary I-ching gives Sali transcribed *Su-li* as the Sanskrit equivalent for Hu: the transcription for Sali is generally Su-li but in one place it is, perhaps by mistake, *Sunlin.* As to what Sali or Su-li means we seem to be left in ignorance. Alberuni mentions a country Sūlika which he places in the north, and another Sūlika which he puts in the north-west, but the latter name, which is taken from the Bṛihat-Samhitā

---

[1] Nan-hai-ch'i-kuei *Chs.* 9, 10, 25, and Takakusu pp. 49, 68, 69, 119.

should perhaps be read Mūlika.[1] It seems probable that the Su-li of our pilgrim corresponds to the "Sārts" of later times. This is a term applied, we are told, by the nomads of Central Asia to all dwellers in towns and villages without regard to race or origin. But, according to M. de Ujfalvy, the Tajiks are not counted as Sārts. These Tajiks, it is important to remember, are Iranians (Eranians) of three kinds, (1) indigenous Iranians, (2) Persian colonists, and (3) the descendants of Persian slaves. It is interesting to compare M. de Ujfalvy's "Carte ethnographique de l'Asie centrale" with Yuan-chuang's narrative and the description of the Su-li with that of the Sārts.[2] But although the descriptions may correspond it does not seem right to regard Su-li as a transcription of Sārt. Like another word to be noticed hereafter it may stand for the Turkic Suliq in the sense of "having water", a term which seems to be very appropriate to at least a portion of the Su-li region but not to all. We should probably regard the pilgrim's statement that the country was called Su-li as a mistake and the name should perhaps be regarded as applying only to the inhabitants and their language.

## THOUSAND SPRINGS.

Returning to the text of our Records we read that a journey of above 400 *li* westward from "Su-she city" brought the pilgrim to the "Thousand Springs". The district with this name was above 200 *li* square; it had Snowy mountains on its south side and level land on the other sides; it had a rich mouldy soil and trees everywhere; in the latter part of spring the place was an embroidery of flowers. There were a thousand springs and ponds and hence the name of the district; the Khan of the Turks came here every year to escape the summer heat. The place contained flocks of tame deer many of which wore bells and rings; the deer were cherished by the Khan who forbade the slaughter of any of them under the penalty of capital punishment, and so the deer lived their natural lives.

---

[1] Alberuni Vol. I. pp. 300, 302: Ind. Ant. Vol. XXII. p. 190.

[2] Le Kohistan, Le Ferghanah et Kouldja pp. 59, 187.

From the Life we learn that the local native name of this charming district, here called *Ch'ien-Ch'uan* (千泉), was Ping-yü (屏聿). This evidently represents Bing-ghyul which is the Turkic equivalent for *Ch'ien-ch'uan* or "Thousand Springs". There is little mention of the district bearing this name in Chinese literature. We find it stated in the history of the Sui dynasty that in the year A. D. 619 the She-hu khan of the West Turks removed his Court to the Thousand Springs, described as being to the north of the Shih (石), that is, Tashkend country.[1] Moreover in the XII$^{th}$ *chuan* of these Records we are told that the Ts'ung-Ling range 'extended on the north to the Hot sea (the Issik-kül) and Thousand Springs'.

M$^{r}$ Schuyler finds the district here named Thousand Springs in the country to the north of the Alexandrofsky range and between Auliéata and Ak-su. Of his journey from the former of these two places to the latter he writes—"All along my right was the beautiful Alexandrofsky range, with many of its summits then white with snow. At almost every step I crossed rivulets trickling down from the hills, showing well the truth of the old name, 'the thousand sources'."[2] With this we may compare D$^{r}$ Bretschneider's opinion—"Vivien de St. Martin, in his geographical notes appended to Stan. Julien's translation of Hüan Thsang's narrative identifies *Ts'ients'üan* with a place *Ming bulak*, south of Lake Karakul, thus carrying the traveller far north-west, and then locates his *Ta-lo-sz* between the aforesaid lake and the Jaxartes. But this view is untenable. Ming bulak meaning 'Thousand Springs' in Mongol and other languages of the East, is a quite frequent name for places in Mongolia and Central Asia. It seems to me that the Thousand Springs of the Chinese traveller, bordered on the south by snowy mountains, whilst on the other sides all was level land, must be rather looked for somewhere on the northern slope of the high

1 See T'ung-chien-kang-mu *ch.* 38 (sui Kung Ti 2$^{d}$ year).

2 Turkistan Vol. II. p. 123.

mountain stretching from Lake Issik-kül westward, and marked on Russian maps as *Alexander's Chain*".[1]

## THE KHAN.

Before leaving this district we must take notice of the short description which the Life gives of the pilgrim's meeting with the Khan of the Turks.

It relates that at the Su-she-water city, called here the *Su-she* city, the pilgrim met with the Turk Sh'eh-hu Khan then on a hunting expedition. His military equipment, we are told, was very grand. The Khan wore a green satin robe; his hair which was ten feet long was free: a band of white silk was wound round his forehead hanging down behind. The ministers of the presence, above 200 in number, all wearing embroidered robes and with plaited hair stood on his right and left. The rest of his military retinue clothed in fur, serge, and fine wool, the spears and standards and bows in order, and the riders of camels and horses stretched far away out of ken. The Khan was delighted to meet Yuan-chuang and invited him to stay in the encampment during his absence which would be only for two or three days, giving him into the charge of a Minister of the presence named Ha-mo-chih. After three days the Khan returned and Yuan-chuang was taken to his tent. The gold embroidery of this grand tent shone with a dazzling splendour; the ministers of the presence in attendance sat on mats in long rows on either side all dressed in magnificent brocade robes while the rest of the retinue on duty stood behind. You saw that although it was a case of a frontier ruler yet there was an air of distinction and elegance. The Khan came out from his tent about thirty paces to meet Yuan-chuang who after a courteous greeting entered the tent. As the Turks are fire-worshippers they do not use wooden seats, we are told, as wood has the principle of fire, and they use double mats as seats: but for the pilgrim the Khan provided an iron-framed bench with a mattress. After a short interval envoys from China and Kao-ch'ang were admitted and presented their despatches and credentials which the Khan perused. He was much elated and caused the envoys to be seated, then he ordered wine and music for himself and them and grape-syrup for the pilgrim. Hereupon all pledged each other and the filling and passing and draining of the winecups made a din and bustle, while the mingled music of various

---

[1] Med. Res. Vol. I. p. 228 note.

instruments rose loud: although the airs were the popular strains of foreigners yet they pleased the senses and exhilarated the mental faculties. After a little, piles of roasted beef and mutton were served for the others, and lawful food such a cakes, milk, candy, honey, and grapes for the pilgrim. After the entertainment grape-syrup was again served and the Khan invited Yuan-chuang to improve the occasion, whereupon the pilgrim expounded the doctrines of the "ten virtues", compassion for animal life, and the Paramitas and emancipation. The Khan raising his hands bowed and gladly believed and accepted the teaching. He detained the pilgrim some days and wanted to keep him permanently. "You need not go to the *In-t'ê-ka* country", he urged, "that land is very hot, its 10th month being as the 5th of this place; judging from your appearance I fear you will not survive a visit; its people are contemptible being black and uncivilized". But the pilgrim replied that notwithstanding all this he wanted to seek the traces of the Buddha and learn his religious system. Then the Khan sought out among his retainers a young man who had spent some years in Ch'ang-an and could speak Chinese and other languages. This young man he made *Mo-to-ta-kuan* and appointed him to go with the pilgrim as far as Kapistet entrusting him also with despatches about the pilgrim. The Khan, moreover, gave Yuan-chuang a dark-red silk monk's suit and fifty webs (*p'i* 疋) of soft silk, and he and his ministers escorted the pilgrim above ten *li* on his way.

The "Sheh-hu Khan" of this passage was probably a relative of that *To-lu* (咄 陸) Khan of the West Turks who died in A. D. 635. His title is written *Ye-hu* (葉 護), in other places also 葉 護, but we are always told that the characters are to be read *Sheh-hu*. This term, which is of very frequent occurrence in historical works treating of the Turks, is generally interpreted as meaning *ta-ch'ên* (大 臣) or "high official". We are told that it denoted the highest rank of Turkish officials under the Khan, and the person bearing this title was usually a son, brother, or other near relative of the Khan.[1] He was commonly the satrap or governor of a Province, but we read also of the Right and Left Shehhu at the Khan's court.[2] There

---

[1] Ma I. l. *ch.* 343. 344.

[2] Ma I. l. *ch.* 347: T'angshu *ch.* 217. Here it is Uigour dignitaries who style themselves "Left and Right Sheh-hu". In the Life

is much probability in the supposition that the word represents the old Turkic Yabgu or Jabgu found in certain old inscriptions, and this word also denotes a viceroy or Governor.[1]

For the words "his military equipment was very grand" the Chinese is *Jung-ma-chên-shêng* (戎馬甚盛) which Julien translates—"Les chevaux de ces barbares étaient extrêmement nombreux." This rendering seems to be faulty and to spoil the description. *Jung-ma* is originally a "war-horse", and the term is used in this sense in classical literature. Then it came to denote the army and all the material equipment for a war, and it is also used to denote "a campaign," a "state of active warfare."[2] As the context here shews the pilgrim found reason to admire the army which attended the Khan and the army included soldiers mounted on elephants and horses along with standard-bearers and others. It seems better, accordingly, to translate the clause by some such words as "his military equipment was magnificent." In the Records we find the expression *ping-ma-ch'iang-shêng* (兵馬强盛) with a similar meaning.

As to the Khan's hair the D text makes it to have

---

also we have the Governor of Tokhara, a grandson of the "Sheh-hu Khan" assuming the title of "Sheh-hu" (Life *ch.* 5: Julien I. p. 268). The pilgrim seems to have made a distinction between the "Sheh-hu Khan" or Governor of several Provinces and the "Sheh-hu", the Governor of one Province under the former. This distinction, however, is not strictly observed by him and it seems to be unknown to others.

[1] Thomsen's Inscriptions de l'Orkhon, p[s] 102, 146, 192: Hirth's Nachworte &c. op. c. S. 22, 45.

[2] Two examples may suffice. In the 46[th] chapter of the Tao-tê-ching we find the *draught-horse* of peace and the *Jung-ma* or "war-horse" used in an illustration of the effects of good government and of disorder respectively. The words of this passage *Jung-ma-shêng-yü-chiao* (戎馬生于郊), "the war steeds are born on the wild frontiers," often shortened to *Jung-ma-tsai-chiao* are often used to denote the existence of a state of border warfare. Then "in the midst of war" is expressed by 在戎馬之間.

been above ten feet long,[1] but the C text, which Julien seems to have had, was taken by him to mean that it was the silk band which was ten feet long. This reading, however, is evidently wrong, the word *i* (以), as the parallel clause shews, being an improper interpolation.

The term here rendered "Ministers of the presence" is *ta-kuan* (達官) for which Julien gives "officiers" and "officiers de haut rang," but neither of these is so good as his discarded rendering "officiers introducteurs." In a Chinese-Sanskrit Vocabulary this word is given as the equivalent of the Sanskrit word *Sammata* in the sense of "held in esteem" or "honoured." It is also given as the rendering of the Sanskrit Amantrayitā and of the Turkish equivalent *Tasrifatyi*. But the word, which is also written *Ta-kan* (達干) is evidently, as has been conjectured, the Turkish word Tarkhan or Darghan. The *Ta-kuan* or Tarkhan were not necessarily officials of high degree, but they were men whom the Khan delighted to honour, who attended him on state occasions and introduced those summoned or invited to his presence. They had the right of entry to the Khan's presence, and they had also the privilege of sitting in his presence at an audience, banquet, or other state function.[2] When the pilgrim is leaving, the Khan, as we have seen, appoints a young retainer to be *Mo-to* (摩咄)-*ta-kuan* and accompany the pilgrim to Kapis. This word *Moto*, which we sometimes find used as if it were a personal name, is perhaps for the Turkish word *Mutarjinn* which means "an interpreter".

The words here rendered "spears and standards" are *sho-tu* (槊纛), but it seems to be possible that the writer used them in the sense of "raised standard". The word *tu* is the Turkish tūgh, a standard formed by a long pole surmounted by a receptacle containing a yak's tail. This

---

[1] Cf. Ogilby's Persia p. 81.

[2] De Courteille Dict. Turk. or e. p. 318: Hirth, op. c. p. 55: Thomsen op. c. ps. 59, 185: Schlegel, Die Chin. Ins. ad. d. Uigur Denkmal, S. 9 et al.

standard was one of the insignia of relatives of the Khan and distinguished military officers.

The author of the Life tells us, we have seen, that the Khan had a fine bearing and presence "although he was a frontier ruler." In the original the words for "frontier ruler" are *K'ung-lü-chih-chün* (穹廬之君) which Julien translates—"un prince barbare, abrité sous une tente de feutre", which seems to be a double translation. *K'ung-lü* is a well-known literary term for *Pien-ti* or "border land" as contrasted with Shên-chou or China. But it is also used to denote "a felt tent," and then "an encampment," "camp-life."[1] As *K'ung* means "vast" or "lofty" and *lü* means a "hut" or "cottage" we may with some probability regard the compound in the sense of a "felt tent" as a foreign word. We find it also written *Kung-lü* (弓閭) and these two terms may perhaps represent the Turkish word *Külube* which means a "tent of felt." But in phrases like that of our text the term should perhaps be regarded as having the signification of "outlying," that is, "barbarous territory."

We come next to the words here loosely rendered by "the mingled music of various instruments." These are *K'in-mei-tou* (or *tu*)-*li* (㰯佅兜離) which Julien renders—"la musique des barbares du midi et du nord, de l'orient et de l'occident," but this is evidently not correct. We know that the old term for the music of the north barbarians was *k'in* (禁), for that of the East barbarians *mei* (韎 or 昧), for that of the southern barbarians *jen* (任), and for that of the west barbarians *chu-li* (侏 or 株離).[2] It will be seen that our passage has not the word *jen*, and that its characters are not those of the rest of the description here quoted. A glossary to the passage tells

---

1 Ku-shih-yuan (古詩原) *ch.* 6 and *ch.* 2: Ch'ien Han-shu *ch.* 96. Jih-chih-lu (日知錄) *ch.* 29. With the description of the Khan given in our text we may compare Master A. Jenkinson's account of Solyman the Great Turke in Hakluyt's Principall Voyages, &c. p. 81 (1st ed.).

2 Ma T. l. *ch.* 148: Kanghsi Dict. s. v. 株.

us that *k'in-mei* is the name of a barbarian music, and our *tu-li* is the recognized transcription of the Sanskrit word *turyā* meaning "music." This last word had been known to the Chinese for some centuries before Yuan-chuang's time. It is possible the *k'in*, *mei*, and *tu-li* of our passage may be the *k'in*, *mei*, and *chu-li* of other books and that the words are used here in a peculiar manner. Our four characters may thus mean simply "the music of the foreign instruments" or something similar.

It will be noticed that among the "pure food" of which the pilgrim partakes at the Khan's banquet was a preparation of milk. In taking this he was not acting in strict accordance with Mahāyānist discipline, and I-ching states positively that milk was not a lawful article of food to a bhikshu.[1]

When the feast was over the pilgrim, at the Khan's request, as we have seen, gave him an exposition of some of the leading features of Buddhism. The first in the list of subjects is the *shih-shan* (十善) or "Ten Virtues" that is, the ten excellent precepts which the Mahāyānist undertook to observe. These were not to kill, not to steal, not to commit impurity, not to be false in language, not to be double-tongued, not to use bad language, not to use fine glosing speech, not to covet, not to be angry, not to take heretical views.[2]

The narrative in the Life with which we are now concerned gives us a very interesting picture of that strange people called by the Chinese *T'u-küe*, Turks. This people had a remarkable but short career the main incidents of which are well known. In the 5th century of our era the Turks were slaves in the iron mines and forges of another tribe, the *Juan-juan* or *Niu-yen*, on the south of the Gold mountain near the modern Barkul. They rebelled against their masters and were successful. Their dash and prowess soon made them a power, and they harried the surrounding

---

1 Nan-hai-ch'i-kuei, *ch.* 1.

2 Fa-kie-tzŭ-ti-chu-mên, *ch.* 1 (No. 1572).

regions to the borders of China. Then we find a king in China sending an envoy to them in A. D. 545 and this is the first appearance of the Turks in Chinese history.[1] A few (24) years afterwards envoys from the rulers of Persia and the Roman Empire arrived at the seat of government of these Turks.[2] About this time also the Wei king in China received and entertained magnificently a Turkish ambassador with a large suite at Ch'ang-an-foo and gave a princess to the Khan in marriage. The splitting up of the great Turkish host occurred a few years afterwards, about the end of the sixth century, and the term "West Turks" began to be used from that time. The power of the Turks grew rapidly until it extended from Liao-tung to the West (Caspian) Sea, but within little more than two centuries it passed away.

The account of the Khan and his doings here reminds one of descriptions of Persian chiefs in other books, and this Khan seems to be in some respects rather Persian than Turkish. We see him, for example, like a satrap, a Persian "Prefectus Provinciæ," practising his soldiers in hunting; and the chase is with him apparently a military exercise. The "Thousand Springs" was a Paradeisos with plenty of water, thickly grown with trees and full of wild animals. The pretty story in the Records about the deer in this place going about free and secure, adorned with bells and rings, shews us that the Khan did not hunt merely for the game to be taken. But the story may be a misinterpretation of an old Persian custom to which the Khan adhered. Of this custom we find mention by Ogilby in the following passage—"In the beginning of the month *Ramadhan*, which is our Lent, the king goes to *Abicurong* in the mountains to take the fresh air, and to hunt, in which sport he spends several days, attended by some thousands of people. At the ears of those beasts which the king takes alive he hangs golden plates, on which are

---

1 T'ung-chien-kang-mu, *ch.* 32, p. 62.

2 Gibbon. Decline and Fall, *ch.* xlii.

engraven certain marks, and then setting them at liberty again, often he retakes them; nay some have been taken who have had the marks of king Thamas, Ismail Sefi, and other ancient princes."[1]

The Life represents the West Turks as fire-worshippers and as abstaining from the use of wooden seats on account of their reverence for the element of fire inherent in wood. But here there is evidently a mistake. The Persians were fire-worshippers, but we read of the Turks as worshipping the "blue heaven," their ancestors, and other objects, and as miners and blacksmiths they cannot have been fire-worshippers. But it is acknowledged that some at least of the Turks, perhaps under Persian influence, became worshippers of fire: and a Turkish tribe, the Karakirghiz, although nominally Mahometan still adheres to rites of the old worship.[2] The Turks at the Su-she city sat cross-legged on mats or cushions because it was their custom. Out of consideration for the Chinese guest the Khan ordered a bench for him such as was used by Buddhist monks. In like manner the king of Hyrcan in 1566 shewed courtesy to M[r] A. Jenkinson when the latter was presented to him. The king "kept his court at that time in the high mountains in tents"; he was "richly apparelled with long garments of silke and cloth of golde imbrodered with pearls and stone." M[r] Jenkinson proceeds—"Thus the king with his nobilitie sitting in his pavilion with his legs acrosse, and perceiving that it was painefull for me so to sit, his highnesse caused a stoole to be brought in and did will me to sit thereupon after my fashion."[3]

---

[1] Ogilby's Persia p. 79.
[2] Schuyler's Turkistan Vol. II. p. 137.
[3] Hakluyt op. c. p. 367.

# CHAPTER IV.

## CHUAN I CONT[D]

### TARAS TO KAPIS.

The account in the Records proceeds to relate that from Bing-ghyul or Thousand Springs the pilgrim continued his journey westward and after going 140 or 150 *li* he arrived at the city of *Ta-lo-ssŭ*. This city was eight or nine *li* in circuit: here traders and Tartars (or, trading Tartars) from other countries lived pell-mell: in natural products and climate the city much resembled *Su-she*.

The *Ta-lo-ssŭ* of this passage is undoubtedly the Taras or Talas of several old writers and travellers. D[r] Bretschneider, properly rejecting M. Saint-Martin's identification of Taras, is disposed to place the site of the city near that of the present Aulié-ata on the river Taras, and D[r] Schuyler is of the same opinion.[1] This seems to be correct enough for practical purposes, but the old Taras (or Talas) was probably some miles to the south-east of the modern town Aulié-ata. It should be added that while the distance between *Su-she* and Taras in this passage is 540 *li* the distance between the *Sui-ye* city and Taras is given elsewhere as only 310 *li*.[2]

Our narrative proceeding tells us that above ten *li* to the south of Taras was a small isolated town inhabited by above 300 Chinese. These men had originally been taken captive by the Turks and carried off to this district: they had afterwards

---

[1] Med. Res. Vol. I. p. 18 note and p. 228 note. See Schuyler's Turkistan Vol. II. p. 120.

[2] T'ang-Shu, *ch.* 43 and 221.

banded together and had settled in and fortified this town: they had then changed their style of dress for that of the Turks but they had still retained their native speech and ways of life.

In connection with these statements it will be remembered that while Yuan-chuang was at Su-she a Chinese envoy arrived and had audience of the Khan. This may have been the envoy sent by the Emperor T'ai Tsung in A.D. 631 to obtain from the Turks the release of all their Chinese captives. In the time of the Sui dynasty the Turks had invaded China, penetrating far into the country and carrying off many myriads of Chinese prisoners. It was to ransom these that the great Emperor sent his ambassador to the Khan in the year mentioned. The historian tells us that the number of men, women, and children released from captivity among the Turks on this occasion was above 80000. Among those thus happily restored to their homes were probably the 300 Chinese of this little town near Taras.[1]

## PAI-SHUI-CH'ÊNG.

Proceeding on his journey and going in a south-west direction for above 200 *li* from the little Chinese town the pilgrim reached the *Pai-shui-ch'êng* or "White water city." This was six or seven *li* in circuit, and the district excelled Taras in fertility of soil and in climate.

As we learn from other sources this was a well-watered region with a rich fertile soil.[2] Long ago Rémusat identified this "White water city" with the "Isfidjab" or "Esfidjab" of Arabian writers, this name also meaning "White water."[3] M. St. Martin adopts this identification and it has been generally followed. Then this "Isfidjab" has been declared to be the *Sairam* which is now, D^r^ Bretschneider tells us, "a little town in Russian Türkestan, north-east of Tashkend and about 6½ (but in another

---

1 T'ung-chien-kang-mu, *ch.* 39 (T'ang-T'ai Tsung's 5th year).

2 T'ang-shu *ch.* 221.

3 Rech. Lang. Tart. p. 286.

place he says 13) English miles east of Chimkend."[1] It is perhaps better, however, to find the representative of the *Pai-shui-ch'êng* of Yuan-chuang in the modern Mankeut. This town, which is also called Ak-su or "White water," is about 15 miles to the north-east of Chimkend. This last town is also regarded by some as being on or near the site of the "White water city."

## KUNG-YÜ.

Continuing to travel south-west our pilgrim went on from "White water" city for more than 200 *li* and arrived at the city *Kung-yü* or *Kung-ya* (恭御), which was five or six *li* in circuit. In this district the downs and marshes had a rich loamy soil and were densely covered with forests.

Of this city no one seems to know anything and even the name is not quite certain as instead of Kung-yü we find in one authority *Kung-ching* (恭敬).[2] It is probable, however, that this latter form is only a freak of a copyist and that the former is the correct reading. As we find *Ch'üan-ch'êng* (泉城) or "City of the spring (or springs)" given as the name of this city we are probably justified in regarding *Kung-yü* as standing for the Turkic word Kūyu which denotes a *well* or *spring*, the native name of the city being Kūyu-shahr. It is remarkable that the Fang-chih here does not mention the "White water city" and makes *Kung-yü* to be above 200 *li* to the south-west of Taras or half the distance given by the pilgrim.

## NU-CHIH-KAN.

Our pilgrim next proceeds to relate that a journey of 40 or 50 *li* south from Kung-yü city brought him to the country of *Nu-chih-kin* or *kan* (笯赤建). This country was above 1000 *li* in circuit and it had a soil rich and fertile, a dense vegetation and fruits and flowers in great luxuriance: grapes were thought much of although plentiful. There were a hundred odd cities

---

[1] Med. Res. Vol. I. p. 74 and II. p. 94. See also Schuyler's Turkistan I. p. 75 and 393.

[2] Ma T. l. *ch.* 336.

and towns each with its own governor: but although the towns and their districts were mutually independent and distinct political divisions yet the collective name for all was the "*Nu-chih-kan* Country."

Of a district in this region bearing the name Nu-chih-kan, perhaps pronounced like Nujikkend, little if anything seems to be known beyond what is recorded here by our author. M. Saint-Martin, however, writes of Nu-chih-kan thus—"Nous retrouvons indubitalement ce lieu dans la *Noudjkeh* (pour Noudjkend) mentionnée par le Mésalek-alabsar entre Taras et Khodjend, mais sans indication précise quant à l'emplacement."[1] This Nujkend, it has been suggested, may possibly represent the Turkic compound Nujabahkend, meaning "the territory of the nobles", a restoration which seems to suit our pilgrim's description.

## CHE-SHIH (TASHKEND).

The pilgrim goes on to state that from Nu-chih-kan going west above 200 *li* he came to the *Che-shih* country. This was above 1000 *li* in circuit, reaching on the west to the *She* (or *Ye*) river, being greater in extent from north to south than from east to west: in natural products and climate it was like Nu-chih-kan: its cities and towns were some tens in number, each with its own chief magistrate and without any general chief, but all subject to the Turks.

The country here described has been long ago correctly identified with the modern Tashkend. Our pilgrim calls it *Che-shih* (赭 時), as we are told to read the characters, or Chesh. This is evidently the *Che-she* (者 舌)[2] of earlier writers with its capital *Che-chih* (赭 支): the latter, Dr Hirth's "Tjadj," is also used to designate the country.[3] The name is also written *Che-chih* (柘 支) and its capital *Che-che* (柘 折), and some western writers call the capital "Seket." The river of this country is here called *She* or *Ye* (葉) short for *Ye-ye* or *Ye-she*, the Jaxartes. Another

---

[1] Julien III. p. 276.

[2] T'ung-chien-kang-mu, *ch.* 25: Ma T. l. *ch.* 338 and 339.

[3] Nachworte op. c. S. 70.

transcription is *Yao-sha* (樂 殺), and the river is also known as the Sihon and the Syr-daria. On entering China, we read in one treatise, it is called *Chên-chu* (眞 珠), but another account makes *Chên-chu* to be a river of Tashkend alone.[1]

A note to our text tells us that the Chinese for Chesh kuo was *Shih*(石)*-kuo*. The fact that the word Tash and its equivalent *Shih* mean *a stone* or *stone* has led to some rather fanciful writing about this country. Thus Alberuni, who makes the philosophic remark that names of countries "change rapidly, when, for instance, a foreign nation with a different language occupies a country," adds—"Their tongues frequently mangle the words, and thus transfer them into their own language, as is, *e. g.* the custom of the Greeks. Or they keep the original meaning of the names and try a sort of translation, but then they undergo certain changes. So the city of Shāsh, which has its name from the Turkish language, where it is called Tāsh-kand, i. e., *Stone-city*, is called *Stone-tower* in the book γεωγραφία."[2] The Geography here mentioned is that by Ptolemy (about A. D. 150) who tells of a "stone tower" on the road of the caravans between India and Serica: but other writers place the tower at the starting point of the caravans proceeding to the country of the Seres. M. St. Martin considers that this identification of Tashkend with Ptolemy's "Stone tower," the Turris lapidea of later geographers, is not "sans beaucoup de probabilité." But serious objections have been made to this identification and probably it is now abandoned. The Turris lapidea as it appears in old maps is far to the south or south-east of Tashkend, the district of Old Tashkend. Moreover, not to mention any more objections, Tashkend, as has been pointed out by others, is always a city or district, never a fort or tower.[3] M. St. Martin repeats the statement

---

1 T'ang-shu, *ch.* 221.

2 Vol. I. p. 298.

3 See Paquier op. c. p. 24.

that Tashkend means "stone castle," while Dr Bretschneider says it means "stone city,"[1] and gives "stony country" as the translation of our Chesh. But there does not seem to be anything in the accounts of the city and district to justify the use of the epithets "stone" or "stony." The land was noted for its fertility and its grain crops made it the granary of the country: among its products are enumerated cotton, silk, woollen stuffs and articles of leather. In Old Tashkend the dwelling-houses are all made of mud, and the mosques and other stone buildings are built of what we may call second-hand stones.[2] The names given to the city and district have a different explanation, and represent a proper name. This was the personal name of one of the nine members of a powerful family of the *Ge-ti* or *Yue-chih* (月支) nation. The head of the family, the eldest brother, was chief of the clan the members of which were known by their territorial designation *Shao-wu* (昭武), that being the name of their original home north of the K'i-lien or Celestial Mountains. When conquered by the Hiung-nu (or, as some writers tell us, by the Turks), and driven away from their native region, they descended to the country between the Ts'ung-Ling and the river Oxus, occupying Kang-kü (Samarkand) and all the surrounding country. The head of the clan ruled in Samarkand and the other chiefs had principalities round about the metropolitan State, Shih or Chesh or Tash being the personal name of the brother who ruled over the district bearing this name. We even find Che-she described as Kang-kü or as a part of that country. In the 6th and 7th centuries also we find this district called the *An* (安) Country, An being the name of another of the Shao-wu brothers, but this did not supplant the other name. Thus Shih-kuo and Tashkend denote the *country* or *domain* of Shih or Tash.[3]

---

[1] Julien III. p. 276: Med. Res. Vol. II. pag. 55 et al.

[2] Hellwald's Centralasien S. 341, 351, 397: Baber Intr. p. XL. See also Schuyler's Turkistan *ch.* 3.

[3] T'ang-shu l. c.: Sui-shu, *ch.* 83: Ma T. l. l. c. In the Sui-shu

## BETWEEN TASHKEND AND SAMARKAND.

We now come to a part of the pilgrim's narrative which presents some serious difficulties. He relates that—

> "From this (i. e. the Old Tashkend country) to the *Fei-han* country south-east is above 1000 *li*." This country, which was above 4000 *li* in circuit, was surrounded by mountains on all sides: it had a rich productive soil with flowers and fruits in great quantity, and it produced sheep and horses: it was windy and cold and the people were stout-hearted: in speech they differed from other countries, and they were ill-featured. For some tens of years the county had been without a sovereign, and the local chiefs struggled for superiority: their districts and cities were determined by rivers (川) and natural defences.

The country which Yuan-chuang here calls *Fei-han* has been identified with Ferghana, corresponding in some measure to the present Khanate of Khokand. Ferghana became known to the Chinese in the second century B. C. by the name Ta-yuan (大宛) its capital being *Kuei-shan* (貴山), probably pronounced *Kusan.*[1] Another old name for the country was *Kü-so* (渠搜) but this is perhaps only the name of the capital slightly altered.[2] In later times we find the country called *Po-han* (撥汗) or (鏺扞) and *Pa-han-na* (拔汗那), and *P'o-lo-na* (破洛那), and in A.D. 744 the Chinese imposed on it the designation *Ning-yuan* (寧遠).[3] The modern Chinese name is *Huo-han* (霍罕), in Cantonese *Fok-han*, which apparently represents the word Ferghana.[4]

Now the pilgrim does not expressly state that he actually visited Fei-han, but some readers of the Records have understood him as describing it from personal observation, while others regard him as writing from hearsay. There

---

and the Wei-shu *ch.* 102 the surname of the king of this country s *Shi* or stone, but he does not belong to the Shao-wu clan.

[1] Shih-chi, *ch.* 123. In this work Kangkü is placed 2000 *li* north-west from Ta-yuan. Ch'ien Han-shu *ch.* 96.

[2] Ma T. l. ch. 338.

[3] T'ang-shu, *ch.* 221 : T'ang-chien-kang-mu *ch.* 20, 42, and 43.

[4] Ta-ch'ing-i-t'ung-chih, *ch.* 351: Li-ko-yen-piao, *ch.* 3.

are several circumstances in the narrative which seem to indicate that he did not visit the country called Ferghana. Thus he makes Fei-han to be 1000 *li* south-east from Tashkend, and this is double the distance, given in the T'ang-shu and other works, of Ferghana from Tashkend. Then he describes his Fei-han as having mountains on all sides, but Ferghana was free from mountains on the west side. Moreover he represents the country as having been for above a score of years in a state of anarchy, an active rivalry for chieftainship going on among the various cities. But we know from Chinese history that within a few years of the pilgrim's visit to this region there was a king of Ferghana, that the king was murdered by the West Turks, and that he was succeeded on the throne by his son.[1] The royal family belonged to the great Shao-wu clan. Thus we are apparently justified in regarding Yuan-chuang's account of the country as information derived from persons living outside of the district described.

The narrative proceeds—

> From this (i. e. Fei-han) going west above 1000 *li* one comes (or, the pilgrim came) to the *Su-tu-li-se-na* country. This he describes as being 1400 *li* in circuit with the *She* (Jaxartes) river on its east. The *She* river rises in the north end of the Ts'ung-Ling and flows north-west a great muddy rapid stream. In natural products and popular ways *Su-tu-li-se-na* resembled Tashkend: there was a king but he was under the Turks.

The name of the country here transcribed Su-tu-li-se-na (窣堵利瑟那) was perhaps a Sanskrit word like Sutushan meaning "happy," "easily satisfied", or Sutrishna which means "dry," "thirsty." It is apparently the same name which is transcribed *Su-tu-shih-ni* (蘇都識匿), *Su-tui-sha-na,* and *Soh-tu-sha-na.* Another name for the district was *Ka-pu-tan-na* (劫布呾那), and it was called by the Chinese the "Tung Ts'ao (東曹) Country," Ts'ao being one of the Shao-wu brothers.[2] This is evidently the "Se-

1 T'ang-shu l. c.: Ma T. l. l. c.
2 T'ang-shu, l. c.: Ma T. l. l. c.

troushteh" of Ibn Haukal who says the country has no navigable river but has "running streams and fountains and meadows and groves" with mines of gold, silver, copperas, and sal-ammoniac. "It is a mountainous region, bounded on the east by part of Ferghana; on the west by the borders of Samarkand: on the north by Chaje (i. e. Tashkend); on the south it lies near Kish."[1] M. St. Martin identifies the district with the Osrushna or Satrushna of Musulman writers, the modern Uratupe or Uratépé, the Ura-Tube of our maps.[2] The identification is evidently practically correct, and the distance and direction of Ura-Tube agree with the pilgrim's account. But the Life, which does not mention Fei-han, makes Yuan-chuang go from Tashkend direct to Sutrishan which it places 1000 *li* west from Tashkend. Here there is evidently a mistake due apparently to the accidental omission of Fei-han. In some Chinese works Sutrishan is placed 500 *li*,[3] and in some 400 *li*[4] to the west of Ferghana and adjacent to Tashkend on the north.

The narrative in the Records proceeds—

> North-west from the Sutrishan country you enter a great desert destitute of water and vegetation, a vast blank where only by following the mountains and observing the skeletons can the course be directed. Going above 500 *li* you reach the *Sa-mei-kan* country.

The Life agrees with this account in representing the pilgrim as going north-west from Sutrishan 500 *li* through a great sandy desert to the Sa-mei(or mo)-kan country. This is, as has been shown long ago, the Samarkand of history. Now it is quite true that there is a great sandy desert to the north-west of the Ura-Tube country, but one could not reach Samarkand going north-west from that country. M. St. Martin does not help us here for he carelessly makes the pilgrim put Samarkand to the *south*

---

1 Oriental Geography (tr. Ouseley) ps. 261. 263.
2 Julien III. p. 278.
3 T'ung-chih-liao l. c.
4 T'ang-shu, l. c.

of Sutrishan or Ura-Tube. His words on this subject are—"D'Auratépé ou Asrouchna à Samarkand la distance est d'environs 45 lieues au sud-sudouest: Hiouen-thsang marque 500 (37 lieues) de *Sou-tou-li-se-na* à *Sa-mo-kien* en marchant au sud."[1] In a note to the passage with which we are now engaged Julien apparently makes a mistake in stating that M. St. Martin would substitute *south-west* for the *north-west* of the text. Bretschneider quotes this note and declares the change to be unnecessary. He, however, gets over the difficulty of the text by cutting out the important but puzzling words *"going above 500 li you come to the Sa-mei-kan country."* A traveller proceeding to Samarkand from Ura-Tube would perhaps go north-west as far as Jizak and then turn south-west, performing a journey of about 120 miles. The fact that Yuan-chuang does not seem to have known of the springs of bad brackish water in the northern part of the desert he describes might lead one to think that if he made the journey between the two places he skirted the southern side of the desert. This inference would be strengthened by the mention of mountains and of course by the direction mentioned, viz. north-west.

But taking all circumstances into consideration we must rather decide to regard the whole passage beginning with—"From this above 1000 *li* to Feihan," and ending with "going above 500 *li* you come to Sa-mei-kan" to be an account obtained from others, and not the result of a personal visit. We should, accordingly, perhaps regard the pilgrim as going direct from Tashkend to Samarkand. From this point of view our text must be regarded here as defective, and the last clause of our passage should read—'From Tashkend going above 500 *li* south-west he came to the Sa-mei-kan country.' The distance seems to be too short, but we find that it agrees with accounts given in other Chinese works.[2]

---

[1] Julien III. p. 279.

[2] e. g. in the T'ang-shu l. c.

## SAMARKAND.

The country at which Yuan-chuang now arrived is called by him *Sa-mo* (or *mei*)-*kin* (or *kan*) (颯秣建), a name which has been taken to represent "Samarkand." We may, however, regard the region indicated by the term "Samokan country" to be identical with the Samarkand district without holding that the two names are identical. According to popular accounts the name Samarkand was derived from an Arabian hero and was not given to the city in this district until about A.D. 643. In Chinese literature this name does not appear until the time of the Mongols. It was introduced by them and it was explained as an Arabian word meaning *fan-hua* (繁華) that is, *bustling, full of life, thronged.*[1]

A note to our text tells us that the Samokan country was called in Chinese *K'ang-kuo* (康國) which is the K'ang and K'ang-kü Kuo of the Han and other histories. This K'ang-kü territory had been at one time a large region embracing the districts since known as Ferghana, Kohistan, Tashkend, Samarkand, and other States.[2] But it had become split up among several members of the Shao-wu clan, and in the beginning of the seventh century A.D. the K'ang country was, roughly speaking, that region bounded on the north by the Chash (or Tash) kingdom, on the east by Kohistan, on the south by Kesh, and on the west by Bokhara.

Up to Yuan-chuang's time K'ang seems to have been the only name by which this country was known to the Chinese generally. Other names had been introduced into

---

[1] See the Ching-ting-yuan-shih-yü-chie (欽定元史語解) *ch.* 4, but see also *ch.* 6.

[2] It was originally, however, a small state kept in restraint by the Yue-chih (Getæ) on the south and by the Hiung-nu on the east, and its inhabitants were nomads. See Shih-chi, *ch.* 123. Kangkü was one of Asoka's outlying Provinces which he proposed to hand over to Kunāla.

literature but they could not be said to have been generally adopted. One of these new names was Samokan (薩末鞬) the same with that used by Yuan-chuang, and another was *Si-wan* (or *man*)-*kin* (悉萬斤), neither of which seems to be explained.[1] After Yuan-chuang's time we find other names such as *Sin-ssŭ-kan* (尋思干), and *Sie-mi-ssŭ-kan* (薛迷思干), and these are said to stand for the Turkish Semez-kand meaning "Fat land."[2] *Siman* is another form of the word for *fat* and the Simankin mentioned above may also mean Fat-Land. But Sie-mi-ssŭ-kan is also interpreted as meaning Sun-Land from *Sams* one of the names for the Sun in Arabic. This last term is also given by some writers as a designation for Tashkend rather than for Samarkand. The interpretation already mentioned as given for the name Samarkand apparently takes the Sanskrit form Samara-kanda as the correct one. The word Samara means a *concourse*, a *flocking together*, and Yuan-chuang's Samokan may be for another Sanskrit word with a similar meaning viz. Samāgama.

An old name for the capital of this country is *Su-hie* (蘇薤), that is, Su-hak or Sugat, supposed by some to be for the Sogd of old writers.[3] It is at least doubtful, however, whether this was the city which afterwards became known as Samarkand. In other Chinese writers Suhak was only one of the royal cities of this country.[4] With these the capital has other names such as *Aluti* (阿祿迪) and Pi-t'an (畀闐) in the Ravani land (樂越匿地).[5]

Our author describes the country of Samarkand as being 1600 or 1700 *li* in circuit, greater in extent from east to west

---

[1] T'ang-shuh, *ch.* 221: T'ung-chien-kang-mu *ch.* 39 (T'ang T'ai Tsung 5th y.) where the commentator gives *Si-fang*(方)-*kin* as the name for *Si-wan-kin*.

[2] See Med. Res. Vol. I. p. 76 note, p. 77, 131 and Vol. II. p. 58, 256. See also Schuyler's Turkistan Vol. I. p. 236.

[3] Ch'in-Shu, *ch.* 97: Sui-shu, *ch.* 83. Hirth, Nachworte op. c. S. 85. *Su-hie* is also given as a city of the Tashkend country.

[4] Ma T. l. *ch.* 338.

[5] Ch'ien Han-Shu *ch.* 96: *T'ung-ch'ien-kang-mu*, *ch.* 4.

than from north to south. Its capital was above 20 *li* in circuit, exceedingly strong and with a large population. The country was a great commercial entrepôt, was very fertile, abounding in trees and flowers, and yielding many fine horses. Its inhabitants were skillful craftsmen, smart and energetic. All the Hu (胡) States regarded this country as their centre and made its social institutions their model. The king was a man of spirit and courage and was obeyed by the neighbouring states. He had a splendid army the most of his soldiers being *Chei-kie* (Chak or Tak 赭羯) men. These were men of ardent valour, who looked on death as a going back to their kindred, and against whom no foe could stand in combat.

The term *Che-ka* of this passage is evidently a foreign word and it is interpreted in other books as meaning *Chan-shi* (戰士), "soldier" or "warrior."[1] But another supposition is that it stands for Chalak, the name of a town to the north-west of the city of Samarkand. The district in which Chalak lay was at this time famed for its tall strong men who were much sought after as soldiers. The characters read *Che-ka*, however, seem rather to stand for a word like Ṭakka, the name of a country.

The Life represents the people of Samokan as being Fire-worshippers. Other accounts describe them as being Buddhists in the sixth and seventh centuries although they worshipped also the gods of other religions and their own ancestors. They probably were not all Fire-worshippers, but they were evidently haters and persecutors of Buddhism at the time of Yuan-chuang's visit. There were two monasteries in the capital and when the young Brethren of Yuan-chuang's party went to perform their religious services in one of these the people drove them out and burned the monastery. The king, however, punished the evil-doers and heard the pilgrim expound Buddhism and extol Buddha, and even allowed him to hold a religious public service for the ordination of Brethren to serve in the monasteries.

This king was the head of the Shao-wu clan and the name of the particular branch to which he belonged was

---

[1] T'ang-Shu, l. c. Here the word is written 柘羯.

Wên (溫).[1] The Western Turks had at this time gained the ascendancy in these regions and had become all-powerful. Policy and ambition made this king wed a daughter of the Turkish royal family and the result was that the Samokan (K'ang) country became a vassal to the West Turks. In the year A.D. 631 the king sent an embassy to China praying to be received as a vassal, but the Chinese Emperor for wise and patriotic reasons declined to accede to the request.[2]

The words here rendered "looked on death as going back to their kindred" are *Shih-szŭ-ju-kuei* (視死如歸). The expression means that the *Che-ka* men regarded death as a natural event, as a return to the state from which they had come. It is a literary phrase and is sometimes varied by the addition of *chung* (終), "the end."

Before continuing the narrative of his journey towards India our pilgrim proceeds to give short accounts of several countries in the region around Samokan and connected with that country. His information about these districts was probably obtained from living authorities during his stay at the capital of Samokan (or Samarkand). Commencing with the first country in a southerly direction he tells us that

> "South-east from Samarkand you go to the *Mi-mo-ha* (弭秣賀) country." This country, which was situated in the mountains, was 400 or 500 *li* in circuit, long from north to south and narrow from east to west. In the products of the land and the ways of the people it resembled Samokan.

The Life does not mention this place and Yuan-chuang, it will be seen, does not tell us how far it was from Samokan. In other Chinese books its situation is described as being 100 *li* to the south or south-east of Samarkand, 500 *li* from Ura-Tube on the north-west (a mistake for north-east) and 200 *li* from Kesh on the south-west, or according to one authority 400 *li* from Kesh on the south.[3]

---

1 Wei-Shu, *ch.* 102.

2 T'ung-chien-kang-mu, *ch.* 39: T'ang Shu l. c.

3 T'ang-shu, l. c.: T'ung-chih-liao, l. c.: Ma T. l. l. c.

A note to our text tells us that the Chinese name for Mimoho was *Mi*(米)-*kuo*, Mi's country, Mi being another scion of the Shao-wu clan. Its foreign name also is given elsewhere as *Mi-mo* (彌末) and it probably was something like Maimak or Memagh. From other sources we learn that the capital, the name of which was *Po-si-tê* (鉢息德), was about two *li* in circuit and was on the west side of the Na-mi (那密) River. This country which was formerly a part of the great K'ang kingdom fell into the hands of the West Turks while Yuan-chuang was on his pilgrimage.[1]

M. Saint-Martin identifies Mimoho with Moughian or Maghin, "à 38 lieues de Samarkand vers l'est en inclinant au sud."[2] This town, the Maghian of our maps, is much too far from Samarkand if we accept the statement that Mimo was 100 *li* or about twenty miles from that place. Maghian is about sixty miles south-east from the site of old Samarkand which was a little to the north and northwest of the present city.

The narrative in the Records continues—

> From this [going] north you arrive at the *Kie* (*Ki* or *Ka*)-*putan-na* (劫布呾那) country.

A note to the text tells us that the Chinese name for this country was *Ts'ao*(曹)-*kuo*, kingdom of Ts'ao, who was another brother of the Shao-wu family. This information, however, is unsatisfactory as there were at this time in this region four Ts'ao kingdoms, known as East, Middle, West Ts'ao and Ts'ao simply. Of these the first corresponded to the Sutrishan or Ura-Tube district, which, as has been seen, was also called Kaputana. The Ts'ao of the note was apparently understood to include the Middle and West Ts'ao.

When the narrative states that "north from this" you go to Kaputana the word *this* is apparently to be taken as meaning Samokan. In the Fang-chih the direction is

---

[1] Tung-chien-kang-mu *ch.* 40 (T'ang T'ai Tsung, 16th y.)

[2] Julien III. p. 280.

given as North-west and this is perhaps right. M. Saint-Martin takes the words "from this" to refer to *Mi-mo* or Maghian, and supposes the Kaputana country to be a city "Kebond" about the situation of which nothing is known.[1] But it is better to understand our author as taking Samarkand as the point of departure; and the Kaputana country is then probably represented by the present Mitan and the surrounding district. The Ts'ao country, we are told, was to the north-west of Kang-kü and Middle Ts'ao to its north. Mitan is about thirty miles north-west from the modern Samarkand and in the district which includes Chalak once famous for its good soldiers.

Our author continues his account—

> Going west from this country for above 300 *li* you come to the *K'u-shuang-ni-ka* or *Ku-san-ni-ka* (屈霜你伽) country.

In other treatises we find this name written *Kuei-sang-ni* (貴霜匿) read Kusannik.[2] The Chinese name, we are told in a note to our text was *Ho*(何)-*kuo*, the kingdom of Ho, another scion of the Shao-wu clan. The great Buddhist monk named Sangha, who came to China in A.D. 660, declared himself to be a native of this country, and claimed to be a member of the Ho family.[3]

M. Saint Martin supposes the Kusannik of our author to be the "Koschanieh or Kochania" halfway between Samarkand and Bokhara. The Life, which has omitted all mention of Mimoha and Kaputana makes Kusannik to be above 300 *li* west from Samokan. This, I think, is also the meaning of the passage in our text; and about 60 miles west of Samokan, or north-west from Samarkand, would bring us to the neighbourhood of the modern Panjshamba district.

Our text proceeds—

> From this country, that is apparently, Kusannik it is above 200 *li* to the Hoh-han (喝捍) country.

---

1 Julien III. p. 281.

2 Ma T. l. *ch.* 338: T'ang-shu, *ch.* 221.

3 Sung-kao-sêng-chuan, *ch.* 18.

The note to the text tells us that the Chinese name for this country was *Tung-An*(東 安)-*kuo* or "East-An kingdom." *An*, as we have seen, was the name of one of the Shao-wu brothers, and this chief evidently had a large principality. *Hoh-han* was only a part and was called the "Small country." It was south of the *Na-mi* river, and its capital had the same name also written *Hoh-han* (喝 汗) and probably pronounced like Khakan or Khagan.[1] M. Saint-Martin identifies this district with that of the modern Kermineh or Kerminah, and he is probably nearly correct.

West from Hoh-han 400 *li* was the *Pu-hoh* (捕 喝) country.

This country which, a note to our text tells us, was called by the Chinese the "Middle *An* kingdom," is placed by the T'ang-Shu 100 *li* to the south-west of Hoh-han. It is the country which is called *Niu-mi* (忸 蜜) in some books, and it is also called the An and the Great An kingdom. For the *Pu-hoh* of our text we find *Pu-huoh* (布 豁) and these two probably represent an original like Bōkh or Bokhar.[2] M. Saint-Martin and Dr Bretschneider identify the country with the modern Bokhara,[3] and they are doubtless right: but the Bōkh of our pilgrim was apparently to the north of the present city and district of Bokhara.

Our author continues—

From this country (i. e. Bōkh) west above 400 *li* is the Fah-ti (伐 地) country.

This is the reading of the A, B, and D texts, but instead of *Fa-ti* the C text has *Ṣu*(戍)-*ti* in on place and *Wu* (or *Mu* 戊)-*ti* in another. Then the Life, which also reads *Fah-ti*, reduces the distance from Bōkh from 400 to 100 *li*. The usual note to the text tells us that the Chinese name for the country was "Hsi-an-kuo" or "West An kingdom." In the T'ang-Shu we find the above *Wu*

---

1 Ma T. l. l. c.: T'ang-Shu, l. c.

2 Ma T. l. l. c.: T'ang-Shu, l. c.

3 Julien III. p. 282; Med. Res. Vol. II. p. 62.

(or *Mu*)-*ti* given as the name of one of the nine Shao-wu chiefs; and it also mentions a *Su-ti* district in this region.[1] Taking *Fah-ti* as the reading we may regard this transcription as possibly representing a name like *Paptei*. St. Martin finds the modern representative of Fah-ti in Bētik, "lieu situé sur la droite de l'Oxus, à une trentaine de lieues au sud-ouest de Boukhara." But we should probably regard the *Fa-ti* of our text as having had a situation in the neighbourhood of the present Darganata district on the west side of the Oxus. This Fa-ti (or Su-ti) is perhaps the principality designated *Niao-na-ga* or *Wu-na-ga* (鳥 or 烏 那 遏) which was to the west of the Oxus about 400 *li* South-west from the *An* country.[2]

The narrative proceeds—

> From this, that is, Fah-ti it is over 500 *li* south-west to the *Huo-li-si-mi-ka* (貨 利 習 彌 伽) country. This lay along the banks of the Oxus being 20 or 30 *li* east to west and above 500 *li* north to south.

M. Saint Martin substitutes *north-west* for the south-west of this passage, and he is doubtless right.[3] All the texts, however, have *south-west* and the Life has *west*, but the T'ang-Shu places this country 600 *li* to the north-west of *Su-ti* (Fa-ti). In the B, C, and D texts there is a Chinese note to the text which contains only the words for "in Chinese," but A supplies the name which had dropped out. This is *Huo-sin*(火 尋)-*kuo*, this kingdom of *Huo-sin* (or *sün*), one of the princes of the Shao-wu family. The country here called *Huo-li-si-mi-ka* or Khorismika(?) has been identified with the modern Khanate of Khiva corresponding to the Kharesm or Khorazm of ancient authors.[4] In the T'ang-Shu *Huo-li-si-mi* and *Kuo-li* (過 利) are given as synonyms for *Huo-sin*, and the country is described as being south of the Oxus and as having bullock-waggons

---

1 T'ang-Shu l. c.

2 Ma T. l. l. c.: T'ung-chih-liao, l. c. In the Sui-Shu l. c. Wu-na-ka (or-ga) is one of the Shao-wu princes.

3 Julien III. p. 283.

4 Med. Res. II. p. 91.

which were used by travelling merchants.[1] In some of the lists of the Shao-wu princes the name Huo-sin does not occur.

## KASANNA.

The pilgrim now resumes the narrative of his journey. He relates that

> from the Samokan country he went south-west above 300 *li* to the *Ka-shuang-na* or Kasanna (羯霜那) country. This was 1400 or 1500 *li* in circuit and it resembled Samarkand in its natural products and the ways and customs of the people.

All texts and the Fang-chih seem to agree in the reading "from Samokan," but the Life makes the pilgrim proceed from Kharesm. This, however, is undoubtedly wrong and quite impossible. In the Chinese note to our text we are told that the Chinese name for this country was *Shih*(史)*-kuo*, the kingdom of Shih, another of the nine Shao-wu chiefs. From other sources we learn that the country was called also *K'a-sha* (佉沙) and *K'ê-shih* (渴石)[2] which are perhaps only different forms of a name like Kesh. This is perpetuated in the modern name of the district, Kesh, derived directly perhaps from the name of the city *Ki-shih* (乞史) which was built in the 7th century. The capital, corresponding to the present Shahr-i-sebs or Shehr, lay about ten *li* south of the *Tu-mo* (獨莫) River.[3] This is probably the present Kashka-daria "on which the city is founded." Kesh was formerly a dependency of Kangkü which lay 240 *li* to the north of it.

## THE IRON PASS.

Our pilgrim's narrative proceeds—

> From Kesh he proceeded south-west above 200 *li* and entered a range of mountains. Here his path was a narrow risky track; there were no inhabitants and little grass or water. Travelling

---

1 T'ang-Shu, l. c.
2 T'ang-Shu, l. c.
3 Med. Res. Vol. II. p. 273.

among the hills in a south-east direction for above 300 *li* he entered the Iron Pass (lit. Iron Gate). Along this Iron Pass on either side is a very high precipitous mountain. Although there is a narrow path in it this is still more inaccessible. The rocks which rise up on both sides are of an iron colour; when the gates were set up they were also strengthened with iron, and numerous small iron bells were suspended on them. The name it bears was given to the Pass on account of its impregnable nature.

Yuan-chuang apparently went from Kesh to the neighbourhood of the place now called Ghuzar Fort, and then turning south-east followed the Ghuzar river until he reached the Iron Pass. But the Life does not make any mention of the change of direction from south-west to south-east. The words for "Although there is a narrow path" are in all my texts *Sui-yu-hsia-ching* (雖有狹徑), but Julien's text seems to have had instead of *sui* the word *li* (離). So his translation of the clause which seems to give better sense is—"Elles (i. e. the "deux montagnes parallèles") ne sont séparées que par un sentier qui est fort étroit, et, en outre, hérissé de précipices." But one does not see how there could be "précipices," and *sui* is the correct reading.

In Dr Bretschneider's learned treatise, to which reference is so often made in these pages, the reader will find much information about the Iron Pass (or Gate).[1] It is the Buzgola-Khana or Goat-house of the Hindus and it is known by other names. According to some its width varies from 40 to 60 feet and it is about two miles in length: a stream flows through it and it contains a village. The Life represents the actual gate as being made of the raw iron of the mountains plated with iron and furnished with iron bells, and hence, according to it, came the name of the pass or rather Gate. But the pilgrim used *mên* in the sense of Pass or Passage and he understood this

---

[1] Op. c. I. p. 82 and II. p. 274. See also Reclus, Geog. T. VI. p. 502. Rémusat, Nouv. Mel. As. T. 1. p. 238; Sui-Shu *ch.* 83; T'ang-Shu l. c.; Hirth's Nachworte op. c. p. 84ff.

to have the epithet Iron because it was strong and impregnable. Later travellers relate that the Pass was guarded by a barrier (or barriers) of the iron-stone of the place clamped or faced with iron. But no one after Yuan-chuang's time seems to have seen an actual gate hung with bells, and we read only of a tradition that there had once been a great gate. This Pass once checked the Tu-kue or Turks in their western advances, and kept them and Tokharans apart; and it became famous in the time of the Mongol conquests. In Chinese works of the T'ang and later periods it is often called the *T'ie-mên-kuan* or "Pass of the Iron Gate." It is thus described by a recent writer—"The famous ravine of the Iron Gate winds through a high mountain chain, about twelve versts to the west of Derbent. It is a narrow cleft, 5 to 36 paces wide and about two versts long. It is known now as Buzghala Khána (i. e. the house of Goats). Its eastern termination is 3540 feet above the sea; its western termination 3740 feet. A torrent, Buzghala Khána bulák flows, through it."[1]

## TU-HUO-LO (TOKHARA).

Our narrative proceeds to describe that

> going out of the Iron Pass you reach the *Tu-huo-lo* country. This was above 1000 *li* north to south and 3000 *li* east to west; it reached on the east to the Ts'ung-Ling, on the west to Persia, on the south to the Great Snow Mountains (the Hindu-Kush) and on the north to the Iron Pass; the river Oxus flowed through the middle of it from east to west; for several centuries the succession to the sovereignty had been interrupted and the country was divided into 27 States with separate chiefs and all subject to the Turks, "When the climate becomes warm there is much sickness. and at the end of winter and beginning of spring there is constant rain (in C. "a succession of hoarfrost and rain"); hence in all the countries south of this to *Lan-p'o* much heat-sickness is a natural characteristic; hence the Buddhist Brethren go into Retreat of the Rainy season on the 16th day of the 12th month and go out on the 15th day of the 3rd month; this is because there is much rain then, thus making their

---

1 Tarikh-i-Rashid by Elias and Ross p. 20.

religious precepts conform to the seasons." The people were pusillanimous and ill-favoured, but they were in a manner reliable and were not given to deceitful ways. They had a peculiar spoken language and an alphabet of 25 letters, their writing was horizontal from left to right, and their records had gradually increased until they exceeded those of *Su-li* in number. They had for clothing more calico (*tieh*) than serge; their currency consisted of gold, silver, and other coins which were different from those of other countries.

The *Tu-huo-lo* (覩貨邏) of this passage is undoubtedly the Tokhara of old western geographers. In the Chinese note to the text we are told that an old and incorrect name was *T'u-huo-lo* (吐火羅), which is the transcription used in the Sui-Shu. There are also other transcriptions of the name such as the *T'u-hu-lo* (吐呼羅) of early writers, but the differences are not important. In certain Chinese translations of Buddhist treatises the name is given *T'u-ka-lê* (兜佉 (or 呿) 勒) or Tukhar.[1] The Sanskrit name is Tukhāra another form of which is Tushāra. This word has the meanings of *frost*, *snow*, and *mist* or *vapour*.

The extent and boundaries of the country named Tokhara found in other works differ considerably from those given by our pilgrim.[2] It was supposed to correspond partly to the great Ta-Hsia of early Chinese records,[3] and portions of the present Bokhara and Badakshan seem to have been once included under this name. Saint Martin and Yule[4] are positive in asserting that Yuan-chuang's Tokhara was the country of the Yetha, but this is against Chinese authority. In the Wei-Shu and Sui-Shu, for example, we have distinct accounts of Tokhara and of the Yetha, and the people of the former are referred to the Small Yue-ti, while the Yetha are said to have been of the original Yue-ti stock. The Yetha

---

1 Ta-chih-tu-lun, *ch.* 25 (No. 1169); Vibhāsha-lun, *ch.* 9 (No. 1279 tr. A.D. 383).

2 Ma T. l. *ch.* 339.

3 T'ang-Shu, *ch.* 221; T'ung-chien-kang-mu, *ch.* 40 (T'ang T'ai Tsung 16th year).

4 Julien III. p. 285; J. R. A. S. Vol. VI. p. 94.

and Tokharians lived together; but the former were nomads, while the latter were dwellers in towns.

The part of the passage within inverted commas reads in Julien's version thus—"La température étant constamment tiède, les épidémies y sont très fréquentes. A la fin de l'hiver et au commencement du printemps, il tombe des pluies continuelles. C'est pourquoi au sud de ce pays, et au nord de *Lan-po*, il règne beaucoup d'épidémies. De là vient que tous les religieux entrent dans les demeures fixes le seizième jour du douzième mois, et en sortent le quinzième jour du troisième. Cet usage est fondé sur l'abondance des pluies. Les instructions qu'on leur donne sont subordonnées aux saisons."[1] Now the text does not seem to assert that the temperature of this large region was *constamment tiède*, and that consequently epidemics were frequent. Such a statement, moreover, would be at variance with other passages in this *chuan* such as the descriptions of Kie-chih and Bamian. It is true, however, that Ma Tuan-lin, on the authority of others, represents the Tokhara country as having a hot climate; but that was evidently only in the summer, for the inhabitants were able to store ice for use during the hot weather. What our author apparently wanted his readers to understand was that the climate became warm or mild in early spring when the rainy season began: this change in the temperature produced much illness which was called "Heat (or Spring) sickness." In all my texts the reading here is *wên-chi* (温疾), but Julien's text may have had *wên*(瘟)*-chi*, and this is rightly translated in his note "maladies épidémiques." Because the early spring was the rainy season of these countries the Buddhist Brethren in them made that their time of Retreat from the Rain.

[1] The text of the passage is—氣序旣温疾疫 (in B 吐) 亦衆冬末春初霖 (in C 霜) 雨相繼故此境己南濫波己北其國風土並多温疾而諸僧徒以十二月十六日入安居三月十五日解安居斯乃據其多雨亦是設教隨時也.

In India the rainy season was in the summer, and this was the time of year in which Retreat was to be observed according to the Vinaya. By changing the time of Retreat these Brethren departed from the letter but conformed to the spirit of their regulations.

For a long time the name Tokhara seems to have practically gone out of use, and the country which once bore the name is now to some degree represented by Badakshan.[1] Even in our pilgrim's time it was properly not the name of a country but of a great tribe or people occupying a certain large territory.

Proceeding with his description of the region the pilgrim tells us that

> following the course of the Oxus down northwards you come to *Ta-mi* (Termed or Termez).[2] This country was above 600 *li* long (from east to west) and 400 *li* broad (from north to south), and its capital was above 20 *li* in circuit longer than broad. There were above ten monasteries with more than 1000 Brethren: its topes and images of Buddha were very remarkable and exhibited miracles.
>
> To the east of *Ta-mi* was the *Chih-ga-yen-na* country, above 400 *li* long by 500 *li* wide, its capital being above ten *li* in circuit. It had five monasteries but the Buddhist Brethren were very few.
>
> To the east of it was the *Hu-lu-mo* country, above 100 *li* long and 300 broad with a capital above ten *li* in circuit. Its king was a *Hi-su* Turk: it had two monasteries and above 100 Buddhist Brethren.
>
> To the east of it was *Su-man* which was above 400 *li* long by 100 *li* broad, its capital being 16 or 17 *li* in circuit; its king was a *Hi-su* Turk; there were two monasteries and very few Buddhist Brethren.
>
> To the south-west and on the Oxus was *Ku-ho-yen-ná*. This country was above 200 *li* long and 300 *li* wide, its capital being above ten *li* in circuit. It had three monasteries and above 100 Buddhist Brethren.
>
> To the east was *Huo-sha*, a country above 300 *li* long by 500 *li* wide, its capital being 16 or 17 *li* in circuit.
>
> On its east was the *Ko-tu-lo* country above 1000 *li* long and

---

[1] See Med. Res. Vol. II. p. 99.

[2] For the various States here mentioned and briefly described by the pilgrim see Yule in J. R. A. S. Vol. VI. Art. V.

the same in width, its capital being 20 *li* in circuit. It reached on the east to the *Ku-mi-tê* country in the Ts'ung-Ling.

The *Ku-mi-tê* country was above 2000 *li* long and 200 *li* wide; it was in the Ts'ung-Ling mountains; its capital was above 20 *li* in circuit: on the south-east it was near the Oxus and on the south it adjoined the *Shih-k'i-ni* country.

To the south across the Oxus were the countries called *Ta-mo-si-t'ie-ti, Po-to-chuang-na, Yin-po-kan, Ku-lang-na, Hi-mo-ta-la, Po-li-ho, Ki-li-si-mo, Ko-lo-hu, A-li-ni, Mêng-kan.* South-east from the *Huo* (Kunduz) country were the *K'uo-si-to,* and *An-ta-lo-fo* countries, the circumstances about these being related in the account of the return journey.[1] South-west from *Huo* was the *Fo-ka-lang* country which was above 50 *li* long and 200 *li* broad, its capital being above ten *li* in circuit. South of it was the *Ki-lu-si-min-kan* country which was above 1000 *li* in circuit, its capital being 14 or 15 *li* in circuit. To the north-west of it was the *Hu-lin* country which was 800 *li* in circuit with its capital five or six in circuit. It had above ten monasteries with more than 500 Buddhist Brethren.

In the Life we are merely told that the pilgrim travelled some hundreds of *li* from Tokhara, crossed the Oxus and came to the *Huo* country (Kunduz). This was the residence of *Ta-tu* (呾度) the *Shê* (設) or General in command, the eldest son of the She-hu Khan and a brother-in-law of the king of Kao-ch'ang.[2] This king had given

---

[1] See *Chuan* XII: *ch.* XVIII.

[2] The whole of this paragraph is taken from the Life, *ch.* II. Julien I. p. 62f. In this passage the word *Ta-tu* is apparently treated as a personal name but it was rather a generic name qualifying a title. It is found with a slight variation of transcription prefixed as here to She, and also to Khan. We must regard it as a foreign word, but we may hesitate to accept its identification with Tardush or Tardu. This latter term is generally used to designate a Turkish tribe or horde, but it also occurs in an inscription as the name of a Kirghiz envoy. The Ta-tu of our passage cannot be regarded as having a tribal significance, and here as in other places it seems to qualify the title to which it is prefixed. See T'ung-chien-kang-mu, *ch.* 40 (T'ang T'ai Tsung 15th y.); Thomsen's Inscriptions de l'Orkhon ps. 63, 114, 146; Hirth Nachworte S. 130f.

The Shê of this passage is of frequent occurrence in Chinese history treating of the Turks. It is explained as meaning *soldier* or *General,* but the title is always applied to a very high military officer usually a near relative of the Khan. This *Shê* is regarded

a letter of introduction, but when Yuan-chuang arrived the Kao-ch'ang princess was dead and the General was ill, and hearing of the pilgrim's arrival with a letter he with his male and female retinue made uncontrollable lamentation. He invited the pilgrim to rest for a time, promising that if he recovered he would accompany the pilgrim to India. The General recovered by the help of the exorcisms of an Indian Buddhist monk, but he was poisoned by a young queen at the instigation of a stepson.[1] Then this stepson *T'ek'in,* the son by the Kao-ch'ang princess being a child, usurped the position of General and married his step-mother (the young wife whom he had induced to murder her husband and his father). On account of the funeral services for the General the pilgrim was detained here more than a month. In this time he made the acquaintance of a great Buddhist monk named Dharmasangha who had a very high reputation as a profound scholar in Buddhism. But Yuan-chuang found him to be only superficially acquainted with the Hīnayānist books, and he knew nothing of Mahāyānism. When the pilgrim was ready to continue his journey he asked the new General for escort and post accommodation[2] on the way southwards towards India. The General strongly recom-

---

as a transcription of an old Turkish word Shad. Thomsen, Inscriptions, p. 146; Hirth, Nachworte S. 45.

1 According to the text the Shê or Military governor after his marriage with the Kaochang princess had taken a new Khatun or queen. This young concubine urged on by the son of a senior queen poisoned her lord, and thereupon the young prince took his father's place to the concubine and people. He is here called *T'ê-kin* (特勤) as if this were his personal name. But *T'ê-kin* is said to be for the Turkish word Tagin (or Tegin) meaning *Prince,* and it is of frequent occurrence as a high title. See Schlegel's Stéle funeraire p. 6; Thomsen's Inscriptions p. 73.

2 For "post accommodation" here the original is *Wu-lo* (鄔落). This is a word common to the Mongols and Turks and is known as *ula* or *ulak.* It denotes the contributions of service imposed on subjects by government, and includes the supply of men and horses and accommodation for officials when travelling on duty.

mended him to visit the *Fo-ho-lo* country, which belonged to his horde, and had interesting sacred sites. This advice was urged also by certain Brethren from that country who had come to *Huo* in connection with the change of administration, and Yuan-chuang acted on the advice, and joined these Brethren on their return.

Most of the countries here described as lying between the Iron Pass and Bamian are mentioned again in the account of the return journey, and it is not necessary to refer to them further at present.

## FO-HO (BALKH).

The narrative in the Records proceeds to relate that

West (i. e. from *Hu-lin*) you reach *Fo-ho*. This country was above 800 *li* from east to west and 400 *li* north to south, reaching on the north to the Oxus. The capital, which all called "Little Rajagriha city," was above twenty *li* in circuit, but though it was strong it was thinly peopled. In natural products the district was rich and the land and water flowers were too many to enumerate. There were above 100 Buddhist monasteries with more than 3000 Brethren all adherents of the "Small Vehicle' system.

Outside the capital on the south-west side was the *Na-fo* (Nava)-Sanghārāma or New Monastery built by a former king of the country. This was the only Buddhist establishment north of the Hindu-Kush in which there was a constant succession of Masters who were commentators on the canon. The image of the Buddha in this monastery was artistically made of (according to one reading, studded with) noted precious substances, and its halls were adorned with costly rarities, hence it was plundered for gain by the chiefs of the various states. In the monastery was an image of Vaiśravana deva which had bona fide miracles and in mysterious ways protected the establishment. The pilgrim tells how not long before the time of his visit this deva had frustrated an armed attempt of the Turkish *She-hu* or governor name *Ssŭ*, the son of a governor, to invade and plunder the monastery.

In the South Buddha-Hall of this establishment were Buddha's washing-basin about one *tou* in capacity: so bright and dazzling was the blending of colours in this basin that one could not well tell whether it was of stone or metal. There was also a tooth of the Buddha an inch long and $^{8}/_{10}$ths of an inch broad, and there was his broom made of *kāśa* grass above two feet long and about seven inches round, the handle being set with pearls. On the six festival days these relics were exhibited to the assembled lay and clerical worshippers. On such occasions the relics moved by the "thorough sincerity" of a worshipper may emit a brilliant light.

To the north of the New Monastery was a tope above 200 feet high which was plastered with diamond-cement. This tope was also ornamented with various precious substances, and it contained relics which sometimes shone with supernatural light.

South-west from the New Monastery was a *ching-lü* (精 廬) or Buddhist temple. This had been built long ago, and had been the resort of Brethren of high spiritual attainments from all quarters. It had been found impossible to keep a record of those who here realized the Four Fruits (that is, became arhats). So topes were erected for those arhats who when about to die made a public exhibition of their miraculous powers; the bases of these topes were very close together and were some hundreds odd in number. But no memorial erection was made in the case of those Brethren, about 1000 in number, who although arhats had died without exhibiting miracles. In this establishment were above 100 Brethren, who were "day and night assiduous at their duties," and one could not tell which was common monk and which was arhat.

The *Fo-ho* (縛 喝) of this passage has been identified with the city and district of Balkh and the identification is probably quite correct. But we cannot properly regard the Chinese word as a transcription of the word Balkh, or of its variant Pahl, or of Vāhlīka the name in the Bṛihat-samhitā and supposed to be the original form.[1] In the Life the name is given as *Fo-ho-lo* and I-ching writes it *Fo-k'o-lo.*[2] These transcriptions seem to require an original like Bokhar or Bokhara, the name of the country which included Balkh. The *Fo-ho* or Balkh of our pilgrim was evidently not very far west or north-west from *Huo* (Kunduz) and it was under the same Turkish governor with that State. The pilgrim, the Life tells us, beheld Balkh as a "Better Land", with its cities and their sur-

---

1 Julien III. p. 289: Alberuni Vol. I. p. 300: Fleet Ind. Ant. Vol. XXII. p. 192.

2 Hsi-yü-ch'iu, *ch.* 1 and Chavannes Mémoires p$^s$. 23, 48.

roundings in bold relief, and its vales and country districts rich and fertile. The description which he gives of the capital and the surrounding district agrees with the accounts of later travellers.[1]

The *Nava-sanghārāma* or New Monastery of this passage is the Nava-vihāra and *Hsin-ssŭ* (with the same meaning) of I-ching, who also represents the establishment as being occupied by Brethren of the Hīnayāna system.[2] In the Life the Buddha's washing basin in this monastery is of a capacity of two *tou*, and another account makes it to have held only a *shêng*. The *tou* of the T'ang period was a little more than nine quarts, and the *shêng* was only about a pint. The basin and the tooth and the broom were exhibited to the worshippers on the sacred days. On these occasions the "thorough sincerity," the full-hearted earnestness of devotees sometimes had power to move the relics to shed a brilliant light. For "thorough sincerity" the term in the text is *Chih-ch'êng* (至誠) a classical expression derived from the "Chung-yung."[3] The Confucianist believed that this "thorough sincerity" enabled its possessor to have a subtle influence over external nature. But to the pilgrim, a Confucianist converted to Buddhism, its power in a believing worshipper extended to the mysterious powers associated with the sacred objects of his adopted religion. This New Monastery, Yuan-chuang tells us, was under the protection of Vaiśravana-deva who kept guard over the establishment. It was to this deva that Indra on the death of the Buddha entrusted the defence of Buddhism in the northern regions, and it was in this capacity that he had charge of the monastery. Here at the time of Yuan-chuang's visit was a very genial learned Brother from the *Che-ka* country from whom our pilgrim received much kindness and assistance in his

---

1 Cf. Q. Curtius B. VII. *ch.* 18; Burnes' Travels into Bokhara *ch.* VIII.

2 Hsi-yü-ch'iu, l. c.

3 *Ch.* 22.

studies. With this Brother, named Prajñākara, Yuan-chuang read certain Abhidharma treatises and also the Vibhāsha-śāstra. There were also in the monastery at the time two learned and esteemed Doctors in Buddhism who treated the Chinese pilgrim with great courtesy.

The term which the Records and the Life use for the Buddhist establishment to the south-west of the New Monastery is, it will be observed, *Ching-lü*. This phrase means "the cottage of the essential," and it is perhaps a synonym of *Ching-shê*, an old and common term with a similar meaning. Our pilgrim may have taken it over from a previous writer who used it in the sense of Vihāra, as Julien translates it here. It is to be observed that the Life does not know anything of the invidious distinction in the treatment given to the relics of the arhats of this temple who died after miraculous exhibitions, and that of the relics of those arhats who passed away without such exhibitions. The pilgrim, as we have seen, describes the 100 Brethren in the establishment at his time as "day and night assiduous at their duties." The words within inverted commas are a quotation with the alteration of one character from a wellknown passage in the Shih-ching and they are a stock literary phrase.[1] He adds that one cannot distinguish among them the ordinary Brother from the arhat. Instead of this last clause Julien has—"Il est difficile de scruter le cœur des hommes vulgaires et des saints," but this platitude cannot be forced out of the text. This simply tells us that all the Brethren were so zealous in the observances of their religion that one could not tell which was common monk and which was arhat.

At a distance of above 50 *li* north-west from the capital was *T'i-wei's* city and above 40 *li* to the north of that was *P'o-li's* city. In each of these towns was a tope above thirty feet high. Now the story of these topes was this. As soon as Ju-lai long ago attained Buddhahood he went to the Bodhi Tree and thence to the Deer Park (near Benares). At this time two householders

---

1 The sentence in the original runs—今僧徒百餘人夙夜匪懈凡聖難測.

meeting him in his majestic glory gave him of their travelling provisions parched grain and honey. Bhagavat expounded to them what brings happiness to men and devas, and these two householders were the first to hear the Five Commandments and Ten Virtues. When they had received the religious teaching they requested something to worship, and Julai gave them of his hair and nail(-pairings). The two men being about to return to their native country begged to have rule and pattern for their service of worship. Julai thereupon making a square pile of his saṅghāṭī, or lower robe, laid it on the ground, and did the same with his uttarāsaṅga or outer robe and his Saṁkachchikam, the robe which goes under the arm-pits, in succession. On the top of these he placed his bowl inverted, and then set up his mendicant's staff, thus making a tope. The two men, accepting the Julai's instructions, returned each to his city, and according to the pattern thus taught by the Buddha they proceeded to erect these two topes, the very first in the dispensation of Sākyamuni Buddha. Above 70 *li* west of the capital was a tope which had been built in the time of Kāśyapa Buddha.

The *T'i-wei* (提謂) and *P'oli* (波利) of this very curious passage are the names of men not of cities. They stand for Trapusha (or Tapassu) and Bhallika (or Bhalluka) and are the transcriptions used by some of the early translators.[1] The former is sometimes translated as *Huang-kua* (黃瓜). "a gourd" or "melon" and in Tibetan as Ga-gong with similar meaning: Bhallika is translated *Ts'un-lo* (村落), "a village," but the Tibetan rendering means "good" or "fortunate" (Bhalluka).[2] These two men were travelling merchants or caravan-chiefs from a far land.[3] The story of their giving the Buddha his first food after he attained Buddhahood is told in many books with

---

[1] They are used in the Hsiu-hsing-pên-ch'i-ching (No. 664. tr. A.D. 197); in the Fo-shuo-t'ai-tzŭ-sui-ying-pên-ch'i-ching, *ch.* 1 (No. 665, tr. cir. A.D. 250).

The two merchants' names are also given as Bhadrasena and Bhadrālik (Yin-kuo-ching, *ch.* 3. No. 666 tr. cir. A.D. 450), and as Kua or "Melon" (Trapusha) and Upali in the Ssŭ-fên Vinaya, *ch.* 31 where the men are brothers.

[2] Sar. Vin. P'o-sêng-shih, *ch.* 5 (No. 1123): Rockhill Life p. 34.

[3] The village of the great alms-giving is also located on the way between Bodhigaya and Benares and its name given as Tapussa-bhalik (多謂娑 for 娑跋利).

some variations. In a late Sinhalese text these pious merchants erected a ṭope over the precious hair- and nail-cuttings in Ceylon;[1] in a Burmese story the monument was erected in Burmah;[2] and in the account which Yuan-chuang gives in *Chüan* VIII a monument was erected at the place where the incident occurred.[3] Some versions represent the two traders as being men from the north, some represent them as brothers, and in some versions there is only one man. The ridiculous story told here of the Buddha's extemporized model of a tope does not seem to be found in any other account of the incident. It gives us, however, the plain outline of the original or early Buddhist tope or pagoda,—a square base surmounted by a cylinder on which was a dome topped by a spire. Julien evidently misunderstood the passage and he had a faulty text. He makes the pilgrim state that Julai took off his saṅghāṭī "formé de pièces de coton carrées". He had the Ming text reading *tieh* meaning "cotton" but the C and D texts have the *tieh* which means to *double, fold, pile.* The topes which these two merchants erected in their respective native places are not represented as the first structures of the kind, but only as the first in the Buddhadom of Śākyamuni. The very next sentence, as we have seen, tells of a Kāśyapa Buddha tope in the same district.

The narrative continues.

> South-west from the capital [of Balkh] coming into a corner of the Snowy mountains you arrive at the *Yue-mei* (or *mo*)-*t'ê* country. This was 50 or 60 *li* long by 100 *li* wide, and its capital was above ten *li* in circuit.

Julien who transliterates the Chinese characters for the name of this country by *Jui-mo-tho,* suggests Jumadha as the foreign word transcribed. But the first character (銳)

---

[1] Hardy M. B. p. 186.

[2] Bigandet Legend vol. i. p. 108.

[3] The version in the Lalitavistara Ch. XXIV, and some other versions of the story do not make mention of the hair and nails relics and the topes.

was read *yue* and the name was probably something like Yumadha. Our author in this passage uses the mode of description which is supposed to indicate that he is giving a second-hand report not the result of a personal visit. But we know from the Life that the pilgrim did go to this country at the pressing invitation of its king who shewed him great kindness.

To the south-west [of *Yue-mei-t'ê*] was the *Hu-shih-kan* country. This was above 500 *li* long and above 1000 *li* broad, and its capital was above 20 *li* in circuit: it had many hills and vales and yielded good horses.

This country, according to the T'ang-Shu, extended on the south-east to Bamian. M. Saint Martin thinks that the *Hu-shih-kan* of this passage may be the district called by the Persians *Juskān* which was "entre Balkh et le district de Méroū-er-Roūd". The pilgrim made a short visit to this country also, we learn from the Life.[1]

North-west [from *Hu-shih-kan*] was *Ta-la-kan*. This country was above 500 *li* long by 50 or 60 *li* wide, and its capital was more than ten *li* in circuit: on the west it adjoined *Po-la-ssŭ* (Persia).

M. Saint-Martin thinks that this name *Ta-la-kan* "nous conduit indubitalement à la *Talekān* du Ghardjistān, ville située à trois petites journées au-dessus de Méroū-er-Roūd, dans la direction de Herat."[2] The name which he has here transcribed may have been Talakan or Tarkan, but it is not likely that the characters were used to represent a word like Talikan or Talekan.

The pilgrim now resumes his journey towards India.

From Balkh he went south more than 100 *li* to *Kie(Ka)-chih*. This country was above 500 *li* long and 300 *li* wide, and its capital was five or six *li* in circuit. It was a very stony, hilly country with few fruits and flowers but much pulse and wheat; the climate was very cold; the people's ways were hard and brusque. There were more than ten monasteries with 300 Brethren all attached to the Sarvāstivādin school of the "Small Vehicle" system.

---

1 Julien III. p. 290. Cf. Yule in J. R. A. S. Vol. vi, p. 102.

2 Julien III. p. 289. Cf. Yule, l. c.; Med. Res. Vol. ii. p. 98.

The word here transcribed *Ka-chih* has been restored as Gachi and Gaz, and Yule took the country to be "the Darah or Valley of Gaz".[1]

## BAMIAN.

Our narrative proceeds to relate that the pilgrim

going south-east from *Ka-chih* country entered the Great Snowy Mountains. These mountains are lofty and their defiles deep, with peaks and precipices fraught with peril. Wind and snow alternate incessantly, and at midsummer it is still cold. Piled up snow fills the valleys and the mountain tracks are hard to follow. There are gods of the mountains and impish sprites which in their anger send forth monstrous apparitions, and the mountains are infested by troops of robbers who make murder their occupation.

A journey of above 600 *li* brought the pilgrim out of the limits of the Tokhara country and into the *Fan-yen-na* country. This was above 2000 *li* from east to west and 300 *li* from north to south. It was in the midst of the Snowy Mountains, and its inhabitants taking advantage of the mountains and defiles had their towns in strong places. The capital, which was built at a steep bank and across a defile, had a high cliff on its north side and was six or seven *li* in length. The country was very cold; it yielded early wheat, had little fruit or flower, but had good pasture for sheep and horses. The people had harsh rude ways; they mostly wore furs and serges, which were of local origin. Their written language, their popular institutions, and their currency were like those of Tokhara, and they resembled the people of that country in appearance but differed from them in their spoken language. In honesty of disposition they were far above the neighbouring countries, and they made offerings and paid reverence with perfect sincerity to [all objects of worship] from the Three Precious ones of Buddhism down to all the gods. Traders coming and going on business, whether the gods shew favourable omens or exhibit sinister manifestations, pay worship (lit. seek religious merit).

The *Fan-yen-na* (梵衍那) of this is, as has been shewn by others, Bamian, and Yuan-chuang was apparently the first to use this transcription. Other transcriptions found in Chinese literature are *Fan-yen* (帆延), and *Wang* (i. e.

[1] Yule l. c.

*Bang)-yen* (縛 衍), each representing a sound like Bam-yan. Our pilgrim represents the inhabitants as using the natural strongholds of the hills and defiles for their places of abode. The district, we learn from the T'ang-Shu, had several large towns, but the people lived chiefly in mountain caves.[1] Writing from reports of recent travellers Colonel Yule tells us: "The prominences of the cliffs which line the valley of Bámián are crowned by the remains of numerous massive towers, whilst their precipitous faces are for six or seven miles pierced by an infinity of anciently excavated caves, some of which are still occupied as dwellings. The actual site of the old city is marked by mounds and remains of walls, and on an isolated rock in the middle of the valley are the considerable ruins of what appear to have been the acropolis, now known as Ghúlghúla."[2] This Ghulghula probably represents part of our pilgrim's capital, the name of which in the 7th century was *Lo-lan* (羅 爛). Ibn Haukal tells us that "Bamian is a town about half as large as Balkh, situated on a hill. Before this hill runs a river, the stream of which flows into Guyestan. Bamian has not any gardens nor orchards, and it is the only town in this district situated on a hill."[3] The Life tells us that when Yuan-chuang arrived at the capital the king came out to meet him and then entertained him in the palace and that in this city the pilgrim met with two learned Brethren of the Mahāsañgika school who were very kind to him. The king was probably regarded by Yuan-chuang as a descendant of the Sākya exile from Kapilavastu who went to Bamian and became its king.

In Bamian there were some tens of Buddhist monasteries with several thousands of Brethren who were adherents of that Hīnayāna school which "declares that [Buddha] transcends the ordinary", that is, the Lokottaravādin School.

---

1 T'ang-shu, *ch.* 221.

2 See "The Rock-cut Caves and Statues of Bamian" in J. R. A. S. Vol. xviii. Art. XIV.

3 Or. Geog. tr. Ouseley p. 225.

For the words here placed within inverted commas the original is *Shuo-ch'u-shih* (說出世). This expression, as has been shewn by others, is used to translate the Sanskrit Lokottaravādin. Julien interprets this and its Chinese equivalent as meaning those "dont les discours s'élèvent au dessus du monde".[1] Burnouf renders the term by "ceux qui se prétendent supérieures au monde".[2] Eitel translates it "Those who pretend to have done with the world".[3] But all these interpretations judged by the accounts of the school seem to be wrong and misleading. Wassiljew explains the term better as meaning "those who argue about emergence from the world, that is, argue that in the Buddhas there is nothing which belongs to the world".[4] So also Rockhill using Tibetan texts explains the term thus—"Those who say that the blessed Buddhas have passed beyond all worlds (i. e. existences), that the Tathāgata was not subject to worldly laws are called ["Those who say that the Tathagata] has passed beyond all world, or *Lokottaravādins.*"[5] The school which bore this name is described as an offshoot from the Mahāsañgika or Church of the Great Congregation of Brethren which arose in the Madhyadeśa or "Mid-India" of Chinese writers. The name was given to the sect from the prominence which its founders gave to the doctrines that the Buddhas were not begotten and conceived as human beings, that there was nothing *worldly* in them, but that they were altogether *above this world*, world-transcending. In Chinese Lokottaravādin became *Shuo-ch'u-shih* (or *Ch'u-shih-shuo*) as in Yuan-chuang's translation, or *Ch'u-shih-chien-yen-yü* or *Ch'u-shih-chien-shuo.*[6] The former means

---

1 Mélanges p. 330, 333.

2 Bur. Int. p. 452.

3 Handbook Ch. Buddhism s. v. Lokottara-vādinah.

4 Wass. Bud. S. 250.

5 Rockhill Life p. 183. I have taken some liberty with Mr Rockhill's text as there is apparently something omitted.

6 See the Shih-pa-pu-lun (No. 1284) and I-pu-tsung-lun-lun (No. 1286).

"stating that [Buddha] transcends the world" and the latter means "talk [of Buddha] transcending what is in the world." In the "Mahāvastu" we have apparently a sort of text book of this sect, though the treatise represent itself to be portion of the Vinaya.[1] It teaches with iteration the doctrine of the unworldliness or super-worldliness of the Tathāgatas or Great Rishis, and consists mainly of legends of the past and present lives of the Buddha. As Vasumitra shews, the Lokottaravādins, like the other sects which branched off from the Mahāsañgika body, differed from the latter only in the accidentals not in the essentials of doctrine and precept. The peculiar doctrine about the Buddhas must be excepted. In the lists of the Buddhist schools given in the Dīpavamso the Lokottaravādin school is not mentioned.

The description in the text proceeds.

> On the declivity of a hill to the north-east of the capital was a standing image of Buddha made of stone, 140 or 150 feet high, of a brilliant golden colour and resplendent with ornamentation of precious substances. To the east of it was a Buddhist monastery built by a former king of the country. East of this was a standing image of Sākyamuni Buddha above 100 feet high, made of *t'u-shih*, the pieces of which had been cast separately and then welded together into one figure.

The large Buddha image of this passage is evidently the "big idol, male" which Captain Talbot measured with his theodolite and found to be 173 feet high. A picture of this image is given at p. 341 in Vol. xviii of the R. A. S. Journal in the Article already quoted from. Captain Talbot states that the image was "hewn out of the conglomerate rock, but the finishing, drapery, &c., was all added by putting on stucco". Our pilgrim's statement that the image was of a "brilliant golden colour" agrees with its name "Surkbut" or "Gold image", and this is said to be probably the meaning of another of its names the Red Idol.[2] The second image, we have seen, was made of

---

[1] Mahāvastu ed. Senart: T. I. Intn p. 2, p. 159.

[2] J. R. A. S. Vol. xix. p. 162, 164.

*t'u-shi.* This word written 鍮石 (or 鋀) is here rendered by Julien *laiton*, but in some other passages he translates it by *cuivre jaune.* Native dictionaries and glossaries also give different and conflicting explanations of the two characters. These are sometimes treated by native scholars as two words, but they evidently stand for one word which is apparently a foreign one, perhaps the Turkish word *tūj* which denotes *bronze.* Chinese interpreters use *t'u-shi,* called also *t'u-ssŭ* ( | 似), to translate the Sanskrit *rīti,* "bell-metal", "bronze", and also as the equivalent of tāmrika from tāmra which means "copper". It is also described as a "stone like gold", and as a metal made from copper, being yellow when of good quality. It seems to be sometimes used in the sense of "copper ore", but in these Records we may generally render it by *bronze.* This bronze image has been identified with the "female figure 120 feet high" of Captain Talbot, who says this, like the other image, was hewn out of the conglomerate rock. It is also the White Idol of the Persian account which also makes it to have been cut in the rock and calls it a female figure. It is about 1/4 of a mile to the left of the larger image. We cannot explain away Yuan-chuang's statement that the image was made of metal by the hypothesis that it was of stone covered with metal. If the Shah-mameh is the image east of the monastery then Yuan-chuang was misinformed as to its material.

The description continues.

> In a monastery 12 or 13 *li* to the east of the capital was a recumbent image of the Buddha in Nirvaṇa above 1000 feet long. Here the king held the Quinquennial Assembly at which he was wont to give away to the monks all his possessions from the queen down, his officials afterwards redeeming the valuables from the monks.

In the D text and in the Fang-chih the monastery of the Nirvāṇa Buddha is only two or three *li* east from the capital, and this is probably correct. In the Life the Nirvāṇa image is at the monastery near which was the tūj or bronze Buddha. The length of the Nirvāṇa image is enormous, especially if we are to regard it as having been within the walls of a monastery. Perhaps, however, the figure was only carved in a rock which formed the back wall of the temple. In any case we probably do well to agree with Colonel Yule's suggestion that the Azdaha of the present inhabitants of this district is the Nirvāṇa Buddha of our traveller. The Azdaha, which is described as being on the flat summit of a nearly isolated rock, is "a recumbent figure bearing rude resemblance to a huge lizard, and near the neck of the reptile there is a red splash as of blood." We cannot, however, imagine that the pilgrim on seeing a figure like this would call it Buddha in Nirvāṇa.

> In this monastery there was also Śāṇakavāsa's sanghāṭi in nine stripes, of a dark red colour, made of cloth woven from the fibre of the śanaka plant. This man, a disciple of Ānanda, in a former existence gave to a congregation of Brethren on the day of their leaving Retreat śanaka robes. By the merit of this act in 500 subsequent births, intermediate and human, he always wore clothing of this material. In his last existence he was born in this attire and his natal garment grew with his growth; when he was admitted into the Church by Ānanda the garment became a clerical robe, and when he received full ordination the garment became a nine-striped sanghāṭi. When Śāṇakavāsa was about to pass away he went into the "Border-limit" samādhi and, by the force of his desire aiming at wisdom, he left this robe to last while Buddhism endures and undergo destruction when Buddhism comes to an end. At this time the robe had suffered some diminution, and this was proof to believers.

The Śāṇakavāsa of this passage is the Śanika, Śaṇavāsa, Śoṇavāsi, and Śānavāsika or Śāṇavāsika of other works. According to the generally received account the bearer of this name was the son of a merchant of Rājagaha. He also in early life became a merchant and amassed a large fortune with which he was very generous to the Buddhist fraternity. Ānanda persuaded him to enter the Order and after ordination he devoted himself to his new career with great zeal and earnestness. He mastered all the Canon, and taught and guided a large number of disciples, his chief place of residence being at the monastery he established near Mathura. The greatest of his disciples was Upagupta whom he made his successor as Master of the Vinaya. After this Śaṇakavasa went to Kipin, a northern region including Kashmir, or to Champā, but returned to Mathura. There he died and his remains were cremated and a tope erected over them.[1] In order to account for his name and career a story is told about him in a former life. He was then the chief of a caravan of 500 merchants and on his journey he fell in with a Pratyeka Buddha dying in lonely helplessness. The caravan-chief devoted himself to the suffering saint, and nursed him with great kindness. This Pratyeka Buddha had an old worn garment of śāṇa, a kind of cloth made from the śan hemp, and the caravan-chief wished him to change it for a new cotton robe. But the saint declined the offer, not wishing to part with the old robe which was associated for him with all his spiritual progress. The caravan-chief expressed his strong desire that when he next was born in this world he should be in all respects like this Pratyeka Buddha. By the merit of his kindness to the Pratyeka Buddha and his prayer he was led to join the Buddhist Order and to wear all his life the linen robe in which he was ordained, and hence he had the name Śāṇakavāsin or "Wearer of linen". The legends about him having been six years in his mother's womb, and having been born in a linen shirt, are only in some of the accounts. This arhat, who lived within 100 years after the Buddha, figures in the Divyāvadāna and in the Buddhist books of Nepāl, Tibet, and China,[2] but he seems to be unknown to the Pali scriptures. We can scarcely regard him as identical with Sonika, the thera of Rājagaha, mentioned in the Mahāvaṃsa and other works, although in some circumstances there is a resemblance.[3] The word *shê-na-*

---

1 Fu-fa-tsang-yin-yuan-ching (or chuan), *ch.* 2 (No. 1340 tr. A.D. 472); A-yü-wang-chuan (No. 1459 tr. A.D. 300).

2 Divyāv. p. 349: Bud. Lit. Nep. p. 67; Rockhill Life p. 161.

3 Mah. *ch.* IV.: Dip. V. 22.

*ka* in the arhat's name is also explained as meaning *tzŭ-jan-fu* (自 然 服) or "natural",—"self-existing clothing", as if for sanaka from sanā which means "eternal", "self-existent".

The words here rendered "in 500 existences intermediate and human" are peculiar and merit attention. In all the texts and in the Life the original is *yü-wu-pai-shên-chung-yin-shêng-yin* (於五百身中陰生陰), and Julien translates this by "pendant cinq cents existences successives". But this is not all that the author states, and the sense in which I understand the words is evidently something like what the construction requires. It is also apparently the sense in which the author of the Fang-chih understood the passage, for he transcribes it *wu-pai-chung-yin-shên-shêng* or "500 intermediate states and human births". The *Chung-yin*, called also *chung-yu* (中 有), is the *antarābhava* or intermediate state, the life elsewhere which intervenes between two existences on this world. Human death or *ssŭ-yin* (死 陰) is the dissolution of the skandha (*yin*) which form the living body; and this is followed in due time by a new human birth, the *shêng-yin*, in which the skandha are recombined. In the period which elapses between these two events that which was, and is to be again, the human being, lives on in some other sphere or spheres of existence, and this unknown life is the *chung-yin*. This in the language of the Buddhists is the road which lies between but connects the two villages of Death and Re-birth. The term will be further explained when we come to *Chuan* VII.

## KA-PI-SHIH (KAPIS).

The narrative proceeds to relate that the pilgrim

going east from this entered the Snow Mountains, crossed a black range and reached *Ka-pi-shih*. This country was above 4000 *li* in circuit with the Snowy Mountains on its north and having black ranges on its other sides; the capital was above ten *li* in circuit. It yielded various cereals, and fruit and timber, and excellent horses and saffron; many rare commodities from other regions were collected in this country; its climate was cold and windy; the people were of a rude violent disposition, used a coarse vulgar language, and married in a miscellaneous manner. The written language was very like that of Tokhara; but the colloquial idiom and the social institutions of the people were different. For inner clothing they wore woollen cloth (*mao-tieh*), and for their outer garments skins and serge. Their gold, silver, and small copper coins differed in style and appearance from those of other countries. The king, who was of the Kshatriya caste, was an intelligent courageous man, and his power extended over more than ten of the neighbouring lands; he was a benevolent ruler and an adherent of Buddhism. He made every year a silver image of Buddha 18 feet high, and at the Moksha-parishad he gave liberally to the needy and to widows and widowers. There were above 100 Monasteries with more than 6000 Brethren who were chiefly Mahāyānists; the topes and monasteries were lofty and spacious and were kept in good order. Of Deva-Temples there were some tens; and above 1000 professed Sectarians, Digambaras, and Pāmśupatas, and those who wear wreaths of skulls as head-ornaments.

The words "from this" at the beginning of the above passage apparently mean from the monastery with the sacred relics. The Life tells us that the journey from the capital of Bamian to the confines of the country occupied about 15 days. Two days' journey outside the Bamian boundary the pilgrim lost his way in the snow and after being set right he crossed a black range into *Ka-pi-shih* or Kapis. This is all the information we have about the distance of the latter country from Bamian. By the words "black range" in this passage we are apparently to understand those mountains of the Snowy range which were not covered with perpetual snow. It will be noticed that although the pilgrim travelled east through the Snowy Mountains into Kapis it was a "black range" that was to the west of that country.

The country here designated *Ka-pi-shih* (迦畢試) does not seem to have been known to the Chinese generally by that name. We find the *Ka-pi-shih* of our author, however, in some later books used to denote a country said to be Kipin.[1] In some older books the country is called

1 K'ai-yuan-lu, *ch.* 1 (No. 1485).

*Ka-pi-shih* (迦臂施),[1] and is described as a great rendezvous for traders. The Sanskrit name is given as Karpisaya and this is transcribed in Chinese by *Ka-pi-shê-ye* (劫比舍也). As Kanishka is Kanerka so Kapis may be Kafir a name which is preserved in the modern Kafiristan. As to the area of the country Cunningham tells us that if Yuan-chuang's "measurement be even approximately correct, the district must have included the whole of Kafiristan, as well as the two large valleys of Ghorband and Panjshir, as these last are together not more than 300 miles in circuit".[2]

Among the products of the country here enumerated is one called *Yü-chin*, that is, "saffron". The translators, however, give "Curcuma" as the meaning of the word and it is so rendered by others in various books. As we have to meet with the word again the reasons for translating it by "saffron" are to be given hereafter.

Our narrative proceeds.

About three or four *li* east of the capital under the north mountain was a large monastery with above 300 Brethren all Hīnayānists. Its history the pilgrim learned was this. When Kanishka reigned in Gandhāra his power reached the neighbouring States and his influence extended to distant regions. As he kept order by military rule over a wide territory reaching to the east of the Ts'ung-Ling, a tributary state of China to the west of the Yellow River through fear of the king's power sent him [princes as] hostages. On the arrival of the hostages Kanishka treated them with great courtesy and provided them with different residences according to the seasons. The winter was spent in India, the summer in Kapis, and the spring and autumn in Gandhāra. At each residence a monastery was erected, this one being at the summer residence. Hence the walls of the chambers had paintings of the hostages who in appearance and dress were somewhat like the Chinese. When the hostages returned to their homes they fondly remembered their residence here, and continued to send it religious offerings. So the Brethren of this monastery with grateful feelings had kept up religious services on behalf the hostages every year at the beginning and end of the Rain-season Retreat. To the south of the east door

---

1 Su-kao-sêng-chuan, *ch.* 2 (No. 1493); K'ai-yuan-lu, *ch.* 7.

2 Anc. Geog. Ind. p. 17.

of the Buddha's-Hall of the Monastery, under the right foot of the image of the Lord over the Gods, was a pit containing a buried treasure deposited there by the hostages. There was an inscription which stated that when the monastery fell into disrepair the treasure was to be used for its repairs. In late times a frontier king had coveted the treasure and tried to steal it, but the figure of a parrot in the God's crown by flapping his wings and screaming frightened the king and his soldiers; the earth also quaked and the king and his soldiers fell down stiff; when they recovered they confessed their guilt and went away home.

The Life tells us that the Hīnayāna monastery of this passage was called *Sha-lo-ka* (沙落迦), a word of which no explanation is given. It was in this monastery that our pilgrim was lodged and entertained during a portion of his stay at the capital. In the Life also there is only one hostage and he is a son of a Chinese emperor and it was by him the monastery was built. The story in the Records evidently supposes the reader to understand that the hostages were the sons of a ruler of a feudal dependency of China or of rulers of several such states. Here also I think there is properly only one hostage-prince and the use of the plural in the latter part of the passage is perhaps a slip. The monastery may be the establishment called in some works the *T'ien-ssŭ* and the *Wang-ssŭ*, or Royal Vihāra. Its name *Sha-lo-ka* is apparently not to be taken as a word qualifying *vihāra*, but as the designation of the whole establishment comprising the hostage's residence, the sacred buildings and the monks' quarters. It is possible that the Chinese transcription may represent the Indian word *śālāka* or "small mansion" used in the sense of a "temporary royal residence."

The Life also gives the story of the buried treasure and tells of the attempts to make use of it by the Brethren. At the time of the pilgrim's visit money was wanted to repair the tope and Yuan-chuang was requested to lay the case before the Lord; he did so and with such success that the required amount was taken without trouble.

The narrative next tells us of caves in the mountains to the north of the Hostage's Monastery. Here the hostages practised samādhi, and in the caves were hidden treasures guarded by a yaksha. On a mountain two or three *li* west of the caves was an image of Kuan-tzŭ-tsai P'usa; to devotees of perfect earnestness the P'usa would come forth from the image and comfort them with the sight of his beautiful body. Above 30 *li* south-east from the capital was the Rāhula monastery with its marvel-working tope, built by a statesman named Rāhula.

Above forty *li* south from the capital was the city called *Si-p'i-to-fa-la-tzŭ* (霫蔽多伐剌祠). When the rest of the region was visited by earthquakes and landslips this city and all round it were quite undisturbed.

For the name of the city here transcribed Julien, who transliterates the last character *sse*, suggests Sphītavaras as the possible Sanskrit original, and Saint Martin proposes Śvetavāras. But the last character *sse* or *tzŭ* is one of those which the Chinese do not like to use in transcriptions and it is probably a Chinese word in the sense of *temple*. The other characters may stand for Śvetavat, one of the epithets of Indra, the god who rides a white (sveta) elephant. Thus the name of the city would be Śvetavat-ālaya, the Abode or Shrine of Indra.

To the south of this city and at a distance of above 30 *li* from it was the *A-lu-no* Mountain, steep and lofty, with gloomy cliffs and gorges. Every [New] year the summit increased in height several hundreds of feet appearing to look towards the *Shu-na-si-lo* Mountain in *Tsao-ku-t'a*, and then it suddenly collapsed. The explanation given to the pilgrim by the natives was this. Once the god *Shu-na* arriving from afar wanted to stop on this mountain, but the god of the mountain becoming alarmed made a convulsion. *Shu-na* deva then said to him—'You make this commotion because you do not want me to lodge with you; if you had granted me a little hospitality I should have filled you with riches; now I go to the Tsao-ku-t'a country to the Shu-na-si-lo mountain, and every [New-]year when I am receiving the worship and offerings of the king and statesmen you are to be a subordinate spectator'. Hence the A-lu-no mountain increases its height and then suddenly collapses.

For the "New-year" of this rendering the original is simply *sui* (歲) "year", but it was evidently at a particular time of the year that the mountain prolonged its summit. A native scholar was of the opinion that the word *sui* in this passage meant *harvest*, the time when thank-offerings were made to the god for the good crops. But it is perhaps better to take the word in the sense of *New-year*, Mount Aruṇa having to do homage openly to Shu-na deva when the latter was receiving the New-year's worship of the king and grandees of Tsao-ku-t'a. The *A-lu-no* of this passage is evidently, as has been conjectured, for Aruṇa which means "red, the colour of the dawn". In Alberuni we read of the Aruṇa mountain to the west of Kailāsa and described as covered with perpetual snow and inaccessible.[1] *Shu-na*, also pronounced *Ch'u-na*, may be for Śuna, and *Shu-na-si-lo* may be for Śunasīrau, a pair of ancient gods associated with farming. But *si-lo* is perhaps for śilā, "a rock", the name of the mountain being Shuna's rock. This Shuna or Ch'una was the chief god among the people of Tsao-ku-t'a, but he was feared and worshipped beyond the limits of that country. A deity with a name like this is still worshipped in some of the hill districts beyond India, I believe. He was perhaps originally a sun-god, as Aruṇa was the dawn, and the name Shun still survives in Manchoo as the word for Sun.

Returning to the Records we read that

> above 200 *li* north-west from the capital was a great Snowy Mountain on the top of which was a lake, and prayers made at it for rain or fine weather were answered. The pilgrim then narrates the legend about this lake and its Dragon-kings. In the time of Kanishka the Dragon-king was a fierce malicious creature who in his previous existence had been the novice attending an arhat of Gandhāra. As such in an access of passion and envy he had prayed to become a Nāga-king in his next birth, and accordingly on his death he came into the world as the Dragon-king of this lake. Keeping up his old bad feelings he killed the old Dragon-king; and sent rain and storm to destroy the trees and the Buddhist monastery at the foot of the mountain. Kanishka enraged at the persistent malice of the creature proceeded to fill up his lake. On this the Dragon-king became alarmed and assuming the form of an old brahmin he remonstrated earnestly with the king. In the end the king and the Dragon made a covenant by which Kanishka was to rebuild the monastery and erect a tope; the latter was to serve as a lookout, and when the watchman on this observed dark clouds rising on

---

[1] Vol. ii, p. 143.

the mountain the gong was to be at once sounded, whereupon the bad temper of the Dragon would cease. The tope still continued to be used for the purpose for which it was erected. It was reported to contain flesh-and-bone relics of the Ju-lai about a pint in quantity, and from these proceeded countless miracles.

In Julien's translation of the passage from which the above has been condensed there occurs a sentence in which the original does not seem to have been properly understood. The words here rendered "assuming the form of an old brahmin he remonstrated earnestly with the king" are in Julien's translation "prit la forme d'un vieux Brāhmane, *se prosterna devant l'élêphant du roi et addressa à Kanichka des reprêsentations*". For the words which I have put in italics the Chinese is *K'ou-wang-hsiang-êrh-chien* (叩王象而諫) literally "striking the king's elephant he remonstrated". But the meaning is simply "he sternly reproved" or "earnestly remonstrated with". The expression corresponds to the common Chinese phrase *K'ou-ma-chien* literally "striking his horse reprove". But there is no *striking* of either horse or elephant, the expression being figurative. To make the brahmin kotow to the elephant is neither Chinese nor Indian and it spoils the story. The phrase *K'ou-hsiang* occurs again, in *Chuan* VI. and Julien again make the same curious mistake. His translation (p. 326) is there even less appropriate than it is here.

To the north-west of the capital on the south bank of a large river was an Old King's Monastery which had a milk-tooth one inch long of Sakya P'usa. South-east from this was another monastery also called "Old King's", and in this was a slice of Julai's ushnīsha above an inch wide of a yellow-white colour with the hair pores distinct. It had also a hair of Julai's head of a dark violet colour above a foot long but curled up to about half an inch. The ushnīsha was worshipped by the king and great officials on the six fast days. To the south-west of this monastery was the Old Queen's monastery in which was a gilt copper tope above 100 feet high said to contain relics of Buddha.

It is curious to find our pilgrim here telling of a slice of Buddha's ushnīsha as existing in Kapis. I-ching also writes of the Julai's *ting-ku* or ushnīsha as being in this country.[1] Our pilgrim, we shall see presently, agreeing with Fa-hsien makes the city Hilo in another country possess the ushnīsha apparently in a perfect state. As Hilo was a dependency of Kapis we may regard I-ching's pilgrims as paying reverence to the ushnīsha of Hilo and getting their fortunes from it. But we cannot understand how a monastery in Kapis had a piece of the ushnīsha at the same time that the whole of it was in Hilo. Then a century or so after our pilgrim's time Wu-k'ung found the ushnīsha relic of Sakya Ju-lai in the *Yen-t'i-li* vihāra of Kanishka in Gandhāra. It was near the capital of Gandhāra also that Wu-k'ung saw the Dragon-king monastery which Yuan-chuang places 200 *li* north-west from the capital of Kapis.[2]

To the south-west of the capital was the *Pi-lo-sho-lo* Mountain. This name was given to the mountain from its presiding genius who had the form of an *elephant* and was therefore called *Pi-lo-sho-lo*. While the Julai was on earth this god once invited him and the 1200 great arhats to his mountain, and here on a large flat rock he gave the Julai worship and entertainment. On this rock king Asoka afterwards built a tope above 100 feet high. This tope, which was supposed to contain about a pint of the Buddha's relics, was known to the people at the time of Yuan-chuang's visit as the *Pi-lo-sho-lo* tope.

To the north of this tope and at the base of a cliff was a Dragon Spring. In it the Buddha and the 1200 arhats cleansed their mouths, and chewed their tooth-sticks, after eating the food supplied to them by the god; their tooth-sticks being planted took root, and became the dense wood existing at the time of the pilgrim's visit. People who lived after the Buddha's time erected at the place a monastery to which they gave the name *Ping* (or *P'i*)-*to-ka* (鞞鐸佉).

The *Pi-lo-sho* (or *so*)-*lo* of this passage, translated by the Chinese as "Elephant-solid", has been restored by Julien as *Pīlusāra*. This was the name of the tutelary god of the mountain and of the mountain itself, and it was the name given to the Asoka tope erected on one of the rocks of the mountain.

---

[1] Hsi-yü-ch'iu, *ch*. 1, 2, and Chavannes Mémoires p. 24, 105.

[2] Shih-li-ching; Chavannes in J. A. T. VI. p. 357.

A note added to the Chinese text here tells us that *Ping* (or *P'i*)-*to-ka* is in Chinese *Chio-yang-chih* (嚼楊枝) literally "chew willow twig". This is the term used to describe the Buddha and his arhats chewing their tooth-sticks in the operation of cleansing their mouths, and it is the common phrase in Chinese Buddhist works to denote this operation. One of the Chinese names for the tooth-stick which the bhikshu was ordered to use daily was *Yang-chih* or "willow-twig", but in India at least the tooth-stick was not made of willow. We are not obliged to accept the native annotator's translation of the foreign word here, and it is apparently not correct. It will be noticed that the name *Ping-to-ka*, according to our pilgrim, was given to the monastery built here by people who lived after the time of the Buddha and his arhats, and apparently at a period when there was a thick clump of trees at the place. The transcription in the text may possibly represent the word Piṇḍaka used in the sense of a *clump of trees*, the monastery being called the Piṇḍaka-vihāra.

---

# CHAPTER V.

## CHUAN II.

### GENERAL DESCRIPTION OF INDIA.

#### Its names.

The pilgrim having now arrived at the frontiers of the great country which he calls *Yin-tu* (India) gives his readers a "Pisgah-sight" of the land before taking them through its various kingdoms. And first he tells them of its name and its meaning and probable origin. His statements about the name may be roughly rendered as follows—

> We find that different counsels have confused the designations of *T'ien-chu* (India); the old names were *Shên-tu* and *Sien* (or *Hien*)-*tou*; now we must conform to the correct pronunciation and call it *Yin-tu*. The people of Yin-tu use local appellations for their respective countries; the various districts having different customs; adopting a general designation, and one which the people like, we call the country *Yin-tu* which means the "Moon".

This rendering differs in some respects from that given by Julien which is neither very clear nor correct. Here, however, as in several other passages of the Records, it is not easy to make out the precise meaning of the author's statements. It is plain, however, that he is not dealing with names given to India generally but only with those used in Chinese books. Then his words would seem to indicate that he regarded T'ien-chu, Shên-tu, and Sien-tou as only dialectical varieties or mistaken transcriptions of Yin-tu, which was the standard pronunciation. Further his language does not seem to intimate, as Julien understood it to intimate, that Yin-tu was the name for all India used by the inhabitants of the country. In some other works we find it stated that Yin-tu was the native name for the whole country, and Indu-deśa given as the original Sanskrit term. Our author may have had this opinion but this does not seem to be the meaning of his statements here. On the contrary he apparently wishes us to understand that the natives of India had only designations of their own States, such as Magadha and Kausambhi, and that they were without a general name under which these could be included. It was the peoples beyond, as for example the Turks, who gave the name Yin-tu, and the Hu who gave Sin-tu, to a great territory of uncertain limits. Then the Buddhist writers of Kashmir, Gandhāra, and other countries beyond India proper, seem also to have sometimes used the name Yin-tu. But, as I-ching tells us, although this word may mean "moon" yet it was not the current name for India. In Buddhist literature India is called Jambudvīpa, and portions of it Āryadeśa and Madhyadeśa.[1] One of the other names for India to be found in Buddhist literature is Indravardhana. But in the Chinese accounts of letters or missions sent by Indian rajahs to the court of China the rajahs are only represented as styling themselves kings of special countries in India. Thus the great Śilāditya, who treated our pilgrim with great honour, is made in Chinese history to call himself king of Magadha.

Let us now examine in detail Yuan-chuang's statements about the terms he quotes as used in China to denote India and the history of these terms. The old name, as he tells us, is that which he, following precedent, writes *Shên-tu* (身毒) as the characters are now pronounced. This word emerges in Chinese history in the account which the famous envoy Chang Ch'ien (Kien) gives of his experiences in the Ta-hsia country (Bactria). In that we

1 Nan-hai-ch'i-kuei, *ch.* 25; Hunter's Ind. Emp. p. 33.

read that when Chang returned from his mission to the West he reported to Han Wu Ti (apparently about B. C. 123) that when in Ta-hsia he had seen bamboo poles and cloth from a district which is now comprised in the Province of Ssŭchuan. He had been told, he relates, that these commodities had been obtained at Shên-tu, as the name of the place is given in the ordinary texts of his report to the Emperor. Now Chinese writers tell us, and Western scholars have adopted and repeated the statements, that the Shên-tu of this story was India, and that all the other designations for that country in Chinese books such as Hsien-tou, Hsien-tu, Kan-tu, Küan (or Yuan)-tu, T'ien-chu, T'ien-tu, and Yin-tu are only phonetic corruptions of Shên-tu. These opinions seem to have been lightly formed and heedlessly followed, and it may be useful for us to enquire whether they have a good basis.

In the first place then we find that there is doubt as to what was the precise form of the name of the country in Chang's statement. So instead of the character for *Shên* in Shên-tu given above we meet with several various readings. Such are 齕 and 訖 which probably represent one sound, something like *Get* or *K'at.* Now a foreign name like *K'atu* or *Gachu* as a name for India seems to have been in use. Then a third various reading for the Shên of Shên-tu is K'ien or Kan (乾) which may have been originally a copyist's slip for one of the characters read *K'at.*[1] We find also a fourth various reading for the syllable Shên of Shên-tu, viz—Küan or Yun (捐).[2] But the country described in Chinese literature under the name Yun-tu was evidently one to the east or north-east of all that has been called India.[3] Then accepting the character now read Shên as the genuine text of Chang's

[1] Shih-chi (史 記), *ch.* 123, Commentary. In the T'ung-chien-kang-mu, *ch.* 4, Yuan-shou (元 狩) 1st y., this passage of the Shih-chi is quoted with the reading *Kan-tu* (乾 篤) instead of *Shên-tu.* See also Kanghsi Dict. s. v. 身.

[2] Han-Shu, *ch.* 96.

[3] T'ung-chih-liao, the Tu-yi-liao, *ch.* I; Han-Shu, l. c.

report we are told that in this name it is to be pronounced like *in* or *yin*. This does not seem very improbable. But an etymological authority tells us that the character in question has, in this name, the sound *T'ien*.[1] There may be some truth in this statement. But it is not supported by authority, and seems rather fanciful.

The district or region which the envoy Chang reported as named, let us continue to say, Shên-tu, is briefly described by him and others of the Han period. It was several thousand *li* south-east from Bactria, near a river (or sea); its inhabitants used elephants in fighting. Some writers describe them as Buddhists; and they were in many respects like the people of Bactria, or like the Geti (Yue-ti) according to another account. Their country was about 2000 *li* south-west from what is now the Ch'êng-tu and Ning-yuan districts in Ssŭchuan, and it had a regular trade with the merchants of the Ch'êng-tu district, some of whom seem to have settled in it. Further, this country was not far from the western border of the Chinese empire in the Han time, and it was on the way from China to Bactria. So though the name Shên-tu came to be afterwards given to India yet in its first use it apparently denoted a small region in what is now Yunnan and Burmah.[2]

The name Hsien-tou was apparently applied to a region different from that designated Shên-tu.[3] Like Hsien-tu (縣度), of which term it is perhaps only a variety, this name was probably used first by the Chinese for the Indus,

---

[1] Wên-ch'i-tien-chu (閒奇典註), *ch.* 2. p. 22. The change of Shên-tu into T'ien-tu may point to a Burmese pronunciation of Śindu as Thindu.

[2] Han-Shu, *ch.* 95; Hou Han-Shu, *ch.* 88; Ma T. l. *ch.* 338 gives much information about India compiled not very carefully from previous authorities; his account is translated in Julien's Mélanges p. 147.

[3] But Hsien (Hien)-tou (賢豆) came to be used as a name for India, and we find it described as a native designation for the whole country properly called Indravardhana. Su-kao-sêng-chuan, *ch.* 2. See also Fang-chih, *ch.* 1.

called Sindhu in Sanskrit. The name was afterwards extended by them to a mountainous region, perhaps Ladak, through which the Indus flows. We find the Hsien-tu country mentioned in the same passages of the Han History with Shên-tu.

We next come to T'ien-chu (天竺) and T'ien-tu (篤) said to represent only one name pronounced something like Tendu or Tintok. We are told by one Chinese writer that the name T'ien-chu was first applied to India in the Han Ho-Ti period (A.D. 89 to 106) but the authority for the statement is not given. Another account makes Mêng K'an (about A.D. 230) the first to identify T'ien-chu with Shên-tu, but this likewise is unsupported by authority. We are also told that the *chu* (竺) of T'ien-chu is a short way of writing *tu* (篤), a statement which is open to very serious doubt.[1] This word *tu* occurs in the ancient classical literature, and native students declare that it represents an earlier *chu*. This is specially noted with reference to the occurrence of *tu* in a wellknown passage of the "Lun-Yü". Then as to the first part of the name there seems to have been an old and perhaps dialectical pronunciation of the character as *Hien* or *Hin*. This pronunciation is found at present in the dialect of Shao-wu foo in the Province of Fuhkeen in which 天竺 is read *Hien-tu*.[2]

But what was the sound originally represented by the character now read *Chu* in the compound T'ien-chu? It seems that no satisfactory and decisive answer can be given at present to this question. We find that in the Han period the character represented several sounds which cannot be said to be very like each other. The upper part *chu* meaning *bamboo* is not significant here, we are told, but only phonetic; and the lower part is significant, and refers the word to the category *earth*. The character might then be read something like *du*, but this account

---

[1] Shih-chi, l. c.

[2] The Chinese Recorder for September 1891, p. 408.

of the syllable may be doubted, as we learn also that the character was read like *tek*, an old and still current pronunciation of the word for *bamboo*. Then this same character was also read as *chuh*, *tuh*, *kat*, and *ko* or *gou*.[1] Something like the last was perhaps the earliest pronunciation of the character, and this is probably a corruption or abbreviation of a form like *kao* (篙) or *kung* (笙). This last form, unknown to the dictionaries apparently, occurs often in Japanese texts of Buddhist books instead of the character for *chu*. Now in the fact that *ko* or *gou* was an old sound of this character we have an explanation of a proper name found in the Tibetan version of the Buddhist "Sūtra in Forty-two Sections". One of the two Indian monks who came to China in the time of Han Ming Ti, and translated or drew up the above scripture, is styled in Chinese text *Chu Fa-lan*. These words apparently represented an Indian name like Dharma-pushpa, that is, Flower of Buddhism. Now the Tibetans transcribing the sounds of the characters for Chu Falan according to their own language wrote apparently *Go-ba-ran* and this became in the modern transcription *Gobharana*. This last word is neither Sanscrit nor Tibetan, but it has been adopted by Feer who has been followed by Beal and Eitel. That Chu in such expressions as Chu-Fa-lan (竺法蘭), is not part of the name, but means "India" or "Indian" we know from its occurrence in other expressions of a similar kind. We may also infer it, in this case, from the fact that it does not occur in some old editions of the above-mentioned scripture, which have only Fa-lan as the name of the Indian monk. So also in another Tibetan work we find him described as "Bhárana Pandita".[2] There is also another word in which we may perhaps

[1] Shuo-wên, ed. Kuei Fu-hsio, s. v. 竺. In the Fo-kuo-chi this character must be pronounced like *Tuh* or *Tak* as it forms the first syllable of the name Takshaśila.

[2] Feer's Le Sūtra en 42 Articles p. 47; Ssŭ-shih-êrh-chang-ching, and Bun. No. 678 and Appx II. col. I; Journal Bengal A. S. No. LI. p. 89; Huth, Geschichte d. Bud. in d. Mongolei, tr. from Tibetan, S. 101.

recognize the *ko* pronunciation of our character *chu*. This word is the old "Tangut", more correctly Tan-ku, which was the Turkish-Persian designation for the country now called Tibet.[1] It is not improbable that, as some have supposed, this Tan-ku is simply the *T'ien-chu* of Chinese writers. And so this last may have been originally a Turkish term, used to denote a country immediately to the west of China, and between that country and Bactria.

*T'ien-tu*, on the other hand was the name of a place in the Eastern Sea mentioned in the "Shan-hai-ching" along with *Chao-hsien* or Korea. This place was afterwards identified wrongly with the *T'ien-chu* of writers on India and Buddhism.[2] But we find mention also of another *T'ien-tu* (written in the same way), a small country to the west of China, which has been supposed by some to be the Shên-tu of Chang Ch'ien.

Whatever the name *T'ien-chu* may have signified originally, however, it came to be given by the Chinese in their literature to the great extent of territory between the Bay of Bengal and the Arabian Sea, and reaching from the Kapis country in the north to Ceylon in the south. Thus used it supplanted the old Shên-tu, and all other names for India among the Chinese; and it continued to be the general literary designation for that country down to the T'ang period when the new name *Yin-tu* was brought into fashion. We even find the term T'ien-chu used with a wider application, and it is employed as a synonym for "Buddhist countries", for example, in a title given to the "Fo-kuo-chi" of Fa-hsien. Nor has the term been quite put out of use by Yuan-chuang's correct name Yintu, and Yuan-chuang himself continues to use it occasionally. We find also each of its component parts

---

1 Georgi's Alph. Tib. p. 10. In the Hai-kuo-t'u-chih it is expressly stated that T'ien-chu has been identified with the modern Hsi-Tsang or Tibet.

2 Shan-hai-ching, *ch.* 18.

sometimes made to do duty for the whole. This *Chung-T'ien* and *Hsi-T'ien* are respectively Middle and West India, while *Chu* in the Han and Ch'in periods and later was commonly used for India or Indian, a way in which *Hsi-T'ien* is also used.

Leaving T'ien-chu to continue as a Chinese name for India, Yuan-chuang puts aside what he considers to be the corruptions of the term Yin-tu, and proceeds to use that form as the correct designation of the country. He goes on to suggest a reason for this word, meaning "moon", having come to be so employed. His explanation is apparently as follows—

> The unceasing revolutions of mortals' existences are a dark long night; were there not a warden of the dawn they would be like the night with its lights which succeeds the setting of the sun; although the night have the light of the stars that is not to be compared to the light of the clear moon. Hence probably India was likened to the moon as [since the sun of the Buddha set] it has had a succession of holy and wise men to teach the people and exercise rule as the moon sheds its bright influences,—on this account the country has been called Yin-tu.

The comparison and explanation of our author, it must be admitted, are sorry things; and they are not improved in any of the translations. But the passage has probably some copyist's mistakes, and we must at least supply a clause which apparently has dropt out of the text. This clause is the important phrase *Fo-jih-chi-yin* (佛日旣隱) which means "when the sun of the Buddha set". I have restored these words within square brackets in the body of the pilgrim's explanation, but it is probable that they occurred at the head of it also. The "long night" of the text is the interminable succession of renewed existences to non-Buddhists, and to the Buddhists the period between the death of one Buddha and the advent of another, but it is rather a state of affairs than a tract of time. It denotes a condition of spiritual darkness to mankind, an endless repetition of mortal life in many varieties; each life ignorant of the one before, and without any hint of the one to follow. There is no Buddha in the world; and so there is no one to end the night, and bring in the dawn of Nirvāna. The Buddha is the *Ssŭ-ch'ên* (司晨) or Warden of the Dawn, the officer in charge of daybreak who ushers in the light of intelligence and the perfect way.

Now on earth, when the "lights of night" succeed the setting of the sun, there are stars, and there is the moon. The stars, however, have only a shining, the brightness of a glow. But the moon has a light which illuminates and influences the world, and which transcends in brightness all other lights of the night. So other lands have had sporadic sages who made a glory for themselves revolving each in his own peculiar eccentric orbit. But India had a regular succession of great Sages who 'followed the great wheel' of ancient authority, each successor only expounding, renewing, or developing the wise teachings of his divine or human predecessors; thus keeping the light of primitive revelation shining among mortals. In Buddhist writings the Buddha is often compared to the moon, while the stars are sometimes the rival teachers of his time, and occasionally his own great disciples.

A later Chinese writer, apparently under the impression that he had the authority of Yuan-chuang for the statement, tells us that *T'ien-chu* means *moon*. But he, like several other authors, explains the giving of this name to India in a different way from that described by the pilgrim. He says that the country was called T'ien-chu or Moon because it was as great and distinguished above the other countries of the world, as the moon is great among the stars of night—"velut inter ignes Luna minores". Other writers, like I-ching for example, are more discreetly wise, and refrain from proposing any explanation of the names for India. Admitting, they say, *Yin-tu* to be a Sanskrit term denoting the *moon*, yet it was not for that reason that the Chinese gave it as a name to the country, nor is the name the universal one. *Yin-tu* is the Chinese name for India as *Chi-na* and *Chen-tan* are terms used in that country to denote China, and apart from such use these names have no signification.[1] This is going too far, and the word India at least has a satisfactory explanation. When our pilgrim enquired about the size and form of the country, he was told that it was shaped like a crescent or, as it is in the text, a half-moon. The term used was apparently Indu-kalā, transcribed *Yin-t'ê-ka-lo* (印特伽羅).[2] This word means a *digit of the moon* or a *crescent*, but it is rendered in Chinese simply by *yueh* or *moon*. It was perhaps this fact which led to the absurd comparison and explanation of our text.

Our author in this passage mentions another general name for India, viz—Country of the brahmins (*P'o-lo-mên-kuo*).

> Among the various castes and clans of the country the brahmins, he says, were purest and in most esteem. So from their excellent reputation the name "Brāhmana-country" had come to be a popular one for India.

Now this is also a foreign designation, and one used by the Chinese especially. It does not seem to have been ever known, or at least current, in India. In Chinese literature we find it employed during the Sui period (A.D. 589 to 618) but it is rather a literary than a popular designation. In the shortened form Fan kuo (梵國), however, the name has long been in common use in all kinds of Chinese literature.

The territory which Yuan-chuang calls *Yin-tu* was mapped off by him, as by others, into five great divisions called respectively North, East, West, Central, and South Yin-tu. The whole territory, he tells us,

> was above 90 000 *li* in circuit, with the Snowy Mountains (the Hindu Kush) on the north and the sea on its three other sides. It was politically divided into above seventy kingdoms; the heat of summer was very great, and the land was to a large extent marshy. The northern region was hilly with a brackish soil;

---

[1] Nan-hai-ch'i-kuei l. c.

[2] Supplement to I-ch'ie-ching-yin-yi, *ch.* 3. This of course is not the origin of the name for India, but it may account for the Chinese use of Yin-tu as a designation for the country.

the east was a rich fertile plain; the southern division had a luxuriant vegetation; and the west had a soil coarse and gravelly.

## Indian Measures of Space.

Our author now proceeds to give the names of measures of space and time which were in use among the people of India or were taught in their standard books of learning and religion.

He begins at the top of the gradation with the Yojana which, he says, had always represented a day's journey for a royal army. The old Chinese equivalent for it, he says, was 40 *li*, the people of India counted it as thirty *li*, while the Buddhist books treated it as equal to only sixteen *li*.

We are not told, however, that in India the Yojana varied in different places and at different times.

Then the Yojana, he states, was divided into eight Krośa, the Krośa into 500 Bows, the Bow into four Cubits, and the Cubit into twenty-four Fingers. Forgetting, apparently, to mention the division of the Finger into three Joints Yuan-chuang proceeds to state the division of the Finger-joint into seven Wheat (properly Barley)-grains. Thence the subdivision by sevens is carried on through the Louse, the Nit, Crevice-dust, Ox-hair [Dust], Sheep-wool [Dust], Hare-hair [Dust], Copper [Dust], Water [Dust], and Fine Dust to Extremely Fine Dust. This last is the ultimate monad of matter and is indivisible.

This enumeration of Indian measures of space was apparently written down from memory, and it does not quite agree with any of the other accounts we have. In the Abhidharmamahāvibhāsha-lun,[1] compiled by the 500 Arhats and translated by Yuan-chuang, we find a similar enumeration, leaving it undecided, however, whether "seven copper-dusts" made one "Water-dust", or seven of the latter made one of the former. In this, and in the other books in which we find the measures of space given, the word for *dust* is added to each of the terms Ox-hair, Sheep-wool, Hare's-hair, Copper, and Water, and I have accordingly inserted it in the version here given of Yuan-chuang's account. Instead of *t'ung, copper*, the D text has *chin, gold*, perhaps

---

[1] Abhidharma-ta-vibhāsha-lun, *ch.* 136 (Bun. No. 1263).

used in the sense of *metal*, and this is the reading of Yuan-chuang's "Abhidharma-tsang-hsien-tsung-lun". Then the "Abhidharma-kośa-lun", which also has *chin* instead of *t'ung*, makes seven "metal-dusts" equivalent to one "water-dust" thus reversing Yuan-chuang's arrangement.[1] The word *dust* here should perhaps be replaced by *atom* or *particle*.

Another enumeration of Indian measures of space is given in the Lalitavistara and its translations Tibetan and Chinese, and another in the Avadāna XXXIII of the Divyāvadāna of Messrs Cowell and Neil.[2] The latter is represented in the Chinese collection of Buddhist books by four treatises. In none of all these works is there anything corresponding to the words "copper" and "water" of our author's list. Moreover each of them makes the Window-Dust or Sunbeam-mote—the "Crevice-Dust" of our author—to be one seventh of a Hare (or Moon)-Dust and equal to seven particles of Fine Dust. Julien took the "copper water" of our text to be one term and translated it by "l'eau de cuivre (Tamrāpa?)", but this is undoubtedly wrong.[3] In this gradation of measures the "Extremely Fine Dust" is a monad of thought, a logical necessity, and has no separate existence in matter. The lowest actual unit of matter is the *anu* of the Divyāvadana, which is the "Fine Dust" of our author. This too, however, though visible to the deva-sight, is invisible to the human sight and impalpable to the other human senses. But it is a material substance, the most minute of all material

---

1 Abhidharma-tsang-hsien-tsung-lun, *ch.* 17 (No. 1266); Abhidharma-kośa-lun, *ch.* 12 (No. 1267).

2 Lalitavistara *ch.* 12: Foucaux's Rgya-cher-rol-pa, p. 142 and note; Fang-kuang-ta-chuang-yen-ching, *ch.* 4 (No. 159); Divyāv. p. 644; Mātanga-sūtra, *ch.* 2 (No. 645).

3 See also the Tsa-abhidharma-hsien-lun, *ch.* 2 (No. 1288); Alberuni, *ch.* XXXIV and XXXVII; Abhidharma-shun-chêng-li-lun, *ch.* 32. In this treatise we have all the measures of space given by Yuan-chuang but the "Metal-dust" is one-seventh of the "Water-dust". It gives also the division of the Finger into three Finger-joints.

sizes and quantities, and the ultimate atom into which dust or metal or water can be analysed. It takes seven of these, according to some, to equal one Atom (truṭi or tuti), and seven of these to make one Sunbeam-mote. If we omit the two words "Copper" and "Water" from our text, and remove the term "Crevice-Dust" to its place, we have an enumeration of measures which agrees substantially with that of the Divyāvadāna up to the Kroṣa. Some of the Chinese texts represent the Kroṣa, translated by *shêng* (聲) a *sound*, to be 2000 Bows, and in some the Barley-grain is subdivided, not as by Yuan-chuang, but into seven Mustard-seeds.

## MEASURES OF TIME.

Our author next goes on to describe the measures of time in India, beginning with the divisions of the Day-night period. Here also he mainly follows Sanghabhadra's treatise[1], and differs from most other writers, Buddhist and orthodox.

> He calls the *Kshaṇa* the shortest space of time and makes 120 of it equal to one *Tatkshaṇa*. Then 60 *Tatkshaṇas* make one *Lava*, 30 *Lavas* make one *Muhurta*, five of these make one "time" (時), and six 'times' make one Day-night. The six 'times' of this last are, we are told, distributed equally between the day and the night. But the non-Buddhist people of India, Yuan-chuang tells us, divided the day and night each into four "times".

It will be seen that Yuan-chuang here puts the Kshaṇa below the Tatkshaṇa, in this agreeing with the Abhidharma treatises of Sanghabhadra and Dharmatara. The Divyāvadāna, on the other hand makes 120 Tatkshaṇas equal to one Kshaṇa, and 60 Kshaṇas equal to one Lava. In some Chinese versions of the sacred books the tatkshaṇa is not mentioned. The kshaṇa is defined as the time occupied by a woman in spinning one *hsün* (尋) of thread, but the word is generally used by Buddhist writers in

---

[1] Abhidharma-shun-chêng-li-lun, l. c. For the measures of Time generally see the references in the above note 3 on p. 142.

the sense of *an instant*, the *twinkling of an eye, the very shortest measurable space of time.*

The word kshaṇa is commonly transcribed in Chinese books as in our text, and it is rarely translated. The *lava* is sometimes rendered by *shih* (時), *time*, and sometimes by *fên* (分), a *division*. So also Muhurta is sometimes translated by *shih*, *time*, but more frequently by *hsü-yü* (須 臾), an *instant* or *moment*, such being also the original meaning of muhurta. But *hsü-yü* when used as a translation of this word does not denote an *instant* but a period of 48 minutes, the thirtieth part of a Day-night. The day is divided into three "times", viz. forenoon, noon, and afternoon, and hence it is called Trisandhya. In like manner the night is divided into three "times" or watches and hence it is called Triyāmā.

Our author next goes on to enumerate the divisions, natural and artificial, of the month and the year in India. He distinguishes between the common four-fold division of the seasons, and the three-fold one used by Buddhists. The latter division was into a hot season (Grīshma) followed by a rainy season (Varsha), and then a cold season (Hemanta). We have next the names of the months of the year in their order beginning with Chaitra. Then comes an interesting passage which, as it appears in our texts, presents some difficulty. The meaning seems to be something like this—

> "Hence the professed Buddhists of India, complying with the sacred instructions of the Buddha, observe (lit. sit) two periods of Retreat, either the early or the later three months. The former period begins on our 16th day of the 5th month, and the latter on the 16th of the 6th month. Previous translators of the Sūtras and Vinaya use "Observe the summer" or "Observe the end of the winter". These mistranslations are due to the people of outlying lands not understanding the standard language, or to the non-harmonizing of provincialisms".

The first sentence of this passage evidently means that the Buddhist monks of India could make either the former or the later three months of summer their period of Retreat. My interpretation of the passage differs a little from that of Julien who substitutes *yü* (雨) *rain*, for the *liang* (兩) *two*, of the text, supporting his change of reading by a quotation of the present passage in a Buddhist Cyclopedia. But one of two copies of this Cyclopedia in my possession gives *liang* and the other has *huo* (或). Moreover all texts of the "Hsi-yü-chi" seem to agree in having *liang* here: and we read in other books of two and even three periods of Retreat. For the monks of India, however, these were all included within the Rain-season, the four months which began with the 16th of their fourth month and ended on the 15th of the 8th month. The full period of Retreat was three months; and Buddha ordained that this period might be counted either from the middle of the fourth or the middle of the fifth month. The conjecture may be hazarded that Yuan-chuang originally wrote *liang-yü*(兩 雨)*-an-chü* that is "two Rain-Retreats" and that a copyist thinking there was a mistake left out the second character. This restoration does not make good style but something of the kind is apparently needed as Yuan-chuang's expression for the Retreat was *yü-an-chü*.

The Sanskrit term for the Retreat is Varshā (in Pali Vassā) which means simply *rains*, the *rainy season*, from *varsha* which denotes, along with other things, *rain* and *a year*. The usual expression for "keeping Retreat" is *varshām vas* (in Pali, vassaṃ vasati) or *varshām sthā*, meaning respectively to reside, and to rest, during the rainy season. For these terms the Chinese give various equivalents such as the *Tso-hsia* and *Tso-la* of some, and the *Tso-an-chü* or *Tso-yü-an-chü* of Yuan-chuang and others. For the Buddhists of India as for the other people of that country the "rainy season" began on the 16th of the month Ashādha (the fourth of their year), and continued for four months. This was chiefly for religious purposes, but to the non-Buddhists of India three months of this period formed also their summer. This may help to explain the use of the phrase Tso-hsia which is a short form for the full expression *Tso-hsia-yü-an-chü* meaning "to observe the Summer Rain Retreat". Then Tso-hsia and Tso-la mean also to pass a year as an ordained monk, the precedence of a brother being settled by his "years in religion". The phrase *Tso-la* or *Tso-la-an-chü* is used specially of the strict anchorite who observed two Retreats, one in the summer and one in the winter. It might be also applied to brethren in strange lands, Tokhara for example, whose Rainy season occurred at the end of the winter. Yuan-chuang seems to think that the terms Tso-Hsia and Tso-La are not correct renderings from the Sanskrit and they certainly are not literal translations. He supposes the mistakes to have arisen either from the translators having been natives of countries remote from Mid-India, and so ignorant of the correct term and its proper pronunciation, or from the use of an expression which had only local application and currency. But the "non-harmonizing of provincialisms" denotes not only the misuse of local terms, but also ignorance of the idioms in one language which should be used to represent the corresponding idioms of another. Thus a Chinese or Indian scholar translating a Sanskrit book into Chinese without a thorough knowledge of the Sanskrit and Chinese idioms would not harmonize the countries' languages. Julien takes "Mid-kingdom" here to mean China but it certainly denotes Mid-India. In that region people called the Rainy season Varshā, but in other places the word was pronounced *vasso*, or *barh*, or *barkh*, or *barsh*. So translators, Yuan-chuang thinks, may have in some cases mistaken the word, or they may have misunderstood either the original, or the Chinese term they were using in translation. Thus the important fact that the Retreat was ordained on account of the Rains is put out of view by the renderings Tso-Hsia and Tso-La. There was not, however, any ignorance of Sanskrit or Chinese in the use of these terms, and good scholars in the two languages such as Fa-hsien and I-ching use Tso-hsia and An-chü indifferently. In countries in which there was no long regular Rainy season the Retreat became of importance as a time for spiritual improvement by study of the sacred books and prolonged meditation, and as giving a year's seniority to the brother among his brethren.

## CITIES AND HOUSES.

We have next a short description of the general characters of the cities and buildings of India. The passage is an interesting one and the meaning may be given somewhat as follows—

"As to their inhabited towns and cities the quadrangular walls of the cities (or according to one text, of the various regions) are broad and high, while the thoroughfares are narrow tortuous passages. The shops are on the highways and booths (or, inns) line the roads. Butchers, fishermen, public performers, executioners, and scavengers have their habitations marked by a distinguishing sign. They are forced to live outside the city and they sneak along on the left when going about in the hamlets. As to the construction of houses and enclosing walls, the country being low and moist, most of the city-walls are built of bricks, while walls of houses and inclosures are wattled bamboo or wood. Their halls and terraced belvederes have wooden flat-roofed rooms, and are coated with chunam, and covered with tiles burnt or unburnt. They are of extraordinary height, and in style like those of China. The [houses] thatched with coarse or common grass are of bricks or boards; their walls are ornamented with chunam; the floor is purified with cow-dung and strewn with flowers of the season; in these matters they differ from us. But the Buddhist monasteries are of most remarkable architecture. They have a tower at each of the four corners of the quadrangle and three high halls in a tier. The rafters and roofbeams are carved with strange figures, and the doors, windows, and walls are painted in various colours. The houses of the laity are sumptuous inside and economical outside. The inner rooms and the central hall vary in their dimensions, and there is no rule for form or construction for the tiers of the terraces or the rows of high rooms. Their doors open to the east, and the throne faces east.

For seats all use corded benches. The royal family, the grandees, officials and gentry adorn their benches in different ways, but all have the same style (or form) of seat. The sovereign's dais is exceedingly wide and high, and it is dotted with small pearls. What is called the "Lion's Seat" (that is, the actual throne) is covered with fine cloth, and is mounted by a jewelled footstool. The ordinary officials according to their fancy carve the frames of their seats in different ways, and adorn them with precious substances.

### Dress and personal characteristics.

The inner clothing and outward attire of the people have no tailoring; as to colour a fresh white is esteemed and motley is of no account. The men wind a strip of cloth round the waist and up to the armpits and leave the right shoulder bare. The women wear a long robe which covers both shoulders and falls down loose. The hair on the crown of the head is made into a coil, all the rest of the hair hanging down. Some clip their mustaches or have other fantastic fashions. Garlands are worn on the head and necklaces on the body.

The names for their clothing materials are *Kiao-shê-ye* (Kansheya) and muslin (*tieh*) and calico (*pu*), Kausheya being silk from a wild silk-worm; *Ch'ü* (or *Ch'u*)-*mo* (Kshauma), a kind of linen; *Han* (or *Kan*)-*po-lo* (Kambala) a texture of fine wool (sheep's wool or goat's hair), and *Ho-la-li* (Ral?) a texture made from the wool of a wild animal—this wool being fine and soft and easily spun and woven is prized as a material for clothing. In North India where the climate is very cold closely fitting jackets are worn somewhat like those of the Tartars (Hu).

The garbs of the non-Buddhists (religieux) are varied and extraordinary. Some wear peacocks' tails; some adorn themselves with a necklace of skulls; some are quite naked; some cover the body with grass or boards; some pull out their hair and clip their moustaches; some mat their side-hair and make a top-knot coil. Their clothing is not fixed and the colour varies.

In this passage, it will be noticed, the clothing materials used by the lay people of India are arranged in four groups. The first is called by the pilgrim "Kausheya clothing and muslin and cloth" (憍奢耶衣及㲲布等). Now kausheya (or kauśeya) is *silk* made from the cocoon of the Bombyx Mori, and *tieh-pu* is *cotton-cloth* or *tieh* and *cotton cloth.* It is perhaps better to regard *tieh* and *pu* as names of two materials, and in another treatise we find Kausheya, *tieh*, and *ts'ui* (毳) grouped together.[1] This *ts'ui* was apparently a kind of coarse cotton cloth, and we find a *ts'ui-ka-pei* or "rough cotton" used to stuff cushions. The term kausheya was applied not only to

[1] Ta-fang-têng-ta-chi-ching, *ch.* 11 (No. 61 tr. cir. A.D. 400).

silk stuffs but also to mixtures of silk and linen or cotton.[1] Our pilgrim evidently makes one group of "silk clothing" and cottons. This is not to be much wondered at when we reflect that he, like the other Chinese of his time and district, knew nothing of the cotton plant and the cloths derived from it. Moreover we should probably regard this description of the dress of the natives of India as derived from an earlier account.

The second kind of clothing material here mentioned is the Kshauma or Linen. This term also is to be regarded as denoting a class. It comprehends, we must suppose, the fabrics made from the Kshumā or flax, the śanā or jute, and the bhangā or hemp. These three plants are mentioned in Chinese translations from the Sanskrit as yielding stuffs from which clothes were made. This word kshauma denotes not only linen but also silk textures.

The third group is the kambala. This word, which denotes "woollen cloth" and "a blanket", is here evidently used in the sense of fine woollen cloth for making clothing. Like the kausheya and the kshauma the kambala clothing was allowed to the Buddhist Brethren.

The fourth kind of stuff mentioned as used for clothing material is called by Yuan-chuang *Ho-la-li* (褐刺縭). There does not seem to be any known Sanskrit word with which this can be identified. As Yuan-chuang spells foreign words the three characters may stand for Ral, a Tibetan word meaning "goat's hair", from Ra, a goat. This *Ho-la-li* or Ral is also probably the *Lo-i* (羅衣) or "Lo (Ra) clothes" of other Buddhist texts. In Sanskrit also we find *rallaka* which denotes a wild animal and a stuff made from its hair, and *rallaka-kambala* which is a fine woollen cloth.

Our pilgrim's description proceeds—

> The clerical costume of the Sha-mên (Śramaṇas) is only the three robes and the Sêng-kio-ki and Ni-p'o-so-na. As to the three robes the Schools adhere to different styles having broad or

---

[1] Sar. Vin. vibhāsha, *ch.* 5 (No. 1135): Sêng-chi-lü, *ch.* 9.

narrow fringes and small or large folds. The sêng-kio-ki goes over the left shoulder covers the armpits, joined on the right and opening on the left side and in length reaching to below the waist. As to the Ni-p'o-so-na, since no belt is worn when it is put on, it is gathered into plaits and secured by one of these, the size and colour of the plaits vary in the different schools.

For the first part of this passage Julien has the following—"Les *Cha-men* (Çramanas) n'ont que trois sortes de vêtements, savoir le *Sêng-kia-tchi* (Sañghāṭi) le Seng-kio-ki (Sañkakchikā), et le *Ni-po-sie-na* (Nivāsana). La coupe et la façon de ces trois vêtements varient suivant les écoles. Les uns ont une bordure large ou étroite, les autres ont des pans petits ou grands". Here the translator spoils the description by interpolating the words "savoir le *Sêng-kia-tchi* (Sañghāṭi)", leaving out the word for "and", and inserting "ces" in the clause "La coupe et la façon de *ces* trois vêtements". The "Three robes" of the Buddhist monk are quite distinct from the two articles of his dress here mentioned by name. The "three robes" are always given as the Antaravāsaka, the Samghāṭi, and the Uttarāsañga. Of these we have already met with the second and third in our traveller's account of Balkh, and there we met also with the article of clothing called *Seng-kio-ki*. This last word is apparently for the original which is Samkachchika in Pali and Julien's Sanskrit Sañkakshikā. This is translated in a Chinese note to our text by "covering armpits". Professor Rhys Davids translates the Pali word by "vest", but the description given seems to suit a rude shirt or jacket with one sleeve which was buttoned or looped on the left shoulder. One name for the vestment as worn by monks in China is *P'ien-shan* (偏衫) or "one-sided jacket".[1] The other article of monk's costume mentioned by name here is the Ni-p'o-so-na or Nivāsana. This is rendered in Chinese by *chün* (裙) an old native term denoting a "skirt" on the lower part of

---

[1] Shih-shih-yao-lan (釋氏要覽), *ch.* 1; Vinaya Vol. ii, p. 272 and Vinaya Texts Vol. iii, p. 351; Sêng-chi-lü l. c.

a robe of ceremony. Nivāsana is a common term for an under-robe or lower garment, but it is here used in its restricted sense as designating the particular kind of skirt or under-robe worn by Buddhist monks. This was, according to regulation, four ells long by one and a half in width, and it reached from the waist to about three finger-breadths above the ankle. As Yuan-chuang here tells us the Schools were distinguished by differences in the wearing of the Nivāsana.[1] Thus, as I-ching tells us, the Sarvāstivādins wore the skirt with a pair of plaits turned out on both sides of it, and the Mahāsanghikas crossed the end of the right side to the top of the left side, tucking it in to keep the skirt in its place. This skirt or Nivāsa had no string or girdle and it was evidently something like the Malay Sarong which, as Colonel Yule tells us, is an old Indian form of dress. This garment also is self-securing, and is not in need of a belt or girdle. The two articles of dress here mentioned and described, viz. the Sañkakshika and the Nivāsana were in addition to the Three Robes which formed originally the full clerical costume of the bhikshu. They are often mentioned in the canonical books, having been allowed apparently as soon as Buddhism began to spread. The mode of wearing the Nivāsana and its colour and fashion caused much discussion and unpleasant feeling in the early church.

The pilgrim's description continues—

> The Kshatriyas and Brahmins are clean-handed and unostentatious, pure and simple in life and very frugal. The dress and ornaments of the kings and grandees are very extraordinary. Garlands and tiaras with precious stones are their head-adornments; and their bodies are adorned with rings, bracelets, and necklaces. Wealthy mercantile people have only bracelets. Most of the people go barefoot and shoes are rare. They stain their teeth red or black, wear their hair cut even, bore their ears, have long noses and large eyes: such are they in outward appearance.

---

[1] Ssŭ-fên-lü, *ch.* 19; Nan-hai-ch'i-kuei, *ch.* 10, 11 and Takakusu; P'i-ni-mu-ching, *ch.* 8.

They are pure of themselves and not from compulsion. Before every meal they must have a wash; the fragments and remains are not served up again; the food utensils are not passed on; those utensils which are of pottery or wood must be thrown away after use, and those which are of gold, silver, copper, or iron get another polishing. As soon as a meal is over they chew the tooth-stick and make themselves clean; before they have finished ablutions they do not come into contact with each other; they always wash after urinating; they smear their bodies with scented unguents such as sandal and saffron. When the king goes to his bath there is the music of drums and stringed instruments and song; worship is performed and there are bathing and washing.

The last sentence of this passage is in Julien's version—"Quand le roi se dispose à sortir, des musiciens battent le tambour et chantent aux sons de la guitare. Avant d'offrir un sacrifice, ou d'adresser des prières (aux dieux), ils se lavent et se baignent". Here Julien evidently had for the first clause the B reading *chün-wang-chiang-ts'ü*, meaning "when the king is about to go out". But in the A, C, and D texts the reading instead of *ts'ü* is *yü*, meaning "to bathe", and this is evidently the correct reading. Then Julien seems to change the author's meaning by making the second clause a new sentence and introducing the word "avant". The author's meaning seems to be that when the king took his bath there was the performance of certain acts of worship.[1]

## WRITTEN AND SPOKEN LANGUAGE &c.

The description next proceeds to tell of the writing and learning of the Hindus.

Their system of writing was invented, as is known, by the deva Brahmā who at the beginning instituted as patterns forty seven [written] words. These were combined and applied as objects arose and circumstances occurred; ramifying like streams they spread far and wide becoming modified a little by place and people. In language, speaking generally, they have not varied from the original source, but the people of "Mid India" are

[1] The text is—君王將浴 or 趨鼓奏弦歌祭祀拜祠沐浴盥洗.

preeminently explicit and correct in speech, their expressions being harmonious and elegant, like those of the devas, and their intonation clear and distinct, serving as rule and pattern for others. The people of neighbouring territories and foreign countries repeating errors until these became the norm, and emulous for vulgarities, have lost the pure style.

The statement here made to the effect that the Sanskrit alphabet was invented by the god Brahmā is repeated in several other books by Buddhist writers. Some tell us that Brahmā was once a rājah on earth, and that he then invented an alphabet of 72 letters called the "Kharu writing" (佉樓書). Disgusted with the bad treatment given to these letters he proceeded to swallow them all; but two, *a* and *au* escaped from his mouth and remained among men.[1] But we are also told that Brahmā invented the Brahma writing first, and that afterwards Kharoshtha produced the script which bears his name.[2] Another account represents the Brahman writing (or Devanagari) to have been the invention of a wise (kovida) Brahmin, and the Kharu writing to have been the work of a stupid (kharu) rishi. This Kharu writing is that mentioned in the Lalitavistara and other books under the name Kharoshtha (or Kharosta). This word is translated by "Ass-ear", and is the name of an ancient rishi who was a great astronomer and astrologist. In some Buddhist treatises we find the invention of letters ascribed to the Buddha, and in some Siva, as in Indian tradition, is credited with the first teaching of spelling and writing.[3] The "forty seven words" of our passage are the twelve symbols which represent the ten vowels, and anusvāra and visarga, and the thirty-five consonants; and so constitute the alphabet. The letters admit of endless combinations to make words as objects require names and circumstances need expression. Some authors give the number of the letters in the

---

1 Pai-lun-su (百論疏).

2 Liu-shu-liao (六書略), *ch.* 5.

3 See Ta-pan-nie-p'an-ching, *ch.* 8 (No. 113); Si-t'an-san-mi-ch'ao (悉曇三密鈔), *ch.* 1; Si-t'an-tsang, *ch.* 1; Si-t'an-tzŭ-chi (字記).

Sanskrit alphabet as less, and others as more, than the number here given; but this is generally regarded as the correct number. With the statements here made by Yuan-chuang about the Sanskrit alphabet and language we may compare the more detailed account given in the third *chuan* of the Life.[1]

It is evident that Yuan-chuang, like other non-Indian Buddhists, had been taught to regard the spoken and written language of "Mid-India" as at once the parent and the standard of all the dialects of "North-India". These latter had departed a little from the correct form in their writing, some of them, as in Gandhāra, having written alphabets so unlike the parent one that they had special names. In oral speech the border lands and outlying regions generally had come to differ much from the people of "Mid-India". They had lost the rich purity of the standard language, and had persisted in erroneous forms of expression until these had come to be taught as the rule.

The description continues—

> As to their archives and records there are separate custodians of these. The official annals and state-papers are called collectivelly *ni-lo-pi-t'u* (or *ch'a*); in these good and bad are recorded, and instances of public calamity and good fortune are set forth in detail.

The *Ni-lo-pi-t'u* of this passage has been rightly restored by Julien as Nīlapiṭa, and the Chinese annotator tells us the word means "Dark-blue store". We find the word Nīlapiṭa in our Sanskrit dictionaries, but the P. W. gives only one illustration of its use, and that is the passage before us.

Proceeding to the education and learning of the people of India our author writes—

> In beginning the education of their children and winning them on to progress they follow the "Twelve Chapters". When the children are seven years of age the great treatises of the Five

[1] Julien I, p. 165; cf. Alberuni Vol. i, p. 170; Bühler's Ind. Palæographie p^s. 1 and 19 to 30.

Sciences are gradually communicated to them. The first science is Grammar which teaches and explains words, and classifies their distinctions. The second is that of the skilled professions [concerned with] the principles of the mechanical arts, the dual processes, and astrology. The third is the science of medicine [embracing] exorcising charms, medicine, the use of the stone, the needle, moxa. The fourth is the science of reasoning, by which the orthodox and heterodox are ascertained, and the true and false are thoroughly sought out. The fifth is the science of the Internal which investigates and teaches the five degrees of religious attainments (lit. the "five vehicles") and the subtle doctrine of karma.

The "Twelve Chapters" of this passage is in the original *Shi-êrh-chang* (十二章) and Julien translates this by "un livre en douze sections". In a note to this rendering he translates a short passage from a well-known Buddhist Dictionary about a book called the "Siddham-chang". This is doubtless the sort of work to which the pilgrim refers as the first book which the children of India learned. The name is made up of Siddham which means, we are told, "Perfection" or "May good fortune be attained", and *chang* the Chinese word for a "section" or "chapter". But Julien makes the whole stand for a Sanskrit compound *Siddhavastu*, a term apparently known only from his use of it. From a passage in I-ching's "Nan-hai-ch'i-kuei" and from other works we learn that the Siddham-chang was the name of a child's primer ABC., the first chapter of which was headed by the word *siddhaṁ.*[1] This word forms an "auspicious invocation", and the Buddhists used it alone or with "Namo Sarvajnāya, "Praise to the omniscient [Buddha]" prefixed, at the beginning of their primers. They used it in a similar way to head such documents as deeds of gift to religious establishments. In these places Bühler took the word to mean "Success", i. e. may there be success, an interpretation which agrees with the accepted Chinese rendering. But Fleet thinks that *siddham* in these places is to be understood as meaning "Perfection has been attained by Buddha", an inter-

1 Nan-hai-ch'i-kuei, *ch.* 34; Si-t'an-san-mi-ch'ao, l. c.

pretation which does not seem to be so good.[1] Instead of siddham the non-Buddhist teachers in India placed "siddhir-astu" meaning "May there be success (or accomplishment)" at the head of their ABCs. Thus these books came to be called Siddham or Siddhir-astu, the former being the name by which they became known to the Chinese. There are many varieties of them and the number of chapters or sections ranges from nine to eighteen, the latter being the number in the work which may be regarded as the standard one in China. This is the *Si-t'an-tzŭ-chi* (悉曇字記) by the monk Chih-kuang (智廣) of the T'ang period taken from the Siddham of Prajnābodhi of South India. A Siddham gives the Sanskrit alphabet, beginning with the vowels and proceeding in the order in which the letters are given in our Sanskrit grammars, then the combinations made by single consonants and vowels, and then those made by two or more consonants with a vowel. In some of the Siddhams made for Chinese use we are told that this word denotes "the alphabet", while in others we are told that it is a designation for the twelve so-called vowels, but the statements are not borne out by any authority, and are evidently not correct. It may be interesting, however, in connection with subject to quote a statement from Álberuni. He relates—"The most generally known alphabet is called Siddha-mātrikā, which is by some considered as originating from Kashmir, for the people of Kashmir use it. But it is also used in Varānasi. This town and Kashmir are the high schools of Hindu science. The same writing is used in Madhyadeśa, i. e. the middle country, the country all around Kanauj, which is also called Aryāvarta".[2] According to I-ching a child began his primer when he was six years of age and learned it within six months.

After mastering the Siddham the Indian child, accord-

---

1 Bühler in Ind. Ant. Vol. x, p. 273; Fleet in Corp. Insc. Ind. Vol. iii, p. 25.

2 Alberuni Vol. i, p. 173.

ing to Yuan-chuang, was introduced to the "great śāstras of the Five Sciences (*Wu-ming-ta-lun* 五明大論). The word *ming* of this phrase is often used to translate the Sanskrit word *vidyā*, but a five-fold classification of vidyā does not seem to be known to Indian literature. We find, however, our pilgrim's list in certain Chinese translations of Buddhist books and the "sciences" are there acquired by aspiring Bodhisattvas.[1] They are called the "Five Science places" or the "Five Science śāstras". In his translation of the present passage Julien has treated the name of each *ming* as the name of a treatise. This is evidently a mistake, and the context shews that *ming* here denotes a *department of knowledge*, and that the *Wu-ming* named are the literatures of five categories of learning and speculation. Yuan-chuang properly places at the head the *Shêng-ming* or "Science of Sounds", i. e. Grammar. Julien agrees with I-ching in giving Śabdavidyā as the original for this term. But Śabdavidyā was apparently the Buddhist name for Grammar which by the people of India generally was called Vyākarana. It is this latter word also which Yuan-chuang elsewhere uses as the original for *Shêng-ming*. The next group is called *Chiao-* or in some texts *Kung-chiao*(工巧)*-ming*, the "Science of the Arts and Crafts". Julien retranslates the Chinese name by Śilpasthānavidyā, which seems to be rather the original for the "Arts-place Science" of the sūtra. The third group is the *I-fang-ming*, "Healing-prescriptions Science", that is Medical science in all its branches. Julien gives as the Sanskrit original for the Chinese name Chikitsāvidyā or Science of Medicine, but this seems to be only a conjecture. The fourth group in our passage is the *Yin*(因)*-ming* or the Science of Reasoning. Julien restores the Sanskrit equivalent as Hetūvidyā which, like *Yin-ming*, means literally "Science of causation". But *Yin-ming* is the technical term used to translate the

---

[1] Fan-wang-ching, *ch.* 2, Glossary; Yoga-shih-ti-lun, *ch.* 38 (No. 1170); P'u-sa-ti-chih-ching, *ch.* 3 (No. 1086 tr. cir. A.D. 415).

Nyāya or Logic of Indian writers, and Julien learned afterwards that it was Nyāya which was the original for *Yin-ming*. The fifth is the *Nei*(內)-*ming* or "Internal Science"; Julien translates "la science des choses intérieures" and gives as the Sanskrit original Adhyātma-vidyā. This word adhyātma means (1) *the highest spirit* and (2) *belonging to oneself*. In Kapila's system ādhyātmika means *self-caused* (in Chinese *i-nei* 依 內), and it is opposed to that which is due to external influences. But in the present passage, as the context shews, and as we learn from other authorities, the *nei-ming* or Inner science is Buddhism. The son of Buddhist parents went through a course of secular instruction like other boys, and he also studied the books of his religion including the metaphysical and argumentative treatises of the great Doctors of Abhidharma. In these he learned all about the Five degrees or "Five Vehicles, the fivefold gradation of moral beings. These "vehicles" or progressive stages are given as lay believer (or "inferior degree"), ordained disciple, Pratyeka Buddha, Bodhisattva, Buddha. They are also said to be Men, Devas, ordained disciples, Pratyeka Buddhas, and Bodhisattvas, and there is further difference of opinion as to the classes of beings which form the successive groups.[1] In the Buddhist śāstras moreover the student found the doctrine of karma stated, defended, and illustrated with a subtlety of intellect and boldness of imagination almost matchless. All the five groups of learning here enumerated were apparently comprised in the training of an Indian Buddhist; and no one could be a leader in the church, or an authority on dogma, who did not shew himself a proficient in these departments of learning. We are told of Kumārajīva that he studied the śāstras of the Five sciences, and of Guṇabhadra it is recorded that in his youth he learned all the śāstras of the Five sciences, astronomy, arithmetic, medicine, exor-

---

1 Shih-chiao-fa-shu, *ch.* 1; Ta-ming-san-tsang-fa-shu, *ch.* 22 (No. 1621).

cisms. The religious training in the Tripiṭaka was according to some authorities a separate affair, while others treat it as a part of the "Inner Science".

Our author's description proceeds.

> The Brahmins learn the four Veda treatises. The first called *Shou* (壽), "Longevity" (the Āyur-Veda) tells of nourishing life and keeping the constitution in order; the second called *Tzŭ* (祠), "Worship" (the Yajur Veda) tells of the making of offerings and supplications; the third called *P'ing* (平) "Making even" (the Sāma Veda) describes ceremonial etiquette, divination, and military tactics; the fourth called *Shu* (術) or "Arts" (the Atharva Veda) tells us of the various skilled arts, exorcisms, medicine. The teacher must have a wide, thorough, and minute knowledge of these, with an exhaustive comprehension of all that is abstruse in them.

The words here rendered "the four Veda treatises" are in the original "*ssŭ-fei-t'ê-lun* (四吠陀論). Julien translates them simply by "les quatres Vêdas", and Beal by "the four Vēda Sāstras". Neither of the translators attempts to explain why the first Veda is here not the Rig but the Āyur. The latter term denotes *life* or *longevity*, as Yuan-chuang translates, and there is an Āyur-Veda. But this is only a supplement or appendix to the Atharva-Veda, and denotes rather the *science* of *medicine* than any particular treatise. It is reckoned as Veda, we learn, because its teachings have been found by experience to be wise and beneficial. Yuan-chuang knew that the Rig was the first, the original Veda, yet he does not even mention it here. His descriptions of the other Vedas also are not good, and it is plain that he knew very little about them and the great literature to which they had given rise. The Sāma Veda, for example, with its Brāhmaṇas and Sūtras, has nothing to do with the subjects which Yuan-chuang assigns to it, and it is concerned only with the worship of Indra, and Agni, and the Soma. When writing this passage Yuan-chuang may have had in view only those Vedic works which were in writing, and were known to or owned by the Brethren in "North India". Some of these Buddhists were converted Brahmins, and it was perhaps by some of them, as has been suggested, that the Vedas were first reduced to writing. The Rig-veda itself still existed only in the memories of the Brahmins, and it was taught entirely by oral communication, but there were commentaries and other Vedic treatises in writing. Moreover we are probably justified in treating the word "Veda" in our text as denoting a group or collection of treatises, each Veda being a title under which several departments of learning were classed. The translators into Chinese sometimes render Veda like vidyā by *ming* (明) which simply means *knowledge, science, intelligence,* as with the Brahmins the Trayi-vidyā or "threefold Science" denotes the Rig, Yajur, and Sāma Vedas. The reader also will observe that Yuan-chuang here does not use the words *books, treatises* with the terms for Ayur, Yajur, Sāma, Atharva.

Our author proceeds to sketch the Brahmin teacher's way of educating his disciples.

> These teachers explain the general meaning [to their disciples] and teach them the minutiæ; they rouse them to activity and skilfully win them to progress; they instruct the inert and sharpen the dull. When disciples, intelligent and acute, are addicted to idle shirking, the teachers doggedly persevere repeating instruction[1] until their training is finished. When the disciples are thirty years old, their minds being settled and their education finished, they go into office; and the first thing they do then is to reward the kindness of their teachers.

We have next some account of a kind of men peculiar to India and long famous in the world. Our author writes—

> There are men who, far seen in antique lore and fond of the refinements of learning, "are content in seclusion", leading lives of continence. These come and go (lit. sink and float) outside of the world, and promenade through life away from human affairs. Though they are not moved by honour or reproach,

---

[1] The original for "doggedly persevere repeating instruction is 拘繫反關. This is the reading of the D text but instead of *fan-k'ai* the Ming edition has 及關 and Julien translates the four words "ils les attachent et les tiennent enfermés".

their fame is far spread. The rulers treating them with ceremony and respect cannot make them come to court. Now as the State holds men of learning and genius in esteem, and the people respect those who have high intelligence, the honours and praises of such men are conspicuously abundant, and the attentions private and official paid to them are very considerable. Hence men can force themselves to a thorough acquisition of knowledge. Forgetting fatigue they "expatiate in the arts and sciences"; seeking for wisdom while "relying on perfect virtue" they "count not 1000 *li* a long journey". Though their family be in affluent circumstances, such men make up their minds to be like the vagrants, and get their food by begging as they go about. With them there is honour in knowing truth (in having wisdom), and there is no disgrace in being destitute. As to those who lead dissipated idle lives, luxurious in food and extravagant in dress, as such men have no moral excellences and are without accomplishments, shame and disgrace come on them and their ill repute is spread abroad.[1]

## BUDDHISM.

Our author passes on to make a few general observations about the internal condition of Buddhism as he heard about it and found it in India. His statements on the subject are meagre and condensed to a fault, and the precise meaning in some cases has perhaps not yet been ascertained. The whole passage should be regarded as forming a separate section, and should not be divided as it has been by the translators. For the present the in-

---

[1] The 'content in seclusion' of this passage is in the Chinese *fei-t'un* (肥遁) which is the *fei-t'un* (肥遯) of the commentary to the 33rd Diagram of the Yih-Ching. The phrase means "to be comfortable and happy in a life of retirement", to be content and cheerful in a voluntary seclusion, in a life of final withdrawal from the contact of bad men in the hurly-burly of an official career.

For the words 'seeking for wisdom while relying on perfect virtue' the original is *fang-tao-yi-jen* (訪道依仁). The phrase *yi-jen*, "depending on (or following) benevolence" is a quotation from the Lun-yü; so also is the expression for "expatiate in the arts and sciences; then "count not 1000 *li* a long journey" is from the first chapter of Mencius; and 'acquired accomplishments' is for the *shih-hsi* (時習) or "constant practise" of the first chapter of the Lun-yü.

formation which it gives may be roughly interpreted to the following effect.—

> As the religious system of Julai is apprehended by people according to their kind, and as it is long since the time of the Holy One, Buddhism now is pure or diluted according to the spiritual insight and mental capacity of its adherents. The tenets of the Schools keep these isolated, and controversy runs high; heresies on special doctrines lead many ways to the same end. Each of the Eighteen Schools claims to have intellectual superiority; and the tenets (or practises) of the Great and the Small Systems (lit. Vehicles) differ widely. They have sitting in silent reverie, the walking to and fro, and the standing still; Samādhi and Prajñā are far apart, and many are the noisy discussions. Wherever there is a community of Brethren it makes [its own] rules of gradation. The Brother who expounds orally one treatise (or class of scripture) in the Buddhist Canon, whether Vinaya, Abhidharma, or Sūtra, is exempted from serving under the Prior; he who expounds two is invested with the outfit of a Superior; he who expounds three has Brethren deputed to assist him; he who expounds four has lay servants assigned to him; he who expounds five rides an elephant; he who expounds six rides an elephant and has a surrounding retinue. Where the spiritual attainments are high, the distinctions conferred are extraordinary.
>
> The Brethren are often assembled for discussion to test intellectual capacity and bring moral character into prominent distinction, to reject the worthless and advance the intelligent. Those who bring forward (or according to some texts, estimate aright) fine points in philosophy, and give subtle principles their proper place, who are ornate in diction and acute in refined distinctions, ride richly caparisoned elephants preceded and followed by a host of attendants. But as for those to whom religious teaching has been offered in vain, who have been defeated in discussion, who are deficient in doctrine and redundant in speech, perverting the sense while keeping the language, the faces of such are promptly daubed with red and white clay, their bodies are covered with dirt, and they are driven out to the wilds or thrown into the ditches. As the moral are marked off from the immoral so the eminent (the wise) and the stupid have outward signs of distinction. A man knowing to delight in wisdom, at home diligently intent on learning, may be monk or layman as he pleases.
>
> For offences against the Vinaya the Community of Brethren has a gradation of penalties. If the offence is slight a reprimand is ordered. For an offence next above this in gravity there is

added a cessation of oral intercourse with the Brethren. When the offence is serious the punishment is that the community will not live with the offender, and this involves expulsion and excommunication. Expelled from a Community, the monk has no home; he then becomes a miserable vagrant, or he returns to his first estate.

This passage contains several phrases and expressions which may seem to require some comment or explanation. Thus in the first sentence we are told that Buddha's "religious system is apprehended by people according to their kind (如來理孝 隨類得 解)", that is, every one understands Buddha's teaching according to his individual nature and capacity. The statement is derived from the canonical Scriptures in which we are told that the Buddha preached in one language, but that all kinds of creatures understood him in their own ways. He spoke, we are told, the "Aryan language" but Chinese, and Yavans, and the peoples of Bactria and Bokhara, heard him as speaking in their own tongues. Moeover each man in a congregation which the Buddha addressed heard his own besetting sin reproved, and the same words called the unchaste to chastity and the avaricious to liberality.[1] This may have been right, and attended with only good consequences while the Buddha was bodily present among men, teaching and preaching and giving rules and precepts. But at Yuan-chuang's time a long period had elapsed since the decease of the Buddha. His teachings had been collected, committed to writing, transmitted and preserved with very unequal faithfulness. Great differences of opinion also had arisen as to whether certain doctrines were or were not the Buddha's teaching. Hence in Yuan-chuang's time the orthodox religion as professed in India was genuine or adulterated according to the moral and intellectual characters of its professed adherents. Some held to what they were taught to believe was the original Canon settled by the first Council. Others doubted and

[1] Abhi-ta-vibh-lun, *ch.* 79; Hua-yen-yi-shêng-chiao, &c., *ch.* 1 (No. 1591).

argued, wrested Scripture from its proper meaning to suit their personal views, and lightly admitted spurious texts to have authority.

We next have mention of the Eighteen *Pu* or Schools which had arisen in Buddhism and of their rivalry. These Schools were famous in the history of Buddhism, and various accounts are given of their origin and growth. We know that the first split in the Church after the Buddha's death led to the formation of the two great Schools of the Sthaviras and Mahāsañghikas. The former in the course of time yielded eleven, and the latter seven Schools; and so there were actually Twenty Schools, but the total number is generally given in the books as Eighteen. Each of these Schools became famous for the propagation and defence of some peculiar doctrine. In Professor Rhys Davids's articles on the Buddhist sects[1] there is an excellent summary of what we know of these Eighteen Schools, with references to other authorities.

Then we have mention of another famous division in the Buddhist Church, viz. the Great and Small Vehicles. Yuan-chuang tells us that "the tenets (or practises) of the Great and the Small Vehicles differ widely". Ta-hsiao-êrh-shêng-chü-chih-ch'ü-pie (大小二乘居 or 舉止區別). Julien translates—"Les partisans du *grand* et du *petit Vehicle* forment deux classes à part", but this does not seem to give the author's meaning. The term *chü-chih* lit. *resting* or *sojourning* denotes here *tenets*, or *outward observances* or *practises*, and *ch'ü-pie* means *very unlike* or *generically different*. Yuan-chuang does not state that the adherents of the two systems formed two classes apart: he knew that in some places they even lived together in one monastery. But he tells us that the tenets of the two Systems, their ways of belief and conduct were far apart. It is a pity that the word Vehicle has come to be generally used as the rendering for the Sanskrit Yāna in the words Mahāyāna and Hīnayāna. We should often

[1] Journal of the Royal Asiatic Soc. 1891 and 1892.

substitute for it some term like Creed or System, and Hīnayāna should be the Primitive and Mahāyāna the Developed System. As is well known, it was the adherents of the latter who gave the name "Small Vehicle" to the creed from which their own grew. Their doctrines and religious observances came to differ very widely from those of the early system. The Mahāyānists had a more expansive Creed, a different standard of religious perfection, and a more elaborate cult than the Hīnayānists. As to particular tenets, they differed very much from the early Buddhists in such matters as opinions about arhats and Bodhisattvas, their views of the relation of the Buddha to mankind, of the efficacy of prayer and worship, and of the elasticity of the Canon. Our author illustrates his statement as to differences in the Great and Little Systems by one or two examples, at least such is the general opinion as to the passage which follows. In the rendering here given its reads—'They have sitting in silent reverie, the walking to and fro, and the standing still: Samādhi and Prajñā are far apart, and many are the noisy discussions'. Julien's translation, which seems to be the result of a serious misconstruction of the passage is—"Les uns méditent en silence, et, soit en marchant, soit en repos, tiennent leur esprit immobile et font abstraction du monde; les autres diffèrent tout à fait de ceux-ci par leurs disputes orageuses".[1] The text, given below, plainly does not admit of this rendering which does great violence to meaning and construction. In this passage *ting*, or "absorbed meditation" (Samādhi), seems to be declared to be far apart from prajñā, *hui* or "transcendental wisdom. But samādhi, although known to early Buddhism, is characteristic of Mahāyānism, and is often found, as here, with *hui*, which is strictly Mahāyānist. We read of a great controversy which was carried on between two Hīnayāna Schools as to the relative merits of samādhi

[1] The text is—有宴默思惟經行住立定慧悠隔諠諍頁殊.

and prajñā. But we should perhaps understand our author here as stating that the Hīnayānist practices of quiet thought, walking up and down, and standing still were far removed from the Samādhi and Prajñā of the Mahayānists.

For the sentence—'Wherever there is a community of Brethren it makes rules of gradation' the original is 隨其衆居各制科防, and Julien translates—"Suivant le lieu qu'ils habitent, on leur a fait un code de règlements et de défenses d'une nature spéciale." This is not in accordance with Buddhism, and it is not a fair rendering of the author's words. These mean that each community of Brethren had its own hierarchy promoted according to a recognized system. The system of promotion, Yuan-chuang explains, was briefly this—the Brethren in any establishment were advanced according to their ability to expound and teach the canonical treatises of the Vinaya, Abhidharma, or Sūtras. In the D text the original is "without distinguishing Vinaya, Abhidharma, Sūtra, in Buddha's canon—(無云律論經是佛經), but the B text has the words *chi-fan* (紀凡) after *Fo-ching*, and C adds the word *kua* (絓) after *fan*. Julien having the reading of the B text translates—"Les règles de la discipline (Vinaya), les Traités philosophiques (Śāstras), les textes sacrés (Sūtras), les Prédictions (Vyākaraṇas), &c. sont tous également des livres du Buddha". He tells us in a note how he gets "les Prédictions", viz. by altering the 紀 of the text to 記. This emendation is quite untenable and unnecessary, as is also the insertion of "&c." by the translator. There is no classification of the Buddhist Scriptures which contains the four heads of division given in Julien's translation. All the canon is contained in the Three Baskets (or Stores), Vinaya, Sūtra, and Abhidharma, and the *Chi* (記) or "les Prédictions" constitute one of the subdivisions of the sūtra.[1] In the passage under consideration the words

[1] But in the passage quoted by Julien and in other places *ching* or sūtra is given as one of the classes of Scripture along with the *Shou-chi* or Predictions; the *ching* is the first of the twelve classes of scriptures the *Chi* (or *Shou-chi*) being also one of the twelve.

*Chi-fan* are not wanted; they were probably inserted to satisfy the demands of style.

The first step in promotion, Yuan-chuang relates, was that a Brother who could teach one treatise (or class of writings) in the Canon "was exempted from serving under the Prior". For the words within inverted commas the original is—*Nai-mien-sêng-chih-shih* (乃免僧知事), and Julien translates—"est dispensé des devoirs de religieux et dirige les affaires du couvent". This faulty interpretation, it will be seen, puts the disciple of one talent above the disciples of two or more talents. The *Sêng-chih-shih* or Karmadāna' in a Buddhist monastery had control of its secular affairs, and the common monks were under his orders for all kinds of menial work. When a Brother proved himself well versed in one subject or department of the canon, and skilled in eloquent exposition of the same, he was, as a first step in advancement, exempted from performing the ordinary work of the establishment. This exemption was granted also in monasteries to which the learned Brother went as a guest. There is an Abhidharma treatise in which we find an illustration of our text. A stranger monk arrives in a monastery and is treated as a guest at first. Afterwards the Prior tells him that according to his seniority he is to take part in the daily routine of the establisment. But the guest said—No, I am not to work; I am a Ph. D., a Lun-shih, and his claim to be exempted was allowed.[1]

For the words here rendered by 'But as for those to whom religious teaching has been offered in vain' the original is 至乃義門虛闢. Julien wrongly connecting these words with what precedes translates "A son arrivée, il passe sous des portes triomphales". It will be readily admitted that *yi-mên* cannot be translated "triumphal gates" and that *hsü-p'i* cannot possibly be rendered by "il passe sous". The term *yi-mên*, lit. "door of meaning" is used in the senses of *article of creed*, *essential doctrine*,

---

[1] Sar. Vin. Mu-tê-kà, *ch.* 6 (No. 1134); Abhi-ta-vib-lun, *ch.* 118.

*course of instruction.* In ordinary Chinese literature the term is not unknown and it is an honourable epithet or distinction. A *yi-mên* is an *unselfish* or *public-spiritual clan*, as a family which keeps together for a long time, five or six generations, living and messing on the same premises. But here *yi-mên* has a Buddhistic use and means "cause of religious instruction". Then *hsü-p'i* is "vainly open", and the clause means "as for those to whom religious teaching has been offered to no purpose". It introduces the words which follow, telling the dreadful fate of the man who does not learn, and yet pretends to be wise.

### The Castes of India.

Our author passes on to give a few particulars about the division of the people of India into castes. His statements may be loosely rendered as follows—

> There are four orders of hereditary clan distinctions. The first is that of the Brāhmins or "purely living"; these keep their principles and live continently, strictly observing ceremonial purity. The second order is that of the Kshatriyas, the race of kings; this order has held sovereignty for many generations, and its aims are benevolence and mercy. The third order is that of the Vaiśyas or class of traders, who barter commodities and pursue gain far and near. The fourth class is that of the Śūdras or agriculturists; these toil at cultivating the soil and are industrious at sowing and reaping. These four castes form classes of various degrees of ceremonial purity. The members of a caste marry within the caste, the great and the obscure keeping apart. Relations whether by the father's or the mother's side do not intermarry, and a woman never contracts a second marriage. There are also the mixed castes; numerous clans formed by groups of people according to their kinds, and these cannot be described.

It will be seen from this passage that Yuan-chuang, like other Chinese writers on India, understood the term *Brāhman* as meaning those who had *brahman* in the sense of a *chaste continent habit of life.* The Kshatriyas were the hereditary rulers, and as such their minds were to be bent on benevolence and mercy. This is in accordance with Manu who lays it down that the king should be a protector to his people.[1] Yuan-chuang here puts the castes in the order given in brahmin books, but in the Buddhist scriptures the Kshatriyas are usually placed above the Brāhmins. The phrase which he applies to the Vaiśyas, whom he calls the trading caste, viz. "they barter what they have not" is one of some interest. The words are *mao-ch'ien-yu-wu* (貿遷有無), and they are to be found in the Shu-ching with the substitution of 貿 for 懋, the two characters having the same sound but very different meanings.[2] Our pilgrim, it will be noticed, makes the Śūdras to be farmers. But in Manu, and in some Buddhist works, the Vaiśyas are farmers, and the business of the Śūdras is to serve the three castes above them.[3]

The sentence here rendered "The members of a caste marry within the caste, the great and the obscure keeping apart" is in the original *hun-chü-t'ung-ch'in-fei-fu-yi-lu* (婚娶通親飛伏異路), lit. "marriages go through the kindred, flying and prostrate different ways". Julien translates the words—"Quand les hommes ou les femmes se marient, ils prennent un rang élevé ou restent dans une condition obscure, suivant la difference de leur origine." This rendering seems to be absurd and it does violence to the text leaving out the two words *t'ung-ch'in* and mistranslating *yi-lu*. What our author states seems to be clear and simple. Marriages take place within a caste, and a Vaiśya man, for example, may marry any Vaisya maid. And he will marry no other. To Yuan-chuang a caste was a *gens* or a clan denoted by one surname (姓) and all who belonged to the *gens* were kindred, they were of one *jāti*. So members of the caste might intermarry provided they were not already related by marriage. But though a man might espouse any maid of his caste, the rich and great married among themselves, and the poor

---

1 *Ch.* 1. 89 et al.

2 L. C. C. Vol. iii, p. 78, Shu-Ching, *ch.* 2.

3 Ch'êng-shih-lun, *ch.* 7 (No. 1274); Manu 1, 91.

and obscure kept to themselves in their marriages. The words *fei*, "flying" and *fu* "prostrate", used for *prosperous* and *obscure* have a reference to the first chapter of the Yih-ching. With what Yuan-chuang tells us here we may compare Manu who lays down the law that "a father ought to give his daughter in marriage to a distinguished young man of an agreeable exterior and of the same class", and of the lady he says—"let her choose a husband of the same rank as herself."[1]

The "mixed castes (*tsa-hsing* 雜姓)" are properly not "castes", but guilds and groups of low craftsmen and workmen. These include weavers, shoemakers, hunters, fishermen, and also water-carriers and scavengers. Alberuni's account of these and his description of the four castes may be used as a commentary to the short account given by our pilgrim.[2]

## The Army.

We have next a short notice of the army of India beginning with its head, the Sovereign. Of the latter Yuan-chuang states according to Julien's rendering—"La série des rois ne se compose que de Kchattriyas, *qui, dans l'origine, se sont élevés au pouvoir par* l'usurpation du trône et le meurtre du souverain. *Quoiqu'ils sont issus de* familles étrangères, leur nom est prononcé avec respect". The italics are mine and they indicate interpolations, unnecessary and unwarranted, made by the translator, who seems to have forgotten the passage he had just translated. What our author states is to this effect—

> The sovereignty for many successive generations has been exercised only by Kshatriyas: rebellion and regicide have occasionally arisen, other castes assuming the distinction

that is, calling themselves kings. The sovereign *de jure* Yuan-chuang thought, was always of the Kshatriya caste, and it was that caste alone which could lawfully produce

---

[1] Manu IX, 88.

[2] Alberuni, *ch.* IX.

a king, but there were instances of men of other castes, Śūdras for example, raising themselves to the throne.

Our author proceeds.

> The National Guard (lit. warriors) are heroes of choice valour, and, as the profession is hereditary, they become adepts in military tactics. In peace they guard the sovereign's residence, and in war they become the intrepid vanguard.
>
> The army is composed of Foot, Horse, Chariot, and Elephant soldiers. The war-elephant is covered with coat-of-mail, and his tusks are provided with sharp barbs. On him rides the Commander-in-chief, who has a soldier on each side to manage the elephant. The chariot in which an officer sits is drawn by four horses, whilst infantry guard it on both sides. The infantry go lightly into action and are choice men of valour; they bear a large shield and carry a long spear; some are armed with a sword or sabre and dash to the front of the advancing line of battle. They are perfect experts with all the implements of war such as spear, shield, bow and arrow, sword, sabre &c. having been drilled in them for generations.[1]

## Social and Legal Matters.

Our pilgrim next sums up the character of the Indian people.

> They are of hasty and irresolute temperaments, but of pure moral principles. They will not take anything wrongfully, and they yield more than fairness requires. They fear the retribution for sins in other lives, and make light of what conduct produces in this life. They do not practise deceit and they keep their sworn obligations.

He then describes the judicial processes and modes of punishment

> As the government is honestly administered and the people live together on good terms the criminal class is small. The statute law is sometimes violated and plots made against the sovereign;

---

[1] For 'They are perfect experts with all the implements of war' the original is 凡諸戎器莫不鋒銳, and Julien translates "Toutes leurs armes de guerre sont piquantes ou tranchantes". But this is manifestly wrong and a little reflection should have shewn Julien that shields and slings, two of the *armes de guerre*, are not *piquantes* or *tranchantes*. On p. 77 of this volume of the Mémoires Julien translates *fêng-jui* by "la superiorité".

when the crime is brought to light the offender is imprisoned for life; he does not suffer any corporal punishment, but alive and dead he is not treated as member of the community (lit. as a man). For offences against social morality, and disloyal and unfilial conduct, the punishment is to cut off the nose, or an ear, or a hand, or a foot, or to banish the offender to another country or into the wilderness. Other offences can be atoned for by a money payment.

The narrative proceeds to describe the four ordeals by which the innocence or guilt of an accused person is determined.

These are by water, by fire, by weighing, and by poison. In the water ordeal the accused is put in one sack and a stone in another, then the two sacks are connected and thrown into a deep stream; if the sack containing the stone floats, and the other sinks, the man's guilt is proven. The fire ordeal requires the accused to kneel and tread on hot iron, to take it in his hand and lick it; if he is innocent he is not hurt, but he is burnt if he is guilty. In the weighing ordeal the accused is weighed against a stone; and if the latter is the lighter the charge is false, if otherwise it is true. The poison ordeal requires that the right hind leg of a ram be cut off, and according to the portion assigned to the accused to eat, poisons are put into the leg, and if the man is innocent he survives, and if not the poison takes effect.

Julien takes a very different meaning out of the text for the last sentence. He understood the author to state that the poison ordeal consisted in placing in the incised thigh of a ram "une portion des aliments que mange le prévenu", poisons having been previously spread over the "portion", and if the ram then died the accused was guilty, and if the poison did not work he was innocent. But this cannot be regarded as the meaning of the text (which is not, however, very clearly expressed). Our author's account of these trials by ordeal in India differs both as to the actual ordeals, and the mode of procedure with them, from the descriptions to be found in other works. Manu, for example, does not give either the weighing or the poison ordeal, but these are mentioned by other authorities.[1]

[1] Manu VIII, 114; Alberuni Vol. ii, p. 159.

## ACTS OF SALUTATION AND REVERENCE.

Our author next tells us about the ways of shewing respect and doing homage among the people of India. He relates—

> There are nine degrees in the etiquette of shewing respect. These are (1) greeting with a kind enquiry, (2) reverently bowing the head, (3) raising the hands to the head with an inclination of the body, (4) bowing with the hands folded on the breast, (5) bending a knee, (6) kneeling with both knees (lit. kneeling long), (7) going down on the ground on hands and knees, (8) bowing down with knees, elbows, and forehead to the ground, (9) prostrating oneself on the earth. The performance of all these nine from the lowest to the highest is only one act of reverence. To kneel and praise the excellences [of the object] is said to be the perfection of reverence. If [the person doing homage] is at a distance he bows to the ground with folded hands, if near he kisses (lit. licks) the foot and rubs the ankle (say, of the king). All who are delivering messages or receiving orders tuck up their clothes and kneel down. The exalted person of distinction who receives the reverence is sure to have a kind answer, and he strokes the head or pats the back [of the person paying respect], giving him good words of advice to shew the sincerity of his affection. Buddhist monks receiving the courtesies of respect only bestow a good wish. Kneeling is not the only way of doing worship. Many circumambulate any object of reverential service, making one circuit or three circuits, or as many as they wish if they have a special request in mind.

Our author's statement here that the nine degrees of showing respect enumerated by him made one act of worship or reverence does not appear in Julien's translation. The original is *fan-ssŭ-chiu-têng-chi-wei-yi-pai* (凡斯九等極惟一拜), and Julien connecting this with the words which follow renders the whole thus—"La plus grande de ces démonstrations de respect consiste à s'agenouiller devant quelqu'un après l'avoir salué une fois et à exalter ses vertues". This sentence cannot possibly be regarded as a translation of the text which Julien evidently did not understand. According to Yuan-chuang's statement there were nine degrees of showing respect but to go through all these constituted only one service of worship or reverence. Perhaps no one of the nine was ever performed alone as an act of respect, and we often find in Buddhist literature four or five actions performed to make one service of reverence.[1] But we may doubt whether the whole nine acts were often gone through as one act of worship. The Buddhist Brother, however, spoke of performing the *chiu-pai* or "nine reverences" to his abbott or other senior in religion. This phrase is found in popular literature, e.g. in the Shui-hu-chuan, and it is apparently sometimes used like our "your obedient humble servant". Although Yuan-chuang does not state so expressly, yet his language seems to indicate that the reference in this passage is to the reverence or worship paid to kings, great Brāhmins, and the Buddha. It will be noticed that he does not make any mention of the signs of respect to a superior shewn by taking off one's shoes, or by uncovering the right shoulder.

### Sickness and Death.

We have next a few particulars as to the ways in which the people of India treat their sick and dead. Our author tells us—

> Every one who is attacked by sickness has his food cut off for seven days. In this interval the patient often recovers, but if he cannot regain his health he takes medicine. Their medicines are of various kinds, each kind having a specific name. Their doctors differ in medical skill and in prognostication.
>
> At the obsequies for a departed one [the relatives] wail and weep, rending their clothes and tearing out their hair, striking their brows and beating their breasts. There is no distinction in the styles of mourning costume, and no fixed period of mourning. For disposing of the dead and performing the last rites there are three recognized customs. The first of these is cremation, a pyre being made on which the body is consumed. The second is water-burial, the corpse being put into a stream to float and dissolve. The third is burial in the wilds, the body being cast away in the woods to feed wild animals.

---

[1] P'i-ni-mu-ching, *ch.* 4 (No. 1138); *Life ch.* III and Julien I, p. 144.

When the sovereign dies the first thing is to place his successor on the throne in order that he may preside at the religious services of the funeral and determine precedence. Meritorious appellations are conferred on the living; the dead have no honorary designations. No one goes to take food in a family afflicted by death, but after the funeral matters are again as usual and no one avoids [the family]. Those who attend a funeral are regarded as unclean, they all wash outside the city walls before entering [the city].

As to those who have become very old, and whose time of death is approaching, who are afflicted by incurable disease and fear that their goal of life has been reached, such persons are content to separate from this world, and desire to cast off humanity, contemptuous of mortal existence and desirous to be away from the ways of the world. So their relatives and friends give them a farewell entertainment with music, put them in a boat and row them to the middle of the Ganges that they may drown themselves in it, saying that they will be born in Heaven; one out of ten will not carry out his contemptuous views.

The Buddhist Brethren are forbidden to wail aloud (i. e. over a departed one); on the death of a parent they read a service of gratitude; their "following the departed" and "being earnest about his death" are securing his bliss in the other world.

The clause "one out of ten will not carry out his contemptuous views" is a literal rendering of the original *Shih-yu-ch'i-yi-wei-chin-pi-chien* (十有其一未盡鄙見). Julien, connecting the first part of this with what precedes and the latter part with what follows, translates—"*On* en *compte* un sur dix. *Il y en a d'autres qui*, n'ayant *pas encore* complètement renoncé *aux erreurs du siècle*, sortent de la famille et adoptent la vie des religieux". The words which I have placed in italics are the translator's interpolations, and the last clause is for the words *Ch'u-chia-sêng-chung* which belong to the next sentence. This treatment of the text quite destroys its meaning. What the author states is that out of ten old men who declare that they are sick of life, and want to leave it, only one is found acting inconsistently at the critical moment, saying that he is sick of life, and yet shrinking from suicide by drowning in the Ganges.

The Buddhist Brother, we are told, may not lament

over the death of a parent, but he shews his grateful remembrance by a religious service, and his filial piety by obtaining for a deceased parent a happy hereafter. The expressions "following the departed" and "being earnest about his death" are taken from the first *chuan* of the Lun-yü. There Tseng-tzŭ says that "if there be earnestness about the death [of a parent] and a following of the departed one (i. e. parent) the moral character of the people will return to a state of thorough goodness". By "earnestness about the death of a parent" the Confucianist meant being careful to have all the funeral rites duly observed; and by "following the departed parent" he meant keeping up the solemn services of worship to the deceased. These were services in which a man shewed his perfect filial piety, but the professed Buddhist carried out his views of filial piety and a future state in securing to his parents happiness in other spheres of existence.[1] To the Confucianist the death of a relative was the "end" of the relative, but to the Buddhist death was only a passing to another life.

## Revenue and Taxation.

Our author next gives us a few particulars about the fiscal matters of Government in India.

> As the Government is generous official requirements are few. Families are not registered, and individuals are not subject to forced labour contributions. Of the royal land there is a fourfold division: one part is for the expenses of government and state worship, one for the endowment of great public servants, one to reward high intellectual eminence, and one for acquiring religious merit by gifts to the various sects. Taxation being light, and forced service being sparingly used, every one keeps to his hereditary occupation and attends to his patrimony. The king's tenants pay one sixth of the produce as rent. Tradesmen go to and fro bartering their merchandize after paying light duties at ferries and barrier stations. Those who are employed in the government service are paid according to their work. They go abroad on military service or they guard the palace;

[1] Lun-Yü, *ch.* 1.

the summonses are issued according to circumstances and after proclamation of the reward the enrolment is awaited. Ministers of state and common officials all have their portion of land, and are maintained by the cities assigned to them.

In this passage the words for "every one attends to his patrimony" are in the original *chü-t'ien-k'ou-fên* (俱佃口分), and Julien translates "tous cultivent la terre pour se nourrir". This is not a correct rendering of the words and is at variance with what follows about the traders. The *k'ou-fên* in China was originally the farm of 100 *mou* given out of government lands to a married couple to maintain the family and keep up the ancestral worship. This farm was called *k'ou-fên-shih-ye-chih-t'ien* (口分世業之田) or "the arable land which is hereditary property for the maintenance of the family". Then *t'ien* (佃) which means "to cultivate", means also "to administer" or "manage", and *t'ien-k'ou-fên* is "to look after the family property", *k'ou-fên* being used in a general sense.

As to one sixth of the crop being paid by the king's tenants as rent we find mention of this in Manu and other authorities.[1]

## GENERAL PRODUCTS OF INDIA.

Our author now proceeds to tell us something of the commodities which India produces and first of its vegetable products. He writes—

As the districts vary in their natural qualities they differ also in their natural products. There are flowers and herbs, fruits and trees of different kinds and with various names. There are, for example, of fruits the āmra or mango, the āmla or tamarind, the Madhūka (Bassia latifolia), the badara or Jujube, the kapittha or wood-apple, the āmala or myrobalan, the tinduka or Diospyros, the udumbara or Ficus glomerata, the mocha or plantain, the nārikela or Cocoa-nut, and the panasa or Jack-fruit. It is impossible to enumerate all the kinds of fruit and one can only mention in a summary way those which are held in esteem among the inhabitants. [Chinese] jujubes, chestnuts, green and red persimmons are not known in India. From Kashmir on, pears,

---

[1] Manu VII. 130, 131, VIII. 308.

plums, peaches, apricots, grapes are planted here and there; pomegranates and sweet oranges are grown in all the countries.

As to agricultural operations, reaping the crops, preparing the soil (lit. ploughing and weeding), sowing and planting go on in their seasons according to the industry or laziness of the people. There is much rice and wheat, and ginger, mustard, melons, pumpkins, kunda (properly the olibanum tree) are also cultivated. Onions and garlic are little used and people who eat them are ostracised.

Milk, ghee, granulated sugar, sugar-candy, cakes aud parched grain with mustard-seed oil are the common food; and fish, mutton, venison are occasional dainties (lit. are occasionally served in joints or slices). The flesh of oxen, asses, elephants, horses, pigs, dogs, foxes, wolves, lions, monkeys, apes is forbidden, and those who eat such food become pariahs.

There are distinctions in the use of their wines and other beverages. The wines from the vine and the sugar-cane are the drink of the Kshatriyas; the Vaiśyas drink a strong distilled spirit; the Buddhist monks and the Brāhmins drink syrup of grapes and of sugar-cane; the low mixed castes are without any distinguishing drink.

As to household necessaries there is generally a good supply of these of various qualities. But although they have different kinds of cooking implements they do not know the steaming boiler (i. e. they have not large boilers such as are used in large households in China). Their household utensils are mostly earthenware, few being of brass. They eat from one vessel in which the ingredients are mixed up; they take their food with their fingers. Generally speaking spoons and chop-sticks are not used, except in cases of sickness when copper spoons are used.

Gold, silver, *t'u-shih* (bronze?), white jade, and crystal lenses are products of the country which are very abundant. Rare precious substances of various kinds from the sea-ports (lit. seabays) are bartered for merchandize. But in the commerce of the country gold and silver coins, cowries, and small pearls are the media of exchange.

The words "From Kashmir on" in the first paragraph of the above passage seem to mean "from Kashmir on towards China". But Julien understood the words in a very different sense and translated the passage containing them as follows[1]—"Depuis que les deux espèces de poiriers

---

[1] The words are 梨柰桃杏蒲萄等果迦溼彌羅國已來往往間植石橊甘橘諸國皆樹.

*li* et *nai*, le pêcher, l'amandier, la vigne et autres arbres à fruits ont été apportés du royaume de Cachemire, on les voit croître de tous côtés. Les grenadiers et les orangers à fruits doux se cultivent dans tous les royaumes de l'Inde." In this, not to notice other faults, we have the words "ont été apportés" interpolated to the serious detriment of the author's meaning. Yuan-chuang knew better than to state that pears, and plums, and the other fruits mentioned had been brought from Kashmir into India and there cultivated everywhere. Throughout the Records there is only, I believe, a single mention of any of these fruit-trees in India. This one instance is to be found in the account of *Chi-na-po-ti* in *Chuan* IV (Julien II, p. 200), and there the peach and pear are represented as having been first introduced into India from China. In no account of India, so far as I know, down to the present time are the above trees enumerated among those grown commonly throughout the country. Ibn Batuta does not mention them and they are not given in Sir. W. Hunter's account of India. But they are grown in many countries between Kashmir and China, and in *Chuan* XII of the Records we find several instances mentioned. On the other hand pomegranates, which are said to grow wild in the Himalayan region, and sweet oranges have been extensively cultivated in India for many centuries.

---

# CHAPTER VI.

### CHUAN II CONT[D].

### LAMPA TO GANDHĀRA.

OUR pilgrim has now reached the territory which he, like others before and after him, calls India. But it is important to remember that the countries which he describes from Lan-p'o to Rajpur both inclusive were not regarded by the people of India proper as forming part of their territory. It was only by foreigners that these districts were included under the general name *India.* To the inhabitants of India proper the countries in question were "border lands" inhabited by barbarians. This was a fact known to Yuan-chuang, but he named and described these States mainly from information obtained as he travelled. The information was apparently acquired chiefly from the Buddhist Brethren and believing laymen resident in these countries. To these Buddhists Jambudvīpa was India and the miracles and ministrations of the Buddha extended over all the great region vaguely called Jambudvīpa. Moreover the great foreign kings who had invaded India from the north had included these States in their Indian empire and the memory of these kings survived in the Buddhist religious establishments.

## LAN-P'O (LAMPA).

From Kapis the pilgrim continued his journey going east above 600 *li* through a very mountainous region; then crossing a black range he entered the north of India and arrived in the *Lan-p'o* country.

Yuan-chuang writes this name 濫波, and this apparently is for him the name both of the country and its capital. Some other authors write 嵐婆,[1] and the local pronunciation was perhaps something like Lampa or Lumba. The word is supposed to represent the old Sanskrit *Lampāka*, and the *Lambatai* of Ptolemy,[2] and the district has been identified with the modern Laghman (or Lughman), the Lamghanat of Baber. This emperor mentions the curious tradition which derives the name Lamghanat from Lam, father of Noah, whose tomb was supposed to be in the country.[3] But no probable explanation of the name Lampa (or Lumba) seems to have been given, and the word is probably foreign, that is, non-Indian.

Lampa is described by the pilgrims as being above 1000 *li* in circuit, having on the north the Snow mountains and on the other sides black ranges.

Another writer of the T'ang period represents this country as of much greater dimensions than those here given and as extending on the north to Kunduz and lying west of the *Wu-je-chih* or Anavatapta Lake.[4] So also in Baber's time Lamghanat was a large region of much greater extent than Yuan-chuang's Lampa or the modern Lughman.

The capital, Yuan-chuang tells us, was above ten *li* in circuit. For several centuries the native dynasty had ceased to exist, great families fought for preeminence, and the state had recently become a dependency of Kapis. The country produced upland rice and sugar-cane, and it had much wood but little fruit; the climate was mild with little frost and no snow; the inhabitants were very musical but they were pusillanimous and deceitful, ugly and ill-mannered; their clothing was chiefly of cotton (*pai-tieh*) and they dressed well. There were above ten Buddhist monasteries and a few Brethren the most of whom were Mahāyānists. The non-Buddhists had a score or two of temples and they were very nnmerous.

---

1 See e. g. Sung-Shih, *ch.* 490.

2 A. G. I. p. 42: Mc Crindle's India from Ptolemy p.p. 104, 106.

3 Baber p. 141—143.

4 Fang-chih, *ch.* 1.

In the common texts here the author is made to state that the non-Buddhists were *very few*, but the old reading is found in the A text, viz. *to*, "many" and it is evidently the right one. This reading moreover is confirmed by the Fang-chih which quoting from our pilgrim's account of this country tells us that in it "the non-Buddhists were remarkably numerous".

This country does not seem to have ever been much known to the Chinese generally; and it is rarely mentioned even in the translations of the Buddhist books, or in the accounts of the travels and in the biographies of eminent worthies of the Buddhist religion. There was, however, at least one distinguished Buddhist scholar who is called a Brahmin from the Lampa country and who is recorded as having visited China. This pious and learned Brother, we are informed, in the year A.D. 700 assisted in the translation from Sanskrit into Chinese of a celebrated treatise of magical invocations.[1] Lampa was evidently a district of some importance and it may have been known by some native or local name.

## NAGAR.

The pilgrim, according to the narrative in the Records, proceeded from Lampa south-east above 100 *li*, crossing a high mountain and a large river, and reached the *Na-kie(ka)-lo-ho* country.

The Life here represents Yuan-chuang as going south from Lampa and crossing a small range on which a tope to commemorate the spot at which the Buddha having travelled on foot from the south rested on arriving in these regions. Then the Life makes the pilgrim continue his journey from this range still going southward for above

[1] The title of this treatise is "Pu-k'ung-chüan-so-t'o-lo-ni-ching" (Bun. No. 314). The translator's name is given as Li-wu-t'ao and he is called a brāhmin of Lan-p'o in "North India". It is doubtful, however, whether the Chinese text of No. 314 was actually the work of this man; see the note appended to the work. See also Su-ku-chin-yi-ching-t'u-chi (No. 1488).

twenty *li*, descending the hills and crossing a river into the *Na-ka-lo-ho* country.

This country, which we may suppose to have been called by a name like Nagar, is one of considerable interest; and as the account given of it in the Records and the Life is peculiar, and rather puzzling, it may be useful to examine the account at some length.

In the Records Yuan-chuang describes Nagar as being above 600 *li* (about 120 miles) from east to west and 250 or 260 *li* (about 50 miles) from north to south. The country was surrounded on all sides by high mountains steep and difficult of passage. Its capital was above 20 *li* in circuit, but there was no king and the State was a province of Kapis. Grain and fruits were produced in abundance, the climate was mild, the people were of good character, courageous, slighting wealth and esteeming learning, reverencing Buddha and having little faith in other religious systems. But although there were many Buddhist establishments the Brethren were very few. There were five Deva-Temples and above 100 professed non-Buddhists.

About two *li* to the east (in the Life, south-east) of the capital stood a great stone tope above 300 feet high which had marvellous sculptures. Close to this tope on the west side was a vihāra and adjoining the vihāra on the south was a small tope. The former of these two topes was said to have been built by king Asoka at the place where Sakya P'usa, having spread in the mud his deer-skin mantle and his hair for Dīpankara Buddha, received from the latter the prediction of Buddhahood. At the periodic annihilations and restorations of the world the traces of this incident are not effaced, and on fast days showers of flowers descend on the spot, which is regarded with great reverence. The small tope was at the spot where the mantle and hair were spread on the mud, [the other tope] having been erected by king Asoka in a retired place off the highway.

Yuan-chuang next takes us into "the city" and tells us of the foundations which still remained of the grand tope which, he was informed, had once contained a tooth-relic of the Buddha. Close to these was a remarkable small tope of unknown origin, and popularly supposed to have come down out of space. The narrative in our text next takes us to a tope above ten *li* south-west of "the city". This tope marked the spot at which the Buddha alighted from his aerial voyage from Mid-India to this country. Near the tope of the Descent on the east side was another tope to commemorate the spot at which, on the occasion of the meeting, the P'usa bought five lotus flowers for an offering to Dīpankara Buddha.

Continuing in a south-western direction from "the city", and at a distance of above twenty *li* from it, the pilgrim takes us to a small range of rocky hills containing a stone monastery with lofty halls and tiers of chambers all silent and unoccupied. Within the grounds of this establishment was a tope 200 feet high built by king Asoka.

Going on again south-west from this monastery we come to a ravine with a torrent the banks of which were steep rocks. In the east bank was the cave inhabited by the Gopāla dragon, very dark and with a narrow entrance, and with water trickling from the rock to the path. In this cave the Buddha had left his shadow or rather a luminous image of himself in the rock, once a clear and perfect resemblance, but at the period of our pilgrim's visit to the district the wonderful likeness was only dimly visible and only at certain times and to certain persons. Outside the Shadow Cave were two square stones on one of which was a light-emitting impress of the Buddha's foot. On either side of the Shadow Cave were other caves which had been used by the Buddha's great disciples as places for ecstatic meditation (samādhi). In the immediate neighbourhood of the Shadow Cave also the pilgrim found various topes and other objects associated with the Buddha's personal visit to this district.

Following the narrative in the Records we have now to return to "the city". Starting again from it and going in a south-east direction for above thirty *li* we come to a city called *Hi-lo* (or *He-lo*). This city, which was four or five *li* in circuit had a strong elevated situation with charming gardens and ponds. Within it was a two-storeyed building in which were carefully preserved the Ushnīsha-bone of the Buddha, his skull, one of his eyes, his mendicant's staff, and one of his clerical robes. To the north of this Relic-house was a wonder-working tope which could be shaken by a touch of the finger.

There are one or two discrepancies between the account here given and that in the Life. Thus in the Records the Buddha comes to Nagar country through the air and alights at a spot ten *li* south-west from "the city", but in the Life he arrives on foot at a place north of Nagar. Then as to Hilo, the Life differs from the Records in placing this city at about 12 *li* distance south-east from the Flowers Tope.

The Nagar of our text, it is agreed, is represented by the region in modern times called Nungnehar, that is, Nine Rivers. In Baber's time Nungnihar, "in many histories written Nekerhar", was a tuman of Lamghan (Lampa).[1] The Nagar country thus included the present district of Jelalabad, the valley of the Cabul River from Darunta on the west to Mirza Kheyl on the east and, according to Mr Simpson, it "might reach from about Jugduluck to the Khyber".[2] Our text makes Yuan-chuang visit two cities of this country, the capital and Hilo the former capital. As to the latter all investigators seem to be agreed that the Hilo of Yuan-chuang and the other pilgrims is represented by the modern Hiḍḍa (or Heida or Hada), a place situated about five miles south of Jelalabad.

As to the site of the city called Nagar supposed to have been the capital of the country "in the Buddhist period" there is some diversity of opinion. The Na-kie (ka)-lo-ho of Yuan-chuang is evidently the Na-kie(ka) of Fa-hsien who uses the name for city and country. It is also the Na-kie city and the Na-ka-lo-ho of the Sung-yun narrative in the "Ka-lan-chi", and also the Na-kie of a Vinaya treatise translated in A.D. 378.[3]

Julien makes Na-ka-lo-ho stand for Nagarahāra, and in a note he tells us that in the Sung annals we find Nang-go-lo-ho-lo which answers exactly to the Indian orthography furnished by the inscription discovered by Captain Kittoe. Julien is of course followed, and his identification accepted, by subsequent writers; and on his and Lassen's authority the P. W. gives Nagarahāra as the name of a kingdom. But this word cannot be made out of Yuan-chuang's four characters which apparently give the full name. Then as to Nang-go-lo-ho-lo the writer in the

---

[1] Baber p. 141.

[2] J. R. A. S. Vol. xiii. Art. VII.

[3] Fo-kuo-chi, *ch.* 13; Ka-lan-chi, *ch.* 5; Pi-ni-ye-ching (the "Chie-yin-yuan-ching". Bun. No. 1130).

"Sung Shi" quotes a Buddhist monk who evidently wrote without knowledge. The passage referred to by Julien puts Udyāna, which was immediately to the north of Gandhāra, twelve days' journey to the east of that country. Then it places Gandhāra at a distance of twenty days' journey eastward from Nang-go-lo-ho-lo and it makes the latter to be ten days' journey to the east of Lampa.[1] But Yuan-chuang's Nagar was only five or six days' journey north-west from Gandhāra and about twenty miles south or south-east from Lampa. Thus Nang-go-lo-ho-lo does not agree with Nagar either in distances or directions and its situation is imaginary and impossible. Then the Nagarahāra of Kittoe's Sanskrit inscription of about the 8th or 9th century is evidently not the Nagar of Yuan-chuang and the other Chinese pilgrims. The inscription represents Vīradeva, son of Indra Gupta a Brahman of Bengal, as becoming a Buddhist and going to the "holy convent called Kanishka" (śrīmat Kanishkam upagamya mahā-vihāram) in Nagarahāra.[2] Now there is no mention by any of the pilgrims of a great Kanishka monastery in Nagar, city or country. But there was a celebrated one in Gandhāra near Purushapur and the Nagarahāra of the Kittoe inscription is evidently the Gandhāra country.

Cunningham places the capital of Yuan-chuang's Nagar "at Begrām, about two miles to the west of Jalalabad".[3] Saint Martin supposes it to have been a little to the west of this Begrām. Mr Simpson, who writes after careful inspection and study of the locality, places the site of the Nagar capital west of Begrām on a rocky elevation at the junction of the Surkhāb and Cabul rivers. No one of these identifications meets all the requirements of the descriptions, but each is supported to a certain extent by the statements in the Records.

If we take the narrative in the Records and read it in

---

[1] Sung-Shih, l. c.

[2] J. A. S. Ben. Vol. xvii, p. 494.

[3] A. G. I. p. 44.

connection with that in the Life we find that there were three cities in this district visited by the pilgrim. These are the capital, the city of the Dīpankara Buddha, and Hilo the city of the Ushṇīsha relic. Now as the Records make mention of only the first and third of these by name it may perhaps be taken for granted that Yuan-chuang mixed up in his mind the first and second when writing out his notes. So the term "the city" seems to stand sometimes for the capital but more frequently for the city of Dīpankara. The confusion apparently affected the compilers of the Life also.

Combining the two narratives we find that Yuan-chuang on entering the country apparently went directly towards the capital. This he describes, as has been stated, as "above 20 *li* [in circuit]". The word *Chou* for "in circuit" is found only in the D text, but some such term is needed and the use of *Chou* agrees with Yuan-chuang's usual way of describing towns and districts. The reader will observe, however, that we are not told anything about the natural and artificial characteristics of the capital, about its situation or surroundings. This silence is very extraordinary if we regard the city to have been on the site proposed and described by Mr Simpson.

Now the description of the place which this explorer gives seems to be that of a fortress rather than a city. And Nagar was perhaps at this time a strong fortress, and it was called the capital because it was the official residence of the Governor appointed by the king of Kapis. Yuan-chuang apparently did not enter this city as he begins his description of the sacred objects of the country with those outside of "the capital". The last character in Yuan-chuang's Na-ka-lo-ho may stand for *kot* which means a *fortress*, and names like Nagkot, Nagarkot are met with in several regions of "North India".[1] The Nagar of our text may be the Nagarkot which Alberuni mentions as containing the annals of the Shāh dynasty of Kābul.

---

[1] See e. g. Nagarkot in Alberuni, Vol. ii, p. 11.

Moreover the Adinapūr of Baber was apparently on the site of Yuan-chuang's Nagar (or Nagar-kot) and it was a fort. Baber describes the fort as "situated on an eminence, which, towards the river, is forty or fifty gez (100 feet or upwards), in perpendicular height", a description which agrees with that given by M[r] Simpson of the Nagar rock. This fort Baber tells us was the official residence of the darogha or commandant of the district.

Let us now substitute "Nagar fortress" for "the Capital" and "the city" in the first part of the pilgrim's narrative. We find then that the great Asoka tope was about two *li* or nearly half a mile to the east (or south-east) of the fortress. Turning to Masson and Simpson we find that they give a tope called "Nagara Goondée" which is apparently about three furlongs to the east or south-east of the Nagar rock.[1]

From the Flower Tope near the Asoka Tope the pilgrim, according to the Life, set out south-east for Hilo, the city of the Ushṇīsha relic. On the way apparently, but this is not quite clear, he learns of the Gopāla Dragon cave with the miraculous likeness of the Buddha. Wishing to visit this, Yuan-chuang had to go out of his way to the Têng-kuang (燈光) city in order to obtain a guide. The term Têng-kuang is used to translate the word Dīpankara, name of a very early Buddha, but we need not suppose that it represents the name of the city. Now the Têng-kuang city was apparently that called Na-kie(ka) by previous pilgrims, and it was apparently a little to the west of the site of the modern Jelalabad. One name for it was Padmapur or Lotus city. This is given by some Chinese as *Hua-shi-ch'êng*, or Flower City; and it is said to be another name for the capital of the Nagar country. A more common name for Dipankara's City in Buddhist books is Dīpavatī from *dīpa*, a *torch* or *light*. We may for the present, however, use Padmapur to represent the name of the city, as we have no means of knowing what

---

1 Masson's Ar. Ant. p. 100 et al.

the name actually was, that is, supposing it not to have been simply Nagar.

This Padmapur then, let us assume, was the Na-ka city which had the ruins of the Tooth-tope, a tope which had been seen by Fa-hsien in perfect condition. It was this city also from which Hilo was distant about 30 *li* to the south-east. Then from it Yuan-chuang went south-west to the Shadow-Cave, and from this south-east to Hilo.

Now going from Padmapur south-west at a distance of above 20 *li* was a small rocky hill which had a great Buddhist monastery with an Asoka tope above 200 feet high. This monastery and tope may be represented by the ruins at Gunda Chismeh of Mr Simpson's map, "the smooth rounded mound of a tope and the rectangular mound of a vihara". Some distance from this on the east bank of a torrent was the Dragon's cave with the luminous picture of the Buddha on the rock. Fa-hsien places the cave about half a Yojana south from the Nakie city. His words are "Half a Yojana south of Nakie city is a cave *as you follow the course of the hills towards the south-west*". The words in italics are for the Chinese 博山西南向 which our translators understood to mean a *great mountain towards the south-west.* The phrase *poh-shan* is certainly used in the sense of a "great mountain" and this is its proper meaning. Here, however, as in some other cases the construction seems to require that the words be taken in the sense of *going along a hill* (or series of hills). This word *poh* is probably, as has been stated already, the *poh* of *hui-poh* (迴薄) of *Chuan I* of these Records, and also the *poh* (搏) of various passages in the Fo-kuo-chi and other works.

There does not seem to be any satisfactory explanation of the names Nagar and Hilo. If the former be for Nagara its memory may be kept up in the modern designation Begrām which like Nagara means a "city". Or the syllable Nag or Nak may possibly be for the Indian word nāga which denotes the *sun,* a *snake,* a *mountain,* an *elephant.* Masson says that the old name for the country was Ajūna and Saint Martin and Cunningham think this word may be a corruption of another old name for it, viz. Udyānapur or "the city of the Garden". But no one seems to give any authority for this last old name and it is apparently unknown to Chinese authors and translators. It may be added that this district is referred to in some Chinese books as in the Yue-shi (Getæ) country of North India. It is also called *Ye-p'o-kan-t'ê* (業波乾陀), that is perhaps, Yavakāṇḍa, and it is said to be to the west of Udyāna.

As to Hilo, Cunningham would have us regard this word as a transposition of the Sanskrit word Haḍḍa, meaning a "bone". But there were several Hilos in North India, and the relic supposed to have given the name is not called in Sanskrit by any term containing a word for "bone". It was the Ushṇīsha of the Buddha that Hilo contained along with other relics of the Buddha. Some Chinese translators, it is true, call the relic "the bone of the top of Buddha's head," but others give a different rendering, or keep the original word. The full name and some of the translations will be given a few pages farther on. We may perhaps regard the name in our text as for Hilā which was probably a local pronunciation for Śilā. This word means a *rock* or *rocky eminence*, and the name suits the description of the place.

## BODHISATTVA AND DĪPANKARA.

From the account given of the Nagar country by our pilgrim we see that the district had several objects of attraction to a Buddhist. The principal of these objects were the mementos of the P'usa's meeting with Dīpankara Buddha, the luminous image of Gautama Buddha in the Dragon's cave, and his Ushṇīsha-bone. A few additional observations about each of these may be of interest to the student.

The story of the P'usa in an exceedingly remote period of time in his existence as a Brahman student meeting the Dīpankara Buddha and giving him worship and service is a well known one. It is found in the Sanskrit Mahāvastu[1] and Divyāvadāna,[2] in the Pali Jātakas,[3] and in several forms in Chinese translations from Indian originals. No one of all these treatises, so far as I know, places the scene of this meeting in a country called Nagar. In the different accounts various names are given to the city of the incident. Thus it is called Rammanagara (or Rammavatī or Rammagama).[4] This would seem to point to Ayodhya, the modern Oudh, but the Jātaka places Ramma-city in "the frontier territory". The city is also called Dīpavati or Dīpavat[5] from *dīpa*, a *light*. It is also Padma-pura or Lotos-city, in Chinese Lien-hua-ch'êng or Hua-shi-ch'êng.[6] The last name means simply Flower city and it is properly applied to Pāṭalipur. It is said, however, as has been seen, to be an old name for Nagar city and it was given on account of the Lotus Ponds of the city.

The P'usa as brahmin student, variously named Megha, Su-medha and otherwise, on his way to see Dīpankara Buddha met a maiden carrying seven lotus flowers for the service of a shrine in the palace grounds. The P'usa bargained with the maiden for five of her flowers that he might have them to throw on the Buddha as he passed in procession. At the spot where the flowers were bought, an act involving great consequences in the distant future, king Asoka had built a tope. It is remarkable that the Pali Jātaka does not make any mention of the purchase and offering of the lotus flowers.

Then there was the place at which the P'usa spread out his deer-skin mantle and his hair on the muddy road

---

1 Mahāvastu T. I, p. 193.

2 Divyāv. p. 246.

3 Rhys Davids' Birth Stories p. 7; Bigandet's Legend, Vol. i, p. 7.

4 Mahāvamsa Int. p. XXXII.

5 Yin-kuo-ching (Bun. No. 666).

6 Fo-shuo-t'ai-tzŭ-sui-ying-pên-chi-ching, *ch.* 1 (Bun. No. 665); Tsêng-yi-a-han-ching, *ch.* 11 (Bun. No. 543); Hsing-chi-ching, *chs.* 2, 3 (Bun. No. 680).

to preserve Dīpankara's feet from being defiled. On the road by which this Buddha was proceeding to the capital on this memorable occasion were several dirty muddy places which the people were trying to make clean. The brahmin student, at his own request, was allowed to put right a hollow in the road made by running water. Unable to fill up this muddy gap on the approach of the Buddha, he spread out in it his deerskin mantle, and then lay down prostrate with his long hair spread out for the Buddha to step on. Though the world had passed away and been renewed since the time of Dīpankara and Megha (or Sumati) yet the depression in the road remained visible, being renewed with the renewal of the world. Close to the spot was a small tope of great antiquity, the successor of the original wooden stake, and not far from it was a very magnificent tope built by king Asoka.

This myth of the P'usa and the Dīpankara Buddha seems to be very unbuddhistical, and its origin should perhaps be sought outside of religion. We remember that one of Gotama's royal ancestors was a king Dīpankara who with "his sons and grandsons also twelve royal princes governed their great kingdom in Takkasilā best of towns."[1] A picture of this king, with a conquered chief prostrate before him, may have suggested the story. Such a picture may be seen in Plate VII fig. 5 of the "Ariana Antiqua." Compare with this the illustration of Dīpankara and the P'usa in Burgess's "Buddhist Cave Temples" p. 66. Here the Buddha does not tread on the hair of the prostrate devotee at his side. The story is explained by some as originally an allegory to express Gautama's resolve to undergo all things in this world of impurities in order to obtain perfect wisdom and teach the way thereof to mortal creatures. A simpler theory is that the brahmin student laid down his deer-skin mantle and his hair before the Buddha to declare to the latter the student's resolve to give up Brahminism and become a professed Buddhist.

---

[1] Dīpavaṃsa p. 131.

As such he must shave his head and cease to wear garments made of the skins of animals.

## THE SHADOW CAVE.

According to Yuan-chuang's account the Gopāla-Dragon cave, with the likeness of the Buddha shining at times in the rock opposite the entrance, was on the east side of a torrent among the heights to the south-west of the Nagar, that is, the Padma city. Mr Simpson thinks that the range of hills which extends from the Ahin Posh Tope south of Jelalabad south-west to Sultanpur does not suit Yuan-chuang's description of the surroundings of this cave. But his objections seem to be based mainly on the occurrence of the words *cascade* and *mountain* in the translations. There is nothing, however, corresponding to either of these terms in the original either of the Life or Records. The road from the city was a bad one and dangerous, but it led to a hamlet with a monastery. Not far from this, above the steep bank of a foaming torrent, was the cave.

The Gopāla Dragon of this cave, Yuan-chuang tells us, and the story seems to be his only, was originally a cowherd in this district at the time of the Buddha. Annoyed at a reproof from the king he vowed terrible vengeance. Then going to the Tope of Prediction he prayed to become a dragon; and immediately fulfilled his prayer by committing suicide, and returning to the world as a malignant demon determined to make havoc. Hearing of his spiteful cruel designs, the Buddha came through the air from Mid-India, converted the dragon, and left him a luminous likeness of himself immanent in the inner rock of his cave. Yuan-chuang saw the likeness of the Buddha and a great deal more. According to the tradition the Buddha was alone in the cave when he caused his likeness to go into the rock, but Yuan-chuang saw also in the wonderful manifestation the P'usas and saints who attended the Buddha in his ministrations.

In the "Ka-lan-chi" the narrative at the part about the Nagar country has this statement—"On to *Kü-lo-lo-lu*, saw the cave of Buddha's shadow, advancing 15 paces into the hill, the entrance facing west". Burnouf, who treats this short passage as corrupt, makes "Gopāla Cave" out of the four Chinese characters represented in the above transcription. This he effects by treating the first *lo* as a mistake for *p'o* and the last character *lu* as a mistake for *chü*, a *deer* for a *cave* as he represents it. But if we take the Chinese characters as we find them they give us Kulāla-lok, that is, the Pottery people. Now this reminds us of an interesting passage in the Chinese version of the Life of King Asoka.[1] There Yasa tells the king how the Buddha, just before his death, converted the Dragon-king Apalāla, the Potter, and the Chandāla Dragon-king. Burnouf translating from the Sanskrit text of this passage has "the potter's wife the Chandāli Gopāli" while the editors of the Divyāvadāna treat Kumbhakāri (Potter's wife) as a proper name.[2]

With reference to this cave and its surroundings the following passage from the "Ariana Antiqua" may be found of some interest—"Tracing the skirts of the Siah koh, is a road leading from Bála Bágh to Darunta, and thence across the river of Kabul and Jelalabad to Laghman. From Bála Bágh to the ferry at Darunta may be a distance of seven miles. At about five miles on this road, coming from Bála Bágh, we meet the topes of Kotpur, situated a little on our right hand. The first is in the midst of cultivation about one hundred yards from the road; a deep ravine, through which flows a stream derived from the Surkh Rúd (red river), separates it from its two companions. These stand on a dák, or barren level, overspread with fragments of

---

[1] A-yü-wang-ching, *ch.* 2 (No. 1343). In *ch.* 6 of this treatise the chandāla Dragon-king is called *Ku-p'o-lo* (Gopāla), and in *ch.* 1 of the "A-yü-wang-chuan" he is the "Ox-Dragon" of Gandhavat. In the "Tsa-a-han-ching", *ch.* 23 (No. 544) Buddha subdues the dragon Apalāla, "the potter chandāla", and the Gopāli dragon.

[2] Bur. Int. p. 377: Divyāv. p. 348. See Legge's 'Fa Hian', p. 29.

potter's ware; and here coins, rings, and other relics are sometimes found. The spot was, therefore, an ancient place of sepulchre."[1] In the 'Life of Asoka', however, the Gopāla cave is located in Gandhāra.

In another Chinese Buddhist work we learn that the Buddha once went to "North India" to the Yue-shi (Getæ) country and thence to the west of this. Here he overcame a fierce wicked Rākshasī, spent a night in her cave, and left his shadow on a rock in it like that in the Gopāla cave.[2] In another Buddhist treatise, moreover, there is mention of a district called Na-kie-lo or Na-kie-han (or a)-lo. Here also was a rākshasī cave, and Buddha came from India to convert the rakshasī and left his luminous image in the cave.[3] This cave was in the side of the mountain Ansu, in the Champak grove of the old rishi, close to a Dragon's lake, and north of the Blue-Lotus fountain. The district in which this cave was situated was evidently not the Nagar country of our pilgrim. He also mentions two other caves with luminous images of Buddha in other parts of India.

There is also something not quite clear in his location of the cave in Nagar. He seems to describe it as in the east bank of a torrent, yet he tells us that there was to the west of it a large flat stone on which the Buddha spread his robe to dry. According to Fa-hsien also there was a tope, 100 paces west of the cave, which was made by Buddha and his disciples as a pattern. Near this, moreover, was a monastery with above 700 monks in it, of which Yuan-chuang does not make mention.

## THE USHṆĪSHA-BONE.

The next of the great objects of interest to Buddhists in this country was the Ushṇīsha-bone of the Buddha in

---

1 Ar. Ant. p. 64. The conclusion drawn in the last sentence of this passage is not quite justified by the premises.

2 Ta-chih-tu-lun, *ch.* 9 (Bun. No. 1169).

3 Kuan-Fo-san-mei-hai-ching, *ch.* 7 (No. 430).

Hilo. This is called by Yuan-chuang and the other pilgrims Buddha's *ting-ku* (頂骨) or ***Bone of the top of the head.*** The Sanskrit term is Ushṇīsha-śīrshas or Ushṇīsha-śiraskatā. As to the latter part of these compounds there is no doubt, the words being from *śiras*, the *head.* But in the literature of India the word ushṇīshā has two meanings. (1) the hair done up into a coil on the top of the head and (2) a peculiar kind of turban or other head-dress. But the Buddhas cut off their hair and did not wear caps or turbans.[1] So a new use was given to the term in Buddhism, and it was applied to the cranial protuberance which was one of the thirty-two distinguishing marks of a Buddha. This protuberance was supposed to be a sort of abnormal development of the upper surface of the skull into a small truncated cone covered with flesh and skin and hair. But some, like Yuan-chuang, regarded it as a separate formation on, but not a part of, the top of the skull. This Ushṇīsha-śirsha among the Buddhists was one of the thirty-two marks not only of a Buddha but also of a Chakravartin and a Mahā-purusha. But, as Senart has pointed out, it is not in the list of the signs of the Great Man (Mahā-purusha) in Brahminical writings such as the "Brihat Samhitā".[2]

According to Yuan-chuang's description the Ushṇīsha in Hilo was

> twelve inches in circumference, with the hair-pores distinct, and of a yellowish white colour. It was kept in a casket deposited in the small tope made of the seven precious substances which was in the second storey of the decorated Hall. Pilgrims made a fragrant plaster, and with it took a cast of the upper surface of the bone; and according to their Karma read in the traces on the plaster their weal or their woe.

In addition to the term already given as a rendering for Ushṇīsha there are several other Chinese translations

---

[1] In Max Müller's Dharma-samgraha p. 54 *ushnīsha* is translated by "Cap". This rendering is not supported by any Buddhist authority, and it is at variance with the descriptions and explanations given in the Buddhist books.

[2] Essai sur la leg. du Bud. p. 111.

or interpretations of the Sanskrit word. Thus we have *ting-jou-chi* (頂肉髻) that is, "the flesh top-knot on the top of the head", and *ju-chi-ku* or "the bone of the flesh top-knot."[1] The Buddha is also described as having, as one of the thirty-two marks, "on the top of his head the ushṇīsha like a deva sun-shade",[2] or as having "on the top of his head the ushṇīsha golden skull-top bone";[3] and we also read that on the top of the Buddha's head is "manifested the ushṇīsha", that is, manifested occasionally as a miraculous phenomenon. It is also stated that the ushṇīsha is not visible to the eyes of ordinary beings.[4]

Nearly two hundred years before Yuan-chuang's time a Chinese pilgrim by name *Chih-mêng* (智猛) had seen, it is recorded, the Ushṇīsha-bone along with other relics of the Buddha in Kapilavastu, but this must be regarded as a mistake of a copyist.[5] Two later pilgrims *Tao-lin* and *Hsüan-chao*, the latter a contemporary of Yuan-chuang, visited Kapis and there paid reverence to the ushṇīsha or skull-top bone of the Buddha.[6] By Kapis we are probably to understand Nagar then a part of the Kapis kingdom. Then a century after Yuan-chuang's time *Wu-k'ung* went to see "Sakya Julai's skull-top bone (or Ushṇīsha) relic" in the city of Gandhāra.[7]

It is interesting to observe that we do not find mention of any Buddhist monks as being concerned in any way with this precious relic. Fa-hsien, indeed, places it in a *ching-shê* or temple, but this was apparently only the name which he gave to the building because it contained the relic. Yuan-chuang does not make mention of any sacred

---

1 Hsing-chi-ching, *ch.* 9: Kuan-Fo-san-mei-hai-ching, *ch.* 1, where the *ting-shang-jou-chi* is one of the 32 marks of a *ta-chang-fu* (大丈夫) or Mahāpurusha; Chang-chao-fan-chih-ch'ing-wên-ching (Bun. No. 734).

2 Fa-chi-ming-shu-ching (No. 812).

3 Chung-hsü-ching, *ch.* 3 (No. 859).

4 Ta-ming-san-tsang-fa-shu, *ch.* 48 (No. 1621).

5 Kao-sêng-chuan, *ch.* 3.

6 Hsi-yü-ch'in, *ch.* 1, 2.

7 Shih-li-ching, and J. A. T. VI, p. 357.

building; he refers only to a tall two-storey building and this is apparently the high two-storeyed Hall of Fa-hsien. The latter pilgrim also mentions the small tope of the seven precious substances in which the casket containing the ushṇisha was kept. This little tope is described by Fa-hsien as being moreover free, opening and shutting, and about five feet in height.[1]

The official custodians of the relic paid all expenses by charging the devout pilgrims according to a fixed tariff for seeing the relic, and for also taking an impression of its upper surface in clay or wax, and they acted in like manner with the other Buddha relics under their care.

The "Bone of the top of Buddha's skull", in shape like a wasp's nest or the back of the arched hand, which was shown to believing pilgrims in Hilo was of course an imposture. It was perhaps the polished skull-cup of some ancient Sakian chief preserved originally as an heir-loom.[2] We have seen that a segment of the Buddha's skull-bone was preserved as a sacred relic in the Kapis country.

## GANDHĀRA.

The pilgrim's narrative in the Records proceeds to relate that "from this" (that is, from somewhere near the site of the modern Jelalabad) he went south-east among hills and valleys for above 500 *li* and came to the *Kan-t'o-lo* (Gandhāra) country. This country was above 1000 *li* from east to west and above 800 *li* north to south, reaching on the east to the *Sin* (in the D text,

---

[1] Fo-kuo-chi, *ch.* XIII. The term which is here rendered by "free" is *chie-t'oh* (解脫). In the translations of the passage the *chie-t'oh-t'a* becomes "tours de delivrance", "Final emancipation tower". and "Vimoksha tope". Nothing is known of such topes or towers; and there is no meaning in the translations. A *chie-t'oh-t'a* is a tope, not closed up, but provided with a door opening and shutting as required. Other topes containing relics were securely fastened, but this one was *released* from the bonds of solid masonry so far as the relic was concerned.

[2] It was made of flesh and bone, was of the capacity of the hollow of the hand, of a dark colour, round, and very beautiful. (Abhi-ta-vib. *ch.* 177).

*Sin-tu*) river. The capital *Pu-lu-sha-pu-lo* (Purushapur) was above 40 *li* in circuit; the royal family was extinct and the country was subject to Kapis; the towns and villages were desolate and the inhabitants were very few; in one corner of the royal city (*Kung-ch'êng*) there were above 1000 families. The country had luxuriant crops of cereals and a profusion of fruits and flowers; it had much sugar-cane and produced sugar-candy. The climate was warm with scarcely any frost or snow; the people were faint-hearted, and fond of the practical arts; the majority adhered to other systems of religion, a few being Buddhists.

The *Kan-t'o-lo* of this passage is doubtless the Gandhāra or Gāndhāra of Indian writers. In a Chinese note we are told that the old and incorrect name was Gandhavat (*Kan-t'o-wei*) and that the country was in "North India". But in several Chinese treatises *Kan-t'o-wei* or the short form *Kan-t'o* is the designation of a large and rather vague region which does not always correspond to the Gandhāra of our pilgrim. Thus Fa-hsien, for example, uses it to denote a city and district in this region quite distinct from the Purushapur district.[1] In the Ka-lan-chi we find Gandha, and also Gandhāra, used to designate both a city and the country in which the city was situated.[2] The Wei-Shu places the district of Gandha to the west of Udyāna and makes it quite distinct from Kapin.[3] Then Gandhavat and Gandhāra are names of a vague "north country" in which was the inexhaustible treasure-store of the nāga-rāja Elāpatra.[4] In some books we find Gandhāra associated with Kapin (Kashmir) either as a part of the latter or as a neighbouring state. Thus the apostle Madhyantika was deputed to go to "Kapin Gandhāras cha", and here I think the syllable *che* (or *cha*) in the Chinese translations stands for the Sanskrit word *cha* meaning

1 Fo-kuo-chi, *ch.* 12.

2 *Ch.* 5.

3 *Ch.* 102.

4 See A-na-pin-ti-hua-ch'i-tzŭ-ching (No. 649): Tsêng-yi-a-han-chin, *ch.* 49 (No. 543): Fo-shuo-Mi-lê-ta-ch'êng-Fo-ching (No. 209): Divyāv. p. 61.

"and".[1] In Wu-k'ung's 'Itinerary' Gandhāra is described as the eastern capital of Kapin, the winter residence of the king of that country, but to the west of Kashmir.[2] The name Gandhāra is an old one in Buddhist literature and it is found in one of the Asoka Edicts.[3] It is interpreted in some places as meaning "Earth-holder",[4] but while there is a Sanskrit word *dhāra* meaning "holding" there does not seem to be any Sanskrit word like *gan* meaning "Earth". Taken as Gandhavat the name is explained as meaning *hsiang-hsing* (香行) or "scent-action" from the word gandha which means *scent, small, perfume.*[5]

In some books we find the name *Shih-shih*(石室)*-kuo* or "Cave country" applied to Gandhāra and the capital called *Shih-shih-ch'êng* or Cave city,[6] and this is evidently another name for Takshaśilā. An old or native name for Gandhāra is given as *Yé-p'o-lo* (業波羅) perhaps for Abār, but this seems to have been local and temporary. We are told, in fact, that it ceased to be used after the country was conquered by the *Ye-ta* (嚈噠 or 悒怛) that is, the Yets or Gats apparently near the end of our 5th century.[7] Further in some Chinese books Gandhāra is said to be the *Hsiao-yue-ti* country, the district of the offshoot of the Yue-ti or Getæ, or at least to include the region so called.[8] The *Ye-ta*, who were a powerful people in Central Asia in the 5th century, are also said to have been of the Yue-ti stock,[9] but some regard them as of Turkish, and others as of Tibetan origin.

In the above passage the words taken to denote that

---

[1] Shan-chien-lü-vib, *ch.* 2 (No. 1125): cf. Mah. *ch.* XIII.

[2] Shih-li-ching.

[3] No. 5 of the Rock Edicts. Fleet in Ind. Ant. Vol. xxii, p. 178.

[4] A-yü-wang-ching, *ch.* 10 (commentary).

[5] Su-kao-sêng-chuan, *ch.* 2 (No. 1493).

[6] A-na-pin-ti-hua-ch'i-tzŭ-ching; A-yü-wang-hsi-huai-mu-yin-yuan-ching (No. 1367).

[7] Ka-lan-chi, *ch.* 5; Wei-shu, *ch.* 102.

[8] Wei-shu l. c.; T'ung-chih-liao s. v. 小月氏.

[9] T'ung-chien-kang-mu s. Liang Wu Ti 普通 3rd year.

Gandhāra had "much sugar-cane and that it produced sugar-candy (lit. stone-honey)" are 多甘蔗出石蜜. The translators in their renderings here have inserted a gloss which makes Yuan-chuang state that the sugar-candy was made by the people from the sugar-cane. Julien translates the words—"il produit aussi beaucoup de cannes à sucre et l'on en tire du *miel en pierre* (du sucre solide)." Here the words "l'on en tire" are not warranted by the text which has merely the ordinary word *ch'u*. This word here as in other passages of the Records simply means "it (that is, the country) yields or produces". We know also from other sources that the Chinese at this time did not know of sugar as a product of the sugar-cane. In consequence of information obtained from India the Emperor T'ang T'ai Tsung sent a mission to that country to learn the art of making sugar and candy from the Sugar-cane. This candy was merely molasses dried or "sugar in pieces". It was at first "hard (or stone) honey" to the Chinese, as sugar was honey to the ancient westerns.[1]

The *Pu-lu-sha-pu-lo* or Purushapur of our text has been supposed to be the Parshawar of later writers, the Purushāvar of Alberuni, and the Peshawer of modern times.[2] Fa-hsien uses the term "Purusha country"; and makes this a distinct place four days' journey south from his Gandhavat country. Sung-yun does not seem to have known the name Purusha, and he uses Gandhāra for country and capital. As has been stated, the Nagarahāra of Kittoe's Sanskrit inscription is evidently the city and district called Purushapur. This name is interpreted as meaning "the city of the Hero", in Chinese *Chang-fu-kung* (丈夫宮) or Hero's Palace,[3] the Purusha or "Hero" being Vishṇu as the conqueror of the terrible Asura.

Yuan-chuang proceeds to state that

---

[1] Pên-ts'ao-kang-mu, *ch.* 33; T'ang-Shu, *ch.* 221 second part.

[2] A. G. I. p. 47 ff. for this and Gandhāra generally: Alberuni Vol. ii, p. 11.

[3] Su-kao-sêng-chuan, *ch.* 2.

of the Buddhist Masters in India who since old times had written śāstras (*lun* 論) there were Nārāyaṇa-deva, *Wu-cho* (Asanga) P'usa, *Shih-ch'in* (Vasubandhu) P'usa, Dharmatāra, Manoratha(?), and Pārśva the Venerable who were natives of this district.

Julien translates this passage as follows—"Depuis l'antiquité, ce pays a donné le jour à un grand nombre de docteurs indiens qui ont composé des Traités (*Çastras*); par exemple à Nārāyaṇa Deva, Asañga, Vasoubandhu, Dharmatrāta, Manorhita, Ārya Parçvika, &c. &c." There is nothing in the text, however, corresponding to the *grand nombre*, the *par exemple*, or the *&c. &c.* of this rendering. Instead of the word *pu* (不), which is in Julien's Chinese text, there should be *yu* (有), the reading of the A and D texts. Of the writers of śāstras or disquisitions mentioned here only three are known as authors of Buddhist books which have come down to us, viz. Asanga, Vasubandhu, and Dharmatāra. The Nārāyaṇa-deva appears again in this treatise as a deva or god, and it is perhaps the incarnation of Vishnu so named that is represented here as a philosophical Buddhist writer, or Yuan-chuang may have heard that the "Dharma-śāstra" which bears the name of Vishnu was written by the god. But we must remember that Nārāyaṇa is a name common to several ancient philosophers of India. The other śāstra-writers of Gandhāra will meet us again as we proceed.

There were above 1000 Buddhist monasteries in the country but they were utterly dilapidated and untenanted. Many of the topes also were in ruins. There were above 100 Deva-temples, and the various sects lived pell-mell. In the north-east part of the capital were the remains of the building which once contained the Buddha's Alms-bowl. After the Buddha's decease the Bowl had wandered to this country, and after having been treated with reverence here for some centuries, it had gone on to several other countries, and was now in *P'o-la-ssŭ* (Persia).

The Buddha's Bowl was seen by Fa-hsien in a monastery in Purusha, where it was in the care of the Buddhist Brethren. Kumārajiva saw it in *Sha-le* or Kashgar, and

Chih-mêng saw it in Kapin.[1] Our pilgrim here represents the Bowl as having passed away from Purushapur and as being in Persia, but the Life instead of Persia has Benares. According to other authorities the Buddha's Bowl moved about from place to place, passing mysteriously through the air, and working miracles for the good of the people until it passed (or passes) out of sight in the palace of the Dragon-king Sagara. There it will remain until the advent of Maitreya as Buddha when it will appear again to be a witness. According to some texts the Bowl was broken once by the wicked king Mihirakula, but the pieces seem to have come together again. As no one less than a Buddha could ever eat from this Bowl, so no one less than a Buddha could move it from its resting-place; borne by the hidden impulses of human karma it floated about from one chosen seat to another as Buddhism waxed or waned.[2]

About eight or nine *li* to the south-east of the capital was a large and very ancient sacred Pipphal Tree above 100 feet high with wide-spreading foliage affording a dense shade. Under it the Four Past Buddhas had sat, and all the 996 Buddhas of the Bhadra kalpa are to sit here; the images of the Four Buddhas in the sitting posture were still to be seen. When Sakya Julai was sitting under this tree with his face to the south he said to Ananda—"Four hundred years after my decease a sovereign will reign, by name Kanishka, who a little to the south of this will raise a tope in which he will collect many of my flesh and bone relics". To the south of the Pipphal Tree was the tope erected by Kanishka. Exactly 400 years after the death of the Buddha Kanishka became sovereign of all Jambudvīpa, but he did not believe in Karma, and he treated Buddhism with contumely. When he was out hunting in the wild country a white hare appeared; the king gave chase, and the hare suddenly disappeared at this place. Here among the trees the king discovered a cow-herd boy with a small tope three feet high he had made. "What is this you have made?" asked the king. The boy replied telling the Buddha's prophecy, and informing

---

1 Fo-kuo-chi, *ch.* 12: Kao-sêng-chuan, *ch.* 2, 3.

2 See "Fo-mie-tu-hou-kuan-lien-sung-ching" (No. 124); Lien-hua-mien-ching, *ch.* 2 (No. 465).

Kaṇishka that he was the king of the prophecy, adding that he had come to set in motion the fullfilment of the prophecy. With this the king was greatly pleased; he straightway became a Buddhist, and proceeded to accomplish the prediction. Trusting to his own great meṛits, he set about building a great tope round the site of the boy's small tope, which was to be concealed and suppressed by the great tope. But as the latter rose in height the small tope always topped it by three feet. The king's tope was one and a half *li* in circuit at the base, which was 150 feet high in five stages, and the tope had reached the height of 400 feet. The boy's tope was now suppressed and the king was greatly pleased. He completed his tope by the addition of twenty five gilt copper disks in tiers, and having deposited a *ho* of relics inside, he proceeded to offer solemn worship. But the small tope appeared with one half of it out sideways under the south-east corner of the great base. The king now lost patience and threw the thing up. So [the small tope] remained as it was (i. e. did not all come through the wall) with one half of it visible in the stone base below the second stage, and another small tope took its place at the original site. Seeing all this the king became alarmed, as he was evidently contending with supernatural powers, so he confessed his error and made submission. These two topes were still in existence and were resorted to for cures by people afflicted with diseases. South of the stone steps on the east side of the Great Tope were two sculptured topes, one three and the other five feet high, which were miniatures of the Great Tope. There were also two images of the Buddha, one four and the other six feet high, representing him seated cross-legged under the Bodhi Tree. When the sun shone on them these images were of a dazzling gold colour, and in the shade their stone was of a dark violet colour. The stone had been gnawed by gold-coloured ants so as to have the appearance of carving, and the insertion of gold sand completed the images. On the south face of the ascent to the Great Tope was a painting of the Buddha sixteen feet high with two heads from one body. Our pilgrim narrates the legend connected with this very curious picture as he learned it at the place.

Above 100 paces to the south-east of the Great Tope was a white stone standing image of Buddha eighteen feet high, facing north, which wrought miracles, and was seen by night to circumambulate the Great Tope. On either side of the latter were above 100 small topes close together. The Buddha images were adorned in the perfection of art. Strange perfumes were perceived and unusual sounds heard [at the Great Tope], and divine and human genii might be seen performing pradakshiṇa round it. The Buddha predicted that when this tope had been seven times burned, and seven times rebuilt, his religion would come to an end. The Records of former sages stated that the tope had already been erected and destroyed three times. When Yuan-chuang arrived he found there had been another burning, and the work of rebuilding was still in progress.

The description of the origin and structure of the Kanishka Tope in this passage is not very full or clear; and the interpretation here given differs in some important points from Julien's rendering. There are, however, other accounts of this unique building which may help to supplement our author's narrative. The white hare which appeared to Kanishka and led him to the fated spot was the agent of Indra; so also was the herd-boy who had made the small tope. Or rather the boy was Indra himself, and as the builder and the material were not of this world the tope could not be like the common buildings of its class. One authority describes it as being made of cow-dung; but when an unbeliever pressed it to try, the hollow which he made with his fingers could not be filled up, and remained to testify to the miraculous character of the tope.[1]

According to our pilgrim Kanishka's Tope was 400 feet high with a superstructure of gilt-copper disks, the base being in five stages and 150 feet in height. Julien makes the words of the text mean that each of the five stages was 150 feet high, but this is not in the original and does not agree with the context. Then the passage which tells of the miracle of the small tope coming out half-way through the wall of the Great Tope is thus rendered by Julien—"Quand il (i. e. the king) eut achevé cette construction, il vit le petit *stoupa*, qui se trouvait au bas de l'angle sud-est du grand, s'élever à côté et le dépasser de moitié." But the text does not place the small tope at the south-east corner of the great one, and the king is described as building it "autour de l'endroit où était le petit *stoupa*". Then the words *pang-ch'u-ch'i-pan* (傍出

[1] The Hsi-yü-chih quoted in Fa-yuan-chu-lin, *ch.* 38.

其半) lit. "side put out its half" cannot possibly be made to mean "s'élever à côté et le dépasser de moitié". This rendering moreover spoils the story which tells us that the king had finished his tope, and was pleased with his success in enclosing the small tope, when the latter was seen to thrust itself half through the stone wall of his tope. Then we learn that on seeing this "the king's mind was ruffled and he threw the thing up". The Chinese for this clause is *wang-hsin-pu-p'ing-pien-chi-chih-ch'i* (王心不平便卽擲棄), and Julien translates: "Le roi en eprouva une vive contrariété et ordonna sur-le-champ de l'abattre". Here the word *ordonna* is a bad interpolation, and the term *chih-ch'i* has been misunderstood. It means, as usually, to *give up, renounce, abandon*. The king had built his great relic-tope, but he could not carry out the ambitious design he had to *mi-fuh* by his power the small tope which, unknown to him, was the work of the god Indra, so he wanted to abandon the whole affair. In the Fang-chih the king is wrongly represented as *putting aside* (*chih-ch'i*) the small tope when proceeding to build his own. At the time of Yuan-chuang's visit the small tope half-out through the wall still remained in that position, and the second small tope was to be seen at the original site of the first one. The position he assigns to his second small tope does not agree with the statement that Kanishka enclosed the site of the original small tope within the inclosure of his Great Tope. Perhaps the small tope appearing half-way out through the wall of the great one may have been a sculpture in alto-relievo in the latter. Mr Simpson in the XIVth Vol. of the Journal of the R. A. S. has described such sculptured topes, and given us a sketch of one.

Yuan-chuang's account of the Great Tope and the little one associated with it from the beginning agrees in the main with Fa-hsien's account, but does not much resemble the descriptions in other works. We must remember, however, that what he records is largely derived from others, while his predecessors saw the Great Tope in the splendour of its perfect condition. One account represents the base of the Tope as 30 (for 300) feet in height, above this was a structure of polished and sculptured stone in five storeys, then a structure of carved wood about 120 feet high, then came the roof on which was erected a spire bearing fifteen gilt disks. Sung-yun, like Yuan-chuang, makes the height of the main building to be 400 feet; above this Sung-yun saw an iron pillar 300 feet high supporting thirteen tiers of gilt disks (lit. gold basins). He makes the total height 700 feet, while others make it 550, 632, 800, and 1000 feet. One of the names by which the tope was known was the "Thousand Foot Tope" (百丈佛圖). It was also called the *Chio-li* (雀離) Tope. This term *Chio-li* we have seen was applied to the pair of vihāras at Kuchih (Kutzŭ), and it is used to designate other vihāras and topes. If the name were always written as above we could regard it as a native term meaning "piebald, brown and yellow", *chio* denoting a sparrow and *li* an oriole. But the characters vary and the word is expressly said to be foreign and to mean *striped* or *chequered* in two or more colours. This sense would suit the Great Tope with its dark-coloured stone variegated by yellow tracings. It is apparently this building which is called in a Buddhist work the "Earth and Stone Tope". This will recall to the reader the very interesting general description of the topes of this region given in the Ariana Antiqua, a description which also illustrates our pilgrim's account of the Great Tope.[1]

In a Vinaya treatise the prediction of the building of this tope is made by the Buddha not to Ananda but to the Vajrapāṇi P'usa. The Buddha going about with this P'usa from place to place in "North India" came to the hamlet of the *Ho-shu-lo* (渴樹羅), that is, the Kharjūra or wild date tree. Here the two sat down; and Buddha, pointing to a small boy making a mud tope at a little distance, told the P'usa that on that spot Kanishka would erect the tope to be called by his name.[2]

---

[1] Wei-shu l. c.; Ka-lan-chi, l. c.; Ar. Ant. p. 56.

[2] Saz. Vin. Yao-shih, *ch.* 9.

The description in the Records goes on—

> To. the west of the Great Tope was an old monastery built by Kanishka; its upper storeys and many terraces were connected by passages to invite eminent Brethren and give distinction to illustrious merit, and although the buildings were in ruins they could be said to be of rare art. There were still in the monastery a few Brethren all Hīnayānists. From the time it was built it had yielded occasionally extraordinary men, and the arhats and śāstra-makers by their pure conduct and perfect virtue were still an active influence.

This old monastery is apparently the "Kanik-caitya" of Alberuni, the "vihāra of Purushāvar" built by king Kanik. It was also the "Kanishka-mahā-vihāra" of Kittoe's inscription, "where the best of teachers were to be found, and which was famous for the quietism of its frequenters". Within the modern city of Peshawer is an old building called the Ghor Khattri (the Gurh-Katri of Baber) and known also as the Caravanserai (or the Serai). This was once a Buddhist monastery "with numerous cells". Does it represent the great Kanishka vihāra?

> In the third tier of high halls of the Kanishka vihāra was the chamber once occupied by the Venerable *P'o-li-ssŭ-fo* (Pārśva): it was in ruins, but was marked off. This Pārśva was originally a brahmin teacher, and he remained such until he was eighty years old. Then he became converted to Buddhism and received ordination. The city boys hereupon jeered at him as an old and feeble man, and reproached him with wishing to lead an idle life, unable to fulfill the duties of a monk in practising absorbed meditation and reciting the sacred Scriptures. Stung by these reproaches the old man withdrew into seclusion, and made a vow not to lay his side on his mat until he had mastered the canon, and had attained full spiritual perfection and powers. At the end of three years he had completely succeeded, and people out of respect called him *Reverend Side* (or *Ribs*) because he had not laid his *side* on his mat for so long a time.

The *P'o-li-ssŭ-fo* (Pārśva) of this passage is called in other works *P'o-she* (波奢) which may be for Passo the Pali form of Pārśva.[1] As this word means *side* it is translated into Chinese by *Hsie* (脇) which also means

---

[1] Pi-p'o-sha-lun, or Vibhāshā-śāstra, *ch.* 1 (No. 1279).

*side* or *ribs*. The Buddhist Doctor with this name was also called *Nan-shêng* or "Hard to be born", which is perhaps a translation of Durjāta. He was so called because, for misdeeds in a former existence, he was six (or sixty) years in his mother's womb, and was born with gray hair. Regarded as one of the Patriarchs he is placed by some ninth, and by others tenth, in the line of succession, and as such he is said to have been a native of "Mid India" and to have lived in the 5th century B. C.[1] But these statements are to be set aside as comparatively late inventions. From other sources we learn that Pārśva was a native of North India, and that he was a contemporary of king Kanishka, at whose Buddhist Council he assisted. His date is thus the first century A.D., and he is said to have lived 400 years after the Buddha's decease. All authorities agree that he was a bhikshu of great zeal and devotion, an ardent student and an indefatigable propagator of Buddhism, eloquent and expert in argument. Among the numerous converts he made the greatest was the celebrated Aśvaghosha who was a brahmin teacher having an unchallenged preeminence in his own country in Mid India. Pārśva, however, defeated him in a public discussion, and according to agreement Aśvaghosha became his disciple, and was ordained as a bhikshu.[2] Pārśva is cited by our pilgrim as a maker of śāstras; but no treatise bearing his name is known to have come down to us, and there does not seem to be any particular work ascribed to him in the Chinese books although he is often quoted in some of these.[3] Nor is there anything, so far as we know, to confirm or warrant Yuan-chuang's story of Pārśva being ordained at the age of 80 years, and

---

[1] In "Fo-tsu-t'ung-chi" (No. 1661), *ch.* 34, and in "Fu-fa-tsang-yin-yuan-ching" (No. 1340) Pārśva is the ninth Patriarch; in the "Chih-yue-lu", *ch.* 3, he is the tenth.

[2] Ma-ming-p'u-sa-chuan (No. 1460). See also Tār. S. 59 and Was. S. 52 note and 231.

[3] E. g. in the Abhi-ta-vib., and the Abhi-shun-chêng-li-lun (No. 1265).

the city boys jeering at him in consequence. We do read in a work already cited that when Pārśva was on his way to Mid India the boys at one town made fun of him for wearing shoes, and carried these off from him.

> On the east side of Pārśva's chamber was the old house in which *Shih-ch'in* (世親) *P'usa* (Vasubandhu) composed the *A-p'i-ta-mo-ku-shi-lun* (Abhidharmakośa-śāstra), and posterity in reverential remembrance had set a mark on the old house.

As Yuan-chuang has told us, Vasubandhu was a native of this country, having been born in Purushapur. His father's name was Kausika and his mother's Bilindi, and he was the second of three brothers all named Vasubandhu. The eldest became celebrated as the great Buddhist teacher Asanga, the youngest was called Bilindibhava from his mother's name, and the middle one remained Vasubandhu simply. This last following the example of his elder brother became a Buddhist monk, and was at first an adherent of the Vaibhāshikas of the Sarvāstivādin School.[1]

The Abhidharmakośa-śāstra, or "Disquisition on the Treasury of Buddhist Philosophy", mentioned here, originated with 600 aphorisms in verse composed by Vasubandhu as a Sarvāstivādin Vaibhāshika. These were sent by the author from Ayodhyā to the Kashmir Vaibhāshikas who were greatly pleased with them. But as the aphorisms were very terse and hard to understand, the Brethren requested the author to expand them into a readable form. Vasubandhu in the meantime had become attached to the Sautrāntikas, and when he expanded his aphorisms into a prose treatise he criticised some of the doctrines of the Kashmir Vaibhāshikas from the point of view of a Sautrantika. This book also was written in Ayodhyā in the reign of Vikramāditya or his son Balāditya. It was regarded by the Vaibhāshikas of Kashmir as hostile to them, and it was refuted by the learned Sanghabhadra

---

[1] Ta-shêng-pai-fa-ming-mên-lun (No. 1213) Int^n; P'o-su-p'an-tou (Vasubandhu)-fa-shi-chuan (No. 1463); Was. S. 240.

who composed two treatises against it and in defence of the Vaibhāshikas. But Vasubandhu's treatise continued to have a great reputation and it was held in esteem by the adherents of both "Vehicles". Several commentaries were written on it in Sanskrit, and it was twice translated into Chinese, the first translation being by the great Indian Buddhist Paramārtha, and the second by our pilgrim. In this treatise the author does not shew any hostility to the Vaibhāshikas, and he frankly acknowledges his indebtedness to them.[1]

The Vasubandhu of this passage, who will meet us again, is not to be confounded with the Buddhist of the same name who is given as the 21st of the Patriarchs of the Buddhist Church.

About fifty paces south from Vasubandhu's house was the second tier of high halls; here the śāstra-master *Mo-nu-ho-la-t'a* (末笯曷剌他) (Manoratha) composed a "vibhāsha-lun". This Master made his auspicious advent within the 1000 years after the Buddha's decease; in youth he was studious and clever of speech. His fame reached far and clericals and laymen put their faith in him. At that time the power of Vikramāditya king of Srāvasti was widely extended; on the day on which he reduced the Indias to submission he distributed five lakhs of gold coins among the destitute and desolate. The Treasurer, fearing that the king would empty the Treasury, remonstrated with him to the following effect—Your Majesty's dread influence extends to various peoples and the lowest creatures. I request that an additional five lakhs of gold coins be distributed among the poor from all quarters; the Treasury being thus exhausted new taxes and duties will have to be imposed; this unlimited taxation will produce disaffection; so Your Majesty will have gratitude for your bounty, but Your Ministers will have to bear insulting reproaches. The king replied that giving to the needy from the surplus of public accumulation was not a lavish expenditure of public money on himself, and gave the additional five lakhs in largesse to the poor. On a future occasion the king, while out hunting, lost trace of a wild boar and rewarded the peasant who put him on the track with a lakh of gold coins. Manoratha had once paid his barber a like sum for shaving his

---

[1] See Abhi-kü-shê(kośa)-lun (No. 1267), and Abhi-kośa-shih-lun (No. 1269); Abhi-kośa-lun-pên-sung (No. 1270).

head, and the State annalist had made a record of the circumstance. This fact had wounded the king's pride, and he desired to bring public shame on Manoratha. To effect this he called together 100 learned and eminent non-Buddhists to meet Manoratha in discussion. The subject selected for discussion was the nature of the sense-perceptions about which, the king said, there was such confusion among the various systems that one had no theory in which to put faith. Manoratha had silenced 99 of his opponents and was proceeding to play with the last man on the subject, as he announced it, of "fire and smoke". Hereupon the king and the Non-Buddhists exclaimed that he was wrong in the order of stating his subject for it was a law that smoke preceded fire. Manoratha, disgusted at not being able to get a hearing, bit his tongue, sent an account of the circumstances to his disciple Vasubandhu, and died. Vikramāditya lost his kingdom, and was succeeded by a king who shewed respect to men of eminence. Then Vasubandhu solicitous for his Master's good name came to this place, induced the king to summon to another discussion the former antagonists of Manoratha, and defeated them all in argument.

The name of the great Buddhist master here called *Mo-nu-lo-ha-t'a*, and translated by Yuan-chuang *Ju-yi* (如意) or "As you will", has been restored by me as Manoratha. Julien here as in the Vie having the B reading *Mo-no-ho-li*(利)*-t'a* restores the name as Manorhita. This seems to be a word of his own invention, but it has been adopted by the P. W., and by subsequent writers on our pilgrim's narrative. The Chinese characters of Julien's text, however, cannot be taken to represent this word, and they might stand for a word like Manoriddha. This would perhaps suit Yuan-chuang's rendering, and also the Tibetan term Yid-on. But Manoratha is the name given by Burnouf from the Abhidharma-kośa-vyākhya, by Paramārtha, who translates it by *Hsin-yuan* or "Mental desire", and by Schiefner in his translation of Tāranātha.[1] But the Tibetan books make the bearer of the name to be a native of South India and a contemporary of Nāgasena. This Manoratha is not to be regarded as the same

---

[1] Bur. Int. p. 567; Life of Vasubandhu (No. 1463); Tār. S. 3, 298.

person as the Manor or Manura who is represented as the 21st (or 22d) Patriarch.

Yuan-chuang here ascribes to Manoratha the composition of a *Vibhāsha-lun*, that is an expository Buddhistic treatise. Julien very naturally took this term to be the name of a particular treatise which he calls the "Vibhāshā śāstra". There is a learned and curious work in the Canon with the name "Vibhāshā-lun", the authorship of which is ascribed to *Shi-t'o-pan-n'i* (尸陀槃尼) restored by Julien as "Siddhapaṇi", and by some to Kātyāyani-putra, but not to Manoratha.[1] Nor is this last the author of the treatise bearing the name "Vibhāshā-vinaya", or of any other work in the sacred Canon.

According to Yuan-chuang Manoratha flourished (*lit.* was seen to profit, 利見 a phrase from the Yih-Ching) within 1000 years after the decease of the Buddha. This, taking the Chinese reckoning, would place the date of the śāstra-master before A.D. 150.

The pilgrim relates of Vikramāditya that "on the day on which he reduced the Indias to submission he distributed five lakhs of gold coins"—For these words the Chinese is *shih-ch'ên-chu-In-tu-jih-yi-wu-yih-chin-ch'ien-chou-kei* (使臣諸印度日以五億金錢周給). Julien, who instead of *chu*, the reading of the A, C, and D texts, had *yi* (詣) of the B text, translates—"Quand un de ses envoyés arrivait dans (un royaume de) l'Inde, il distribuait chaque jour cinq cent mille pièces d'or pour secourir les pauvres, les orphelins et les hommes sans famille." This is very absurd and is not in the text. The first character here *shih* is not needed, and is not in the D text; and the meaning seems to be very clear that, on the day on which India became subject to him, the king distributed five lakhs of gold coins among his own needy and desolate. Then the narrative makes the Treasurer try to frighten the king by proposing that he should distribute another lakh, among the poor from all quarters, thereby

[1] Bun. No. 1279 and 收 9 of Jap. Reprint.

exhausting the Treasury and causing oppressive taxation. The Treasurer's speech, which is rather absurd, seems to be clearly expressed; but Julien does not seem to have understood its meaning. A little farther on we have the reasons alleged by the king for summoning the non-Buddhists and Buddhists to a public debate. He said "he wanted to set right seeing and hearing and study (lit. travel in) the real objects of the senses" (欲收視聽遊諸眞境), the diverse theories on sense perceptions having led to confusion and uncertainty. The king's language refers to the great controversies about the senses and their objects, and the word he uses for the latter, *ching* (境), is that employed in Yuan-chuang's translation of the Abhidharmakośa-lun. There were great differences of opinion among the rival schools as to the relations between the senses and their respective objects. Thus, for example, as to sight, it was discussed whether it was the eye or the mind which saw, and whether the "true realm" of sight was colour or form. For the purpose at least of suppressing Manoratha, the philosophers at the debate were agreed on the point that smoke should precede fire.

> From the Kanishka Monastery Yuan-chuang went north-east above 50 *li*, crossing a large river, to the city which he calls *Pu-se-ka-lo-fa-ti* (Pushkaravati). This was about fourteen or fifteen *li* in circuit, was well peopled, and the wards were connected by passages. Outside the west gate of the city was a Deva-Temple with a marvel-working image of the Deva. To the east of the city was an Asoka tope on the spot where the Four Past Buddhas had preached. The Buddhist sages who in old times came from "Mid India" to this district and taught mortals were very numerous. It was here that Vasumitra composed his "Chung-shih-fên-Abhidharma-lun". Four or five *li* north of the city was an old monastery in ruins and with only a few Brethren who were all Hīnayānists. In it Dharmatrāta composed the "Tsa-abhidharma-lun".

The Pushkaravatī of this passage, which the Life makes to be 100 *li* from the Kanishka Monastery, is evidently the *Fo-sha-fu* of the Ka-lan-chi and the Pukaravati of other works, and it is supposed to be represented by the modern Hashtnagar. Here according to our text Vasumitra composed his "*Chung-shih-fên* (衆事分)-Abhidharma-luṇ" or "Abhidharma-prakaraṇa-pada-śāstra". It is worthy of note that Yuan-chuang, who is sparing in his references to his predecessors, uses here the translations of the title of this work given by Guṇabhadra and Bodhiyaśa, the first translators of the treatise. For his own version Yuan-chuang used a more correct translation of the title "Abhidharma-*p'in-lei-tsu*(品類足)-lun"[1]. Yuan-chuang here ascribes to Dharmatrāta the authorship of a work which he calls "Tsa-abhidharma-lun". But no treatise with this name is known to the collections of Buddhist scriptures, and it is perhaps a mistake for "Tsa-abhidharma-hsin(心)-lun"; there is in the Canon a work with this name and it is ascribed to Dharmatrāta (or Dharmatāra) as author.[2]

> Beside the monastery was an Asoka tope some hundreds of feet high, the carved wood and engraved stone of which seemed to be the work of strangers. Here Sākya Buddha in his P'usa stage was born 1000 times as a king, and in each birth gave his eyes in charity. A little to the east of this were two stone topes, one erected by Brāhma and one by Indra, which still stood out high although the foundations had sunk. At the distance of 50 *li* to the north-west of these was a tope at the place where the Buddha converted the *Kuei-tzŭ-mu* or "Mother of Demons", and forbade her to kill human beings. The people of the country worshipped this Demon-mother and prayed to her for offspring.

The word "thousand" in the statement here about the thousand gifts of his eyes by the Bodhisattva in as many previous existences as a king is perhaps a mistake. Describing the commemorating tope our author tells us that the *tiao-mu-wên-shih-p'oh-yi-jen-kung* (彫木文石頗異人工). These words seem to have the meaning given to them above, but they have also been taken to mean "the carved wood and engraved stone are superhuman work". Julien's translation, which is the tope "est fait en bois sculpté et en pierres veinées; les ouvriers y ont déployé un art extraordinaire" seems to be far wrong.

The *Kuei-tzŭ-mu* or "Mother of Demon-children" of this passage is evidently the goddess whom I-ching identifies with the Ha-li-ti (Hārītī) of the Sarvāstivādin Vinaya.[1] This goddess, in the time of the Buddha, was a Yakshinī living near Rajagriha, and married to a Yaksha of Gandhāra. Her name was *Huan-hsi* (Nandā?) or "Joy", and she was supposed to be a guardian deity to the people of Magadha. But as the result of a spiteful wish in a previous life she took to stealing and eating the children of Rājagaha. When the people found that their goddess was secretly robbing them of their offspring to feed herself and her 500 sons, they changed her name to Hārītī or Thief. On the petition of the victims the Buddha undertook to put an end to the Yakshini's cannibal mode of life.[2] In order to convert her he hid her youngest and favourite son, in one account called Pingala, in his alms-bowl, and gave him up to the mother on her promise to renounce cannibalism and become a lay member of his communion. Then to provide for the subsistence of the mother and her numerous offspring the Buddha ordained that in all monasteries food should be set out for them every morning. In return for this service the Yakshini and her sons were to become and continue guardians of the Buddhist sacred buildings. The Sar. Vin. does not make any mention of Hārītī undertaking to answer the prayers of barren women for children, but in one of the sūtras the Kuei-tzŭ-mu agrees to comply with the Buddha's request in this matter.[3] I-ching tells us that the name Kuei-tzŭ-mu was used by the Chinese before they had the story of Hārītī, and a goddess of children with that name is still worshipped by Chinese women. She is com-

---

[1] Nan-hai-ch'i-kuei, *ch.* 1 and Takakusu p. 37.

[2] Sar. Vin. Tsa-shih (No. 1121), *ch.* 31.

[3] See the "Kuei-tzŭ-mu-ching" (No. 759) where the scene is laid in the 不凳 country; Tsa-pao-tsang-ching (No. 1329) *ch.* 9 where the baby is Pin-ka-lo (Pingala) and the name of the country is not given; Tsa-a-han-ching, *ch.* 49 where the scene is in Magadha and the demon-mother's baby is *Pi-lêng-ka*. See also Waddell's 'Buddhism of Tibet' p. 99; and Ch'i-Fo-so-shuo-shên-chou-ching, last page (No. 447).

monly represented by a standing image with a baby in her arms and two or three children below her knees as described by I-ching. As the word *kuei* has only unpleasant associations ever since the T'ang period the Chinese have occasionally substituted for it in the name of this goddess the word for *nine*, calling her *Kiu-tzŭ-mu*, "Mother of nine (that is, many) sons"

> Above 50 *li* north from the scene of the conversion of the Kuei-tzŭ-mu was another tope. This marked the place at which the P'usa in his birth as Śama while gathering fruit as food for his blind parents was accidentally shot by a poisoned arrow aimed by the king at a deer of which he was in pursuit. The perfect sincerity of the P'usa's conduct moved the spiritual powers and Indra provided a remedy which restored the son to life.

It will be remembered that Brahminical literature has a similar story about Krishṇa. The Jātaka is a well known one and is related in several books.[1]

> From the Śamaka (or Śama) Tope a journey of above 200 *li* south-east brought the pilgrim to the city called *Po-lu-sha* (Palusha). To the north of this city was a tope to mark the place at which the P'usa in his birth as Prince *Su-ta-na* (Sudāna) bade adieu on being sent into exile for having given the elephant of the king his father to a brahmin. At the side of this tope was a monastery with above fifty Brethren all adherents of the "Small Vehicle". Here the Master of Śāstras, Īśvara, composed the "Abhidharma-ming-chêng-lun".

The Palusha of this passage was apparently about 100 *li* to the south-east of Pushkaravatī. Cunningham has proposed to identify it with the modern Palo-dheri which is about forty miles from Pushkaravati or Hashtnagar. As it is also, however, apparently about forty miles south-east from the Samaka tope, Palo-dheri may correspond to the site of Palusha.

The name Sudāna of the text is explained in a note as meaning "having good teeth", but this, as has been pointed out by others, is evidently wrong. Better renderings are

---

[1] See Wilkins' Hind. Myth. p. 188, 209; Jātaka Vol. VI. p. 71; P'u-sa-sau-tzŭ-ching (No. 216); Liu-tu-chi-ching, *ch.* 5 (No. 143).

*Shan-yü* and *Shan-shih* (善與 or 亅施), both meaning *liberal* or *generous.* As Sudāna is apparently an epithet for the prince whose name was Viśvantara (Wessantara), so *Shan-ya* or "Good-teeth" may have been the name of the much prized white elephant which the prince gave away to the brahmin from the hostile country.

As to the Abhidharma treatise which Yuan-chuang here ascribes to the śāstra master Īśvara no work with the name "Abhidharma-ming-chêng-lun" seems to be known to the Buddhist canon. Instead of the *ming-chêng* (明證) of the ordinary texts the D text has *ming-têng* (燈), making the name to be the "Abhidharma Shining lamp śāstra".

Outside the east gate of the Palusha city was a monastery with above 50 Brethren all Mahāyānists. At it was an Asoka tope on the spot at which the brahmin, who had begged the son and daughter of the Prince Sudāna from him on the *Tan-to-lo-ka* (Dantaloka) mountain, sold the children. Above twenty *li* north-east from Palusha was the Dantaloka mountain on which was an Asoka tope at the place where Prince Sudāna lodged. Near it was the tope where the Prince having given his son and daughter to the Brahmin the latter beat the children until their blood ran to the ground; this blood dyed the spot and the vegetation still retained a reddish hue. In the cliff was the cave in which the Prince and his wife practised samādhi. Near this was the hut in which the old rishi lived; above 100 *li* north from it beyond a small hill was a mountain; on the south of this was a monastery with a few Brethren who were Mahāyānists; beside this was an Asoka tope where the rishi *Tu-chio* (Ekaśringa) once lived; this rishi was led astray by a lustful woman and lost his superhuman faculties, whereupon the lustful woman rode on his shoulders into the city.

In their renderings of the text of the above passage the translators have made a serious mistranslation which injures the narrative. They make the pilgrim state that the tope at the east gate of Palusha was at the place where *Prince Sudāna sold his two children to a brahmin.* But the Prince never did anything like this, and the Chinese states clearly that it was the brahmin who sold the children after having begged them from their father on the mountain. This agrees with the context and with the story in the Scriptures. According to the latter the brahmin on the instigation of his wife went to the Danta mountain to beg the Prince to give him the son and daughter of whom the Prince and his wife were very fond; and by his urgent entreaty he prevailed on the father, in the absence of the mother, to give up the children to serve in his household. But when the Brahmin brought them to his home his clever wife saw they were of superior birth, and refused to keep them as slaves. Hereupon the brahmin took them away to sell, and against his will, under the secret influence of Indra, he found himself with the children at the royal city, where they fell into the hands of the king their grandfather. This happy incident led to the recall of the all-giving Prince and his faithful devoted consort.

Then the stone-hut on the Danta mountain was not merely one which had been inhabited by "a rishi". It was the hut supposed to have been once occupied by the old rishi Akshuta, in Chinese transcription *A-chu-t'ê*, the Acchuta of Fausböll. This was the aged hermit who welcomed the banished Prince and family on their coming to stay on his mountain.

The name of this mountain is given by Yuan-chuang as *Tan-to-lo-ka*, which Julien restored as Dantaloka; the restoration has been adopted by the P. W., and by subsequent writers. But the old and common form of the name in Chinese translations is *T'an-t'eh* (檀 特), and the original may have been Daṇḍa. The "Mountain of punishment" would be an appropriate designation, and the suggestion is strengthened by the Tibetan rendering "forest of penance". Our pilgrim places the mountain at a distance of above twenty *li* north-east from Palusha; but instead of twenty we should probably read 2000 *li* as in the Fang-chih. All the legends represent the mountain of exile as being far away from any town or place of human habitation. It was beyond the Chetiya country, or in Udyāna, or in Magadha. In the Jātaka it is called Vaṁkaparvata, and a Chinese authority explains *T'an-t'eh-shan* as meaning "the dark shady mountain (*yin-shan*)".[1]

In his remarks about the rishi whom he calls "Single-horn" (or Ekaśringa) our pilgrim is apparently following the "Jātaka of Rāhula's mother". In this story, the scene of which is laid in the Benares country, the ascetic of mixed breed, human and cervine, is named Unicorn on account of the horn on his forehead. He has attained great power by his devotions and becoming offended he stops the rain. The king is told that in order to save his country from a prolonged drought he must find a means by which the rishi's devotions will be stopped. A very clever rich "lustful woman" comes forward and undertakes to seduce the saint. She takes 500 pretty girls with her, and by means of love potions, disguised wines, and strong love-making she overcomes the rishi and makes him fall into sin. Beguiling her lover-victim to the city of Benares she pretends on the way to be faint and the rishi carries her on his shoulders into the city.[2] In other versions of this curious wellknown legend the lady who woos and wins the simple, innocent, but very austere and all-powerful, hermit is a good princess, the daughter of the king of the country. For her father's sake and at his request she undertakes the task of wiling the saint from his austerities and devotions: he is captivated, becomes the princess's lover, marries her and succeeds her father on the throne. In most versions of the story the saint to be seduced is called Rishyaśringa, the Pali Isisinga; the lady who leads him astray is Śāntā in the Chinese translations and some other versions, but Nalinī or Nalinikā in other versions.[3] In the "Jātaka of Rāhula's

---

[1] Liu-tu-chi-ching, *ch.* 2: T'ai-tzŭ-su-ta-na-ching (No. 254) in this work the elephant's name is *Su-tan-yen*; Hardy M. B. p. 118; Jāt. Vol. VI last jātaka where the mountain is Vaṁkapabbato; Feer's Chaddanta-jātaka p. 81; Schiefner Tib. Tales p. 257.

[2] Ta-chih-tu-lun, *ch.* 17; cf. Hsing-chi-ching, *ch.* 16.

[3] Kshemendra's Kalpalatā in J. B. T. S. Vol. i. P. II, p. 1, here the rishi is Ekaśringa, the lady is the Princess Nalinī, and the two

mother" the rishi and his tempter are respectively the Bodhisattva and his wife Yasodhara, but in the Jātaka it is the wise father of the rishi who is the Bodhisattva, and the rishi and the lady are a certain bhikshu and his former wife.

Above 50 *li* to the north-east of Palusha (Julien's Varusha?) was a great mountain which had a likeness (or image) of Maheśvara's spouse Bhīmā-devī of dark-blue stone. According to local accounts this was a natural image of the goddess; it exhibited prodigies and was a great resort of devotees from all parts of India; to true believers, who after fasting seven days prayed to her, the goddess sometimes shewed herself and answered prayers. At the foot of the mountain was a temple to Maheśvara-deva in which the Ash-smearing "Tīrthikas" performed much worship.

Going south-east from the Bhīmala (or Bhīma) Temple 150 *li* you come to *Wu-to-ka-han-t'u* (or *ch'a*) city, twenty *li* in circuit and having the Indus on its south side; its inhabitants were flourishing and in it were collected valuable rarities from various regions.

A journey of above 20 *li* north-west from *Wu-to-ka-han-t'u* brought one to the *P'o* (or *Sha*)-*lo-tu-lo* city, the birth place of the rishi Pāṇini who composed a *shêng-ming-lun* (Treatise on Etymology). At the beginning of antiquity, our author continues, there was a very luxuriant vocabulary. Then at the end of the kalpa, when the world was desolate, and void the immortals became incarnate to guide mankind; and from this written documents came into existence, the flow of which in after times became a flood. As opportunity arose Brahma and Indra produced models. The rishis of the various systems formed each his own vocabulary; these were emulously followed by their successors, and students applied themselves in vain to acquire a knowledge of their systems. When the life of man was a century Pāṇini appeared; of intuitive knowledge and great erudition he sorrowed over the existing irregularities and desired to make systematic exclusions and selections. In his studious excursions he met Siva to whom he unfolded his purpose; the god approved and promised help. So the rishi applied himself earnestly to selecting from the stock of words and formed an

---

are the Bodhisattva and Yasodhara of after births, cf. App$^x$ I of the same Vol.; Mahāvastu T. III, p. 143; Bud. Lit. Nep. p. 63; Takakusu in Hansei Zashi Vol. xiii, No. 1; Jāt. Vol. v, p. 123 where the lady is Nalinikā, p. 152 where she is the apsarā Alambusā.

Etymology in 1000 stanzas each of 32 words; this exhausted modern and ancient times and took in all the written language. The author presented his treatise to the king who prized it highly and decreed that it should be used throughout the country; he also offered a prize of 1000 gold coins for every one who could repeat the whole work. The treatise was transmitted from master to disciple and had great vogue, hence the brahmins of this city are studious scholars and great investigators.

The pilgrim goes on to tell a story which he heard on the spot. Within the city of *P'o* (or *Sha*)-*lo-tu-lo* was a tope where an arhat had converted a disciple of Pāṇini. Five hundred years after the Buddha's decease a great arhat from Kashmir in his travels as an apostle arrived at this place. Here he saw a brahmin teacher chastising a young pupil: in reply to the arhat's question the teacher said he beat the boy for not making progress in Etymology. The arhat smiled pleasantly and in explanation said—You must have heard of the treatise on Etymology made by the rishi Pāṇini and given by him to the world for its instruction. The brahmin replied—"He was a native of this city; his disciples admire his excellences, and his image is still here". To this the arhat answered—This boy of yours is that rishi. He added that in his previous existence Pāṇini had devoted all his energies to worldly learning but that from some good Karma he was now the teacher's son. He then told the teacher the story of the 500 Bats who long ago allowed themselves to be burned to death in a decayed tree through delight in hearing a man read from the Abhidharma. These 500 Bats came into the world in recent times as human beings, became arhats, and formed the Council summoned by king Kanishka and the Reverend Pārśva in Kashmir which drew up the Vibhāsha treatises. The arhat added that he was an unworthy one of the Five Hundred, and he advised the teacher to allow his dear son to enter the Buddhist church. Then the arhat disappeared in a marvellous manner and the teacher became a Buddhist and allowed his son to enter the Buddhist church; he became a devoted believer, and at the time of the pilgrim his influence in the district was still a very real one.

The image or likeness of Bhīmā-devī here mentioned was apparently a dark-blue rock in the mountain supposed to have a resemblance to that goddess. Julien, however, understood the passage to mean that there was a *statue* and he makes the author state that the people said—"la statue de cette déesse s'est formée toute seule". But what the people said was that "this goddess' likeness (or image) was a natural (or self-existing) one"—此天像者自然有也 (in B text 形 instead of 也).

Then the Bhīmala of the next paragraph in the B text, the others having Bhīma, is taken by Julien to be a mistake for Bhimā. But the texts are quite correct, Bhīma and Bhīmala being names of Siva. There is no mention in the text of a temple to Bhīmā, but there is a temple to Siva at the foot of the mountain and from it the journey begins.

The name of the city here transcribed *Wu-to-ka-han-t'u* (or *ch'a*) (烏鐸迦漢荼 or 茶) is tentatively restored by Julien as Uḍa-khāṇḍa, but the characters give us a word much liker Udaka-khaṇḍa. In two texts of the Life the name of the city is given as *Wu-to-ka-han-p'êng* (蓬). Saint Martin and Cunningham consider that this city was on the site of the later Ohind (or Waihand), but the identification seems to be doubtful.

In the next paragraph we have Pāṇini's city called in Julien's text *P'o-lo-tu-lo*. As the great Grammarian is supposed to have been a native of Śalātura Julien proposed to regard *P'o* here as a mistake for Sha; in this he is probably right as the A text here has *Sha*. All the other texts, however, have *P'o* (娑 or 婆) and one does not like to regard them all as wrong. Still for the present it is better to regard *Sha* (娑) as the correct reading, the name transcribed being Śalātura. It is remarkable that neither in the part of the Life which tells of the pilgrim's visit to Gandhāra nor in the Fang-chih have we any mention of Pāṇini and his birth place. But in the third *chuan* (Book) of the Life we read of "the rishi Pāṇini of the *P'o-lo-mên-tu-lo* city of Gandhāra in North India" (北印度健馱羅國婆羅門覩羅邑波膩尼仙). These words are in Julien's rendering "dans le royaume de *Gandhara*, de l'Inde du Nord, un Brāhmane nommé le Rĭchi *Po-ni-ni* (Pānini) de la ville de *Tou-lo* (Śālātoula)". Here the learned translator must have known that he was doing violence to the text and that the word *P'o-lo-mên* or Brāhmana could not possibly be severed from *tu-lo* and made to apply to Pāṇini who here, as in the Records, is styled a *rishi.* It is perhaps possible that the *mên* in the text is a copyist's interpolation and that the original reading was *P'o-lo-tu-lo* as in the common texts of the Records.

When our author writes of the Immortals, the devas of long life, becoming incarnate, he is referring to the restoration of our world after its last destruction. The first beings to occupy the new earth were the time expired devas of one of the Heavens and they did not become incarnate in the ordinary sense; they came to earth with the radiance and beauty of gods and with the aerial ways of celestial beings.[1] But they did not come to teach men and it was a very long time after their descent when human beings first began to have a written language.

The reader of this passage about Pāṇini will observe that the pilgrim gives the date of king Kanishka as 500 years after Buddha's decease. This is not in accordance with the common Chinese chronology of Buddhism which makes the death of the Buddha to have taken place in the ninth century B. C.

---

[1] Ta-lu-t'an-ching, *ch.* 6.

# CHAPTER VII.

## CHUAN (BOOK) III.

### UDYĀNA TO KASHMIR.

From Udakakhaṇḍa city a journey north over hills and across rivers (or valleys) for above 600 *li* brought the traveller to the *Wu-chang-na* country. This country was above 5000 *li* in circuit; hill and defile followed each other closely and the sources of river-courses and marshes were united. The yield of the cultivated land was not good; grapes were abundant, but there was little sugar-cane; the country produced gold and iron (in the D text, gold coins) and saffron; there were dense woods and fruits and flowers were luxuriant. The climate was temperate with regular winds and rain. The people were pusillanimous and deceitful; they were fond of learning but not as a study, and they made the acquisition of magical formulæ their occupation. Their clothing was chiefly of *pai-tieh* (calico). Their spoken language was different from, but bore much resemblance to, that of India, and the rules of their written language were in a rather unsettled state.

A note added to our text tells us that Wu-chang-na means "park", the country having once been the park of a king, (viz. Asoka, according, to the 'Life'). The Wu-chang-na of the narrative is perhaps to be read Udana and it stands for Udyāna which means "a park". Other forms of the name in Chinese works are *Wu-t'u* or *-ch'a* (荼 or 茶) perhaps for Uḍa.[1] *Wu-ch'ang* (長) used by Fa-hsien, *Wu-ch'ang* (塲) in the Ka-lan-chi, *Wu-tien* (or *yun*)-*nang* (塡 or 唄 曩) used by Shih-hu of the later Sung period, and

---

[1] T'ung-chien-kang-mu, T'ang Kao Tsung Tsung-chang 2d y.

the unusual form *Wu-sun-ch'ang* (孫塲). But the territory denoted by these varieties of name does not always correspond to the *Wu-chang-na* of our text. In some Chinese translations this country is vaguely denominated "*Yue-ti* (Getæ) Country".[1] There may possibly have been a native name like Uda from which the Sanskrit form Udyāna and the Pali Uyyāna were formed. Our pilgrim's Udyāna, according to Cunningham, comprised the present districts of Pangkora, Bijāwar, Swât, and Bunir.[2] The country is represented by Yuan-chuang as not yielding good crops, and this is not in agreement with the accounts in other works which describe it as a well watered region yielding good crops of rice and wheat.[3]

> The people of Udyāna held Buddhism in high esteem and were reverential believers in the Mahāyāna. Along the two sides of the *Su-p'o-fa-su-tu* river there had formerly been 1400 Monasteries but many of these were now in ruins, and once there had been 18 000 Brethren but these had gradually decreased until only a few remained; these were all Mahāyānists who occupied themselves with silent meditation; they were clever at reciting their books without penetrating their deep meaning; they lived strictly according to their rules and were specially expert in magical exorcisms. There were five redactions (*pu*) of the Vinaya taught, viz. the *Fa-mi* (Dharmagupta), the *Hua-ti* (Mahīśāsika), the *Yin-kuang* (Kāśyapīya), the *Shuo-yi-ch'ie-yu* (Sarvāstivādin) and the *Ta-chung* (Mahāsaṅgkika) Vinaya. Of Deva-Temples there were above ten and the various sectarians lived pellmell.

The river here called *Su-p'o-fa-su-tu* according to the B, C, and D texts is the Śubhavastu, the Swāt of modern geography. In the old A text the reading is *Su-p'o-su-tu* representing a form like Svastu. The name Swāt is applied not only to the river but also to the district through which it flows.

The five redactions of the Vinaya which the pilgrim found in force in this country are the more or less hete-

---

[1] E. g. in the Ta-chih-tu-lun, *ch.* 9.

[2] A. G. I. p. 81. For recent observations on this country see H. A. Deane in J. R. A. S. for 1896 p. 655.

[3] Wei-Shu, *ch.* 102.

rodox editions ascribed to five disciples of Upagupta. Instead of Mahāsaṅgkika we find Vatsiputra, but this name is supposed to be used as an equivalent for Mahāsaṅgkika. This five-fold Vinaya is often mentioned in Buddhist treatises and another enumeration of it is Sthavira, Dharmagupta, Mahīśāsika, Kāśyapīya, and Sarvāstivādin.[1] I-ching, who gives a fourfold division of the Vinayas, says he never heard of the five-fold division in India: his four chief schools (or redactions) are the Sthavira, the Sarvāstivādin, the Mahāsaṅgkika, and the Sammatiya.[2] It will be noticed that according to our pilgrim all the Buddhists in Udyāna were Mahāyānists and yet followed the Vinaya of the Hinayānists; Fa-hsien represents the Brethren here as Hīnayānists.[3]

> This country had four or five strong cities of which *Mêng-kie* (or *ka*)-*li* was chiefly used as the seat of government. This city was 16 or 17 *li* in circuit and had a flourishing population.

The *Mêng-kie-li* of the text may represent a word like Mangkil. Cunningham has identified the city with the modern Manglaur (or Minglaur), a large and important village at the foot of one of the north-west spurs of the Dosirri mountain between Swāt and Boner, and Major Deane thinks that the identity is undoubted.

> Four or five *li* to the east of the capital was a tope of very many miracles on the spot where the P'usa in his birth as the Patiently-enduring rishi was dismembered by the *Ka-li* king.

Julien understood the words of this passage, 爲羯利王割截肢體, to mean that the rishi cut off his own limbs on behalf of the king. But the word *wei* (爲) here, as often, is used to convert the following active verb into a passive one and has the sense of "was by"; so used the word is said to be in the *ch'ü-shêng* and to be equivalent to *pei* (被) in the sense of "by". The "Patiently-enduring rishi" is the Kshānti or Kshānti-vādin (Pali, Khantivādi),

---

1 Fang-yi-ming-yi, *ch.* 4 Sec. 41; Seng-chi-lü, *ch.* 40.

2 Nan-hai-ch'i-kuei Int., and Takakusu Int. p. XXI, and p. 7.

3 Fo-kuo-chi, *ch.* 8.

or Kshānti-bāla or Kshāntivat of the Buddhist scriptures, and called Kuṇḍakakumāra in the Jātaka. The "*Ka-li* king" is the king named Kali or the king of the country named Kali or Kalinga. The word Kshānti means "patient endurance", and Kali is interpreted as meaning "fighting", or "quarreling". We find the story of this wicked king Kali hacking to pieces the good hermit who was endeavouring to make himself perfect in patient endurance told in several Buddhist books with some variations of detail. It forms the Kshāntibala chapter of the *Hsien-yü-ching* or "Sūtra of the Wise and the Foolish",[1] and it is the "Khantivādi Jātaka" in the Pali Jātaka.[2] In these books the scene of the action is laid in the vicinity of Benares, and in some of the other accounts the name of the locality is not given. The Sūtra of the Wise and the Foolish calls the king Kali, but the Jātaka and some other authorities call him Kalābu, in Chinese transcription *Ka-lan-fu* (迦藍浮). The wording of our author's text here recalls the reference to the story in the 14th chapter of the Chin-kang-ching or Vajra-chchedikā, and there the Sanskrit text leaves no doubt as to the meaning of the words. In the Jātaka the king orders his executioner to flog and mutilate the patient rishi and the king personally only administers a parting kick. But in other versions it is the king himself who in his wrath hacks off the various limbs of the Kshānti rishi who is not in all versions the P'usa destined to become Gautama Buddha.

A note to the B text here tells us that there is a gap after the words of this paragraph, but the note is not in the other texts, and there is no reason to suppose that anything has fallen out. It is to be observed that neither Fa-hsien nor Sung-yun makes any mention of the Kshanti rishi tope in this country.

From Mangkil, the pilgrim tells us, a journey north-east of about 250 *li* brougt him to a mountain in which was the *A-p'o-*

---

[1] Hsien-yü-ching, *ch.* 2: Der Weise u. d. Thor, S. 60.
[2] Jātaka, Vol. iii, p. 39.

*lo-lo* (Apalāla)-Dragon Spring, the source of the Swāt river. This river flows away from its source south-west; it keeps its coldness through spring and summer, and morning and evening (in one text, every evening) the flying spray, rainbow-tinted, sheds brightness on all sides. The dragon of the spring in the time of Kāśyapa Buddha was a man named *King* (or *Keng*)-ki (Gañgi? Julien), able by his magical exorcisms to control dragons and prevent them from sending violent rains. For his services in this way the inhabitants had given him fixed yearly contributions of grain. But the contributions fell off, and the magician, enraged at the defaulters, expressed a wish to be in his next birth a wicked malicious dragon, and in consequence he was reborn as the dragon of this spring, the white water from which ruined the crops. Sakyamuni Buddha came to this district to convert the dragon; on this occasion the Vajrapāṇi god struck the cliff with his mace, and the dragon becoming terrified took refuge in Buddhism. On his admission to the church the Buddha forbade him to injure the crops, and the dragon asked to be allowed to have these once every twelve years for his maintenance; to this petition Buddha compassionately assented. And so once every twelve years the country has the "white water" infliction.[1]

Major Deane says that the distance and direction here given by our pilgrim "bring us exactly to Kalām, the point at which the Utrot and Laspur (Ushu in our maps) streams meet. The junction of these is the present head of the Swat river."

The word Apalāla means *without straw*, and it is rendered in Chinese by *Wu-tao-kan* (無稻芋) meaning "without ricestraw". Another translation is *Wu-miao* (無苗) that is "without sprouting grain". The name seems to have been given to the dragon of the Swāt on account of the ravages among the crops made by the floods of that river. We read in the Sarvata Vinaya[2] that the Buddha, on a certain occasion near the end of his career, took with him his attendant Yaksha named *Chin-kang-shou* or Vajrapāṇi, and went through the air to the country

---

[1] For this Jātaka see Fo-shuo-p'u-sa-pên-hsing-ching, *ch.* 2 (No. 432); Ta-chih-tu-lun, *ch.* 14; Liu-tu-ching, *ch.* 5 (No. 143); Hsien-chie-ching, *ch.* 4 (No. 403). In the Ch'u-yao-ching, *ch.* 23 (No. 1321) the story is told of Siddhārtha while preparing to become Buddha.

[2] Sar. Vin. Yao-shih, *ch.* 9.

beyond the Indus to subdue and convert this dragon. When Buddha arrived at the palace of the dragon the latter became greatly enraged, and caused fierce showers of rain and hail to descend on the Buddha. Determined to put the dragon in terror Buddha caused the Yaksha to smite the adjoining mountain with his adamantine club, whereupon a vast fragment of the mountain fell into the dragon's tank. At the same time Buddha caused a magic fire to appear all around the place. Then the dragon, frightened and helpless, came to Buddha's feet, gave in his submission, and was converted with all his family. It is worthy of note that in this Vinaya story the dragon-king is required by Buddha to take up his abode in Magadha. This dragon is also called *A-p'o-lo* and we find the Spring which was his residence located in the "Yue-ṣhi (Getæ) country of North India" or simply in "North India". The "A-yü-wang-chuan" places the home of this dragon in Udyāna, but the "A-yü-wang-ching" and the Divyāvadāna do not mention his country. In a Vinaya treatise, apparently from Pali sources, we read of a dragon called Alāpalu in Kapin (Kashmir), who is overcome and converted by the great arhat Madhyantika (Majjhantika) who had come as an apostle to introduce Buddhism.[1] This legend seems to be a version of the story here narrated, Majjhantika taking the place of the Buddha.

Julien in his translation of the description of the Swāt river here seems to have followed the text of the Life rather than that of his author. The latter does not state that *an arm* of the river flows to the south-west; it is, as the passage and context show, the river itself which so flows. Nor does Yuan-chuang state that "dans ce pays il gêle au printemps et en été", for that would be at variance with his former statement about the climate of the country; it is the river which is cold through spring and summer. Moreover, although *fei-hsüe* does mean "flying snow", it also means "flying spray", and that is its

[1] Shan-chien-lü-vibhāsha, *ch.* 2 (No. 1125).

meaning here. There was apparently a cascade near the source of the river; and the morning and evening (or, the evening) sun daily shone on the dense white spray tossed up in the air, and made it bright and beautiful with the colours of the rainbow.

The "white water" of this district is referred to by other authorities. Thus Alberuni[1] quotes Jīvaśarman to the effect that "in the country of Svāt, opposite the district of Kīrī (?) there is a valley in which 53 streams unite; during the 26th and 27th days of the month Bhādrapadā the water of this valley becomes white, in consequence of Mahādeva's washing in it, as people believe". According to the Fang-chih it was the rains which the dragon sent that made the water plague.

> Above 30 *li* south-west from the Apalāla dragon spring, and on the north bank of the river, was a large flat stone with the Buddha's footprints; these, the size of which varied with the religious merit of the measurer, were left by the Buddha when he was going away after having converted the dragon; a building had been erected over them and people from far and near came to make offerings. Above 30 *li* farther down the river was the rock on which Buddha had washed his robe, the lines of the robe being still distinct like carving.
>
> Above 400 *li* south from Mangkil was the *Hi-lo* mountain; the stream of the mountain valley flows west; as you go up it eastward flowers and fruits of various kinds cover the water-course and climb the steeps; the peaks and precipices are hard to pass, and the ravines wind and curve; you may hear the sound of loud talking or the echo of musical strains: square stones like couches (in D, topes) made by art form an unbroken series over the gulley. It was here that Ju-lai once gave up his life for the hearing of a half-stanza of doctrine.

The stone with the miraculous footprints of the Buddha and the rock on which he had washed his robe and spread it out to dry are described in the Fo-kuo-chi and the Ka-lan-chi, and the accounts in these works should be compared with our pilgrim's narrative. For the words "the streams of the gorge flow west and as you go up them eastward", Julien has "Les eaux de la vallée se

---

[1] Alberuni Vol. ii, p. 182.

partagent à l'ouest et remontent ensuite du côté de l'orient." This cannot, however, be taken as the meaning of the text which is 谷水西派逆流東上 lit. "the water of the mountain-valley goes off to the west; going up east against the course of the stream —". The pilgrim is probably here describing a part of his journey from Udakahantu to the capital of Udyāna. In the last sentence of the present passage we have reference to a curious Jātaka. In a very far off time when there was no Buddha in the world the P'usa was a brahmin student living on the Himavat; he knew all secular lore, but had never heard the teaching of Buddhism. He expressed his great desire to learn at any cost some of the doctrines of that religion, and Indra, wishing to prove the sincerity of the brahmin's desire, disguised himself as a hideous rākshasa, came to the Himavat, and appeared before the Brahmin. On behalf of the latter he uttered half of the stanza beginning with the words "all things are impermanent"; the brahmin was delighted and asked for the other half. But the rākshasa refused to utter this until the brahmin promised to give himself up as food to the rakshasa in reward for the recital. When the second half of the stanza was uttered the brahmin threw himself from a tree towards the rākshasa; but the latter in his form as Indra saved the devotee's life.[1]

> Above 200 *li* south from Mangkil at the side of a mountain was the *Mo-ha-fa-na* (Mahāvana or Great Wood) monastery. Ju-lai long ago as P'usa was the *Sa-fo-ta-chih* king; to avoid his enemy he gave up his kingdom and going into obscurity came to this place; here he met a mendicant brahmin, and having nothing whatever to give the brahmin, he made the latter bind him and deliver him up to the king his enemy, the reward offered for the exiled king being the latter's alms to the brahmin.

The Monastery of the Great Wood according to Major Deane "was apparently on the western, or north-western, slopes of the present Mahaban. Numerous ruins exist on

---

[1] See the Ta-pan-nie-p'an-ching, *ch.* 14 (No. 113); Hsüan-chi-pai-yuan-ching *ch.* 4 (No. 1324); Ta-chih-tu-lun, *ch.* 12.

the lower slopes and also on the higher portions of Mahaban". But Dr Stein thinks that Mahāban is too far away, and that the Mahāvana monastery was at Pinjkoṭai at Sunigram.[1] In the B and D texts the name of the good king is given as *Sa-fo-ta-chih* (薩縛達之), but instead of *chih* the other texts have *ta* repeated. The name is interpreted as meaning "All-giving", and the original was either Sarvadā, as in some places, or Sarvadada as in other passages. Our pilgrim's version of this pretty jātaka agrees with the story in the Buddhist books except that in these the locality is not given.[2]

> North-west from the Mahāvana monastery, and 30 or 40 *li* down the mountain, was the *Mo-yü* (摩愉) monastery with a tope above 100 feet high, and at the side of it a large square stone on which were the Buddha's footprints. These were left when the Buddha treading on the stone sent forth a Koṭi of ray of light which illumined the Mahāvana Monastery while he related his former births to men and devas. At the base of the tope was a stone of a pale yellow colour yielding a constant exudation; it was here that the Buddha as P'usa hearing Buddhist doctrine wrote the sacred text with a splinter from one of his bones.

A note added to the text here tells us that *Mo-yu* is in Chinese *tou*, a general name for all kinds of pulse. Julien reads the second character of the word as *su* and regards the transcription as representing the sanskrit word Masura which means *lentils*. But all my texts have *Mo-yu* and this agrees with the Glossary. The native interpretation may be a mistake, and the Chinese characters may represent *Mayū* for Mayūkha, a word which means *brightness, a ray of light*. This suggestion is strengthened by the statement which our pilgrim makes about the Buddha here shedding a bright light which lit up the Mahāvana Monastery. The incident of the Buddha in one of his previous births taking a splinter of one of his bones to write out a Buddhist text is taken from a Jātaka mentioned in several of the Chinese writings. In some

1 Ind. Ant. Vol. xxviii, pp. 14, 58.
2 See Ta-chih-tu-lun, *ch.* 12 and 33.

versions of the story the P'usa's name is *Ai* (or *Lo*)-*fa* (愛 or 樂 法), "Loving or Rejoicing in dharma"[1], but in other versions he is *Yü-to-lo* (or *Yu-to-li*), and in the 'Der Weise u. d. Thor' he is Udpala.[2] As the price of hearing a sacred text of Buddhism the P'usa agreed to write the text with a pencil made from one of his bones on paper made from his skin and with his blood for ink. The person who made this hard bargain was a brahmin or the Devil disguised as such.

Sixty or seventy *li* to the west of the *Mo-yü* Monastery was an Asoka tope to mark the spot at which the P'usa in his birth as *Shih-p'i-ka* (Śivika) king sliced his body to ransom a pigeon from a hawk.

A note added to the Chinese text here tells us that *Shih-p'i-ka*, the correct form for the old *Shih-p'i*, means "giving", but we are not bound to accept either the correction or the interpretation. The story of the Rajah of Śivi (or Raja Śivi) saving a pigeon chased by a hawk, and then cutting off portions of his own flesh to weigh against the pigeon, and finally putting his skeleton in the scales in order to have an equivalent in weight for the bird which still remained heavier, is told or referred to in many Buddhist books. It is found also in old Brahminical literature and Dasaratha is reminded by his queen how

"His flesh and blood the truthful Saivya gave
And fed the hawk a suppliant dove to save".

According to the common versions of the story the hawk was Indra bent on proving or tempting the king, and the pigeon is in some versions Agni, in others Visvakarma, or a "frontier king".[3] In the "Liu-tu-chi-ching" the king's name is given as Sarvadā. In the "Hsien-yü-ching", and in other works, the capital of Sivi is Dīpavatī

---

[1] Ta-chih-tu-lun, *ch.* 16 and 49.

[2] Hsien-yü-ching, *ch.* 1; Der Weise u. d. T., S. 15; P'u-sa-pên-hsing-ching, *ch.* 3 where the P'usa is the rishi *Yu-to-li* (優 多 梨).

[3] Liu-tu-chi-ching, *ch.* 1.

or Devapati, the Devawarta of "Der Weise u. d. Thor".[1] Fa-hsien makes the scene of this deed of charity to have been in the *So-ho-to*, that is probably Svāt, country, to the south of his Udyāna.[2] In some works Sivi is a personal name, in others the name of a people or country, and there is a king Sivi among the supposed ancestors of Gautama Buddha.[3] Yuan-chuang apparently understood his Sivika to be a personal name or epithet.

> Above 200 *li* north-west from the Pigeon-ransom Tope and in the *Shan-ni-lo-she* valley was the *Sa-pao-sha-ti* monastery with a tope above 80 feet high. It was here that Ju-lai in his existence as Indra encountered a year of famine with pestilence. In order to save the people's lives the P'usa as Indra changed himself into a great serpent lying dead in the valley; the starving and distressed, in response to a voice from the void, cut from his body pieces of flesh which were at once replaced, and all who ate were satisfied and cured. Near this Monastery was the *Su-mo* great tope where Ju-lai in his Indra life in a time of plague changed himself into a *Su-mo* serpent and all who ate his flesh were cured. By the side of the cliff at the north of the *Shan-ni-lo-she* valley was a tope with powers of healing. It was here that Ju-lai in his existence as a king of peacocks pecked the rock and caused water to flow for the refreshment of his flock; there was a spring and the traces of the peacock's feet were to be seen on the rock.

The *Shan-ni-lo-she* of this passage may be, as Julien suggests, for Sanirāja, and the *Sa-pao-sha-ti* for the word Sarpaushadhi. This latter means "serpent medicine", and this agrees with the rendering in the Chinese note to the ordinary texts. The D edition gives the translation as "Earth Medicine", but this is probably the result of some copyist's error. The *Su-mo* of the text is perhaps for Soma, although Julien restores it as Sūma and translates *Su-mo-shê* by "water serpent".

Major Deane supposes our pilgrim's Sanirāja to be "the Adinzai valley entered from Swat at Chakdara". In this

---

1 Hsien-yü-ching, *ch.* 1; Der Weise u. d. T., S. 16.

2 Fo-kuo-chi, *ch.* 9.

3 Dip. p. 132.

Chakdara district, he tells us, there is a large tope which is still known to some of the people by the name Suma.

In a Buddhist sūtra[1] we read of the Bodhisattva in his birth as Indra becoming a great reptile called *Jen-liang-chung* (仁良蟲) interpreted as meaning "the reptile benevolent and of healing efficacy". When the Kuru country was afflicted with plague Indra caused a voice from the void to call the people to cut from his (that is, the reptile's) body, and eat the flesh, and be cured. The people flocked to the carcase, and eagerly cut pieces of its flesh which never suffered diminution, new flesh replacing the pieces cut away. A similar story is found in other books; but the inexhaustible benevolent animal is usually a large fish.[2]

> About sixty *li* south-west from Mangkil city and on the east side of a great river was the tope erected by Uttarasena, king of this country, to enclose his share of the relics of the Buddha's body, and near this was the tope which that king built to mark the spot at which his large white elephant bearing the precious relics had suddenly died and become a rock.

There does not seem to be any mention either of Udyāna or of Uttarasena in the various accounts given in the various Nirvāṇa treatises of the division of the Buddha's relics. But other authorities relate how a female elephant named *Mo-tu* (or Mata) bearing relics of Buddha to a north country died suddenly on the way, was afterwards reborn as a human creature and became an arhat with an enormous appetite.[3] Yuan-chuang also tells in another

---

1 Ta-pao-chi-ching, *ch.* 8 (Bun. No. 23(3)).

2 Hsien-yü-ching, *ch.* 7; Der Weise u. d. T., S. 215; P'u-sa-pên-hsing-ching, *ch.* 3.

3 Abhi.-ta-vib., *ch.* 42. Major Deane tells us that on the Swat River "between Ghaligai and Shankardar, the natives of the country describe the remains of a stūpa as still standing; and this is undoubtedly that referred to by the Pilgrim—for the Pilgrim records next a large rock on the bank of the great river, shaped like an elephant. This rock is a conspicuous landmark existing near the river, about twelve miles from the village of Thana, and near Ghaligai", op. c. p. 660.

place of an arhat of Kashmir who in a previous existence had been a king's elephant, and had been given to a monk to carry some Buddhist scriptures. When the elephant died he was reborn as a human being, entered the Buddhist church, and rose to be an arhat.

West from Mangkil above 50 *li* and across a large river was the *Lu-hi-ta-ka* (Rohitaka or Red) tope above 50 feet high erected by Asoka. At this place Ju-lai in his birth as *Tzŭ-li* (Compassion-strength) king drew blood from his body to feed five Yakshas.

The *Tzŭ-li*, "whose strength is compassion", of this passage is the king Maitra-bala (or Maitribala) of certain Jāṭakas. This king, who lived in an unknown past and in an undefined country, had administered his kingdom so perfectly that the Yakshas in it were reduced to starvation, as they could not obtain human blood and life on which to subsist. At last five of these creatures came to the king and laid their sad case before him. The king in utter pity made five incisions in his body and refreshed the Yakshas with his blood. Having done this he taught them the way of mercy to creatures, and induced them to take the vows of good life as Buddhists. Very long afterwards when the king came into the world and became Buddha these five Yakshas were born as human creatures and became Ajñāta Kaundinya and his four companions, the first disciples of the Buddha.[1]

In this passage "Rohitaka tope" probably denotes "the tope of Rohitaka". This was the name of a town or village and in an interesting passage of the Sarvata Vinaya it is placed in India south of Kashmir.[2] It was here that Buddha, while lodged and entertained by a good Buddhist Yaksha, gave his disciples leave to eat grapes purified by fire and to drink grape-syrup. The grapes offered to the disciples on this occasion are said to have been brought

---

[1] P'u-sa-pên-shêng-man-lun, *ch.* 3 where the P'usa is king *Tzŭ-li* (慈力); Hsien-yü-ching, *ch.* 2 where the king's name is Mi-k'a-lo-po-lo but rendered in Chinese by Tzŭ-li; Jātakamāla (Kern) S. 41.

[2] Sar. Vin. Yao-shih, *ch.* 9.

from Kashmir by the Yakshas, and the fruit was new to the disciples. Major Deane thinks that the village of the tope is that now called Hazara and adds that the natives describe the tope as still existing.[1]

> Above thirty *li* to the north-east of Mangkil was the *O-pu-to* (Adbhuta or Marvellous) stone tope above forty feet high. The Buddha had preached and taught here, and after his departure the tope emerged from the ground and became an object of worship. West from this stone tope across a great river thirty or forty *li* was a Buddhist temple (*ching-shê*) in which was an image of the Bodhisattva Avalokiteśvara (Kuan-tzŭ-tsai P'usa) of mysterious power with miraculous manifestations; it was an object of pilgrimage for Buddhists and its worship was continuous.
>
> North-west from this image 140 or 150 *li* was the *Lan-po-lu* mountain on which was a dragon-lake above 30 *li* in circuit. The pilgrim then tells the story of the exiled Sakya from Kapilavastu who came to this place, married the dragon's daughter, assassinated the king of Udyāna and reigned in his stead; this king was the father of Uttarasena. After this we have the story of the mother of king Uttarasena being converted by the Buddha and regaining her sight.

The marvellous stone tope of this passage, Major Deane tells us, is said to be still in existence, but this may be doubted. Above 30 *li* west from this tope was the Buddhist temple which Deane following B. wrongly calls "Vihāra", and about 140 *li* north-west from this we have the Lan-po-lu mountain. "This measurement", Major Deane writes, "brings us exactly to the head of the Aushiri valley, which drains into the Panjkora near Darora. How the Pilgrim got his distance over several valleys and intervening high spurs, it is difficult to conjecture. But on the hill to which it brings us there is found a large lake, more than a mile in length."

Our pilgrim represents the conversion of Uttarasena's mother and the restoration of her sight as having occurred at Mangkil. In the Sarvata Vinaya the conversion of the queen-mother is stated to have occurred in a city called

---

[1] Op. c. p. 660.

*Tao-ku-lu-ko* (稻穀樓閣) or "Grain-loft" which was apparently in this region.[1]

## TA-LI-LO (DĀREL).

The narrative in the Records now proceeds.

North-east from Mangkil over hills and across gulleys ascending the Indus by hazardous paths through gloomy gorges, crossing bridges of ropes or iron chains, across bridges spanning precipices or climbing by means of pegs for steps, a journey of above 1000 *li* brings you to the *Ta-li-lo* valley, the old seat of government of Udyāna. The district yields much gold and saffron. In the valley is a great Monastery by the side of which is a carved wooden image of *Tzŭ-shih* P'usa (Maitreya Bodhisattva) of a brilliant golden hue and of miraculous powers; it is above 100 feet high; it was the work of the arhat Madhyāntika who by his supernatural power thrice bore the artist to Tushita Heaven to study Maitreya's beautiful characteristics; the spread of Buddhism eastwards dates from the existence of this image.

It is worthy of note that the Life represents Yuan-chuang as only learning of the road to *Ta-li-lo*, whereas the text of the Records seems to imply that he actually travelled from Mangkil to that place. One text of the Life also makes the distance between the two places to be only ten *li*, but in the D text it is 1000 *li* as in the Records. The *Ta-li-lo* valley is apparently, as Cunningham suggests, the *To-li* country of Fa-hsien and the modern Dārel; it may be also the *Ta-la-t'o* (Dard?) of a Buddhist śāstra.[2] The great wooden image of Maitreya in this district was a very celebrated one, and it is strange to find our pilgrim making it 100 feet high while Fa-hsien makes it only 80 feet high.[3]

## PO-LU-LO (BOLOR).

Proceeding east from Ta-li-lo across mountains and gulleys going up the Indus, by flying bridges over precipices, a journey of above 500 *li* brought you to the *Po-lu-lo* country. This was

---

1 Sar. Vin. l. c.

2 A. G. I. p. 82; Abhi-ta-vib., *ch.* 79 (*Ta-la-t'o* 達剌陀).

3 Fo-kuo-chi, *ch.* 6.

above 4000 *li* in circuit and was situated in the Great Snow Mountains, it was long from east to west and narrow from north to south; it produced wheat and pulse and gold and silver. The people were rich, the climate was cold; the inhabitants were rude and ugly in appearance; they wore woollen clothes, their writing was very like that of India but their spoken language was peculiar. There were some hundreds of Buddhist Monasteries; and some thousands of Brethren who were without definite learning, and were very defective in their observance of the rules of their Order.

The *Po-lu-lo* of this passage is apparently, as has been suggested by others, the Bolor of later writers and the modern Balti or Little Tibet. But it may be doubted whether the pilgrim's account was derived from a personal visit; it may have been all obtained at Mangkil. According to the Fang-chih the traveller after a journey of 500 *li* east from Dārel crossed the Oxus east into the *Po-lu-lo* country. The narrative in the Life does not make any mention of this country.

## TAKSHAŚILA.

From this (i. e. Bolor) the pilgrim returned to Utakahantu (Udaka Khaṇḍa) city, went south across the Indus here three or four *li* broad and flowing south-west (in B and C but in D south) pure and clear, to the Takshaśilā country. This was above 2000 *li* in circuit, its capital being above ten *li* in circuit. The chiefs were in a state of open feud, the royal family being extinguished; the country had formerly been subject to Kapis but now it was a dependency of Kashmir; it had a fertile soil and bore good crops, with flowing streams and luxuriant vegetation; the climate was genial; and the people, who were plucky, were adherents of Buddhism. Although the Monasteries were numerous, many of them were desolate, and the Brethren, who were very few, were all Mahāyānists.

The *Ta-cha-shi-lo* (Takshaśilā or Taxila) of this passage seems to be described by the pilgrim as adjacent to Gandhāra, but Fa-hsien makes Takshaśilā to be seven days' journey east from his Gandhāra.[1] These two travellers treat Takshaśilā as a district separate from Gandhāra,

---

[1] Fo-kuo-chi, *ch.* 11.

but in several of the Buddhist books it appears as a part or city of that country. Fa-hsien explains the name as meaning "cut off head" as if the second part of the word were śira. Another author translates it by *sio-shih* (削石) or "severed rock",[1] and another by *ts'o-shih* (鑿石) or "chiseled rock;[2] it is rendered by "rock-cave",[3] and interpreted as meaning "the Rock of the Takkas". The Pali form of the name is Takkasilā. In very old times, it is fabled, a city called Bhadraśilā was on the site afterwards occupied by Takshaśilā,[4] and in modern times the latter has also had the name Mārīkala.[5] Baron Hügel thought that the site of the old city corresponded with that of the present Rawal-Pindi,[6] but Cunningham places the site of Takshaśilā at the modern Shahdheri, a mile to the north-east of Kālaka-serai. There seems to be much in favour of Cunningham's identification which has been generally accepted.[7] According to the statements in the Buddhist books Takshaśilā was at one time an important trading centre, and a great seat of learning specially famed for its medical teachers.[8] It formed a part of Asoka's empire; and that sovereign, and after him his son, were viceroys appointed to reside at it before they succeeded to the throne.[9]

Above 70 *li* to the north-west of the capital was the tank of the *I-lo-po-ta-lo* (Elāpattra) Dragon-king above 100 paces in circuit, its limpid water beautiful with various-coloured lotuses. This dragon was the bhikshu who in the time of Kāśyapa

---

1 Hsing-chi-ching, *ch.* 38.

2 A-yü-wang-ching, *ch.* 10.

3 E. g. in A-yü-wang-hsi-huai-mu-yin-yuan-ching (Bun. No. 1367). It is sometimes doubtful whether the name "Rock-cave" is applied to Takshaśilā or to Gandhāra.

4 Bud. Lit. Nep. p. 310.

5 Alberuni Vol. i, p. 302.

6 Travels in Kashmir and the Panjab p. 230 et al.

7 A. G. I. p. 104; Mc Crindle's Invasion of India by Alexander the Great p. 342.

8 Ta-chuang-yen-lun-ching, *ch.* 8, 15.

9 Divyāv. p. 371; A-yü-wang-chuan, *ch.* 1.

Buddha destroyed an *I-lo-po-ta-lo* tree; hence when the natives are praying for rain or fine weather they have to go with a monk to the tank, and when they have cracked their fingers, and spoken the dragon fair, they are sure to have their prayers answered.

The story here alluded to of the very ancient Buddhist monk who was afterwards reborn as the Elāpattra Dragon-king is told with slight variations in several Buddhist books. The monk was a very pious good ascetic living in a lonely hermitage among Cardamon (Elā) plants or "Ilā trees". He was much given to ecstatic meditation, and on one occasion he remained absorbed in thought all the morning and until it was the afternoon. He then arose, took his bowl, and went in the usual manner into the town or village, to beg his daily food. The people, seeing him beg for food out of hours, upbraided him, and made disagreeable remarks about his violation of the rules of his Order. The monk became annoyed and irritated by these remarks, and went back to his hermitage. Here he paced up and down as usual, but being in a bad temper he could not endure the touch of the leaves of the Elā (or "Ilā trees"). So he tore them off and angrily strewed them on the ground. When the Buddha Kāśyapa came to remonstrate with him for injuring the plants, and tried to bring him to a proper frame of mind, the monk was rude to the Buddha, and refused to take his reproof. For the two offences, eating food in the afternoon and breaking off the Elā leaves (or scorning the Buddha's reproof for doing so), the monk was reborn as a Dragon-king. In this form he had a monstrous, hideous, and distressing body with seven heads from each of which grew an "Ilā tree", and so long was his body that it reached from Benares to Takshaśilā, a distance of above 200 Yojanas. While the Buddha was at Benares this Elāpattra dragon came thither seeking for the explanation of an incomprehensible verse, and having assumed the form of a universal sovereign, he presented himself in the congregation of the Buddha. The latter, however, caused the dragon to resume his proper form, and then informed him that at the advent of Maitreya he would be released from the dragon existence. Elāpattra then undertook to lead a life of gentleness and mercy not doing harm to any creature.[1] In all the Chinese transcriptions the name Elā (or Ilā)-pattra is given both to the tree which the bhikshu injured and to the dragon-king, but there does not seem to be any plant or tree with the name Elāpattra. I-ching transcribes the name of the dragon *I-lo-po* as if for Elāpat, and he uses a different transcription for the name of the great Treasure.

From the Dragon-Tank Yuan-chuang proceeded south-east for above thirty *li* to a place between two ranges of hills where there was an Asoka tope above 100 feet high. This marked the spot at which, according to the Buddha's prediction, when Maitreya comes as Buddha one of the four great natural Treasures of valuables will be in existence.

The four great Treasures here alluded to are those of Elāpattra in Gandhāra, Pāṇḍuka in Mithila, Piñgala in Kaliñga, and Śañkha in the Kasi (Benares) country.[2] According to some authorities it was at Sāvatthi that the Buddha made to Anāthapiṇḍaka the announcement of the existence of these four hidden Treasures to be revealed at the time when Maitreya comes to be Buddha, but other versions of the story differ.[3] So also some accounts represent the Treasures as being already made use of by the people who every seventh year, on the seventh day of the seventh month, drew at will from the Treasures, which did not experience any diminution.[4] When Maitreya comes as Buddha the Elāpattra, Pāṇḍuka, and Piñgala Treasures are to be transferred to that of Śañkha. In the Tsêng-yi-a-han-ching we find the terms *dragon* and

---

1 Fu-kai-chêng-so-chi-ching (福蓋正所集經), *ch.* 11; Sar. Vin. Tsa-shih, *ch.* 21; J. B. T. S. Vol. ii, P. 1, p. 2; Rockhill Life p. 46.

2 See Divyāv. p. 61.

3 Anāthapiṇḍada-hua-ch'i-tzŭ-ching (No. 649); Tsêng-yi-a-han-ching, *ch.* 49.

4 Upasaka-chie-ching, *ch.* 5 (No. 1088). See also Sar. Vin. Yao-shih, *ch.* 6.

*dragon-king* applied to Elāpattra in connection with the Treasure at Takshaśilā in Gandhāra, but in the other accounts there is no reference to a dragon. Some think that Elāpattra was the name of a king, but it was probably the name of the place afterwards extended to the Tank and the dragon of the Tank. It was undoubtedly this Elāpattra Treasure which our pilgrim here mentions as a sacred spot divinely protected and marked by a tope.

Above twelve *li* to the north of Takshaśilā city, the pilgrim continnes, was an Asoka tope which on Fast days sent forth a brilliant light accompanied by divine flowers and heavenly music. Yuan-chuang learned at the place that within recent times a miracle had occurred in connection with this tope. A woman afflicted with a repulsive skin-disease had come to it for purposes of worship; finding the building in a very filthy state she set to work to cleanse it, and having succeeded in this she presented flowers and incense. Thereupon her disease left her, and she became a beautiful woman, breathing a perfume of blue lotus. At the site of this tope, Yuan-chuang tells us, the P'usa as Chandraprabha (Moon-brightness) king cut off his own head as an act of charity, and did this in 1000 similar births.

Fa-hsien simply relates that the P'usa here once gave his head in charity to a man, and adds that this act gave its name to the country, as if Taksha-śira or "Severed head".[1] In another treatise it is the king of the *Kan-yi* (乾夷) country who agrees to give his head to a wicked and importunate petitioner, but when the latter draws his sword to cut off the king's head, a deity intervenes and saves the king's life.[2] In this Jātaka the king is the P'usa, and the cruel petitioner is Devadatta. This story is told with some variations in the "Divyāvadāna Mālā" where the king is Chandraprabha, and his head is actually cut off by the petitioner.[3] In one book we read of Prince Moon-brightness (Chandraprabha) giving his blood and marrow to heal a poor distressed man.[4] It is rather

---

[1] Fo-kuo-chi l. c.
[2] Liu-tu-chi-ching, *ch.* 1.
[3] Bud. Lit. Nep. p. 310.
[4] Ta-chih-tu-lun, *ch.* 12.

curious to find the story which Yuan-chuang here tells about the woman afflicted with a loathsome skin disease cleansing the sacred building and offering flowers and in consequence becoming healed and endowed with beauty and a sweet breath quoted in an Abhidharma-vibhāsha-śāstra.[1]

Near the Head-giving Tope, Yuan-chuang relates, was an old ruinous Monastery occupied by a few Brethren. It was in this monastery that the Sautrāntika Doctor in Buddhism by name *Kou-mo-lo-lo-to* (Kumāralabdha) once composed expository treatises.

The name of this learned Buddhist Śāstra-master as given here is translated in a Chinese note by *Tung-shou* (童·受) or "Received from the Youth", that is from Kumāra, the god of war, the name being Kumāralabdha. In the Life the name is given as *Ku(Kou)-mo-lo-to* and translated wrongly by "youth's life". Kumāralabdha, we learn from another part of the Records, was a native of this country, but he was taken by force to Kabandha where the king of the country gave him a splendid monastery in the old palace grounds. He was, we are told elsewhere, the founder of the Sautrāntika School, and he was celebrated over all the Buddhist world for his genius, his great learning, and his controversial abilities. He was one of the "Four Suns illuminating the world", the three others being Aśvaghosha, Deva, and Nāgārjuna.[2] Kumāralabdha is mentioned by Tāranātha as a Sautrāntika Master by the name Gzon-nu-len or "Youth-obtained", but he seems to be little known in Buddhist literature and history.[3] He may perhaps be the great *Kiu(Ku)-mo-lo-t'o* who is the 18th (or 19th) in the list of Buddhist Patriarchs.[4]

On the north side of the south hill to the south-east of the capital was a tope above 100 feet high erected by king Asoka

---

1 Abhi-ta-vib., *ch.* 114. Here Asoka had built a Chaitya at the place where king Chandraprabha had given 1000 heads (his own head 1000 times).

2 *Ch.* 12; J. Vol. iii, p. 213.

3 Tār. S. 78.

4 Fu-fa-tsang-yin-yuan-chuan, *ch.* 6 (No. 1340).

on the spot where his son Prince *Ku-lang-na* (for *Ku-na-lang*), or Kunāla, had his eyes torn out by the guile of his step-mother; the blind came here to pray, and many had their prayers answered by restoration of sight. Our pilgrim then proceeds to tell his version of the story of Kunāla's career; of Asoka on the advice of his wicked second queen sending his son to govern Takshaśilā, of the blinding of this prince there by the cruel deceitful action of this queen, of the return of the prince and his princess to the king's palace, and of the restoration of the prince's eyesight effected by the Buddhist arhat Ghosha.

Some versions of this pathetic story represent Asoka as sending his son to restore order in Takshaśila on the advice of a Minister of state and without any interference on the part of Tishyarakshā, the cruel, vindictive, libidinous queen, and in some accounts the prince dies after his return home without having any miracle to restore his eyes. His name was Dharmavivardhana, and his father gave him the sobriquet Kunāla because his eyes were small and beautiful, precisely like those of the Himavat bird with that name. The blinding of this pious and virtuous prince was the consequence of bad Karma wrought in a far-past existence. He had blinded 500 deer, according to one story; or an arhat, according to another version; or he had taken the eyes out of a chaitya, according to the Avadāna-kalpalatā. Ghosha, the name of the arhat who restored eyesight to Kunāla, was also the name of a physician of this district who was celebrated as an oculist.[1]

The Takshaśilā city and region were celebrated from old times, and we read of the king of the country who was contemporary with the Buddha coming to Rājagaha on the invitation of king Bimbisāra to see Buddha. This king became a convert and was ordained, but he died by an unhappy accident before he could return to his kingdom. With reference to this country in later times we

---

[1] A-yü-wang-chuan, *ch.* 3; A-yü-wang-hsi-huai-mu-yin-yuan-ching (the Prince is sent on the advice of Yasa); Fa-yi-ching (法益經) where the story is like that told by Yuan-chuang; Divyāv. p. 416; Bur. Int. p. 404; Bud. Lit. Nep. p. 61.

have the following interesting passage in Cunningham's "Ancient Geography of India"—"At the time of Asoka's accession the wealth of Taxila is said to have amounted to 36 *kotis* or 360 millions of some unnamed coin, which, even if it was the silver *tangka*, or six pence, would have amounted to nine *crores* of rupees, or £ 9,000,000. It is probable, however, that the coin intended by the Indian writer was a gold one, in which case the wealth of this city would have amounted to about 90 or 100 millions of pounds. I quote this statement as a proof of the great reputed wealth of Taxila within fifty years after Alexander's expedition" (p. 106). The whole of this statement is based on Burnouf's translation of a passage in the Asokāvadāna in the "Introduction à l'histoire du Buddhisme Indien" (p. 373) which reads—"Le roi (i. e. Asoka) fit fabriquer quatre-vingt-quatre mille boîtes d'or, d'argent, de cristal et de lapis-lazuli; puis il y fit enfermer les reliques. Il donna ensuite aux Yakchas et déposa entre leurs mains quatre-vingt-quatre mille vases avec autant de bandelettes, les distribuant sur la terre tout entière jusqu'aux rivages de l'océan, dans les villes inférieures, principales, et moyennes, où [la fortune des habitants] s'élevait à un koṭi [de Suvarṇas]. Et il fit établir, pour chacune de ces villes, un édit de la Loi.

En ce temps-là on comptait dans la ville Takchaśilâ trente-six koṭis [de Suvarṇas]. Les citoyens dirent au roi: Accorde-nous trente-six boîtes. Le roi réfléchit qu'il ne le pouvait pas, puisque les reliques devaient être distribuées. Voici donc le moyen qu'il employa: Il faut retrancher, dit-il, trente-cinque koṭis. Et il ajouta: Les villes qui dépasseront ce chiffre, comme celles qui ne l'atteindront pas, n'auront rien".

It will be observed that in this passage the words "la fortune des habitants" and "de Suvarṇas" are introduced by the learned translator to supplement the language and complete the meaning of his author. But these words do not seem to be warranted by the Sanskrit original, which apparently refers to *inhabitants*, and not to *coins*. This interpretation is supported by two out of the three Chinese translations, the third translation being apparently from a different text. The passage translated by Burnouf would thus mean something like the following—The king had 84 000 boxes made to hold Buddha's relics. These boxes he gave to Yakshas to distribute among all large, medium, and small towns having a koṭi of inhabitants. But the people of Takshaśila said—We are thirty-six koṭis in number and we want thirty-six boxes. The king seeing he could not give a box for every koṭi of inhabitants in his dominions said to the Takshaśilans—No, you must knock off thirty-five koṭis for the rule is to be that a box is to be given only to those places which have exactly a koṭi of inhabitants neither more nor less.[1]

According to one story the people of Takshaśila accepted the king's conditions and received a box of relics. But from other accounts it is to be inferred that they did not obtain any of the relics. Neither Fa-hsien nor our pilgrim refers to the presence in this country of one of the 84 000 boxes containing Buddha's relics distributed by Yakshas for Asoka.

## SIÑHAPURA.

From this (that is, the neighbourhood of Takshaśilā) going south-east across hills and valleys for above 700 *li* you come to the *Seng-ha-pu-lo* (Siñhapura) country; this was about 3500 *li* in circuit with the Indus on its west frontier. The capital fourteen or fifteen *li* in circuit rested on hills and was a natural fortress. The soil of the country was fertile, the climate was cold, the people were rude, bold, and deceitful. There was no king and the country was a dependency of Kashmir.

The text of this paragraph by itself and taken in connection with what follows presents serious difficulties. Although the pilgrim seems to describe himself here as

---

[1] Divyāv. p. 381. In A-yü-wang-chuan, *ch.* 1 and in Tsa-a-han-ching, *ch.* 23 it is a matter of population, and in A-yü-wang-ching, *ch.* 1 it is a question of money. The particular form of expression used seems to be susceptible of both these interpretations.

going south-east from Takshaśila to Siñhapura, yet a little further on he represents himself as returning from the latter to the north of the former. In the Life, at this part of Yuan-chuang's journey, the D text makes him *hear* of (聞) Siñhapura at Takshaśila, but the other texts state that Siñhapura was among (間) the hills and valleys 700 *li* south-east from Takshaśilā. In another passage of the Life Siñhapura is placed about twenty-two days' journey from Takshaśilā and apparently to the east of that city, but the direction is not given.[1] If the rest of the narrative with which we are now concerned be correct it would seem that north-east should be substituted for south-east in the statement of the direction of Siñhapura from Takshaśilā. We cannot imagine Yuan-chuang going 700 *li* (about 140 miles) south-east from Takshaśilā, then turning back to the north of that district, and setting out from it again south-eastwards. From the context here it seems to be clear that Yuan-chuang places Siñhapura to the north of Takshaśilā rightly or wrongly. Moreover the "Fang-chih" which places Siñhapura to the south-east of Takshaśilā, following the Records, yet makes the latter place to be south of the former.

Cunningham, in his "Ancient Geography of India", identifies the capital of Siñhapur with Ketās "situated on the north side of the Salt Range, at 16 miles from Pind Dādan Khan, and 18 miles from Chakowāl, but not more than 85 miles from Shah-dheri or Taxila".[2] This identification, to which Cunningham did not adhere, has since been established by Dr Stein to his own satisfaction and that of Dr Bühler.[3] It is true that distance from Taxila, extent of territory, situation of capital, and one or two other details do not tally, but such discrepancies are not insuperable difficulties to an enthusiastic Indian archæologist.

---

1 *Ch.* 5. The T'ang-Shuh (*ch.* 221) agrees with Yuan-chuang in placing Siñghapura 700 *li* to the south-east of the Taxila district.

2 A. G. I. p. 124.

3 Trübner's Or. Rec. No. 249 p. 6.

> Near the south of the capital was an Asoka tope the beauty of which was impaired although its miraculous powers continued, and beside it was a Buddhist monastery quite deserted. Forty or fifty *li* to the south-east of the capital was a stone tope above 200 feet high built by Asoka. Here were also more than ten tanks large and small—"a scene of sunshine". The banks of these tanks were of carved stone representing various forms and strange kinds of creatures. The struggling water (that is, the river which supplied the tanks) was a clear brawling current; dragons, fish, and other watery tribes moved about in the cavernous depths; lotuses of the four colours covered the surface of the clear ponds; all kinds of fruit trees grew thick making one splendour of various hues and, the brightness of the wood mixing with that of the tanks, the place was truly a pleasure-ground.

The words "a scene of sunshine" in this passage are a quotation and in the original are *ying-tai-tso-yu* (映帶左右) "a sunshine borne left and right". The meaning is that there was a continuous line of brightness along the sides of the tanks and the stream by which they were supplied. Julien understood the passage to mean that the tanks surrounded the tope "à gauche et à droite, d'une humide ceinture". But this seems to be impossible and is not in the original. Our pilgrim saw (or was told) that the mountain stream formed a pool or tank in its course, flowed out from this and formed another, and so on, making above ten tanks, the stream all the way between the tanks being above ground in the daylight. The people had afterwards furnished these tanks with facings for their banks made of curiously carved stone.

Supposing Ketās to be the modern representative of Siñhapura we may compare with Yuan-chuang's account the description which Dr Stein gives from personal observation of the scenery at Mūrti a few miles south-east from Ketās—"The bed of the Ketās brook forms in the narrow and very picturesque Gamdhala valley a number of small tanks, and at a bend, where there are two large basins, stands the hill of Mūrti. From the top of the hill I heard distinctly the murmuring of the brook, which on leaving the chief tank, forces its way between a number of boulders. Dense groups of trees, such as Hiuen Tsiang describes, are reflected in the limpid waters of the tanks, which still swarm with fish". Dr Stein also saw at Ketās "two richly-ornamented stone pillars which were stated to have come from Mūrti". "The sculptures on their capitals differ", he adds, "but are decidedly in the Jaina style, showing seated, naked male figures with garlands in their hands. You will understand that they forcibly reminded me of Hiuen Tsiang's "balustrades of different shapes and of strange character"." The words within inverted commas at the end of this paragraph are an incorrect quotation from Burnouf who puts "balustrades" in italics and within brackets to show that the word is the gloss which he adds to his text. There is nothing whatever corresponding to the word in the Chinese.

> Our pilgrim continues his description and tells us that beside [the tope?] was a Buddhist monastery which had long been unoccupied. Not far from the tope, he says, was the place at which the founder of the "White-clothes" sect having come to realize in thought the principles for which he had been seeking first preached his system, the place being now marked by a memorial beside which a Deva-Temple had been erected. The disciples [of the founder of the White-clothes sect] practise austerities persevering day and night without any relaxation. The system which their founder preached, Yuan-chuang says, was largely taken from the doctrines of the Buddhist canon. He proceeded according to classes and made rules of orderly discipline; the great (i. e. senior) disciples are Bhikshus and the small ones are called Śramaṇeras; their rules of deportment and ritual observances are much like those of the Buddhist system; but they leave a little hair on the head and they go naked, or if they wear clothes these have the peculiarity of being white. By these differences of detail they have gradually become quite distinct (viz. from the Buddhists). The images of their "deva teacher" they have venturned to make like those of Buddha, with the difference as to clothing, the distinguishing marks being the same.

From a careful study of all this passage and the preceding one about the Siñhapur country and the objects of interest which it contained, one feels very much inclined to believe that the pilgrim did not visit the place on this occasion and that he obtained his information about it at Takshaśilā and elsewhere. What he tells us about the "white robed non-Buddhists, *pai-yi-wai-tao* (白衣外道) is very interesting, but it is vague and unsatisfactory. This sect was evidently, as has been pointed out by others, the Śvetāmbaras, a development of primitive Jainism. But who was the founder of it who attained spiritual enlightenment and began to preach his system in this region? The spot had a memorial of the event at the time of Yuan-chuang's visit, or as Julien translates—"Aujourd'hui, on y voit une inscription". But this seems to be more than is in the original—*chin-yu-fêng-chi* (今有封記), which perhaps means only "there is now a memorial of the event set up". Beside this memorial there had been erected a "Deva-Temple". Julien adds—"Les sectaires qui le frequentent", but the Chinese has only *ch'i-t'u* (其徒) which means "his disciples", that is, the followers of the founder of the sect. The pilgrim is telling us now of the Śvetambara and Digambara ascetics generally. Severe austerities were inculcated and practised by the Jains from their first appearance and wherever they lived. The constitution, doctrines, and outward observances of their religion with certain exceptions named had, according to our pilgrim, been appropriated from Buddhism. It is thus plain that Yuan-chuang had been taught that Jainism as a system was later in origin than Buddhism, and was mainly derived from the latter. His remarks on this subject appear very extraordinary when we remember that the Nirgrantha (or Jain) sect figures largely in the Buddhist canonical works. It was evidently a large and influential body in the time of Gautama Buddha, who was an avowed opponent of the system, and argued strongly against its teaching as to the efficacy of bodily austerities. As Yuan-chuang must have known, the Jains had their ritual code and their religious and philosophic creed and organisation at the time of the founder of Buddhism.

It should be noticed that our pilgrim does not make mention of a Jain establishment at Śiñhapur, or of any inhabitants whatever in the neighbourhood of the tope. There were at the place a Buddhist monastery without Brethren and a Deva-Temple, but no Jain temple or monastery is mentioned. Thus Dr Stein's sculptures from Mūrti "decidedly in the Jaina style" and thus enabling him to find "Hiuen Tsiang's long-looked for Jaina temple" must wait for further developments. The Ketās district as described by Dr Stein seems to present some agreement with our pilgrim's Siñhapura in its natural scenery, having a stream, a series of tanks, and dense vegetation. But this does not amount to much; and as it is apparently the only point in which there is any resemblance, it is not enough for a basis of identification.

Our pilgrim proceeds to relate that from this (i. e. the Siñhapura district) he went back to the north confines of the Takshaśilā country, crossed the Indus, and travelled south-east going over a great rocky Pass. Here long ago the Prince Mahāsattva gave up his body to feed a hungry tigress. About 140 paces from this was a stone tope at the spot to which Mahāsattva pitying the wild beast's feeble state came; here piercing himself with a dry bamboo he gave his blood to the tigress, and she after taking it ate the Prince; the soil and the vegetation of the spot had a red appearance as if blood-dyed. Travellers suffering from the wild thorns of the place, whether they are believers or sceptics, are moved to pity.

This story of the compassionate Prince giving his body to save the lives of a starving tigress and her cubs is told with variations in several Buddhist books. The version which Yuan-chuang apparently had before him was that given in the "Hsien-yü-ching" which agrees in the main with Schiefner's translation from the Tibetan.[1] According to the story there was once many kalpas before the time of Gautama Buddha a king of a great country the name of which is not given. But the name of the king was Mahāratna (or Mahāratha), and he had three sons the youngest of whom was called Mahāsattva. This prince grew up to be good and gentle, and very compassionate

[1] Hsien-yü-ching, *ch.* 1; Der Weise u. d. T., S. 21; P'u-sa-pên-shêng-man-lun, *ch.* 1. Cf. Bud. Lit. Nep., p. 247.

to all creatures. It happened that one day he and his brothers were strolling among the hills when they saw near the foot of a precipice a tigress with two cubs. The tigress was reduced to a skeleton, and was so utterly famished with hunger that she was about to eat her young ones. Prince Mahāsattva, seeing this, left his brothers, and desirous of saving the animal's life, and the lives of her cubs, threw himself down the precipice, and then lay still for the tigress to eat him. But she was too weak and exhausted to take a bite out of his body. So he pricked himself with a sharp thorn and thus drew blood. By licking this blood the wild beast gained strength, and then she devoured the prince leaving only his bones. When his parents found these, they had them buried, and then raised a mound or tope at the grave. This Mahāsattva was the Buddha in one of his numerous preparatory stages of existence as a Boddhisattva.

Other versions of the story give the number of the tigress' cubs as seven, the number in the Life. This jātaka, sometimes called the Vyāghrī (or Tigress) Jātaka, is not in the Pāli collection, but the story is in Hardy's "Manual of Buddhism" where the P'usa is a brahmin named Brahma and lives near Dāliddi, a village not far from the rock Munda (otherwise called Eraka).[1] In one version the P'usa is the prince Chandanamati son of king Gandhaśri of Gandhamati (that is, Gandhāra);[2] in another he is a Prince in the Panchāla country, and in another the scene of the self-sacrifice is not localised. The Chinese pilgrim of the Sung period found the precipice from which Mahāsattva threw himself in a mountain to the west of Kashmir.[3]

The word which Yuan-chuang uses in this passage for "tigress" is the unusual one *wu-t'u* (烏菟 or as in D 擇). This word, also written 於虥 pronounced *wu-t'u*, is the

---

1 M. B. p. 94.

2 P'u-sa-t'ê-shên-ssŭ-ngo-hu-ch'i-t'a-yin-yuan-ching (No. 436).

3 Ma T. l., *ch.* 338.

old Central-China name for a *tiger*, and it is also a recognized term but of very rare occurrence.[1]

> To the north of the Body-offering Tope was a stone Asoka tope above 200 feet high with very artistic ornamentation and shedding a miraculous light. Small topes and above 100 small shrines encircled the grave; pilgrims afflicted with ailments made circumambulation, and many were cured. To the east of this tope was a monastery with above 100 Brethren all Mahāyānists.

We have thus two topes at this place to commemorate the self-sacrifice of the P'usa to save the life of the tigress. Cunningham has identified one of these, apparently the stone one, with the great Mānikyāla Tope, and he quotes the Chinese pilgrims' testimony in support of this identification.[2] Now Fa-hsien places the scene of the "body-offering", and the site of the memorial tope, at a spot two days' journey east from his Takshaśilā, which was seven days' journey east from his Gandhāra; Sung-yun, who does not mention any tope, places the scene eight days' journey south-east from the capital of Udyāna; and Yuan-chuang puts it above 200 *li* (about 40 miles) south-east from the north of the Takshaśila country. For Sung-yun's Udyāna Cunningham substitues Gandhāra, for Yuan-chuang's "north of Takshaśilā" he substitutes "Taxila", and he makes the "Indus" of the Records to be a mistake for the "Suhān" River. Then he finds that the three pilgrims have thus exactly described the situation of the great Mānikyāla Tope, which is about 34 miles south-east from Shah-dheri. The identification of this tope with either of those mentioned here by Yuan-chuang seems to be attended with serious difficulties. The large stone tope was built by Asoka and the other one (according to tradition) was built either by a king of Gandhāra contemporary with the Buddha or by Asoka, and the Mānikyāla tope cannot be referred to an earlier period than the first century of our era. The tope near the "grave" or spot in which Mahāsattva's bones were interred was known as the "Sattva-

---

1 See Fang-yen (方 言), *ch.* 8.
2 A. G. I. p. 121.

śarīra Tope" or more fully as the "Tope of the relics of the Bodhisattva having given up his body to the tigress." It was supposed, we are told, to have been built by the king of Gandhāra after he had heard the pathetic story from the Buddha.

The Monastery mentioned in the above passage was visited by the Chinese pilgrim monk by name *Fa-shêng* (法 盛), a native of Kao-ch'ang, about the beginning of the 5[th] century A.D. He found it a large establishment frequented by about 5000 Brethren, and the great tope was then daily visited by crowds of pilgrims coming to be cured of infirmities.

> From this (i. e. the place of the interment of Mahāsattva's bones) the pilgrim proceeded eastward above 50 *li* to an isolated hill. Here was a monastery with above 200 Brethren, all students of the Mahāyāna system, amid luxuriant vegetation and with pellucid streams and tanks. Beside the monastery was a tope above 300 feet high which marked the place where the Buddha once converted a wicked Yaksha, and made him give up the eating of animal food.
>
> Continuing his journey, our pilgrim travelled south-east over hills for above 500 *li*, and arrived at the *Wu-la-shih* country. This was a very hilly region above 2000 *li* in circuit, with little cultivated land; the capital was seven or eight *li* in circuit, but there was no ruler and the country was a dependency of Kashmir; the people were rough and deceitful, and they were not Buddhists. About four *li* to the south-east of the capital was an Asoka tope above 200 feet high, and at its side was a monastery which contained a few Brethren all Mahāyānists.

The *Wu-la-shih* of this passage, in the D text of the Life *Wu-la-cha*, perhaps represents an original like Uras or Uraksh. The word for "over hills" (*shan* 山) is in most of the texts, but not in all. Cunningham identifies this country with the "*Varsa Regio* of Ptolemy, and with the modern district of *Rash*, in Dhantāwar, to the west of Muzafarabād". That is, Yuan-chuang places the district of Uras about 125 south-east from the Takshaśilā country; and Cunningham, without any warning or explanation, places it above 100 miles to the north-east of that country.[1]

---

[1] A. G. I. p. 103.

M. St. Martin, who had made the same identification, suggests that there is a mistake in our author's text which should have *north-east* instead of *south-east.*[1] But this latter is the reading of all the texts, and of the Life, and the Fang-chih. In another passage of the Life, however, we find Kashmir placed 50 yojanas distant from Taksha-śilā in a north-east direction.[2] There are apparently mistakes in the pilgrim's account of some of the places in this part of his narrative with respect to their relative positions; and, on the other hand, the identifications proposed are not to be accepted as absolutely correct. A later investigator, who also silently ignores the pilgrim's statement of direction, thinks that "the country of Urasa corresponded pretty nearly to that of the modern Hazara, if we include in that term the whole tract up to the Indus, now held by the Tamaolis, the Hassarzais, the Akazais and others". This writer regards Haripur as corresponding to Yuan-chuang's capital of Uras, the actual city being now represented by Pir-māmaka, a Mahometan shrine close under the citadel of Haripur. The identification here proposed, it will be seen, practically agrees with that proposed by previous investigators.[3]

> From Uras, the pilgrim goes on to narrate, he continued his journey south-east above 1000 *li* over mountains and along dangerons paths and across iron bridges to the country of Kashmir.

Our pilgrim transcribes this name *Ka-sse-mi-lo* (迦濕彌羅), and the transcription in the T'ang-Shu and other works is *Ko-shih-mi* (箇失蜜).

---

[1] Julien Vol. iii, p. 321.

[2] *Ch.* 5 and Julien Vol. i, p. 262.

[3] Revd C. Swymerton in Ind. Ant. Vol. xx, p. 336.

# CHAPTER VIII.

### CHUAN III CONTD.

## KASHMIR TO RAJAPUR.

### KASHMIR.

For an account of the pilgrim's entry into Kashmir, and his arrival at the capital of that country, we are indebted to the narrative in the Life.[1] This treatise tells us that Yuan-chuang entered Kashmir territory by the rocky Pass which formed the western approach to the country. At the outer end of the Pass he was received by the maternal uncle of the king, who had been sent with horses and conveyances to escort him to the capital. On the way thither the pilgrim passed several Buddhist monasteries in which he performed worship; and at one, the Hushkara (護瑟迦羅)-vihāra, he spent a night. During the night the Brethren of the monastery had dreams in which they were informed by a deity that their guest was a Brother from Mahā-China who, desirous of learning, was travelling in India on a pilgrimage to Buddhist sacred places; the Brethren were also exhorted by the deity to rouse themselves to religious exercises in order to earn by their proficiency the praise of their illustrious guest. This was repeated on each of the few days occupied by the pilgrim and his party in reaching the royal Dharmasāla which was about a yojana from the capital. At this building the king was waiting to receive the pilgrim and conduct him into the city. His Majesty was attended by

---

[1] *Ch.* 2.

his grandees, and by certain Buddhist monks from the capital, and he had a magnificent retinue of above 1000 men. He treated his Chinese visitor with marked ceremonious respect, and mounted him on one of his large elephants when setting out for the city. On his arrival here the pilgrim lodged for one night in the Jayendra (闍耶因陀羅)-monastery, but next day on the king's invitation he took up his quarters in the palace. Then His Majesty appointed some scores of Brethren with the illustrious Bhadanta *Ch'êng* (稱), or ? Yaśa, at their head to wait on his Chinese guest. He also invited Yuan-chuang to read and expound the Scriptures, gave him twenty clerks to copy out Mss, and five men to act as attendants. The pilgrim remained here two years and devoted his time to the study of certain sūtras and śāstras, and to paying reverence at sacred vestiges (that is, places held in reverence by Buddhists).

Neither the Records nor the Life gives the name of the king of Kashmir who so hospitably entertained our pilgrim. It was, apparently, the same king who about this time, as we learn on I-ching's authority, received another Chinese pilgrim, by name Süan-hui (玄會), and entertained him as a guest in the palace for about a year, when some unpleasantness arose which caused Süan-hui to leave and continue his wanderings.[1]

Coming back to the text of the Records we find a Chinese editorial note added to the word Kashmir telling us that Ki(-Ka)-p'in (罽賓) was an old and incorrect name for the country. But in many Chinese treatises Ka-pin is a geographical term of vague and varying extension, and not the designation of a particular country. It is applied in different works to Kapis, Nagar, Gandhāra, Udyāna, and Kashmir. The region first called Kapin was once occupied by the Sakas (塞), a great nomad people who spread themselves over vast regions to the north-west

[1] Hsi-yü-ch'iu, *ch.* 1; Chavannes Mém. p. 46.

from what is now the district of Kashgar.[1] Afterwards applied less vaguely Kapin was the name of a country south of the Ts'ung-Ling and subject to the Great Yue-ti (Getæ), and it is said to have been a synonym for the *Tsao* (漕) of the Sui period.[1] But by several Chinese writers, and translators of Buddhist books into Chinese, both before and after our pilgrim's time, the word Kapin is used to designate the country which he and others call Kashmir. Thus for the "charming Kāśmir-city" of the Divyāvadāna the Chinese translation has simply Kapin. Then we read of the rishi Revata, who lived on a mountain in Kapin, being converted by the Buddha, and building a tope (or chaitya) for the Buddha's hair- and nail-relics. This Revata is "Raivataka, a bhikshu of Śaila Vihāra at Kaśmir", and the "Śaila vihara" was the Cliff (石崖)-Monastery not far from the old capital of Kashmir.[3] But by Chinese writers generally Kapin seems to have been always loosely applied; and even down to the T'ang period the word was used by them to designate a region which did not correspond to that afterwards known to them as Kashmir. Thus in the *Hsi-yü-chih*, a Buddhistical treatise of the Sui period, Kapin is evidently the Kapis of other works, the country of Buddha's skull-bone and of the Chinese Monastery. Even the T'ang-Shu treats Kashmir and Kapin as names of two countries, and gives descriptive particulars about each. In other works of the T'ang period we find Kapin apparently used to denote the Nagar and Kapis of earlier writings.

The word Kashmir is transcribed in Chinese in several ways giving slight differences as Kaśmir and Kashmir, and it is explained as meaning "Who goes in?". It is said to have arisen at the time when Madhyāntika induced the dragon to turn the lake into dry land in the manner to be presently described. When the people saw the arhat

---

[1] Han-Shu, *ch.* 96, P. I.

[2] Divyāv. p. 399; Tsa-a-han-ching, *ch.* 23; Ta-chih-tu-lun, *ch.* 9; Abhi-ta-vib. *ch.* 125; Bud. Lit. Nep. p. 76.

sitting where water had been a moment before, they were afraid to venture to him, and kept exclaiming to each other—*Who goes in?*[1] This etymology, which reminds one of Dean Swift, is curious but not satisfactory. Burnouf suggested that Kaśmir might be for Kāśyapa-mir, and one variety of the Chinese transcriptions is *Ka-ye* (that is *Ka-sa* often used for Kāśyapa)-*mi-lo* (迦葉彌羅) or Kāśyapa-mir, but these characters may simply be for Kaśmir.

The pilgrim gives a short general description of Kashmir in his usual manner. It was, he states, above 7000 *li* (1400 miles) in circuit, surrounded by high steep mountains over which were narrow difficult Passes, and the country had always been impregnable. The capital, which had a large river on its west side, was 12 or 13 *li* from north to south and four or five *li* from east to west. The district was a good agricultural one and produced abundant fruits and flowers; it yielded also horses of the dragon stock, saffron, lenses, and medicinal plants. The climate was very cold in season with much snow and little wind. The people wore serge and cotton (*pai-tieh*); they were volatile and timid, being protected by a dragon they crowed over their neighbours; they were good-looking but deceitful; they were fond of learning and had a faith which embraced orthodoxy and heterodoxy (that is, Buddhism and other religions). The Buddhist Monasteries were above 100 in number, and there were above 5000 Buddhist Brethren; and there were four Asoka topes each containing above a pint (*shêng*) of the bodily relics of the Buddha.

The circuit which our pilgrim here assigns to the country of Kashmir is about 3000 *li* above that given to it by Ma Tuan-lin and other authorities, and it is evidently much too great. The rocky Pass (lit. "stone gate"), by which the pilgrim entered the country, was evidently the western Pass which terminates near the town of Barāmūla (Varāhamūla). This is Alberuni's "ravine whence the river Jailam comes; at the other end of this ravine is the watch station Dvāz, on both sides of the river Jailam. Thence, leaving the ravine, you enter the plain, and reach in two more days Addisthān, the capital of

[1] Yi-ch'ie-ching-yin-yi, Supplement *ch.* 1.

Kashmīr, passing on the road the village of Ushkāra, which lies on both sides of the valley, in the same manner as Baramūlā".[1] In the text of the Life the Prince is represented as meeting the pilgrim at the outer end of the Pass, but as he had horses and carriages with him, we must understand him as waiting for the pilgrim at the Dvār at the inner end of the Pass. In the T'ang-Shu the name of the capital of Kashmir is given as *Po-lo-wu-lo-pu-lo* (撥邏勿邏布羅) that is Barāmūla- (or Varāha-mūla)-pura. Other authorities give *P'i-lo-t'a* (媲邏叱) that is Bhiraṭh, or *Shan-chien* (善堅) meaning "of good solidity", as names for the capital in previous periods.[2] Our pilgrim represents the capital as having a large river on its west side, and the T'ang-Shu tells us that this was the *Mi-na-si-to* (彌那悉多) or, perhaps, Menāsitā.

Among the products of Kashmir specified by the pilgrim in this passage is an article the name of which here as in other passages is given by me as "saffron". The original for this is *Yuh-chin-hsiang* (鬱金香) which Julien and others always render by *Curcuma* or *turmeric*. But this undoubtedly is not the meaning of the term here and in other passages of the Records and Life. The word *hsiang* means "incense" or "perfume", and *Yuh-chin*, pronounced like Guh-kum, evidently represents a foreign word. In Sanskrít one name for *saffron* is *Kuṇkuma*, and *Yuh-chin* in its old pronunciation is to be regarded as a transcription of this word, or of a provincial variation of it like the Tibetan *Gurkum*. That *Yuh-chin-hsiang* is "saffron" is seen also by comparing the Tibetan and Chinese translations of a Sanskrit passage which tells of Madhyāntika's proceedings in Kashmir. The valuable plant which this arhat carries off from the Gandhamādana Mountain, and introduces into Kashmir, is called *saffron*

---

[1] Alberuni Vol. i, p. 207. So Baron Hügel leaving this "Indian Paradise" "passed through a rock which together with the river forms a strong barrier". Travels in Kashmir and the Panjab p. 172 (tr. Jervis).

[2] Abhi-ta-vib., *ch.* 125.

in the Tibetan rendering, and *Yuh-chin* in the Chinese version.[1] The saffron plant, Crocus sativus, has been greatly cultivated in this country from a very early period. Its flowers were long ago used to adorn the necks of oxen at the autumn festival in the country, and they were boiled in aromatic spirits to make a perfume.[2]. This, or some preparation of the flowers, was largely used in northern countries in the service of worship offered before images in Buddhist temples. The flowers of the saffron plant are still largely used in decoctions, both as a condiment and as a pigment, by many of the inhabitants of Kashmir.[3] But the *fei*(緋)-*yuh-chin* or purple saffron was forbidden as a dye-material to the Buddhist Brethren. It seems very likely that the term Yuh-chin-hsiang is sometimes used in a loose manner and applied to turmeric, just as the name "Saffron", we learn, is often given to turmeric and saffflower.[4]

The word for "lenses" in Yuan-chuang's description in the passage under consideration is *huo-chu* (火 珠), lit. "fire pearls", and this is rendered by Julien "lentilles de verre". The pilgrim was here apparently translating the Sanskrit word *dahanopala* which means *fire-stone, burning gem*, and is a name for crystal lenses. These "fire pearls" are described as being like crystal eggs, and one of the tortures of the Hungry Ghosts is that for them the drops of rain turn into "fire pearls".

The reader will observe that our pilgrim, in his enumeration of some of the chief products of Kashmir, has not a word about its grapes and wine. Yet the country was celebrated for its grapes, and it was long the only place

---

[1] Sar. Vin. Tsa-shih, *ch.* 40; Tār, S. 12; A-yü-wang-chuan, *ch.* 4. See Dr Bretschneider in Ch. Notes and Queries, Vol. iii, p. 55 and iv, p. 97.

[2] Abhi-ta-vib, *ch.* 12; Fa-yuan-chu-lin, *ch.* 36.

[3] On the saffron of Kashmir see Lawrence's "Valley of Kashmir" p. 342.

[4] Glossary of Ang-Ind. Terms s. v. Saffron.

in all the parts about India in which wine was made from the juice of the grape.

With reference to the state of Buddhism it is remarkable that our pilgrim gives the number of Buddhist establishments in this country as only 100, while Wu-k'ung, who lived in it for some time above a century later, gives the number at his time as 300.[1]

Kashmir is one of the most important and most famous lands in the history of the spread and development of Buddhism. In the literature of this religion we find frequent reference to the capital, and the country generally, in terms of praise and admiration. The pious, learned, and eloquent Brethren of the region seem to have had a great reputation even at the time of king Asoka, who is represented as calling on the disciples of Buddha dwelling in the "charming city of Kaśmir" to come to his Council.[2] When the Buddha and the Yaksha Vajrapāṇi—not Ananda as Yuan-chuang relates—were returning through the air from the conquest and conversion of the Dragon of Udyāna, as they were over the green vales of Kashmir Buddha drew Vajrapāṇi's attention to them.[3] Into these, the Buddha predicted, after my pari-nirvāṇa an arhat named Madhyāntika will introduce my religion, and the country will become distinguished as a home of the Brethren devoted to absorbed meditation (Samādhi) and prolonged contemplation (Vipassanā). In another book the Buddha is represented as having prophesied that Kashmir would become rich and prosperous as Uttaravat, that Buddhism would flourish in it, the number of the disciples being beyond counting, and that it would become like the Tushita Paradise.[4] The country, he said, would be like Indra's Pleasure-garden, or the Anavatapta Lake district, and it would be a real "great Buddhist Congregation."

The pilgrim proceeds with his narrative and relates the story

[1] Shih-li-ching; J. A. 1895, p. 341 ff.
[2] Tsa-a-han-ching, *ch.* 23; Divyāv. p. 399.
[3] Sar. Vin. Yao-shih, *ch.* 9.
[4] Lien-hua-mien-ching, *ch.* 2 (Bun. No. 465).

of Madhyāntika's coming. According to the native records, he states, Kashmir was originally a dragon-lake. When the Buddha, having subdued the wicked dragon of Udyāna, had arrived above Kashmir on his way through the air to Central India he said to Ananda—"After my decease Madhyāntika, an arhat, will in this place establish a country, settle people, and propagate Buddhism". In the 50th year after Buddha's decease, the pilgrim continues, Ananda's disciple the arhat Madhyāntika, perfect in spiritual attainments, having heard of Buddha's prediction was delighted. He accordingly came hither and took his seat in a wood at a great mountain. Here he made miraculous exhibitions and the dragon seeing these asked the arhat what he wanted. "I want you to grant me room for my knees in the lake", was the reply, i. e. I want to have as much dry land in the lake as will enable me to sit cross-legged. The dragon thereupon proceeded to grant the arhat's request by withdrawing water from the lake, but Madhyāntika by the exercise of his supernatural powers enlarged his body until the dragon had drawn off all the water of the lake. Then the dragon was accommodated in a lake to the north-west of the old one, and his relations and dependents went to live in a small one. The dragon now begged Madhyāntika to remain permanently and receive due service, but the arhat replied that this was impossible as the time was near for his pari-nirvāṇa. At the dragon's request, however, Madhyāntika consented that his 500 arhats should remain in Kashmir as long as Buddhism lasted in the country, the land to become again a lake when Buddhism ceased to exist. Madhyāntika now by his miraculous powers built 500 monasteries, and afterwards he bought foreign slaves to serve the Brethren. Some time after his decease these inferiors became rulers of the country; but neighbouring states despising them as a low-born breed would not have intercourse with them, and called them Kritā or "the Bought".

This account of Madhyāntika does not quite agree with any of the older accounts in Buddhist books. These, however, present some interesting and important points of difference among themselves. Yuan-chuang's narrative follows the version which is to be found with slight variations of detail in the "A-yü-wang-chuan" version of the Asokāvadāna, the Sarvata Vinaya, and in the Tibetan texts translated by Schiefner and Rockhill.[1] In these

[1] A-yü-wang-chuan, *ch.* 4; Sar. Vin. Tsa-shih, *ch.* 40; Tār. l. c.; Rockhill Life p. 166 ff.

Madhyāntika is a disciple of Ānanda, converted and ordained in the last moments of Ānanda's life; he is a master of 500 disciples, and comes with these from the Himavat to the place where Ānanda is about to pass away; on a magic isle in the Ganges Ānanda ordains the master and his disciples and all immediately attain arhatship; they want to pass away before Ānanda, but he gives the master Buddha's commission for him to go and teach Buddhism in Kashmir, and the commission is accepted. The name given to the master, and also apparently to his disciples, is explained as meaning Mid-water (中 水), as if Madhyan-taka (for udaka), because they were ordained and perfected on an island in the Ganges; it is also explained by Mid-day (中 日) as if Madhyan-dina, because the ordination took place at mid-day. But according to the "Shan-chien-lü-vibhāsha", Buddhaghosha, the "Dipavamsa", and the "Mahāvaṇsa", Maddhyāntika, called Majjhantiko the thera, lived in the time of Moggala-putta Tissa, and was sent by that head of the church from Pāṭaliputra to Kashmir and Gandhāra.[1] Then there is a Kashmir Abhidharma treatise in which we have a dragon called "Fearless" in the country. This dragon plagues the 500 arhats in their monasteries; the arhats have no magic powerful enough to drive the dragon away; a foreign Brother comes who has no skill in magic and no supernatural powers whatever; by the power of a pure strict life (śīla) he, using only a polite request, rids the country of the dragon.[2] In the Pali versions of Madhyāntika's story the name of the dragon is Aravāla, the *A-lo-p'o-lu* of the Chinese translation; in the Sarvata Vinaya it is *Hu-lung*, the Hulunta of Rockhill. This dragon was a wicked spiteful creature sending floods to ruin crops, according to the Pali accounts, and he is perhaps the original of the Udyāna dragon.

---

[1] Shan-chien-lü-vib, *ch.* 2; Vinaya, Vol. iii, p. 315; Dip. VIII. 1. 4; Mah. *ch.* XII.

[2] Abhi-ta-vib, *ch.* 44.

Our pilgrim next gives a brief account of the settlement of 500 arhats from India in Kashmir, an event which he assigns to the hundredth year after Buddha's decease in the reign of Asoka king of Magadha. This great and powerful sovereign was a firm believer in Buddhism, we are told, and charitable to all creatures. There were [at his capital] 500 arhats and 500 ordinary Buddhist monks, all of whom were treated by the king with equal reverence and attention. Among the ordinary Brethren was one Mahādeva, a man of great learning and wisdom, a subtle investigator of name and reality who put his extraordinary thoughts into a treatise which taught heresy. All this man's acquaintances followed his heretical reasonings. The king following his personal inclinations and taking the part of those whom he liked, unable to distinguish the arhat from the common monk, summoned all to the Ganges with the intention of causing them all to be drowned. But the arhats, finding their lives in danger, used their supernatural powers, and flew through the air to Kashmir, where they settled on the hills and in the vales. When the king learned this he became distressed, went to Kashmir to apologize to the arhats, and to beg them to return. They, however, stedfastly refused to go back, so the king built 500 monasteries for them, and gave up all Kashmir for the benefit of the Buddhist church.

This is Yuan-chuang's short and condensed abstract, which cannot be properly understood without some knowledge of Mahādeva's career as this is related in the "Abhidharma-mahā-vibhāsha-lun"[1] and other treatises. According to the Abhidharma work, Mahādeva was the son of a brahmin merchant of Mathurā. While still a very young man he took advantage of his father's prolonged absence from home on business and formed an incestuous connexion with his mother. When his father returned Mahādeva murdered him, and soon afterwards he fled with his mother. Finding that a Buddhist arhat had an inconvenient knowledge of his guilty life he promptly killed the arhat. Then finding that his mother was not true to him he murdered her also. By thus taking the lives of his parents and an arhat he had committed three unpardonable offences; in the technical

[1] *Ch.* 99.

language of Buddhism he had "made three immediate karmas" (造三無間業), three ānantarya karmas. Stung by conscience, and haunted by fear, he now skulked from place to place until he reached Pāṭaliputra. Here he resolved to enter religion, and he easily persuaded a monk of the Kukuṭārāma vihara to have him ordained. He now devoted all his energies and abilities to his new profession and, having zeal and capacity, he soon rose to be the head of the establishment, and the leader of a large party in the church at Pāṭaliputra. His intellectual abilities were much above those of the ordinary brethren, but his orthodoxy was doubtful, and his moral character was not above suspicion. Mahādeva claimed to have attained arhatship, and he explained away circumstances which seemed to be destructive of his claim. In answer to queries from younger brethren he enunciated five dogmas, or tenets, which led to much discussion, and at length to open dissension. These tenets were, (1) An arhat may commit a sin under unconscious temptation, (2) One may be an arhat and not know it, (3) An arhat may have doubts on matters of doctrine, (4) One cannot attain arhatship without the aid of a teacher, (5) The "noble ways" may begin by a shout, that is, one meditating seriously on religion may make such an exclamation as "How sad!" and by so doing attain progress towards perfection. These five propositions Mahādeva declared to be Buddha's teaching, but the senior Brethren declared them to be Mahādeva's invention and opposed to the orthodox teaching. There were at the time four "sets" or "parties" of Buddhists at Pāṭaliputra, and these had bitter controversies about the five propositions. When dispute ran high the king, on Mahādeva's suggestion, called an assembly of all the monks to have an open discussion and vote on the subject, the king being a friend and patron of Mahādeva. When the assembly was summoned it was attended by a number of senior Brethren, who were arhats, and by an immense number of ordinary ordained members of the church. The superior Brethren argued and voted against the five propositions, but they were far outnumbered by the inferior members who were all friends of Mahādeva. When the discussion and voting were over the wrangling still continued, and the king ordered all the brethren to be embarked in rotten boats and sent adrift on the Ganges; by this means he thought it would be shewn who were arhats and who were not. But at the critical moment 500 arhats rose in the air, and floated away to Kashmir. Here they dispersed, and settled in lonely places among the vales and mountains. When the king heard what had occurred he repented, and sent messengers to coax the arhats to return to his capital, but they all refused to leave. Hereupon he caused 500 monasteries to be built for them, and gave the country to the Buddhist church. These 500 arhats introduced and propagated the Sthavira school in Kashmir, and the majority of inferior brethren at Pāṭaliputra began the Mahāsaṅghika school.

It will be noticed that in this account we have neither the name of the king nor the date of the schism. But in the "I-pu-tsung-lun" and the "Shi-pa-pu-lun" the king is Asoka, and the time above 100 years after Buddha's decease. Additional information on the subject will be found in Wassiljew's "Buddhismus" and in Schiefner's "Tāranātha".[1] In the "Shan-chien-lü-vibhāsha" and in the passages of the Pali works referred to in connection with Madhyāntika we find mention of a Mahādeva at Pāṭaliputra.[2] But this man lived apparently a good and pious life, and he was sent by Tissa as a missionary to the Andhra country. He preached (or composed) the "Deva-dūta-sūtra" that is the Deva-messenger sūtra, in Chinese *T'ien-shi-ching* (天使經), and he seems to have been successful in propagating Buddhism. This may be the Mahādeva of the northern treatises, the popular and influential abbott of Pāṭaliputra. But the latter dies, and

---

[1] Was. Bud. S. 62; Tār. S. 51 and 293; Rhys Davids in J. R. A. S. 1892, p. 9.

[2] Shan-chien-lü-vib. *ch.* 2; Vinaya Vol. iii, p. 316.

is cremated with peculiar circumstances at the capital, and there is no mention of his mission to Andhra. On the other hand it seems possible that the Brethren, sent away in different directions as apostles, were men who had taken prominent parts in the controversies which had arisen among the Buddhists of Pāṭaliputra. All accounts seem to agree in representing their Mahādeva as a man of unusual abilities and learning; and the story of his great crimes as a layman, and his unscrupulous ambition as an abbott, related in the Abhidharma treatises are probably the malicious inventions of enemies.

Our pilgrim next proceeds to relate the circumstances connected with the great Council summoned by Kanishka. This king of Gandhāra, Yuan-chuang tells us, in the four hundredth year after the decease of Buddha, was a great and powerful sovereign whose sway extended to many peoples. In his leisure hours he studied the Buddhist scriptures, having a monk every day in the palace to give him instruction. But as the Brethren taught him different and contradictory interpretations, owing to conflicting tenets of sectarians, the king fell into a state of helpless uncertainty. Then the Venerable Pārśva explained to His Majesty that in the long lapse of time since Buddha left the world disciples of schools and masters with various theories had arisen, all holding personal views and all in conflict. On hearing this the king was greatly moved, and expressed to Pārśva his desire to restore Buddhism to eminence, and to have the Tripiṭaka explained according to the tenets of the various schools. Pārśva gave his cordial approval of the suggestion, and the king thereupon issued summonses to the holy and wise Brethren in all his realm. These came in crowds from all quarters to Gandhāra, where they were entertained for seven days. They were far too numerous, however, to make a good working Council, so the king had recourse to a process of selection. First all had to go away who had not entered the saintly career—had not attained one to the four degrees of perfection. Then of those who remained all who were arhats were selected and the rest dismissed; of the arhats again those who had the "three-fold intelligence" and the "six-fold penetration" were retained; and these were further thinned out by dismissing all of them who were not thoroughly versed in the Tripiṭaka and well learned in the "Five Sciences". By this process the number of arhats for the Council was reduced to 499.

Yuan-chuang goes on to tell that the king proposed Gandhāra

as the place of meeting for the Council, but that this place was objected to on account of its heat and dampness. Then Rājagaha was proposed, but Pārśva and others objected that there were too many adherents of other sects there, and at last it was decided to hold the Council in Kashmir. So the king and the arhats came to his country, and here the king built a monastery for the Brethren.

When the texts of the Tripiṭaka were collected for the making of expository Commentaries on them, the Venerable Vasumitra was outside the door in monk's costume. The other Brethren would not admit him because he was still in the bonds of the world, not an arhat. In reply to his claim to deliberate, the others told him to go away and come to join them when he had attained arhatship. Vasumitra said he did not value this attainment a spittle—he was aiming at Buddhahood and he would not have any petty condition ("go in a small path"); still he could become an arhat before a silk ball which he threw in the air fell to the ground. When he threw the ball the Devas said to him so as to be heard by all—Will you who are to become Buddha and take the place of Maitreya, honoured in the three worlds and the stay of all creatures—will you here realize this petty fruit? The Devas kept the ball, and the arhats made apologies to Vasumitra and invited him to become their President, accepting his decisions on all disputed points.

This Council, Yuan-chuang continues, composed 100 000 stanzas of Upadeśa śāstras explanatory of the canonical sūtras, 100 000 stanzas of Vinaya-vibhāshā-śāstras explanatory of the Vinaya, and 100 000 stanzas of Abhidharma-vibhāshā śāstras explanatory of the Abhidharma. For this exposition of the Tripiṭaka all learning from remote antiquity was thoroughly examined; the general sense and the terse language [of the Buddhist scriptures] were again made clear and distinct, and the learning was widely diffused for the safe-guiding of disciples. King Kanishka had the treatises, when finished, written out on copper plates, and enclosed these in stone boxes, which he deposited in a tope made for the purpose. He then ordered the Yakshas to keep and guard the texts, and not allow any to be taken out of the country by heretics; those who wished to study them could do so in the country. When leaving to return to his own country Kanishka renewed Asoka's gift of all Kashmir to the Buddhist church.

This account of king Kanishka's Council and its work is very interesting, but it requires to be supplemented by some notes and explanations. There are also some statements of the author which, in the abstract here given, are different from the versions given in Julien's full translation. Thus Yuan-chuang represents the king as summoning the arhats to make *vibhāshā-lun*, that is, discussions on, or expositions of, the Canonical works. Julien, however, makes the author state that the king "voulut composer (un traité intitulé) Vibhāshā çāstra". Here the words which I have put in brackets are an addition by the translator and do injury to the text. Again, when all was ready for the Council to proceed to work, the Venerable Vasumitra, Yuan-chuang tells us, *hu-wai-na-yi* (戶外衲衣) which Julien translates "se tenait en dehors de de la porte et raccommodait son vêtement". But the words mean simply "was outside in monk's costume". The term *na* (sometimes written 納)-*yi* is of very frequent use in this sense of "bhikshu's clothing". Thus the monk's complete dress is called "the five *na-yi* of the cemeteries", and we read of a Brother *na-yi-yen-tso*, "sitting meditating in monk's dress; it was one of the rules of Devadatta's fraternity that the members should for life "don *na-yi*". The expression in our text is used to indicate that Vasumitra was an ordinary bhikshu, not an arhat.[1]

The story which follows about the attempt to exclude Vasumitra from the deliberations of the Council, because he was only an ordinary bhikshu, is a feeble imitation of the story about Ananda at the First Council. In our text Yuan-chuang, going according to Mahāyānist traditions, identifies the Vasumitra of Kanishka's time with Buddha's disciple of the same name. The latter, as the Buddha is represented telling his audience, had in a far past existence been a monkey; as such he acquired a knowledge of and faith in Buddhism, and he received the prediction that in a future birth he would become Buddha; in the time of Gautama Buddha he had been born as a human creature and in due course of time had become a

---

[1] Vasumitra-so-chi-lun, *ch.* 2 (No. 1289); Kao-sêng-chuan, *ch.* 3; Shih-sung-lü, *ch.* 36.

disciple and risen to great eminence. But something remained over from his simious life which led him to play and gambol occasionally, and so give cause of offence. Buddha, however, explained the circumstances, and stated that Vasumitra was so take the place of Maitreya, and finally succeed the latter as Buddha with the name Shih-tzŭ-yue (or merely Shih-tzŭ)-Ju-lai, that is, Lion-moon (or Lion) Tathāgata.[1] Thus the Vasumitra of Yuang-chuang's story having the rank of a Bodhisattva (being a "P'usa-bhikshu as he is called) was above the degree of arhat according to Mahāyānist teaching, and hence his refusal in the story to acquire the "petty fruit". It was probably a survival of simious propensities which made him play with the ball of silk in the very solemn circumstances here related. The story here told about Vasumitra is very like one given in an old Mahāyāna śāstra about this p'usa. But in the latter treatise it is a stone which he throws in the air; the stone is caught and held by devas who tell Vasumitra that he is to seek bodhi, that they are to obtain emancipation through him, and that after twenty kalpas he will become Buddha.[2]

Vasumitra, here as in other places translated *Shih-yu* (世友), is a name common to several illustrious Buddhists in the early periods of the church. The personal disciple of the Buddha already mentioned who is destined to become Buddha may perhaps be the sthavira with this name who is placed by one authority next in succession to Upagupta.[3] Then we have the Śāstra-Master Vasumitra, mentioned in the Records, who composed the "Abhidharma prakaraṇa-pāda-śāstra" already noticed, and the "Abhidharma-dhātukāyapāda-śāstra".[4] It was probably also this author who composed the "*Wu-shih-lun*" to which Dharmatrāta supplied a short expository commentary. This is

---

[1] Fo-shuo-shih-tzŭ-yue-Fo-pên-shêng-ching (No. 414): Tsun-Vasumitra-P'usa-so-chi-lun, Preface (No. 1289).

[2] Wei-jih-tsa-nan-ching (No. 1328).

[3] Dharmatara-shan-ching, *ch.* 1 (No. 1341).

[4] Abhi-chie-shên-tsu-lun (No. 1282).

S

apparently not the Bodhisattva Vasumitra to whom is ascribed the authorship of the "Arya Vasumitra-Bodhisattva-saṅgiti-śāstra".[1] The "Abhidharma-mahāvibhāshā-śāstra" is also said to have been the work of the 500 arhats of Kanishka's Council with Vasumitra at their head. But there is nothing either in this treatise or the Saṅgiti-śāstra to show that these works were written at the time of Kanishka, nor is there anything in either to show that it was wholly or in part the work of Vasumitra. It is only in one text out of four that the Saṅgiti-śāstra appears with Arya Vasumitra on the title-page as author. These two treatises contain references to Vasumitra and quotations from him, and the "Vibhāshā" work mentions him as one of the "Four Great Lun-shi of the Sarvāstivādin School". He was noted among the learned and ingenious Doctors of this School for his theory about the threefold division of time and states of existence. He held that the Past, Present, and Future are all realities and that they differ as to their *wei* (位) "locations", or "Conditions" as Mr Rockhill renders the corresponding Tibetan term. Then there is also the Vasumitra who composed the important treatises "Chih-pu-yi-lun" and "Yi-pu-tsung-lun".[2] Moreover there is the Vasumitra who furnished a commentary to Vasubandhu's celebrated "Abhidharma-kośa-śāstra", but of him little or nothing seems to be known.[3] The Vasumitra who is given as the seventh Patriarch in the succession from Kāśyapa, and who is supposed to have lived in the 6th century B. C., need not be further mentioned.[4]

The unfriendly feeling exhibited by the 499 arhats of Kanishka's Council in our pilgrim's narrative towards Vasumitra reminds us, as has been stated, of Ānanda and the First Council. But the old Mahāyāna Śāstra to

---

[1] See Tsun-Vasumitra-P'usa-so-chi-lun. Cf. Tār. S. 67 ff.

[2] Chih-pu-yi-lun (No. 1285); Yi-pu-tsung-lun (No. 1286).

[3] Bur. Int. p. 566 ff.

[4] Chih-yue-lu, *ch.* 3.

which reference has been made tells us of an envious opposition to Vasumitra on the part of certain junior Brethren, and the hostility is not represented as connected with the Council. In both accounts, however, the genius and learning of Vasumitra are indispensable, and he overcomes the enmity, and gains the admiration of the Brethren.

The pilgrim tells us that when Vasumitra was admitted the Council being duly constituted proceeded to its work which was, not to revise or rearrange the canonical treatises, but to furnish these with commentaries and discussions. Taking the sūtras first the arhats composed 100 000 stanzas of upadeśa or explanatory comments on these. Julien makes the author say they composed "le traité Oupadêça çāstra", and here again the addition of "le traité" spoils the meaning. Although there are upadeśas to several individual sūtras, or to a class of sūtras, there does not seem to have ever been a general upadeśa-śāstra for all the sūtra-piṭaka.

This word *upadeśa* seems to have puzzled some of the early translators from Sanskrit into Chinese, and some of them apparently did not understand its meaning and derivation. One curious explanation of it is that it is "oral instruction to leave lust and cultivate goodness".[1] As the designation of a class of canonical treatises it is translated by Lun-i (論 議) or Discussion. The term was technically used to denote a treatise made by a bhikshu, and explanatory of the teachings of a canonical sūtra, and the work itself might become a recognized sūtra. It was then called a Sūtra-upadeśa to distinguish it from the primitive Upadeśa-sūtras, and it was also called a Mahopadeśa, or Great Upadeśa. An essential requisite of such a work was that its teachings should be perfectly in accordance with those of the accepted canon. An upadeśa presented for approval, and rejected on account of its

---

[1] Sui-hsiang-lun, *ch.* 1 (No. 1280).

heterodoxy is called a Karopadeśa.[1] The Council composed also 100 000 stanzas explaining the Vinaya — "Vinaya-vibhāshā-lun". There is an extant treatise entitled "Sarvata (or Sarvāstivādin)-vinaya-vibhāshā" which may have been regarded as the work of the Council. Unfortunately there is only a Chinese version of this work which is in nine *chuan*, of unknown date, and imperfect. The original, however, was evidently composed at a time long after the Buddha, in a country outside of India, and for the use of foreigners. There is nothing in the work, however, to shew that it was the work of Kanishka's Council.[2]

According to our pilgrim this Council further made 100 000 stanzas of exposition or discussion of the Abhidharma — Abhidharma-vibhāshā-lun. There are several vibhāshā treatises in this section of the canon, and it would seem that there are others which have disappeared. In the existing collections of Buddhist books in China we find a treatise known by its short name "Vibhāshā-lun", its full title being "Vibhāshā-shuo. Abhidharmāshṭakhanda".[3] This book is sometimes wrongly ascribed to Katyāyanīputra who apparently composed the original text to which this work serves as a commentary. The author of the "Vibhāshā-lun" is given as Shi-t'ê-p'an-ni, the native pronunciation being perhaps something Siddhavanni. This man apparently lived in Kashmir and, according to his own statement, about 1000 years after Buddha's death. Another vibhāshā treatise is the short one entitled "Wu-shi (五事)-vibhāshā-lun", composed by the great Dharmatāra.[4] This is an exposition of Vasumitra's "Wu-shi-lun", a treatise which does not appear among the canonical books. Then we have the long and important work called "Abhidharma (or Abhidharmata)-vibhāshā-lun" already mentioned. This treatise, which was evidently

---

[1] Ta-pan-nie-p'an-ching (No. 114); Yi-ch'ie-ching-yin-yi, *ch.* 17; Sar. Vin. Mātrika, *ch.* 6.

[2] Sar. Vin. Vibhāshā (Nos. 1135 and 1136).

[3] Vibhāshā-lun, end of treatise (No. 1279).

[4] Wu-shih-vibhāshā-lun (No. 1283).

written in Kashmir, was composed, according to the translators into Chinese, by 500 arhats. It is an exposition and discussion of Katyāyanīputra's "Abhidharma-jñāna-prasthāna-śāstra", the short Chinese translation for which is "Fa-chih-lun" (發智論). But the "Abhidharma-ta-vibhāshā-lun" was evidently not composed by the Kanishka Council for, not to mention other matters, it relates a miracle which it says occurred *formerly* in the reign of that king.

The word *vibhāshā* is often rendered in Chinese by Kuang-shuo (廣說), *comprehensive statement*, or Kuang-chie (廣解), *comprehensive explanation*. But more appropriate renderings are chung-chung-shuo (種種說) and fên-fên-shuo (分 | |), meaning *statement by classes or sections.*[1] It denotes properly a commentary or discussion on a canonical text, especially on an Abhidharma treatise.[2] The term, however, seems to have become restricted, by some at least, to the Abhidharma commentaries written by certain masters in Buddhism, chiefly of Kashmir, who attached themselves to the Sarvāstivādin School. These Masters are very often called Vibhāshā-shi (師), but they are also sometimes called by other names such as Kashmir-shi. A vibhāshā must apparently be a commentary on an abhidharma treatise elucidating the text by the opinions of various authorities, and it is not necessary that the author should be bound by the views of the Sarvāstivādins or any other school or sect. There are also, as has been seen, Vinaya-vibhāshās, and these are Commentaries or discussions on Vinaya rules as promulgated by certain disciples or enforced by certain schools.

Yuan-chuang's remarks about the learning brought to the making of the explanatory commentaries on the Tripiṭaka do not appear in the translations. The extent of the commentators' investigations is doubtless overstated, but there is evidence of great study and research in the

---

[1] Yi-ch'ie-ching-yin-yi, *ch.* 17.

[2] Tsa-abhi-hsin-lun, Int. et al. (No. 1287).

"Vibhāshā-lun" and "Abhidharma-mahā vibhāshā-lun". In these books we find an extraordinary acquaintance with Buddhist learning of various kinds, and also with Brahminical learning including the original Indian alphabets, the Vedas and their aṇgas.

It is to the statements made by our pilgrim about Kanishka's Council that we are indebted for nearly all our information about the Council. In later Tibetan books we find mention of it and some particulars about it which do not agree with Yuan-chuang's account.[1] In the Life of Vasubandhu also we read of an assembly meeting in Kapin (Kashmir) 500 years after Buddha's decease.[2] It contained 500 arhats and 500 Bodhisattvas with Katyāyanī-putra as President, the Vice-President being Aśvaghosha. These sages compiled the "Sarvata-Abhidharma" and composed for it a commentary—vibhāshā. When the latter was finished it was written out on stone by Aśvaghosha, and placed under guard, and the king, whose name is not given, forbade the carrying away of any part of the treatise out of the country. This account also does not agree with Yuan-chuang's narrative which must be treated with suspicion as probably containing some grave mistakes. The discovery of the copper plates which he mentions, with the treatises inscribed on them, would help much to make known the Buddhism taught in the schools of Kashmir in or about the first century of our era.

Our pilgrim continues his narrative and tells us of the invasion of Kashmir, and the assassination of its Kritiya usurping sovereign, by the king of the Tokhara country Himatala, in the 600th year after the Buddha's decease. We are told that after Kanishka's death a native dynasty had arisen in Kashmir, and its sovereign had become a persecutor of Buddhism. Hereupon the king of Himatala, who was a Sakya by descent and a zealous Buddhist, determined to drive the cruel Kritiya king from his

---

1 Tār. S. 58 ff., 298.

2 Vasubandhu-chuan (No. 1463); Was. Bud. S. 238 ff.

throne and restore Buddhism. By a stratagem, cunningly devised and skilfully carried out, he succeeded in killing the king of Kashmir. He then banished the chief ministers of the Court, and reinstated Buddhism as the religion of the country, and then returned to his own kingdom. But, the pilgrim adds, in the course of time the Kritiyas, who still hated the Buddhists and bore them grudges, regained the sovereignty and at Yuan-chuang's time the country had no faith in Buddhism and gave itself up to other sects.

The Himatala of this passage is a country of which we have some account in the XII$^{th}$ *chuan* (Book) of these Records, and it will meet us again.

The pilgrim now proceeds to mention some of the noteworthy sacred objects connected with Buddhism in this district, and he begins with a Monastery containing above 300 Brethren, and at it a tope built for a Tooth-relic of the Buddha. These buildings, he tells us, were situated on the south side of a mountain to the north of the old capital, and above ten *li* south-east from the new capital. The tooth, brought from India, was preserved in the tope, and Yuan-chuang describes its size and colour. We have also the legend of the acquisition of this relic by a persecuted monk of the country who had gone to India on a pilgrimage.

The Tooth-relic here mentioned was not allowed to remain in Kashmir and was carried away a few years after Yuan-chuang's visit by the great king Śilāditya.[1]

Our pilgrim goes on to describe that about fourteen *li* (about three miles) to the south of the Monastery at the Tooth-tope was a small Monastery which contained a standing image of the P'usa Kuan-tzŭ-tsai (Kuan-yin P'usa). To importunate earnest worshippers this P'usa occasionally caused his golden body to emerge from the image.

On a mountain above thirty *li* south-east from this were the ruins of a fine large old monastery. At the time of the pilgrim's visit, he tells us, only a two-storey building in one corner of it was inhabited, and this contained thirty Brethren who were all students of the Mahāyāna system. It was in this monastery

---

[1] There was a sacred tooth in Kashmir in Baron Hügel's time. The Brahmins of Báramulla, in whose keeping it was, declared that the tooth was that of an ancient jin, but Hügel says it was an elephant's tooth "and of no great age to judge from its appearance."

that the Śāstra-master Sanghabhadra composed the "Shun-chêng-li-lun (順正理論)." To the right and left of the monastery were topes to great arhats, and the relics of these were all still in existence. Hither monkeys and other wild animals brought flowers as offerings of worship, and they did this regularly as if acting under instructions. Many other strange things occurred on this mountain. Thus a wall of rock would be split across and footprints of horses would be left on the top of the mountain. But the latter were deceptive, being tracings made by the arhats and their novices when out on parties of pleasure; such traces left by them as they rode to and fro were too numerous to mention. Above ten *li* east of the Buddha-tooth monastery in the steep side of the northern mountain stood a small monastery. Here the great Śāstra-Master *So-kan-ti-lo* (索建地羅) or Skandhila, composed the "*Chung-shih-fên-p'i-p'o-sha-lun*" (衆事分毘般沙論).

The Śāstra-master Sanghabhadra will come before us again in chapter X. The treatise here mentioned by the name "Chung-shih-fên-p'i-p'o-sha (vibhāshā)-lun" does not seem to be known to the Buddhist canon, at least it is not in the existing catalogues or collections. It was apparently a vibhāshā or disquisition on Vasumitra's treatise already mentioned the "Chung-shih-fên-abhidharma-lun" called also the "Abhidharma-p'in-lei-tsu-lun", the Sanskrit original for which is given as "Abhidharma-prakaraṇa-pāda-śāstra" (Bun. No. 1292). Julien suggests "Vibhāshā-prakaraṇa-pāda as possibly the original title of Skandhila's treatise. This Śāstra-master, also styled "Arhat", of whom very little seems to be known, was also the author of the short but interesting treatise entitled "Shuo-i-ch'ie-yu-ju-abhidharma-lun". But the characters for *Shuo-i-ch'ie-yu* meaning "Sarvāstivādin" are generally omitted and the work is known by its short name "Ju-abhidharma-lun" which is in Sanskrit, according to B. Nanjio, "Abhidharmāvatāra-śāstra". This retranslation of the title, however, may possibly not be the correct one. The book is an introduction or *entrance* (*Ju* 入) to the study of the Abhidharma, and its original title may have been something like "Abhidharmapraveśana-śāstra". It is to our pilgrim that we are indebted for the Chinese translation of this little treatise.[1]

Within the grounds of this little monastery, the pilgrim tells us, was a stone tope over the bodily relics of an ancient arhat. This arhat, who has been referred to already, had been a very large man with the appetite of an elephant: so the people of the time jeered at him as a glutton without a conscience. When the time for his passing away was near he said one day to the people—"I am soon to take the remainderless [to die]; I wish to explain to you the excellent state to which I have personally attained". But the people only jeered the more, and collected together to see what would befall. The arhat then addressed them thus—"I will now tell you the causal connection of my past and present states. In my last existence before this one I had through previous karma the body of an elephant in the stable of a raja of East-India. While I was there a Buddhist monk from Kashmir came to travel in India in search of sacred books. The raja gave me to the monk to carry his books home, and when I reached this country I died suddenly. As a result of my merit from carrying the sacred books I was next born as a human being, and then enjoying the residue of my good fortune I became a Buddhist monk in early life." The arhat goes on to tell the people how he assiduously sought and at length obtained spiritual perfection. The only survival from his former bodily existence was his elephantine appetite, and by the exercise of self-restraint he had reduced his daily food by two-thirds. Finally in the presence of the scoffing and unbelieving spectators he rose in the air and there, in the smoke and blazes of a burning ecstasy, he went into final extinction, and a tope was erected over the relics which fell to the earth.

The story here related bears considerable resemblance to a story told in the Mahā-vibhāshā-śāstra. There a she-elephant named *Mo-t'u* (or *-ch'a*) carries relics of the Buddha from a foreign country to Kashmir where she dies; she is then re-born as a male child and becoming a bhikshu attains arhatship. But the arhat retains the elephant's appetite and requires a *hu* (bushel) of food every day. When he is about to pass away he proposes to explain to certain nuns his "superior condition" but

---

[1] This treatise is Bun. No. 1291. In the name of the author the first syllable is Sa (塞) instead of the So of our text.

they only jeer at him. Then he tells them his history, and so explains his great appetite, which he says he had moderated, reducing his daily food from a bushel and a half to a bushel *per diem.*[1] The reader will remember that Uttarasena brought his share of the Buddha's relics home on an elephant, and that the elephant died on reaching a place not many miles from the capital of Udyāna.

The pilgrim goes on to relate that at a distance of above 200 *li* north-west from the capital was the monastery of the *Shang-lin*, that is perhaps, Merchant's-wood. Here the Śāstra-Master *Pu-la-na* (Pūrṇa) composed an "expository vibhāshā-*lun*" (釋鞞般沙論). To the west of the capital 140 or 150 *li* north of a large river and adjoining the south side of a hill was a Mahāsaṅgika Monastery with above 100 inmates. Here the Śāstra-Master *Fo-ti-lo* composed the "Chi-chên-lun" of the Mahāsaṅgika School.

By the words here rendered "expository vibhāshā-lun" the pilgrim probably only intended to describe the character of the śāstra. not to give the name of the treatise written by Pūrṇa. There does not seem to be any work by this author in existing catalogues and collections of Chinese translations of Buddhist works, and we cannot be certain who is the Pūrṇa here mentioned. A book already mentioned, No. 1282 in Mr Bun. Nanjio's Catalogue, is referred by one authority to a Pūrṇa as its author.

The name of the other Śāstra-Master of this passage, *Fo-ti-lo* Julien thinks may be for Bodhila. In a note to the text the word is explained as meaning "Bodhi-taking". But nothing seems to be known either about the man, or the "Chi-chên-lun" which he composed.

It is worthy of notice that none of the Buddhist monasteries in Kashmir mentioned by Yuan-chuang seem to have been known to other pilgrims and writers; and that Buddhist establishments at or near the capital, and in other parts of the country, mentioned by other authorities were apparently unknown to Yuan-chuang, although they were evidently in existence at the time of his visit. Some

---

[1] Abhi-ta-vib., *ch.* 42.

of the vihāras in Kashmir mentioned in Wu-k'ung's Itinerary were evidently of a date subsequent to that of our pilgrim, but several were much older. Then the pilgrim Süan-hui, already mentioned, visited the monastery of the Dragon-Tank Mountain where the 500 arhats were worshipped, and this monastery does not seem to have been known to our pilgrim. The reader will have noted also that Yuan-chuang when giving the numbers of the Monasteries and Brethren in Kashmir does not tell to which "Vehicle" the Brethren were attached. But we know from other sources that they were mainly Hīnayānists of the Sarvāstivādin School, although as we learn from the Records and Life there were also Mahāyānists. At the capital the Brethren of the two "Vehicles" seem to have been living together, and the greatest among them, *Ch'êng* (or Yaśa?) was evidently a Hīnayānist. The other Brethren mentioned in the Life are Visuddhasimha and Jinabandhu who were Mahāyānists, Suga-(ta-)mitra and Vasumitra who were Sarvastivādins, and Suryadeva and Jinatrāta who were Mahāsangikas.

## PAN-NU-TS'O.

From this (that is perhaps, the vicinity of the capital of Kashmir) the pilgrim travelled, he tells us, through a difficult mountainous district south-west for above 700 *li* to the *Pan-nu-ts'o* country. This region he describes as being above 2000 *li* in circuit, as abounding in hills and mountain valleys, with narrow areas of cultivation. The country yielded grain and flowers; sugar-cane and fruits, except grapes, abounded. The country produced the mango, the fig (here called the udumbara), and the plaintain, and these trees were grown in orchards near the dwelling-houses. The climate was hot, the people were daring and straight-forward, they wore chiefly cotton clothing, and they were sincere believers in Buddhism. The Buddhist monasteries, of which there were five, were in a ruinous condition, and the country was a dependency of Kashmir. In a monastery to the north of the capital were a few Brethren, and to the north of this was a wonder-working tope made of stone.

The *Pan-nu-ts'o* of this passage has been identified with the modern Punach, or Punats as the Kashmiris call it according to Cunningham.[1] Instead of 2000 *li* as the circuit of the country given in some texts of the Records the old reading was 1000 *li*, and this agrees with Cunningham's statement of the size of the district. In some old texts of the Life the name is given as *Pan-nu-nu-tso* (半笯奴嗟) in which the second *nu* may be due to a copyist's carelessness, this character being one of the two characters given to indicate the sound of *nu* 笯.

## RĀJAPURA.

> Our pilgrim goes on to relate that from Punach a journey south-east of above 400 *li* brought him to the *Ho-lo-she-pu-lo* (Rājapura) country. This he describes as being above 4000 *li* in circuit its capital being above ten *li* in circuit. It was a difficult country to travel in as it was very hilly with narrow valleys; it was not fertile and it resembled Punach in products and climate, and like that country it had no sovereign of its own and was subject to Kashmir. There were ten Buddhist monasteries and the Brethren were few in number; there was one Deva-Temple, but the non-Buddhists were very numerous.

The native annotator to our text here makes Rājapura to be in "North India", but the annotator to the Fang-chih represents it as a state outside of India. The country has been identified by Cunningham with "the petty chiefship of Rajaori, to the south of Kashmir".[2] In some texts of the Life the direction of Rājapura from Punach is south instead of the south-east of our text.

Here our pilgrim inserts the following interesting general observation about the countries through which he had lately been passing—

> "From Lampa to Rājapura the inhabitants are coarse and plain in personal appearance, of rude violent dispositions, with vulgar dialects, and of scant courtesy and little fairness; they do not belong to India proper but are inferior peoples of frontier (i. e. barbarian) stocks."

As to this statement we may observe that the native editor of the Records has referred all these countries from

---

[1] A. G. I. p. 128.

[2] A. G. I. p. 129.

Lampa to Rājapura to "North India". Moreover our pilgrim's remarks at the beginning of *Chuan II* seem to indicate that he regarded all these countries as being included in the great region called India. There, however, he was writing as a foreigner, and here he is writing from the point of view of a Indian. The summary character which he here gives of the inhabitants of these countries is not to be fully accepted, and it does not seem to agree with his own descriptions in the preceding pages.

## CHAPTER IX.

### (CHUAN IV.)

## CHÊH-KA (ṬAKKA?) TO MATHURĀ.

From Rājapur the pilgrim proceeded south-east down a hill and across a river 700 *li* to the *Cheh-ka* country. This was above 10 000 *li* in circuit; it lay between the *P'i-po-she* (Bibas) river on the east and the Indus on the west; the capital was above 20 *li* in circuit. The crops of the country were upland rice and spring wheat; it yielded gold, silver, bell-metal (*t'u-shih*), copper, and iron; the climate was hot with much violent wind; the inhabitants had rude bad ways and a low vulgar speech; they wore glossy white clothing made of silk, muslin &c.; few of them believed in Buddhism, and most served the Devas; there were ten Buddhist monasteries, and some hundreds of Deva-Temples. On from this country there were numerous Puṇyasāl's or free rest-houses for the relief of the needy, and distressed; at these houses medicine and food were distributed and so travellers having their bodily wants supplied, did not experience inconvenience.

In the Life we are told that our pilgrim on leaving Rājapur went south-east, and after a journey of two (or three) days crossed the Chandrabhaga (Chenāb) river to the city of Jayapur. Here he spent a night in a non-Buddhist monastery outside the west gate of the city. From this he went on to Śākala in the *Cheh-kal* (in one text *Li-ka*) country, from that to the city Narasimha, and thence eastward to a palāśa wood. Here he had an encounter with brigands and narrowly escaped with his life. From the village beyond this wood he resumed his journey and reached the eastern part of the *Cheh-ka* country. Here he found a large city, and in a mango grove west of it lived a brahmin 700 years old, looking like a man of thirty years, and having all his mental and bodily powers. He had been a disciple of the great Nāgārjuna, and he was well acquainted with the sacred lore of Brahmins and Buddhists. With him Yuan-chuang seems to have studied the "Pai-lun" and the "Kuang-pai-lun", the latter of which our pilgrim afterwards translated.

The clause in the above passage from the Records rendered "they wore glossy-white clothing made of silk, muslin, &c." is in the original *yi-fu-hsien-pai-so-wei-kiao-she-ye-yi-chao-hsia-yi* (衣服鮮白所謂憍奢耶衣朝霞衣等). This is translated by Julien "Ils s'habillent avec des étoffes d'une blancheur éclatante qu'on appelle *Kiao-che-ye* (Kaûçeya-soie), et portent des vêtements rouges comme le soleil levant, &c." But Kauśeya, with which we have met already, and *chao-hsia* are the materials of the white garments worn by the people. The words *chao-hsia-yi* cannot possibly be made to mean "et portent des vêtements rouges comme le soleil levant". *Chao-hsia* denotes the *light vapours of dawn*, the *eastern glow which heralds sunrise*. But it is the name given by the Chinese Buddhist pilgrims and writers to certain fine transparent fabrics which they found in India and other foreign countries. Thus the dancing girls of Fu-nan are described as "using *chao-hsia* for clothing". This material was a very fine white gauze or muslin capable of being dyed; it was soft and transparent like the fleecy vapours of dawn. The images of the P'usas, and other Buddhist worthies, were often made to represent these beings as wearing *chao-hsia-chün* or skirts of transparent material. Such koa vestments may be seen on many of the Buddhist figures found in India and depicted in books. But *chao-hsia* as an article of clothing was evidently a kind of muslin simply fine and light.[1]

---

[1] See the "T'ang-Shu, *ch.* 22, 197 et al.; Fo-shuo-t'ê-lo-ni-ching, *ch.* 2 (No. 363, tr. 653). Cf.—

"And the far up clouds resemble
Veils of gauze most clear and white."

Further, in this passage we have the sentence beginning with—"On from this country there were numerous Puṇyaśālas". For this the original is *tzŭ-kuo-yi-wang-to-yu-fu-she* (此國已往多有福舍). Julien translates the whole sentence thus—"Il y avait jadis, dans ce royaume, une multitude de maisons de bienfaisance (Pounyaçālās), où l'on secourait les pauvres et les malheureux. Tantôt on y distribuait des médicaments, tantôt de la nourriture. Grâce à cette resource les voyageurs ne se trouvaient jamais dans l'embarras". This rendering quite spoils the author's statement which is to the effect that at the time of his travels Rest-houses, at which food and medicine were distributed gratis, abounded in Cheh-ka and the countries of India about to be noticed. These Rest-houses or *Fu-she* are called Puṇyaśālas in *Chuan XII*, but in the account of the present country the Life calls them Dharmaśālas. This latter word, in Pali Dhammaśāla, is the name given to the Hall for preaching, but it seems to be also used to designate the free Rest-houses.

On his way to the capital of this country (which was probably also called Cheh-ka) and about fourteen *li* south-west from it Yuan-chuang came to the old capital called Śākala. Some centuries previously a king named Mo-hi-lo-ku-lo (Mahirakula), who had his seat of government at this city, ruled over the Indians. He was a bold intrepid man of great ability and all the neighbouring states were his vassals. Wishing to apply his leisure to the study of Buddhism, he ordered the clergy of this country to recommend a Brother of eminent merit to be his teacher. But the clergy found difficulty in obeying the command, the apathetic among them not seeking notoriety, and those of great learning and high intelligence fearing stern majesty. Now at this time there was an old servant of the king's household who had been a monk for a long time. Being clear and elegant in discourse and glib in talking, this man was selected by the congregation of Brethren to comply with the royal summons. This insulting procedure enraged the king who forthwith ordered the utter extermination of the Buddhist church throughout all his dominions. Now the king of Magadha at this time, Bālāditya by name, was a just and benevolent ruler and a zealous Buddhist and he rebelled against the order for the persecution of Buddhists. When Mahirakula proceeded to invade the territory of Bālāditya to reduce him to obedience the latter accompanied by several myriads of his subjects withdrew to an island. Mahirakula came in pursuit but he was taken prisoner. On the petition of Bālāditya's mother the prisoner was set free and allowed to go away. His younger brother having taken possession of the throne he took refuge in Kashmir, and here he repaid hospitality by treachery, and having murdered the King he made himself ruler. Then he renewed his project of exterminating Buddhism, and with this view he caused the demolition of 1600 topes and monasteries, and put to death nine koṭis of lay adherents of Buddhism. His career was cut short by his sudden death, and the air was darkened, and the earth quaked, and fierce winds rushed forth as he went down to the Hell of unceasing torment.

This passage reads like a romance founded on a basis of fact. The Mahirakula of our pilgrim has been identified with king Mihirakula of Kashmir, and his king Bālāditya of Magadha is supposed to be possibly the Nara Bālāditya of coins.[1] But there are difficulties in the way of accepting these identifications. There is first the difference in the forms Mahirakula and Mihirakula, but this is perhaps unimportant and need not be further noticed. The form Mahirakula seems to be confined to the pilgrim, and he may have used it to suit his erroneous rendering of the name by *Ja-tsu* or "Great Clan". But the Mihirakula of the Inscriptions began his reign in A. D. 515, while the king of whom Yuan-chuang tells lived "some centuries" before the pilgrim's time. Other authorities also seem to place Mikirakula at a date much before A. D. 515. Thus in the "Lien-hua-mien-ching" or "the sūtra of Lotus-flower-face" Mihirakula, a reincarnation of the Lotus-flower-face arhat, appears as the King who exterminates Buddhism in Kapin (Kashmir) and breaks the Buddha's bowl.[2] This sūtra must have been composed some time before A. D. 574 the date of its translation (according to one account), and the contents seem to indicate that it was

1 See Mr. Fleet on Mihirakula in Ind. Ant. Vol. XV p. 245 f., and the correspondence at p. 346 f.: J. R. A. S. Vol. XXI p. 114—5: J. P. T. S. 1896 p.p. 87, 110: Lawrence's Valley of Kashmir p. 185.

2 Lien-hua-mien-ching *ch.* 2 ((No. 465).

written long after the death of Mihirakula. It relates that after this event seven deva-putras became incarnate in succession in Kashmir, and that they restored Buddhism. The meaning of this evidently is that the king was succeeded by seven sovereigns who were all patrons of Buddhism. Then in the "Fu-fa-tsang-yin-yuan-ching", translated A.D.472, a persecuting king called *Mi-lo-ku* (彌羅崛), that is evidently Mihirakula, destroys the Buddhist sacred buildings and slaughters the Brethren in Kapin (Kashmir).[1] He beheads the 23rd, and last (according to this work), of the great Buddhist Patriarchs, by name Shih-tzu (師子) that is, Simha. This last event according to the "Chih-yue-lu" occurred in A. D. 259.[2] No authority is given for this date and it is not to be implicitly accepted, but it is interesting to note that the Rājatarangini makes twelve reigns intervene between Kanishka and Mihirakula. If we allow an average of 15 years for these reigns we get A.D. 80 + 180 or A.D. 260 for the accession of Mihirakula.

The Life and Records leave the situation of the ruined city of Sākala rather uncertain. The latter work tells us that this city was 14 or 15 *li* south-west from the new capital, of the situation of which, however, we are not told anything. In the Life Sākala is three (or four) days' journey or about 300 *li* (about 60 miles) south-east from Rājapur and on the east side of the Chenāl. Then the *old capital* of the Records does not appear in the Life which on the other hand mentions a large city on the eastern confines of Che-Ka and this city does not appear in the Records. Cunningham, against both the Life and the Records, places Sākala about 120 miles to the *south-west* of Rājapur. He identifies Yuan-chuang's Cheh-ka (or Tsekia), as name of a city, with "the ruins of a large town, called *Asarur* which accord almost exactly with the pilgrim's description of the new town of Tsekia". This Asarur is "exactly 112 miles distant from Rajaori (Rājapur) in a direct line

[1] Fu-fa-tsang-yin-yuan-ching, *ch.* 6 (No. 1340).

[2] Chi-yue-lu, *ch.* 3.

drawn on the map", that is, 112 miles to the south-west of Rājapur. But it is very evident that Yuan-chuangs journey from the latter to the capital of Cheh-Ka was a zig-zag one always, however, tending eastward, and Asarur cannot be the pilgrim's capital of that country.

In Sākala was a Buddhist monastery with above 100 Brethren all adherents of the Hinayāna system. In this Monastery P'usa Vasubandhu composed the "Shêng-yi-t'i-lun" (勝義諦論). A tope beside this monastery marked a place where the Four Past Buddhas had preached, and there were footprints where they had walked up and down.

The śāstra here ascribed to Vasubandhu does not seem to be known to the Buddhist collections. Julien restores the Sanskrit name as "Paramārtha satya śāstra", but this is only a probable conjecture.

The *Cheh-ka* (磔迦) of this passage is *Lih* (礫)-*ka* in one text of the Life, and this latter form is found in other works. It is possible that the original for both transcriptions was a word like Ṭikka or Ṭekka, *ch* and *l* sounds being both used to represent the *ṭ* of Sanskrit. The term in our text has been restored as Tchēka, Ṭakka and Ṭaki. It designated a country which was not in India, but was one of the foreign states which lay between Lampa and India, and should have been included in the pilgrim's general survey at the end of the last *chuan.*[1]

## CHI-NA-P'UH-TI.

From the Che-ka (or Tekka) district Yuan-chuang continued his journey going eastward for above 500 *li* and came to the country which he calls *Chi-na-p'uh-ti* (至那僕底). This district was above 2000 *li* and its capital 14 or 15 *li* in circuit: it produced good crops of grain but did not abound in trees: the inhabitants had settled occupations and the national revenue was abundant: the climate was warm and the inhabitants had feeble timid ways. The learning of the people embraced Buddhism and secular knowledge, and orthodoxy and heterodoxy had each its adherents. There were ten Buddhist monasteries and nine Deva-Temples.

---

[1] For this country see A. G. I. p. 179.

The Chinese annotator here has translated the name of the country by *Han-fêng* (漢 封), and Julien, who reads the characters of the name as *Tchi-na-po-ti* gives the Sanskrit original as "Tchīnapati", meaning "Lord of China". But Han-fêng means *China-fief* not *China-lord*, and the characters for *p'uh-ti* cannot be taken to represent *pati*. They evidently stand for *bhukti* which is translated by *fêng* in the sense of *possession, portion.*[1] So China-bhukti is the China-allotment, and the China-bhukti-deśa was the district assigned to China, that is to the China hostage according to Yuan-chuang's story.

One of the ten monasteries here mentioned was, according to the Life, called *T'u-she-sa-na*, which perhaps stands for Toshāsan meaning "Pleasure-giving". This monastery was apparently at the capital, and Yuan-chuang found in it a monk eminent for learning and piety. The name of this monk was Vinītaprabha, and he was the son of an Indian prince. This monk was the author of two commentaries on Abhidharma works, and Yuang-chuang remained here fourteen months studying with him various Abhidharma treatises.

Going back to the narrative in the Records we have the pilgrim's explanation how the name China-bhukti came to be given to this region.

> When Kanishka was reigning the fear of his name spread to many regions so far even as to the outlying vassals of China to the west of the Yellow River. One of these vassal states being in fear sent a hostage to the court of king Kanishka, (the hostage being apparently a son of the ruler of the state). The king treated the hostage with great kindness and consideration, allowing him a separate residence for each of the three seasons and providing him with a guard of the four kinds of soldiers. This district was assigned as the winter residence of the hostage and hence it was called Chinabhukti. The pilgrim proceeds to relate how Peaches and Pears were unknown in this district and the parts of India beyond until they were introduced by the "China

---

[1] Sanskrit-Chinese Vocabulary. In the C text of the Life instead of *-p'u* we have *-kin* (僅), but this may be only a copyist's mistake.

hostage". Hence, he tells us, peaches were called "Chināni" and pears were called "China-rājaputra".

The Sanskrit names here given for the peach and the pear seem to be known only from this narrative. Later authorities tell us that these fruits are indigenous in the country, and the whole story of the hostage is possibly an invention. One Sanskrit name for the peach is given in a glossary as *āru* and this name is still in use: and a name for the pear is given as *tanasa* but this word does not seem to be known. Further the "Chīna" known to the people of India before the arrival of Chinese pilgrims and afterwards was apparently not the "Flowery Middle Country", but rather a region occupied by a tribe living to the west of the Chinese empire, far west of the Yellow River. This "Chīna" was watered by the rivers Sita and Chakshu and it was one of the countries in the north-east. The name was afterwards extended to the "Flowery Land" apparently by the Buddhist writers and translators of India and Kashmir. Our pilgrim tells his readers that the people of Chinabhukti had great respect for the "East Land" and that pointing to him they said one to another — "He is a man of the country of our former king".

Cunningham thinks that the capital of this country may be represented by the present Patti, "a large and very old town situated 27 miles to the north-east of Kasūr and 10 miles to the west of the Biās river".[1] But notwithstanding the presence of the ubiquitous brick-bats and old wells, this proposed identification need not be seriously considered. It is not at all probable that the name Chinabhukti was ever generally known or used for the district to which it is applied by the pilgrim. He seems indeed to be the only authority for the name. Not only so but a copyist's error in transcribing it has unfortunately been perpetuated. In the Life, and in one place in the old texts of the Records, the first syllable of the word was left out by mistake. It was evidently this mistake

[1] A. G. I. p. 200.

which led to the use of *Na-p'uh-ti* instead of *Chi-na-p'uh-ti* as the name for the country next to Ṭekka in the Fang-chih and in maps and treatises of later times.

## TAMASĀVANA.

**From the capital of Chinabhukti the pilgrim went south-east above 500 *li* to the *Ta-mo-su-fa-na* (Tamasāvana) Monastery. This had above 300 Brethren of the Sarvāstivādin School who led strict pure lives and were thorough students of the Hinayāna. Here each of the 1000 Buddhas of the Bhadrakalpa assembles a congregation of devas and men and preaches the profound excellent Religion. Here also in the 300th year after Sakyamuni Buddha's nirvāṇa the Śāstramaster *Ka-to-yen-na* composed his "Fa-chih-lun". This monastery had an Asoka tope above 200 feet high beside which were the spots on which the Four Past Buddhas had sat and walked up and down. Small topes and large caves in unknown number succeeded each other closely, all having relics of arhats who since the beginning of this kalpa here passed away for ever. Surrounding the Hill-Monastery for a circuit of twenty *li* were hundreds and thousands of Buddha-relic topes very close together.**

In the Life the distance from the capital of Chinabhukti to the Tamasāvana monastery in 50 *li* or only one tenth of the distance here given. Our pilgrim's *Ta-mo-su-fa-na* is undoubtedly the Tamasāvana (or Tāmasavana) or "Darkness-wood" of other authors. This was apparently the name both of the monastery and of the district in which it was situated. The monastery must have been at an early date a noted seat of Buddhism as Brethren from it were among the great Doctors invited by king Asoka to his Council. The description of the summoning of this Council is given in several treatises from one original apparently. It is interesting to note the agreement and difference of these treatises in the matter of the Tamasāvana. In the Divyāvadāna the reading is "Tamasāvane" and the A-yü-wang-ching in agreement with this has *An-lin* or "Darkness-wood", the interpretation given by our pilgrim. But the Tsa-a-han-ching instead of Tamasāvana has *To-p'o-p'oh* which is evidently for Tapova, the original being probably Tapovana. In the A-yü-wang-chuan the "dhirās Tamasāvane" is rendered by *Chou-ye-wu-wei* lit. "day-night fearless", that is, the brave of the Day-night.[1] The phrase in ordinary Chinese would mean "day and night without fear", but here the term *chou-ye* is used in the sense of "the darkness of day". It corresponds to the *chow-an* or "Day-darkness" of another treatise and both terms evidently stand for Tamasā.[2]

With reference to this Monastery we read that the Buddha accompanied by the faithful yaksha Vajrapāṇi passed over a dark green wood on his way through the air to convert the Dragon-king Apalāla. Addressing the Yaksha Buddha prophecied that in that place 100 years after his decease a vihāra would be erected to be called "Darkness-wood" which should be preeminent for absorbed meditation.[3]

The Śāstra-master here called *Ka-to-yen-na* (Katyāyana) was Kātyāyanīputra, and his śāstra here mentioned exists in two Chinese translations one of which is by our pilgrim.[4]

For the words in the text here interpreted as meaning—"Surrounding the Hill-monastery for a circuit of twenty *li* were hundreds and thousands of Buddha-relic topes very close together", Julien has— "Les couvents, qui s'élèvent tout autour de la montagne, occupent un circuit de vingt li. On compte par centaines et par milliers les *stoupas* qui renferment des *che-li* (Çariras-reliques) du Bouddha. Ils sont très-rapprochés et confondent mutuellement leur ombre". This rendering seems to be inadmissible and to give a meaning very different from what the author intended to convey. Yuan-chuang does not make the absurd statement that there were Buddhist monasteries for twenty *li* all round a hill, but he tells us that there were thousands of relic-topes all round the "Hill monastery". The "Hill

---

[1] Divyāv. p. 399: A-yü-wang-ching, *ch.* 3: Isa-a-han-ching, *ch.* 23: A-yü-wang-chuan *ch.* 1 (chou-ye-wu-wei 晝夜無畏).

[2] Ta-chuang-yen-lun, *ch.* 5 (No. 1182), *chow-an* 晝闇.

[3] Sar. Vin. Yao-shih, *ch.* 9.

[4] Bun. No. 1273, 1275.

monastery" was the Tamasāvana; and it was so called by the pilgrim because it was isolated, and not subject to a superior establishment. This use of the word *shan* (山) in the senses of *wild, independent, rustic* is very common, and the phrase *shan-ka-lan* meets us again in these Records. The monastery Tamasāvana as our pilgrim describes it was a spacious comprehensive establishment. It had accommodation for 300 Brethren: it contained a tope and sacred places of the Buddhas, and the caves and memorial topes of numerous deceased arhats; and then all round it for twenty *li* were many thousand Buddha-relic topes. In other treatises the establishment is called a *Wood* or *Hill*, and it was evidently different in character from ordinary vihāras.

## SHÊ-LAN-TA-LO (JĀLANDHARA).

From Tamasāvana a journey of obout 140 *li* north-east brought the pilgrim to the *She-lan-ta-lo* (Jālandhara) country. This country was above 1000 *li* east to west and 800 *li* north to south, and its capital was twelve or thirten *li* in circuit. The region yielded much upland rice with other grain, trees were widely spread, and fruits and flowers abounded; the climate was warm; the people had truculent ways and a mean contemptible appearance, but they were in affluent circumstances. There were above 50 Monasteries with more than 2000 Brethren who made special studies in the Great and Little Vehicles. There were three Deva-Temples with more than 500 professed non-Buddhists of the Paśupata sect. A former king of this country had been a patron of non-Buddhistic systems; afterwards he met an arhat and learning Buddhism from him became a realous believer. Thereupon the king of "Mid-India" appreciating his sincere faith gave him sole control of matters relating to Buddhism in all India. In this capacity (as Protector of the Faith) the king of Jālandhara rewarded and punished the monks without distinction of persons and without private feeling. He also travelled through all India and erected topes or monasteries at all sacred places.

The *She-lan-ta-lo* of this passage was long ago restored as Jālandhara, the name of a city and district in the north of the Panjab.[1] But it may be noted that the Life here

---

[1] A. G. I. p. 136.

and the Fang-chih have *She-lan-ta-na* as if for Jālandhana[1]; in another passage the Life has *She-lan-ta*, and this is the form of the name used by I-ching[2]. In the Sung pilgrim's itinerary the name is given Tso-lan-t'o-la (左攔陀羅) that is, Jālandhana[3].

Of the 50 Monasteries here mentioned one was doubtless the Nagaradhana vihāra mentioned in the Life. In it Yuan-chuang found the learned Brother named Chandravarma with whom he spent four months studying the "Chung-shih-fên-vibhāshā", or Commentary on the "Chung-shih-fên-Abhidharma-lun" already noticed.

Our pilgrim, it will be noticed, represents the Brethren in this district as "making special studies in the Mahāyāna and Hīnayāna". His words are *ta-hsiao-ērh-shêng-chuan-mên-hsi-hsio* (大小二乘專門習學). These words are translated by Julien— "que l'étude particulière du *grand* et du *petit Vehicule* partage en deux classes distinctes". This is a very unhappy rendering and the interpolation of the words "partage en deux classes distinctes" is unwarranted and spoils the author's statement. What he wished us to unterstand was that the Brethren in the various Monasteries devoted themselves as they pleased to particular lines of study in the Mahāyānist and Hīnayānist books.

According to the Life our pilgrim revisited Jālandhara, and on that occasion was well treated by the king of "North-India" who had his seat of government in the city with this name. The king is called Wu-ti or Wu-ti-to (烏地多) restored as Udito. It was evidently the same king who treated courteously, and entertained hospitably, another Chinese pilgrim whose name was *Hsüan-chao* (玄照)[4] whom we have met already.

---

1 Life *ch.* 5 and J. I. p. 260—1.

2 Hsi-yü-ch'iu, *ch.* 1 and Chavannes Mémoires pp. 14, 15 and notes.

3 Ma I. 1., *ch.* 338.

4 Hsi-yü-ch'iu l. c.

# KU-LU-TO.

From Jālandhara the pilgrim travelled north-east, across mountains and ravines, by hazardous paths, for above 700 *li*, and came to the country which he calls *Kulto*. This region, which was above 3000 *li* in circuit, was entirely surrounded by mountains. Its capital was 14 or 15 *li* in circuit. It had a rich soil and yielded regular crops, and it had a rich vegetation abounding in fruits and flowers. As it was close to the Snow Mountains it had a great quantity of valuable medicines. It yielded gold, silver, red copper, crystal lenses and bell-metal (*teu-shih*). The climate grew gradually cold and there was little frost or snow. There were in the country twenty Buddhist Monasteries with above 1000 Brethren of whom the most were Mahāyānists, a few adhering to the Schools (that is, belonging to the Hīnayāna system). Of Deva-Temples there were fifteen and the professed non-Buddhists lived pell-mell. On both sides of the steep mountain-passes were caves [which had been] the lodging-places of arhats and rishis. In this country was a tope erected by Asoka to mark the place at which the Buddha on his visit to the district had preached and received members into his church.

In the statement here made about the climate of the country the words "grew gradually cold" are in the original *chien-han* (漸寒). This is the reading of the A and C texts, but the B and D texts instead of *chien* have *yü* (逾) meaning, *passing*, *excessive*, which is manifestly wrong. The latter was the reading of Julien's text, and as it did not suit the words which follow— "there was little (*wei* 微) frost or snow", he decided to substitute *chêng* (徵) for the *wei* of his text. He then translates— "il tombe souvent du givre et de la neige". But this violent alteration seems to be unnecessary, and *wei* is the reading of all the texts.

In the Fang-chih the name of this country is given as *Ku-lu-to-lo* and also *Ku-lu-lo*. Cunningham considers that the distance and bearing of the district from Jālandhara correspond "exactly with the position of *Kullu*, in the upper valley of the Byas river", and he regards it as the Kulūtā of other writers[1]. This latter term is the name

---

[1] 'Ancient Geography of India' p. 142.

of a country in the north-west division of the Brihat Samhita[1]. As the Sanskrit word *kula* means, along with other things a *heap* or *collection* the *Ku-lu-to* country is perhaps the *Chi-chi* (積 集) or "Accumulation" district of the Sarvata Vinaya. Buddha there goes from the Tamasāvana to the Chi-chi district where he converts and receives into his church a Yakṣha who afterwards builds a monastery. The district also obtained a relic of the Buddha's body for which a tope was built called the *Chi-chi* Tope[2].

The pilgrim now tells us of two countries which he did not visit. Going north, he writes, from Kuluto for above 1800 *li* you come to the *Ko-hu-lo* country: still farther north above 2000 *li* was the *Mo-lo-so* (or-*sha*) country, the roads being very bad and cold.

Cunningham regards the Lo-hu-lo of this passage as "clearly the *Lho-yul* of the Tibetans and the Lāhul of the people of Kullu and other neighbouring states". The pilgrim's Mo-lo-so, Cunningham says— "must certainly be Ladāk." He regards the *so* of the name as a mistake for *p'o*, and Mo-lo-p'o, he says, would give us Mar-po "the actual name of the province of Ladāk". A note to our Chinese text here tells us that another name for Mo-lo-so was *San-p'o-ha*. The two countries here mentioned were of course outside of India.

## SHE-TO-T'U-LU.

From Kuluto the pilgrim travelled south, over a high mountain and across a great river, for above 700 *li*, and reached the country called *She-to-t'u-lu*. This was above 2000 *li* in circuit, bounded on the west by a large river (supposed to be the Sutlej), and its capital was 17 or 18 *li* in circuit. It was an a agricultural and fruit-producing country, and yielded much gold, silver, and other precious substances. The inhabitants were in good circumstances and led moral lives, observing social distinctione and adhering devoutly to Buddhism. In and about the capital were ten monasteries, but they were desolate, and the Brethren were very few. Abont three *li* to the south-east of the capital was an Asoka

---

1 Ind. Ant. Vol. XXII. p. 182.
2 Sar. Vin. Yao-shih, *ch.* 9.

tope above 200 feet high, and beside it were traces of spots on which the Four Past Buddhas had sat and walked up and down.

Nothing seems to be known of the country and city here described, and the suggestions for identification requiring some tampering with the text are not of much value[1]. The restoration of the name as Śatadru has been generally accepted, but the transcription seems to require rather Śatadure, and this is perhaps better than Śatadru which is the name of a river (the Sutlej): the characters, however, may represent Śatadru.

## P'O-LI-YE-TA-LO (PĀRYĀTRA).

From Śatadru the pilgrim proceeded south-west, and after a journey of over 800 *li*, reached the country called *P'o-li-ye-ta-lo* (Pāryatra). This country was above 3000 and its capital about 14 *li* in circuit. It had good crops of spring wheat and other grain, including a peculiar kind of rice which in 60 days was ready for cutting. Oxen and sheep were numerous, and fruits and flowers were scarce: the climate was hot and the people had harsh ways, they did not esteem learning and were not Buddhists. The king, who was of the *Fei-she* (吠奢) (Vaiśya stock, was a man of courage and military skill. There were eight Buddhist monasteries in a bad state of ruin: the Brethren, who were very few in number, were Hīnayānists. There were above ten Deva-Temples and the professed non-Buddhists were above 1000 in number.

The district here described has been identified by M. Reinaud "with Pāryatra or Bairāt" and this identification has been accepted.[2]

The rice of this country which grew and ripened in 60 days could not have been the ordinary upland or dry rice, as Jo thinks, for that was well known to the pilgrim as a product of his own country and of several lands through which he had recently passed. It must have been a special variety, as the Cochin-China rice, to which Julien refers, is a peculiar variety.

---

1 See Julien III. p. 335: A. G. I. p. 144.

2 Julien III. p. 336: A. G. I. p. 337.

## MATHURĀ.

From Pāryatra, the pilgrim continues, a journey of above 500 *li* eastwards brought him to the conntry called *Mo* (or *Mei*)-*t'u-lo* (or Mathurā).

This name is translated in some Chinese glossaries by "Peacock", as if Mayūra. It is also said to be derived from *madhu, honey*, as if the spelling of the name were Madhurā. Mr Growse considers that the word is probably connected with the Sanskrit root *math*, "to churn", "the churn forming a prominent feature in all poetical descriptions of the local scenery".[1] In connection with this it is interesting to observe that in a Buddhist scripture a sick bhikshu is represented as unable to obtain milk at Mathurā.[2] There was also a story of a great giant Madhu from whom the name of the city and district was derived. This also points to the form Madhurā.

Yuan-chuang describes the country of Mathurā as being above 5000 *li* in circuit, its capital being above twenty *li* in circuit. The soil, he says, was very fertile and agriculture was the chief business: mango trees were grown in orchards at the homesteads of the people: there were two kinds of this fruit, one small and becoming yellow when ripe, and the other large and remaining green. The country produced also a fine striped cotton cloth and gold: its climate was hot: the manners and customs of the inhabitants were good: the people believed in the working of karma, and paid respect to moral and intellectual eminence. There were in the district above twenty Buddhist monasteries, and above 2000 Brethren who were diligent students of both "Vehicles". There were also five Deva-Temples and the professed adherents of the different non-Buddhist sects lived pell-mell.

When Fa-hsien visited this country he also found 20 monasteries but he estimated the number of Brethren as about 3000.[3]

We now come to a passage which presents some serious difficulties. It seems to be faulty both in form and sub-

---

[1] Growse's Mathurā p. 73 (2d ed.). See below p. 311.

[2] A-yü-wang-ehing, *ch.* 9.

[3] Fo-kuo-chi, *ch.* 16.

stance and it has perplexed native scholars. For the present we may render it as follows.

> There are three topes all built by Asoka: very numerous traces left by the Four Past Buddhas: topes (or a tope) for the relics of the following holy disciples of Sakya Ju-lai, viz. Sāriputra, Mudgalaputra, Pūrṇamaitriyāniputra, Upāli, Ānanda, and Rāhula: topes for Mañjuśrī and the other P'usas. In the "Three Longs" of every year, and on the six Fastdays of every month, the Brethren with mutual rivalry make up parties, and taking materials of worship with many valuables, repair to the images of their special patrons. The Abhidharma Brethren offer worship to Sāriputra, the Samādhists to Mudgalaputra, the Sūtraists to Pūrṇamaitriyāniputra, the Vinayists to Upāli, the bhikshuṇis to Ānanda, and the śrāmaṇeras to Rāhula: and the Māhāyanists to the various P'usas. On these days the topes vie with each other in worship: banners and sunshades are displayed, the incense makes clouds and the flowers are scattered in showers, sun and moon are obscured and the mountain-ravines convulsed: the king and his state'smen devote themselves to good works.

The difficulties of this passage begin with the first sentence, and a native scholar took from the paragraph a very different meaning from that here given. He understood the author to state that there were three Asoka topes, viz. one for the numerous traces left by the Four Past Buddhas, one for the holy disciples of the Buddha, and one for the P'usas. There is something to be said in favour of this interpretation, but it does not quite suit either the construction or the context. With the present interpretation we have the bald statement that there were three Asoka topes. The Fang-chih places these within the capital; but our text does not give any information as to their situation, or structure, or the purposes for which they were erected. So also the next clause— "very many traces of the Four Past Buddhas" —seems to require at its head either the — "viz. a tope for" of the Chinese scholar, or the "On montre" which Julien prefixes. Then as to the topes for the relics of the great disciples the term for relics is *i-shên* (遺 身) lit. "left bodies", and Julien translates *i-shên stūpa* by "Divers stoūpas renfermant les corps'. But *i-shên* here, as in other passages, means only the *ashes*, *bones* or other relics left after cremation, *shên* being used as the equivalent of the Sanskrit word for *body*, Śarīra, which is also used in the sense of a "bodily relic". Then we have this difficulty, that not only was no one of the great disciples here named buried at Mathura, but also there is no authority for stating that the relics of any one of them were conveyed to this district. Moreover, as the Fang-chih points out, Rāhula was supposed not to have tasted death. This treatise, accordingly suggests that the word for *body* (*shên*) should not be taken here in its ordinary sense, but should be unterstood as meaning a visible symbol, such as an image or other likeness. The reader will observe that our pilgrim represents the worshippers as paying reverence, not to the topes, but to images or pictures apparently set up for the occasion. Fa-hsien in his general survey of "Mid-India" including the Mathurā district, tells us that at the Buddhist vihāras there were topes to Śāriputra, Madgalyāyana (Yuan-chuang's Mudgalaputra), Ananda, and to the Sūtras, the Vinaya, and the Abhidharma. To some of these topes services were offered, but he describes the Śrāmaṇeras as making offerings to Rāhula not to his tope, and he describes the Mahāyānists as offering worship to "Prajñāparamitā, Mañjuśrī, and Kuan-shi-yin".[1]

Then our pilgrim is perhaps wrong in representing the Abhidharmists as worshipping Śāriputra, the Samādhists as worshipping Mudgalaputra, and the Sūtra Brethren as worshipping Pūrṇa-Maitriyāniputra. Sāriputra was distinguished among the disciples for his great spiritual wisdom or prajñā, but he had nothing to do with the Abhidharma, which did not come into existence until after his death. So Mahāmaudgalyāyana was great in magic, in his superhuman powers, but not in samādhi. Maitriyāniputra is sometimes praised as a good expounder of the Master's teaching but he is not specially associated with the sūtras.

Julien takes Manjuśrī to be one of the holy disciples of the Buddha, and the author of Fang-chih; and others

---

[1] Fo-kuo-chi.

have taken the same meaning out of the text. But Manjuśrī was not a human being: he was one of the great Bodhisattvas, often figuring as first or chief of all these Mahāyāna creations.

This passage tells us that the Brethren went in parties to offer worship to their respective patrons in the "Three Longs" of the year and the Six Fast-days of each month. By the "Three Longs" we are probably to understand the first, fifth, and ninth months of each year which were called the "Three Long Months" and the "Three Long Fasts". The Six Fast-days were the 8th, 14th, 15th of each half-month or the 8th, 14th, 15th, 23th, 29th, 30th of each month. This has been made known to us by Julien who obtained his information from a late Chinese Buddhist compilation. In this work under the heading "Nine Fast Days" we find the above three month-fasts and six monthly day-fasts given as making up the "Nine Fast-days". This seems to be rather a peculiar way of reckoning, and Julien gets over the difficulty by changing *month* into "in the month", and making the "nine Fast-days" literally nine days. But then, what is to be done with the Fasts called the "Three long months" or "Three long Fasts"? The reason for the religious observance of these periods by the Buddhist clergy and laity is given in several books. In the three months specified Indra (or according to some Visvamitra, or according to others the four Devarājas) by means of secret emissaries made a careful examination into the conduct and modes of life of the inhabitants of Jambudvīpa (India). So all the people of that continent were on their best behaviour in these months, they abstained from flesh and wine, and even from food lawful in ordinary times, and they offered worship and practised good works. They also kept holiday and visited the shrines of their divinities to pray for earthly blessings. In these months there were no executions of criminals and no slaughter of animals was allowed.[1] Thus

[1] Fo-shuo-chai-ching (No. 577): Shih-shih-yao-lan, *ch.* 3: Fo-tsu-t'ung-chi, *ch.* 33 (No. 1661).

the "Three Long Fasts" were evidently in their origin a popular rather than a Buddhistic institution, and Buddhism may have adopted them to a certain extent as a matter of expediency. They are never mentioned, however, in the canonical treatises.

The "Six Fast-days of every Month" were also popular religious holidays before the time of the Buddha. According to some accounts these days, like the three months, were devoted by Indra's messengers to a roving inspection of the moral and religious conduct of the people of India[1]. The people on their part were careful on these days to fast, and offer worship, and do good works, in the hope of receiving material recompense such as fine weather and good crops. This sort of observance was called the "Cowherd's Fast". But the Parivrājakas of the Tīrthikas devoted these six days to the public reading of their scriptures, and the Buddha followed their example. He ordained that on these days the Pratimoksha should be recited in a select congregation of the Brethren; and he seems also to have appointed the reading of the Dharma on these days, the Uposatha days, to the people[2]

Our pilgrim is apparently wrong in representing the Buddhist Brethren as spending the first, fifth, and ninth months in the manner here indicated. The fifth month was part of the Retreat from the rains, and the Brethren could not break up Retreat for a whole month and go away to a tope or a monastery to pay respect to their special patrons and enjoy themselves with their companions. Fa-hsien makes the festival of Patron-worship occur once a year after Retreat, each set having its own day, and this is more likely to be correct than Yuan-chuang's account. According to Fa-hsien also it was the people who provided the illuminations and flowers for the topes while the clergy preached. These topes, moreover, in his narrative throughout the region of which he is writing were apparently

---

[1] Ssŭ-t'ien-wang-ching (No. 722): Tsêng-yi-a-han-ching, *ch.* 16

[2] 'Vinaya Texts' (S. B. E.) Vol. 1. pp. 239, 240.

attached to or near monasteries, but the topes of our pilgrim's account do not seem to have been connected with any Buddhist establishment.

Returning to our pilgrim's description of this district we read that—

> going east from the capital five or six *li* one comes to a "hill-monastery" the chamber of which was quarried in a steep bank, a narrow defile being used to form its entrance. This monastery had been made by the venerable Upagupta and it enclosed a tope with a finger-nail relic of the Buddha. Through the north rock-wall of the monastery was a cave above 20 feet high by 30 feet wide, within which were piled up fine four-inch slips of wood (that is, tallies). When the Venerable Upagupta was preaching and converting, every married couple which attained arhatship put down a tally here, but for single members of families although they became arhats no record of the fact was kept.

The words for "a hill-monastery" in this passage are *yi-shan-ka-lan* and Julien translates them "un *kia-lan* situé sur une montagne". As has been seen a "hill-ka-lan" was a rural non-descript vihāra not attached to any superior establishment. Then Julien makes the pilgrim locate the Tally-cave "dans une caverne qui est au nord de ce *kia-lan*". The text has *ka-lan-pei-yen-hsien-yu-shih-shih* (伽藍北巖間有石室) that is, in the steep rock on the north of the ka-lan is a cave. The word *yen* does not mean *une caverne* but a steep wall of rock, and the entrance to the Tally-cave was through the rock which formed the north side of the Vihāra-Cave. This interpretation of the text will be found to agree with descriptions given in other treatises.

The site of the Upagupta monastery, as we may call the Hill *ka-lan*, of our author's narrative was apparently the place called the Urumuṇḍa (or Urumaṇḍa or Rurumaṇḍa) Hill, and the Rimurunda of Mr. Rockhill's Tibetan text. The name Urumaṇḍa is rendered in Chinese by "Great Cream" (大醍醐), its literal signification[1], and near the hill there was a "Great Cream" town or village. To describe or indicate this hill various forms of ex-

---

[1] A-yü-wang-ching, *ch.* 9.

pression are used. Thus seen from a distance it was "an azure streak"; it was also a "line of green forest", and a "wood of green trees". On or at this hill, according to some authorities, the brothers Naṭa and Baṭa constructed the Naṭabaṭa-vihāra, to which they afterwards invited Upagupta when he came to live at Mathurā. This is supposed to be the "Hill ka-lan" of our pilgrim but it may have been a separate establishment. This "Hill ka-lan" was evidently the house or vihāra of Upagupta on the Urūmaṇḍa hill, and it was probably a large natural cave improved by art to constitute a monastery. Connected with the monastery was the cave in which the disciples converted by Upagupta's teaching, on their attainment of arhatship deposited each a slip of wood or bamboo.[1] This cave is also represented as a "made house" but this is evidently a mistake[2]. Its dimensions vary in different books, one authority making it 18 *chou* long, by 12 *chou* wide, and 7 *chou* high[3]. In our pilgrim's description we should probably regard "above 20 feet high" as a mistake for "above 20 feet long" other writers giving the length as 24 or 27 feet, the height being about 9 or 10 feet. Then Yuan-chuang's statement, that tallies were kept only of married couples attaining arhatship is very silly and does not agree with the accounts in other Chinese books. According to these every one who through Upagupta's teaching and guiding became an arhat added his tally to the pile. Upagupta had marvellous success as a Buddhist missionary at Mathurā: he converted many thousands of lay people, and through him 18000 disciples attained arhatship. When he died all the tallies deposited by these arhats were taken away and used at his cremation[4]. Yet Yuan-chuang would have us believe that he saw them still filling up the cave.

---

1 Sar. Vin. Yao-shih, *ch.* 9.

2 A-yü-wang-chuan, *ch.* 5.

3 Sar. Vin. l. c. The sh'ou (肘) was about 1½ foot. See also A-yü-wang-ching, *ch.* 6.

4 Sar. Vin. l. c.: Tār. S. 14 f.

In some books the hill on which was the Naṭabaṭa-vihāra occupied by Upagupta is called Śira or Uśira, although we also have mention of the Uśira hill without any reference to a cave or monastery[1]. This Uśira hill was at the side of the "Urumaṇḍa Hill" and the latter name may have included the two hills and the wood or forest adjoining.

General Cunningham considered the site of Upagupta's monastery to be that of the Id-gah or Katra of the present Muttra, and this opinion has been adopted by others. But it is undoubtedly wrong. A later investigator, Mr Growse, writes: "General Cunningham, in his Archæological Report, has identified the Upagupta monastery with the Yasa vihāra inside the Katra: but in all probability he would not now adhere to this theory; for, at the time when he advanced it, he had never visited the Kankāli Tīlā, and was also under the impression that the Fort always had been, as it now is, the centre of the city. Even then, to maintain his theory, he was obliged to have recourse to a very violent expedient, and in the text of the Chinese pilgrim to alter the word 'east' to 'west', because, he writes, "a mile to the east would take us to the low ground on the opposite bank of the Jamuná, where no ruins exist", forgetting apparently Fa Hian's distinct statement that in his time there were monasteries on both sides of the river, and being also unaware that there are heights on the left bank at Isapur and Mahában, where Buddhist remains have been found. The topographical descriptions of the two pilgrims may be reconciled with existing facts without any tampering with the text of the narrative. Taking the Katra, or the adjoining shrine of Bhútesvar, as the omphalos of the ancient city and the probable site of the great stupa of Sáriputra, a short distance to the east will bring us to the Kankāli Tīlā, i. e. the monastery of Upagupta".[2] This is very positive but not quite con-

---

[1] Tār. l. c.: Ta-pei-ching (No. 117).

[2] Growse op. c. p. 112.

vincing, and where did Mr Growse get his "great stupa of Śáriputra"?

This Upagupta monastery is apparently the "Cream-village" vihāra of a Vinaya treatise, one of the many Buddhist establishments mentioned as being in the Mathurā district.[1] It may also perhaps be the Guha vihāra of the Lion Pillar inscriptions.[2] We find it called the Naṭika ṣanghārama, and the Naṭabaṭa (or Naṭibaṭi)-vihāra, as already stated, and the Naṭabhaṭikāraṇyāyatana of the Divyāvadana.[3] It was evidently in a hill among trees and not far from the city of Mathurā, but Yuan-chuang seems to be the only authority for placing it about a mile to the east of the city. This would apparently put the Urumaṇḍa hill on the east side of the Jumna, and the situation assigned to the Monkey Tope in the next paragraph agrees with this supposition.

> The pilgrim's narrative proceeds to state that to the south-east of the cave (that is, the Cave monastery) and 24 or 25 *li* (about five miles) from it was a large dried up pond beside which was a tope. This was the place, Yuan-chuang tells us, at which when the Buddha was once walking up and down a monkey offered him some honey. The Buddha caused the honey to be mixed with water and then distributed among his disciples. Hereupon the monkey gambolled with delight, fell into the pit (or ditch) and died, and by the religious merit of this offering was born as a human being.

The story of a monkey or a flock of monkeys (or apes) presenting wild honey to the Buddha is told with variations in several Buddhist scriptures. In some the scene of the story is laid near Vaiśāli[4] (and our pilgrim, it will be seen, tells of a troop of monkeys offering honey to the Buddha at this place), in some at Śrāvasti[5],

---

1 Sêng-chi-lü, *ch.* 8.

2 J. R. A. S. for 1894 p. 526.

3 Divyāv ch. XXVI and p. 385: Bur. Int. p. 378: Ta-pei-ching.

4 Chung-a-han-ching, *ch.* 8: Sar. Vin. Yao-shih, *ch.* 18. Cf. Records, *ch.* 7.

5 Hsien-yü-ching, *ch.* 12: Der Weise u. d. T. S. 347.

and in some at the Natika village[1]. The following account of the whole matter is taken chiefly from the "Hsien-yü-ching". The Buddha was once visited at Śrāvasti by a Brahmin householder who was son-less and wished to know whether he was to die so. Buddha consoled him with promise of a son who should become a distinguished member of the church. In due time the son was born, and because it was observed that about the time of his birth the honey-vessels in the house became full of honey, he received the name "Honey-prevailing". In Chinese the name is Mi-shêng (蜜勝) and the Sanskrit original is written *Mo-t'ou-lo-se-chih,* that is, Madhuraśachi or "Sweet Influence", viz. born with the good omen of honey. This boy in time became a disciple of the Buddha who explained to Ananda that Mi-shêng in a long-past previous existence had been a bhikshu, that he had then once been disrespectful to a senior Brother. The senior rebuked him gently and Mi-shêng was penitent, but he had to suffer punishment for his thoughtless rude language by 500 births as a monkey. It was in the last of these births that the incident of the honey-offering occurred. The Buddha and his disciples had halted for rest one day under some trees by a tank not far from Śrāvasti. Here a monkey came and took Buddha's bowl and soon after returned with it full of honey and offered it to the Buddha. The latter sent the monkey back first to remove the insects from the honey and afterwards to add water to it. When the honey was thus "pure", that is, fit for bhikshus' use Buddha accepted it and distributed it among his disciples. The monkey was now up a tree again, and seeing his honey accepted and distributed he frisked about with delight until he fell and was drowned in the pit below. But by the merit of the gift of honey he was immediately born again as a human creature and became the disciple Mi-shêng. In another treatise the name of the bhikshu

[1] Sar. Vin. P'o-sêng-shih, *ch.* 12. This may be the Naṭika of Urumanda, the village and the monastery having the same name.

is given as Madhu-Vasishṭha, his family name being Vasishṭha[1], and in another work he is called *Mi-hsing* or "Honey-nature".[2] In one book the monkey skips with delight but does not fall into the water[3], and in another he dies and is born again in Paradise.[4]

The story of the monkey and the honey, here repeated by the pilgrim, being told of Mathurā as an explanation of the name, must have arisen at a time when the form used was Madhurā. There is also another monkey or ape story connected with Mathurā. In a previous existence, the Buddha once explained, Upagupta was born as a monkey (or ape) and became the chief of a troop of monkeys living at Urumaṇḍa. As such he made offerings and shewed much kindness to 500 Pratyeka Buddhas who were living on another part of Urumaṇḍa. The merit of his conduct to these worthies brought the monkey birth as a human being in his next existence, and in it, as the bhikshu Upagupta, he rose to be a most successful preacher, a peerless saint, and a Buddha in all but the bodily signs.[5]

The pilgrim goes on to narrate that to the north of the dried-up pond, and not far from it, was a large wood in which were footsteps of the Four Past Buddhas, left by them as they walked up and down. Hard by these were topes to mark the places at which Śāriputra and the others of the Buddha's 1250 great disciples had practised absorbed meditation. There were also memorials of the Buddha's frequent visits to this district for the purpose of preaching.

The "large wood" of this passage, which lay between the Upagupta Monastery and the Dried-up Pond, may be the forest generally mentioned in connection with Urumaṇḍa. But it is at least doubtful whether any of the 1250 disciples ever practised samādhi in this neighbour-

---

1 Sar. Vin. P'o-sêng-shih, *ch.* 12.

2 Sar. Vin. Yao-shih, *ch.* 18.

3 Chung-a-han-ching, *ch.* 8.

4 Sêng-chi-lü, *ch.* 29.

5 Fu-fa-tsang-yin-yuan-ching, *ch.* 3: Sar. Vin. Yao-shih, *ch.* 9: Divyāv. Ch. XXVI.

hood. The Urumaṇḍa district was a great resort of ascetics devoted to serenity of mind and prolonged meditation, but this was after the time of Upagupta. Then the Buddha's visits to the Mathurā district do not seem to have been numerous, even if we accept records of doubtful authenticity. We are told that he expressed a dislike to the country which had, he said, five defects. The ground was uneven, it was covered with stones and brick-bats, it abounded with prickly shrubs, the people took solitary meals, and there were too many women.[1] We find mention of the Buddha visiting the country on one occasion and lodging in a mango-tope near the Bhadra river.[2] On another occasion he lodged with his disciples in Ass Yaksha's palace (or the monastery of Ass Yaksha) which was apparently outside the capital.[3] He also passed through this country with Ananda when returning from his mission to "North-India", going among the *yung-chün-jen* (勇軍人) or Sūrasenas until he reached Mathurā city.

It is worthy of notice that in his account of Mathurā and the surrounding district the pilgrim does not give the name of any hill, or river, or town, or Buddhist establishment in the country. His information about the district is meagre and his remarks about the Buddhist objects of interest in it seem to be confused and to a certain extent second-hand. He apparently did not visit the capital, and made only a hurried journey across a part of the country. It seems very strange that he does not mention by name the famous Urumuṇḍa (or Urumaṇḍa) Hill, so intimately connected, as we have seen, with the introduction of Buddhism into the district, and evidently an old place of resort for contemplative ascetics of other religious

---

1 Sar. Vin. Yao-shih, *ch.* 10.

2 Tsa-a-han-ching, *ch.* 2 and 24. The mango topes seem to have all disappeared from the Mathurā district.

3 Sar. Vin. Yao-shih, *ch.* 10. This building was properly not a monastery, but a hall or temple. It was apparently on the occasion of the Buddha's returning from the north that he made the stay at Mathurā, converting the wicked Yakshinīs, and preaching his religion.

systems. Nor does he mention the great river which flowed past the east side of Mathurā city. Fa-hsien mentions this river which he calls *Pu-na* (捕 那) short for the Yao (搖)-pu-na (Yabuna) of his translations. Our pilgrim in his translations and in this *chuan* transcribes the name *Yen-mou-na* (Yamunā). Then he does not seem to have heard of such wellknown Buddhist establishments as the vihāra of the *Hsien-jen* (仙 人)*-chü-lao* or Rishi village (or town), or the vihāra of the Grove the *Ts'ung-lin* (叢 林) *-ssŭ*. The former was on the east and the latter on the west side of the Jumna.[1] *Ts'ung-lin* is supposed to be for the Sanskrit Piṇḍa-vana: it could not have been Krishna's Vṛindā-vana, which was on the opposite side of the river.

---

[1] Sêng-chi-lü, *ch.* 8.

# CHAPTER X.

### CHUAN IV CONT[D].

## STHĀNEŚVAR TO KAPITHA.

From the Mathurā country the pilgrim, according to his narrative, proceeded north-east, and after a journey of above 500 *li*, reached the *Sa-t'a-ni-ssŭ-fa-lo* (Sthāneśvara) country. He tells us this country was above 7000 *li* in circuit, and its capital, with the same name apparently, was above twenty *li* in circuit. The soil was rich and fertile and the crops were abundant: the climate was warm: the manners and customs of the people were illiberal: the rich families vied with each other in extravagance. The people were greatly devoted to magical arts and highly prized outlandish accomplishments: the majority pursued trade, and few were given to farming: rarities from other lands were collected in this country. There were (that is, at the capital apparently) three Buddhist monasteries with above 700 professed Buddhists, all Hīnayānists. There were also above 100 Deva-Temples and the non-Buddhists were very numerous.

The capital, the pilgrim goes on to describe, was surrounded for 200 *li* by a district called the "Place of Religious Merit" — *Fu-ti* (福 地). The origin of this name Yuan-chuang learned at the place to be as follows. The "Five Indias" were once divided between two sovereigns who fought for mastery, invading each other's territory and keeping up unceasing war. At length in order to settle the question of superiority, and so give peace to their subjects, the kings agreed between themselves to have a decisive action. But their subjects were dissatisfied and refused to obey their kings' commands. Thereupon the king [of that part of India which included Sthāneśvara] thought of an expedient. Seeing it was useless to let his subjects have a voice in his proposals, and knowing that the people would be influenced by the supernatural, he secretly sent a roll of silk to a clever brahmin commanding him to come to the palace. On his arrival there the brahmin was kept in an inner chamber, and there he composed (that is, by the King's inspiration) a Dharma-sūtra (that is, a treatise on Duty). This book the king then hid in a rock-cave, where it remained for several years until vegetation covered the spot. Then one morning the king informed his ministers at an audience that he had been enlightened by Indra, who told him in a dream about an inspired book hidden in a certain hill. The book was brought forth, and officials and people were enraptured. By the king's orders the contents of the scripture were made known to all, and the sum of them was briefly this—

Life and death are a shoreless ocean with ebb and flow in endless alternation: intelligent creatures cannot save themselves from the eddies in which they are immersed. I have an admirable device for saving them from their woes, and it is this—Here we have for 200 *li* round this city the place of religious merit for generations of the ancient sovereigns, but as its evidences have been effaced in the long lapse of time, people have ceased to reflect on the efficacy of the place, and so have been submerged in the ocean of misery with no one to save them from perishing. Now all who, being wise, go into battle and die fighting, will be reborn among men: slaying many they will be innocent and will receive divine blessings: obedient grand-children and filial children serving their parents while sojourning in this district will obtain infinite happiness. As the meritorious service is little, and the reward it obtains great, why miss the opportunity? Once the human body is lost there are the three states of dark oblivion: hence every human being should be diligent in making good karma, thus all who engage in battle will look on death as a return home—

The the king ordered an enrolment of heroes for battle, and an engagement took place on this ground. The bodies of those killed in battle were strewn about in confused masses, so great was the number of the slain, and the huge skeletons of these heroes still cover the district, which popular tradition calls the Place of Religious Merit.

The whole of this passage about the "Place of Religious Merit" is curious and interesting, giving, as has been pointed out by others, the story which our pilgrim heard on the spot about the wars of the Kauravas and Pāṇḍavas. It reads like an extract from the Bhagavadgītā. The passage which, in the present rendering of it, is treated as being the sum of the inspired teaching of the sūtra, is made by Julien, in his version, to be a proclamation by the king of

Sthāneśvara. The last clause of the passage is treated by him as a separate sentence and he translates it thus—"Là-dessus, tous les hommes combattirent avec ardeur et coururent joyeusement à la mort", that is, before the king called on the people to enlist in his service. This treatment of the text seems to be a very unfortunate one as Yuan-chuang makes a clear distinction between the counsel of the Dharmasūtra (*Fa-ching* 法經), and the king's proceedings after the promulgation of the counsel.

> Four or five *li* to the north-west of the capital, the pilgrim relates, was an Asoka tope made of bright orange bricks, and containing wonder-working relics of the Buddha. Above 100 *li* south from the capital was the *Ku-hun-t'u* (in some texts *-ch'a*) monastery: this had high chambers in close succession and detached terraces: the Buddhist Brethren in it led pure strict lives.

The *Ku-hun-t'u* (or *ch'a*) of this passage may perhaps, as has been suggested, be for Govinda. Another restoration proposed is Gokaṇṭha, and this is the name adopted by Cunningham, but it does not seem possible that the Chinese characters are a transcription of this word. Govinda is a common name for Krishna, but it may have been the name of the village in which the monastery here described was situated.

The Sthāneśvara of this passage has been identified with the modern Thānesar (Tānesar, Tanessar) in Ambala. Cunningham seems to regard this identification as beyond question[1], although in perhaps no point of distance, direction or measurement do the two places correspond. Thānesar is about 180 miles to the north-north-west of Mathurā[2], and Sthāneśvar was about 100 miles to the north-east of that place: the area of the country as given by the pilgrim is too great by one fourth and that of the "holy land" (Yuan-chuang's Place of Happiness, that is Religious Merit) is too small by half. Moreover the *Fu-ti* of the Records cannot be regarded as a translation of

---

1 A. G. I. p. 328: J. III. p. 339.

2 Alberuni Vol. I. p. 199.

Dharma-Kshetra, another name for the Kuru-Kshetra. Besides, this latter name designated a large plain above 100 miles to the south-east of Thānesvar, and the Fu-ti was all round the city Sthānesvara for only about 40 miles. Cunningham in his usual manner proposes to get over some of the difficulties by taking liberties with the pilgrim's text. It is better, however, to regard our pilgrim as being correct in his statement of distance and direction from Mathurā to Sthānesvara, and as deriving his information on other matters from the Brethren in the monasteries. He seems to represent himself as going to the great monastery 100 *li* (about 20 miles) south from the capital. Had he made a journey to the south of Thānesar, he would probably have told us of the celebrated Tank in the district about which Alberuni and Tavernier relate wonderful things.[1]

## ŚRUGHNA.

The pilgrim continuing the story of his travels relates that—

> from this (that is apparently, Sthāneśvara) he went north-east for above 400 *li* and came to the country *Su-lu-k'in-na.*

The Life, which calls this country *Lu-k'in-na,* makes it to be 400 *li* to the *east* of Sthāneśvara. Our pilgrim's transcription has been restored as Śrughna, but this does not seem to be right. Another transcription is *Su-lu-kie (ka)-k'ün,* and this and the transcription in the text seem to point to an original like Srukkhin or Srughin. Cunningham, taking the "from this" of the text to mean from the Govinda monastery, makes the 400 *li* to be counted from that monastery and accordingly gives the distance from Sthāneśvara to Śrughna as only 300 *li.*[2] But the Life, and the Fang-chih, make Yuan-chuang start from and count from Sthāneśvara, and as it seems likely that

[1] Alberuni Vol. II. p. 145: Bernier's Travels (Constable's Or. Misc.) p. 302.

[2] A. G. I. p. 345.

Yuan-chuang did not go to the Govinda monastery, I think we should understand the "from this" of the text to mean from the capital. Cunningham identifies the city Śrughna with the modern village of Sugh which "is surrounded on three sides by the bed of the old Jumna". But as the measurements and distances given by Yuan-chuang, as usual, do not agree with those required by Cunningham, we may perhaps regard the identification as not quite established.

Proceeding with his description of Śrughna the pilgrim tells us that

> it was above 6000 *li* in circuit, bounded on the east by the Ganges and on the north by high mountains, and that through the middle of it flowed the river *Yen-mo-na* (Jumna). The capital, above 20 *li* in circuit, was on the west side of the Jumna, and was in a ruinous condition. In climate and natural products the country resembled Sthāneśvara. The inhabitants were naturally honest: they were not Buddhists: they held useful learning in respect and esteemed religious wisdom. There were five Buddhist monasteries and above 1000 Buddhist ecclesiastics, the majority of whom were Hīnayānists, a few adhering to "other schools". The Brethren were expert and lucid expounders of abstract doctrines, and distinguished Brethren from other lands came to them to reason out their doubts. There were 100 Deva-Temples, and the non-Buddhists were very numerous.

The statement here that the majority of the Buddhist Brethren in Śrughna "learned the Little Vehicle and a few studied other schools" is rather puzzling as all the Eighteen Schools (*pu*) belonged to the Hīnayāna. All the texts, however, agree, and the Fang-chieh shews a wise discretion by omitting the difficult words. By the "other schools" Yuan-chuang may have meant the Sautrāntikas and other schools which had arisen in the later development of Buddhism, and were independent of the old schools and the two "Vehicles". The pilgrim heard expositions of the doctrines of the Sautrāntikas during his stay in the country. But we must also remember that he uses the terms Mahāyāna and Hīnayāna in a manner which is apparently peculiar to himself.

The narrative proceeds — To the south-east of the capital and on the west side of the Jumna outside the east gate of a large monastery was an Asoka tope at a place where the Ju-lai had preached and admitted men into his church. Beside this tope was one which had hair and nail-relics of the Ju-lai, and round about were some tens of topes with similar relics of Śārîputra, Mudgalaputra, and the other great arhats. After the Buddha's decease the people of this country had been led astray to believe in wrong religions and Buddhism had disappeared. Then Śāstra-masters from other lands defeated the Tīrthikas and Brahmins in discussions, and the five monasteries already mentioned were built at the places where the discussions were held in order to commemorate the victories.

A journey of above 800 *li* east from the Jumna (that is, at Śrughna) brought the pilgrim to the Ganges. The source of this river, he adds, is three or four *li* wide: the river flows south-east to the sea, and at its mouth it is above ten *li* wide: the waters of the river vary in colour and great waves rise in it: there are many marvellous creatures in it but they do not injure any one: its waters have a pleasant sweet taste and a fine sand comes down with the current. In the popular literature the river is called *Fu-shui* or "Happiness-water" that is, the water (or river) of religious merit. Accumulated sins are effaced by a bath in the water of the river: those who drown themselves in it are reborn in heaven with happiness: if the bones of one dead be consigned to the river that one does not go to a bad place: by raising waves and fretting the stream (that is, by splashing and driving the water back) the lost soul is saved.

In the Life and the Fang-chih the pilgrim proceeds to the "Source of the Ganges" which is 800 *li* to the east of the Jumna and this is supposed to be what the pilgrim meant to state. But the context and the sequel seem to require us to take him literally as simply coming to the Ganges. It was apparently at a place to the south of the "Source of the Ganges" that he reached that river. This "Source of the Ganges" is supposed to be Gangādvāra or Hardwar, the place where the Ganges emerges from the Sivalik mountains into the plains. The expression here rendered "the waters of the river vary in colour" is *shui-sê-Tsang-lang* (水色滄浪) that is, "the water in colour is Tsang-lang", or clear and muddy. The allusion is to the Tsang-lang river which, as we learn from a boy's song quoted in Mencius, ran sometimes clear and sometimes muddy.[1] Julien translates the words by "La couleur de ses eaux est bleuâtre", a rendering which is not correct from any point of view. Then as the original for *Fu-shui*, "River of religious merit" (lit. Religious merit water) Julien gives Mahābhadrā, which is a name for the Ganges but is not the equivalent of Fu-shui. This term is a literal rendering of the Sanskrit and Pali word Puṇyodaka, *merit-water*, and Puṇyodaka is the name of a river in the world beyond. The reason why the name was transferred to the Ganges is to be found in the next paragraph of our passage, in which the pilgrim describes the spiritual efficacy of the water of the river. In this paragraph the words rendered "by raising waves and fretting the stream the lost souls (or spirits) are saved" are *yang-p'o-chi-liu-wang-hun-huo-chi* (揚波激流亡魂獲濟). Julien connects these words with the preceding clause which states that if the bones of a dead person are consigned to the river that person does not go to a bad place, Julien making the author add — "pendant que les flots se gonflent et coulent en bondissant, l'âme du défunt passe à l'autre rive". The first clause of this is not a translation of the Chinese, and Julien's failure to understand his author has spoiled this passage and his rendering of the story about Deva P'usa which follows.

Our pilgrim, in connection with his remarks about the popular belief in the spiritual virtues of the water of the Ganges, that is presumably at Gangādvāra, relates the following annecdote—

> Deva P'usa of the *Chih-shih-tzŭ-kuo* (or Simhala country), profoundly versed in Buddhist lore and compassionate to the simple, had come hither to lead the people aright. At the time of his arrival the populace, male and female, old and young, were assembled on the banks of the river and were *raising waves and fretting the current*. The P'usa solemnly setting an example bent his head down to check and turn the stream. As his mode of

[1] Mencius, *ch.* 7. P. I.

**procedure was different from that of the rest, one of the Tirthikas said to him—Sir, why are you so strange? Deva answered —My parents and other relatives are in the Siṁhala country, and as I fear they may be suffering from hunger and thirst, I hope this water will reach thus far, and save them. To this the Tirthikas replied — Sir, you are in error and your mistake comes from not having reflected—your home is far away with mountains and rivers intervening—to fret and agitate this water, and by this means save those there from hunger, would be like going back in order to advance, an unheard of proceeding. Deva then replied that if sinners in the world beyond received benefits from this water, it could save his relatives notwithstanding the intervening mountains and rivers. His arguments convinced his hearers; who thereupon acknowledged their errors, renounced them, and became Buddhists.**

The *Chih-shih-tzŭ kuo* or Siṁhala country of this passage has been taken to be Ceylon, the country generally so designated, but it may be here the name of a country in India. Yuan-chuang, as will be seen hereafter, probably knew that Deva was a native of South-India and not of Ceylon.

According to the story here related, when Deva found the people on the river-side splashing the water, he set himself to lead them to right views. He assumed a grave air and an earnest manner, and while the others were merely going through a religious rite, he seemed to be making a serious effort to force the river back. As he evidently desired, his strange manner attracted attention; and he was able to turn the Tirthikas' criticism against themselves. Here Julien gives a rendering which seems to be against construction and context, and makes the story absurd. The Chinese for "giving an example" or "leading aright" here is *chi-yin* (汲 引) which Julien translates "voulut puiser de l'eau". But the phrase is of common occurrence and generally in the sense of "lead by example" or "set in the right course".

In this Srughna (or Ṣrughin) country, we learn from the Life, the pilgrim enjoyed the society of a learned Doctor in Buddhism, by name Jayagupta. The pilgrim remained here one winter, and half of the spring following; and "when he had heard all the vibhāshā of the Sautrantika School" he continued his journey.

With reference to Yuan-chuang's mention of the Buddha having preached at the capital of this country, it may be stated that the story of the Buddha visiting Srughna and there meeting the Brahmin named Indra, who was proud of his youth and beauty, is told in the Divyāvadāna and in the Sarvata Vinaya.[1]

## MO-TI-PU-LO (MATIPUR).

The pilgrim proceeds to narrate that crossing to the east bank of the river (that is, the Ganges) he came to the *Mo-ti-pu-lo* (Matipur) country. This was above 6000 *li*, and its capital above 20 *li* in circuit. It yielded grain, fruits, and flowers, and it had a genial climate. The people were upright in their ways: they esteemed useful learning: were well versed in magical arts: and were equally divided between Buddhism and other religions. The king, who was of the Śūdra stock (that is caste) did not believe in Buddhism, and worshipped the Devas. There were above ten Buddhist monasteries with above 800 Brethren mostly adherents of the Sarvāstivādin school of the Hinayāna. There were also above fifty Deva-Temples and the sectarians lived pell-mell.

The *Mo-ti-pu-lo* or Matipur of this passage has been identified by Saint-Martin and Cunningham with Madāwar or "Mandāwar, a large town in western Rohilkhand, near Bijnor".[2] But in Cunningham's Map No. X, to which he refers us, Madāwar is to the south-east of Srughna and to the south of Gangādvāra, whereas Matipur was to the east of Srughna and east of the "Source of the Ganges", if we are to regard that as the place at which the pilgrim halted before crossing the river. Then, as usual, the areas of the country and its capital do not agree with Cunningham's requirements.

Four or five *li* south from the capital, the pilgrim continues, was the small monastery in which the Śāstra-master Guṇaprabha composed above 100 treatises including the "*Pien - chèn - lun*"

---

1 Divyāv. p. 74: Sar. Vin. Yao-shih, *ch.* 9.

2 A. G. I. p. 348.

(辯眞論) or Truth-expounding Treatise. This Guṇaprabha, Yuang-chuang tells us, from being a very clever boy had grown up to be a man of great intellectual abilities, and of wide and varied learning. He had at first been a student of the Mahāyāna system, but before he had thoroughly comprehended the abstruse mysteries of that system, he was converted to the Hinayāna by the perusal of a Vaibhāsha treatise. After this he composed several tens of treatises in refutation of the Mahāyāna principles, and in defence of the Hinayāna tenets. He was also the author of some scores (several tens and more) of secular books: he set aside as wrong the standard treatises of his predecessors. But in his comprehensive study of the Buddhist canonical scriptures Guṇaprabha had experienced difficulties on above ten points, and of these his prolonged application did not bring any solution. Now among his contemporaries was an arhat named Devasena, who was in the habit of visiting the Tushita Paradise. This Devasena, by his supernatural powers, on one occasion took Guṇaprabha, at the request of the latter, up to the Tushita Paradise to have an interview with Maitreya Bodhisattva, and obtain from the Bodhisattva the solution of his spiritual difficulties. But when presented to Maitreya Guṇaprabha was too proud and conceited to give the Bodhisattva his due reverence, and accordingly Maitreya would not solve his difficulties. As Guṇaprabha remained stubborn in his self-conceit even after one or two unsuccessful visits, and as he would not be guided by the counsels of Devasena, the latter refused to take him any more into Maitreya's presence. Hereupon Guṇaprabha in angry disgust went into solitude in a forest, practised the "Penetration-developing samādhi", but, not having put away pride, he was unable to attain arhatship.

The Tushita Paradise, as is well known, is the Heaven in which the Bodhisattva Maitreya sojourns between his last incarnation on earth and his future advent as Buddha. The Šāstra-master Guṇaprabha in this passage considers himself, as a fully ordained Buddhist bhikshu, to be superior to the Bodhisattva who was enjoying the pleasures of a prolonged residence in Paradise; and accordingly Guṇaprabha persists in his refusal to show to Maitreya the reverence due to a great Bodhisattva, and consequently fails in his career.

The last clause in the above passage is given according to the correction of the Ming editors. This makes the text to read *pu-tê-chêng-kuo* (不得證果), that is, "he could not realize the fruit", viz-of arhatship. The old reading of some texts was *pu-shih*(時)*chêng-kuo*, meaning "he quickly realized the fruit". The D text has *pu-chêng tao-kuo*, which also means "he did not attain to arhatship", and this is doubtles the author's meaning.

In a note to the name of Guṇaprabha's treatise, the "Pien-chên-lun", mentioned in the above passage Julien restores the Sanskrit original as "Tattvavibhañga cāstra". This seems to show that he had forgotten the restoration of the name, given in translation and in Chinese transcription, which he had made in the Life. There he makes the name to be "Tattvasatya çāstra", and this restoration has been adopted by subsequent writers although it does not correspond to the translation of the name given by Yuan-chuang and the Chinese annotator. Now the characters which Julien makes to stand for *satya* are *san-ti-sho* (三弟鑠) for sandeśa, and the name of the treatise was evidently Tattvasandeśa or "Exposition of Truth", Yuan-chuang's *Pien-chên*, with the word for śāstra (*lun*) added.[1] This treatise, which at one time had some fame, expounded the views of the Sarvāstivādin school, but it is unknown to the existing collections.

The Guṇaprabha of Parvata here mentioned is not to be confounded with the great Vinaya master of the same name mentioned by Tāranātha.[2] Burnouf was of opinion that our Guṇaprabha might be the Guṇamati, Master of Vasumitra, mentioned in the "Abhidharmakośa-vyākha", but there does not seem to be any ground for this unlikely supposition.[3] In the 8th *chuan* of our treatise we find a Guṇamati disputing with a great master of the Sañkhya system.

> Three or four *li* north from Guṇaprabha's monastery, Yuan-chuang's narrative proceeds, was a monastery with above 200 Brethren, all Hinayānists. It was in this monastery that the

[1] Life *Ch.* 2: J. I. p. 109.

[2] Tār. S. 126 et al.: Wass. Bud. S. 84.

[3] Bur. Int. p. 566: Le Lotus de la bonne Loi p. 358.

> Sāstra-Master Sanghabhadra ended his life. This Sanghabhadra, it is added, was a native of Kashmir, and a profound scholar in the Vaibhāsha śāstras of the Sarvāstivādin school.

In this passage it is especially important to avoid Julien's rendering. "[Le Traité] Vibhacha çāṣtra" as the treatise of Sanghabhadra to be presently noticed does not deal with the special work called "Vibhāshā-lun".

> Contemporary with Sanghabhadra, Yuan-chuang continues, was Vasubandhu Bodhisattva, devoted to mystic doctrine, and seeking to solve what was beyond language. This man in refutation of the Vibhāshā masters composed the "Abhidharma-kośa-śāstra" ingenious in style and refined in principles. Sanghabhadra was moved by the treatise, and devoted twelve years to its study: then he composed a treatise which he called the "Kośa-pao" or "Bud-hail", śāstra. This work he entrusted to three or four of his cleverest disciples, telling them to use his unrecognized learning, and this treatise, to bring down the old man Vasubandhu from the preeminenee of fame which he had monopolized. At this time Vasubandhu, at the height of his fame, was in Sākala the capital of Cheika; and thither Sanghabhadra and his chief disciples proceed with the view of meeting him. But Vasubandhu learning that Sanghabhadra was on the way to have a discussion with him, hastily packed up and went off with his disciples. To these he excused his conduct by alleging his age and infirmities, and he added that he wished to allure Sanghabhadra to Mid-India where the Buddhist pundits would shew the charater of his doctrines. Sanghabhadra arrived at the monastery at Matipur the day after Vasubandhu had left it, and here he sickened and died. On his deathbed he wrote a letter of regret and apology to Vasubandhu, and entrusted it, with his treatise, to one of his disciples. When the letter and book were delivered to Vasubandhu with Sanghabhadra's dying request, he was moved and read them through. He then told his disciples that Sanghabhadra's treatise though not perfect in doctrine was well written, that it would be an easy matter for him to refute it, but that out of regard for the dying request of the author, and as the work expounded the views of those whom he (Vasubandhu) followed, he would leave the work as it was only giving it a new name. This name was "Shun-chêng-li-lun", the Sāstra which accords with orthodox principles (Nyāyānusāra-śāstra). The tope erected over Sanghabhadra's relics, in a mango grove to the north-east of the monastery, was still in existence.

The above passage has been condensed from Yuan-chuang's text and the reader will observe that; according to Yuan-chuang's information, Sanghabhadra was not, as Tāranātha represents him, the master of Vasubandhu. He is rather the young Doctor in Philosophy who is presumptuous enough to take up arms against the great chief renowned far and wide as peerless in dialectics. There is nothing in the text to shew that he and Vasubandhu were personal acquaintances, or that they ever met. So also in the Life of Vasubandhu the two men are apparently unknown to each other, and never meet.[1] Then as to the "Abhidharma-kośa-śāstra" it will be remembered that according to Yuan-chuang it was composed by Vasubandhu in Purushapur of Gandhāra, and this does not agree with the account in the Life of Vasubandhu. Yuan-chuang also tells us, and the statement has been often repeated, that Vasubandhu composed this treatise in order to refute the Vaibhāshikas. But, as has been stated already, this is not correct.[2] The original verses were compiled by him as a Sarvāstivādin Vaibhāshika, and the Commentary, still mainly Vaibhāshika, gives a development to certain questions from the Sautrantika point of view.

As to the treatise which Sanghabhadra wrote to demolish the Abhidharma-kośa according to Yuan-chuang the original title is given in the text as *Kośa-hail-lun*. In the name "Abhidharma-kośa-śāstra" the word kośa is used in the sense of a *bud*, the verses being buds in which were folded the flowers of Buddhist metaphysics awaiting development. So the Kośa-pao-lun, or Bud-hail-treatise, is to be understood as the work which was to spoil all the hope and promise of the *Kośa*. Vasubandhu, Yuan-chuang tells us, changed the name to "Shun-chêng-li-lun" the "Śāstra which follows Right Principles", and the Life of Vasubandhu gives the title as "Sui-shih-lun" or the "Śāstra which follows the True". These names are probably only different renderings of a name like Nyāyānusāra- or Anusāra-śāstra. But the story about the "Bud-hail" title must be

---

[1] Vasubandhu-chuan (No. 1463).

[2] See ch. VI. p.

discarded as the work itself shews that the author intended the title to be something like Nyāyānusāra-śāstra. Moreover in his subsequent treatise abridged from this he calls his large work "Shun-chêng-li-lun".[1] With the wicked title should go the statements about the author writing the book in a spirit of envious hostility against Vasubandhu. Nothing of this appears in the treatise; and on the contrary, as Vasubandhu stated, the work developes the views of Vasubandhu and those whom he followed. In its observations on the verses of the original treatise it sometimes uses the words of Vasubandhu's own commentary. The work condemns as heterodox certain opinions ascribed to the Sthaviras and the Sūtra-lords (*Ching-chu*), but Vasubandhu is not mentioned by name. Tāranātha mentions a treatise called "Abhidharmakośabhāshyaṭīkā-tattva" which he ascribes to Sthiramati. Another name for it is given as the "Thunder-bolt",[2] and it is perhaps not impossible that this may be the "Bud-hail" treatise ascribed by Yuan-chuang to Sanghabhadra.

The pilgrim's narrative proceeds to relate that beside the mango plantation which contained Sanghabhadra's tope was another tope erected over the remains of a Sāstra-Master named Vimala-mitra. This man, who was a native of Kashmir and an adherent of the Sarvata school, having made a profound study of canonical and heterodox scriptures, had travelled in India to learn the mysteries of the Tripiṭaka. Having gained a name, and finished his studies, he was returning to his home, and had to pass Sanghabhadra's tope on the way. At this place he sighed over the premature death of that great Master under whom he had studied. He lamented also that Vasubandhu's teaching was still in vogue, and he expressed his determination to write a refutation of the Mahāyana system, and to efface the name of Vasubandhu. But he in-

---

[1] Abhidharma-tsang-hsien-tsung-lun (No. 1266). The word *tsang* in this title is evidently a translation of *kośa* and not of *piṭaka*. In the name of the original treatise the word *kośa* has been explained as meaning not only *bud* but also *core*, *sheath*, *integument*, and other things. Sanghabhadra, however, does not seem to have taken the word in the sense of *bud* either in the Anusāra-śāstra or in this abstract.

[2] Tār. S. 130 note, and S. 319 and note.

stantly became delirious, five tongues emerged from his mouth, and his life-blood gushed forth. He had time to repent, and to warn his disciples; but he died and went, according to an arhat, to the Hell which knows no intermission. At the time of his death there was an earthquake, and a cavity was formed in the ground at the spot where he died. His associates cremated the corpse, collected the bones, and erected a memorial (that is, the tope) over them.

It is unusual for a tope to be erected in memory of a man reputed to have gone to Hell, and a Chinese annotator has suggested that *stūpa* here is a mistake for *ti* (地) meaning "place". But the correction is not necessary, as the tope was erected by the personal friends of Vimalamitra, who did not think he had gone to Hell. As this man's dead body was cremated it seems strange that the arhat should have declared he had gone down into the Avichi Hell. It was evidently not the human being Vimalamitra who had so descended, but his *alter ego*, the embodied karma which had been formed and accumulated in successive births.

From the Life we learn that the pilgrim remained several months in this district studying Guṇaprabha's *Pien-chên-lun* or "Tattvasandeśa śāstra", already mentioned, and other Abhidharma commentaries. He also met here the Bhadanta *Mi-to-se-na*, that is Mitasena (or Mitrasena), ninety years old who had been a disciple of Guṇaprabha and was a profound scholar in Buddhist learning.

In the north-west of Matipur, Yuan-chuang proceeds to relate, on the east side of the Ganges was the city *Mo-yü-lo* (or Mayūra) above twenty *li* in circuit. It had a large population and streams of clear water: it produced bell-metal (*t'u-shih*), rock-crystal, and articles of jewelry. Near the city and close to the Ganges was a large Deva-Temple of many miracles, and in its inclosure was a tank the banks of which were faced with stone slabs, the tank being fed by an artificial passage from the Ganges. This was called the Ganges-Gate and it was a place for making religious merit and extinguishing guilt: there were constantly many thousands of people from distant regions assembled here bathing. Pious kings erected Puṇyaśālas in the district for the free distribution of dainty food and medical requisites to the kinless and friendless.

The "Ganges-Gate" of this passage is said to be the Gangādvāra of Indian writers, the modern Hardwar (or Haridvār), the "Source of the Ganges" already mentioned. As Yuan-chuang apparently did not go to Mayūra, we should perhaps regard him as writing about Gangādvāra only from information given to him by others. Cunningham thinks that this Mayūra "must be the present ruined site of Māyāpura, at the head of the Ganges canal".[1] But *Mo-yü-lo* cannot be taken as a transcription of Māyāpura, and this town was on the west side of the Ganges whereas *Mo-yü-lo* (Mayūra) was on the east side of that river.

Our pilgrim proceeds to relate that going north "from this" above 300 *li* he came to the *P'o-lo-hih-mo-pu-lo* country. This was more than 4000 *li* in circuit, with mountains on all sides, its capital being above twenty *li* in circuit. It had a rich flourishing population, and a fertile soil with regular crops: it yielded bell-metal (*t'u-shih*) and rock-crystal: the climate was coldish: the people had rough ways: they cared little for learning and pursued gain. There were five Buddhist monasteries, but there were very few Brethren: there were above ten Deva-Temples and the sectarians lived pell-mell.

The *P'o-lo-hih-mo-pu-lo* of this passage has been restored by Julien, who here transliterates *P'o-lo-ki-mo*, as Brahmapura; and the restoration, said by Cunningham to be correct, has been generally accepted. Although P'o-lo-hih-mo is not the usual transcription for Brahma, we may perhaps regard these sounds as standing here for this word. Brahmapura is the name of a city which is in the north-east division of the Bṛihat Samhitā[2], but in our author it is the name of a country. Cunningham, who treats the *north* of our text as a mistake for *north-east*, finds the country in "the districts of Garhwāl and Kumaon".[3] It is not very clear whether the pilgrim meant us to understand that he started on his journey to this country from Mayūra, or from Matipura. The Fang-Chih took the former as the

---

1 A. G. I. p. 351.
2 Ind. Ant. Vol. XXII. p. 172.
3 A. G. I. p. 355.

starting-place, but it is perhaps better to regard Matipur as the "this" of the text from which the pilgrim goes north 300 *li*. This construction is in agreement with the Life which has no mention of Mayūra.

To the north of this country (Brahmapura), and in the Great Snow Mountains, was the Suvarṇagotra country. The superior gold which it produced gave the country its name. This was the "Eastern Woman's Country" (that is, of the Chinese) so called because it was ruled by a succession of women. The husband of the queen was king, but he did not administer the government. The men attended only to the suppression of revolts and the cultivation of the fields. This country reached on the east to T'u-fan (Tibet), on the north to Khoten, and on the west to San-p'o-ha (Malasa).

The Suvarṇagotra country of this passage is perhaps the Suvarṇabhū or Gold-region in the north-east division of the Bṛihat-Saṇhitā, which Kern regards as "in all likelihood a mythical land".[1] Our pilgrim was taught to identify this district with the "Eastern Woman's-Country" of his countrymen, which is undoubtedly a mythical region. Further the situation of the Eastern Woman's Country is far away from the region in which Yuan-chuang places his Suvarṇagotra. This name is translated properly in a note to the text by "the Golds" that is, the Gold family, but the author evidently regarded the name as meaning "the land of gold".

## KU-P'I-SANG-NA (GOVIŚANA).

From Matipur the pilgrim continued his journey, he goes on to state, travelling south-east for above 400 *li* to the country of *Ku-p'i-shuang*(or *sang*)*-na*. This country was above 2000 *li* in circuit; and its capital, which was 14 or 15 *li* in circuit, was a natural stronghold. There was a flourishing population: everywhere was a succession of blooming woods and tanks: the climate and natural products were the same as those of Matipur. The people had honest sincere ways, they applied themselves to learning and were fond of religious merit: most of them were non-Buddhists, and sought the joys of this life. There

[1] Ind. Ant. Vol. XXII. p. 190.

were two Buddhist monasteries with above 100 Brethren all Hinayānists. Of Deva-Temples there were above 30, and the sectarians lived pell-mell. Close to the capital was an old monastery in which was an Asoka tope to mark the spot at which the Buddha preached for a month on religious essentials. Beside this were sites of the sitting places and exercise grounds of the Four Past Buddhas, and two topes with hair and nail relics of the Julai.

For the *Ku-p'i-sang-na* of our pilgrim's text Julien suggests *Goviśana* as a possible restoration, and Saint-Martin proposes Goviśāna, but a word like Govisanna would be nearer the Chinese sounds. Cunningham thinks that the capital of this country was on the site of "the old fort near the village of Ufain which is just one mile to the east of the modern Kāshipur". The country he thinks, "must have corresponded very nearly to the modern districts of Kāshipur, Rāmpur, and Pilibhit".[1] The Fang-chih here agrees with the Records, but the Life does not mention the journey from Matipur to Govisana.

For the words "religious essentials" in the penultimate sentence of the above passage the original is *chu-fa-yao* (諸法要), which may also be translated "the essentials of things". These words are rendred by Julien— "les vérités les plus essentielles de la loi".

## NGO-HI-CH'I-TA-LO (AHICHATRA?)

From Goviśana, our pilgrim proceeds to tell us, he travelled south-east above 400 *li*, and came to the country which he calls *Ngo*(or *O*)-*hi-ch'i-ta lo*. This country was above 3000 *li* in circuit: its capital, which was in a strong position, was 17 or 18 *li* in circuit. The country yielded grain, and had many woods and springs, and a genial climate. The people were honest in their ways, they studied abstract truth (*tao* 道) and were diligent in learning, with much ability and extensive knowledge. There were above ten Buddhist Monasteries, and more than 1000 Brethren students of the Sammitiya School of the Hīnayāna. Deva-Temples were nine in number, and there were above 300 professed adherents of the other systems Pāśupatas who worshipped Īśvara (Siva). At the side of a Dragon Tank outside the capital was

[1] A. G. I. p. 357.

an Asoka tope where the Ju-lai preached to the Dragon for seven days. Beside it were four small topes at the sitting and exercise places of the Four Past Buddhas.

The first character for the name of the country here described is written 堊 in some texts and 惡 in others, and the sound of these characters is given as *Ngo* or *wo*, or *o* or *yo*. In the Life this syllable is omitted and the name is given as Hi-ch'i-ta-lo, apparently by mistake although it seems to be the reading of all the texts. The Life also makes the pilgrim go from *Brahmapura* south-east above 400 *li* to this country. Julien restores the name in our text as Ahikshetra, but the characters seem to require a word like Ahichhitra. Cunningham adopts the account in the Records and writes the name Ahichatra which, he says, is still preserved although the place has been deserted for many centuries. The district of Ahichatra, he believes, occupied the eastern part of Rohilkhand.[1]

## P'I-LO-SHAN-NA.

From Ahichitra, the pilgrim tells us, he went south (according to the other texts but according to D, east) about 260 *li* and crossing the Ganges went to the south (or according to the B text, south-west) into the *P'i-lo-shan-na* country. This was above 2000 *li* in circuit and its capital above ten *li* in circuit. It resembled Ahichitra in climate and products. The people were mainly non-Buddhists, a few reverencing Buddhism. There were two Buddhist Monasteries with 300 Brethren all Mahāyāna students. There were five Deva-Temples and the sectarians lived pell-mell. In the capital was an old monastery within the inclosure of which stood an Asoka tope at the pilgrim's time in ruins. It was here that the Buddha delivered during seven days the sūtra called *yun-chie-ch'u-ching* (蘊界處經). By its side were vestiges of the sitting and exercise places of the Four Past Buddhas.

The name of the country here described is restored by Julien tentatively as Vīraśāna, but it may have been something like Vilaśāṇa or Bhilasana. *P'i-lo-shan-na* (毗羅刪拏) is the reading in the A, B, and C texts of the Records,

---

[1] A. G. I. p. 359.

and in the Fang-chih, but in the D text of the Records and in the Life the reading is *P'i-lo-na*(那)*-na* which may be for a word like Bhiladaṇa.

Cunningham identifies the capital of the *P'i-lo-shan-na* of our text with "the great mound of ruins called *Atranji-khera* which is situated on the right or west bank of the *Kāli Nadi*, four miles to the south of *Karsāna*, and eight miles to the north of *Eyta*, on the Grand Trunk Road".[1]

The name of the sūtra which the pilgrim says the Buddha delivered at the capital of this country is given as *yun-chie-chcu-ching*. This means "the sūtra of the place of the elements of the skandha", and it may represent a Sanskrit name like Skandhadhātusthāna sūtra (B. Nanjio suggests "Skandhadhātuupasthāna sūtra"), the "sūtra of the basis of the elements of phenomena", that is, of the senses and their objects. No sūtra with a name like this seems to be known to the collections of Buddhist scriptures, and the Fang-chih merely states that the Buddha preached for seven days "the dharma of the elements of the skandha".

## KAPITHA OR SĀNKAŚYA.

From P'i-lo-shan-na, the narrative proceeds, a journey of above 200 *li* south-east brought the pilgrim to the *Kah-pi-t'a* (Kapitha) country. This was more than 2000 *li*, and its capital above twenty *li* in circuit: the climate and products of the district were like those of P'i-lo-shan-na. There were four Buddhist monasteries (that is perhaps, at the capital) and above 1000 Brethren all of the Sammatiya School. The Deva-Temples were ten in number and the non-Buddhists, who lived pell-mell, were Saivites.

Above twenty *li* east (according to the A, B, and C texts, but in the D text, west) from the capital was a large monastery of fine proportions and perfect workmanship: its representations of Buddhist worthies were in the highest style of ornament. The monastery contained some hundreds of Brethren, all of the Sammatiya School, and beside it lived their lay dependents some myriads in number. Within the enclosing wall of the monastery were Triple stairs of precious substances in a row south to north, and sloping down to east, where the Julai descended from the

---

[1] A. G. I. p. 365.

Tayastiṃsa Heaven. The Ju-lai had ascended from Jetavana to Heaven and there lodged in the "Good-Law-Hall" where he had preached to his mother: at the end of three months he was about to descend. Then Indra by his divine power set up triple stairs of precious substances, the middle one of gold, the left one of crystal, and the right one of silver. The Buddha descended on the middle stair, Brahma holding a white whisk came down with him on the right stair and Indra holding up a jeweled sunshade descended on the left stair, while devas in the air scattered flowers and praised the Buddha. These stairs survived until some centuries before the pilgrim's time when they sank out of sight: then certain kings on the site of the original stairs set up the present ones of brick and stone adorned with precious substances and after the pattern of the original stairs. The present stairs were above 70 feet high with a Buddhist temple on the top in which was a stone image of the Buddha, and images of Brahma and Indra were at the top of the right and left stairs respectively and these images like the originals appeared to be descending.

By the side of these was an Asoka stone-pillar of a lustrous violet colour and very hard with a crouching lion on the top facing the stairs: quaintly carved figures were on each side of the pillar, and according to one's bad or good deserts figures appeared to him in the pillar. Not far from the Stairs was a tope where the Four Past Buddhas had sat and walked up and down: beside it was a tope where the Ju-lai had taken a bath: beside this was a Buddhist temple where the Julai had gone into samādhi. Beside the temple was a large stone platform 50 paces long and seven feet high where the Julai had walked up and down, all his footsteps having the tracery of a lotus-flower: and on both sides of it were small topes erected by Indra and Brahma. In front was the place where the bhikshuni Lotus flower-colour (Uttpalavarnī) wishing to be first to see the Buddha on his descent from Heaven transformed herself into a universal sovereign. At the same time Subhūti sitting meditating on the vanity of things beheld the spiritual body of Buddha. The Julai told Utpalavarṇā that she had not been the first to see him for Subhūti contemplating the vanity of things had preceded her in seeing his spiritual body. The Buddha's exercise platform was enclosed by a wall and had a large tope to the south-east of which was a tank the dragon of which protected the sacred traces from wanton injury.

The Life gives the direction in which the pilgrim travelled from *P'i-lo-shan-na* to *Kah-pi-t'a* as east instead of the souh-east of our text, but this may be a slip, the distance between the places being the same in the two books.

Our pilgrim's *Kah-pi-t'a* has naturally been restored as Kapitha, and we may retain the restoration for the present, although the word seems to be otherwise unknown. The transcription may, however, be for *Kalpita,* a word which has, with other meanings, that of "set in order". It was perhaps this name which the translator of a sūtra had before him when he gave *An-hsiang-hui* (安詳會), "Orderly arranged Meeting" as the name of the place of the Buddha's descent.[1] A note to our text here tells us that the old name of Kapitha was *Sêng-ka-she* (僧迦舍). This is a transcription of the name which is given as Sankāśya or Sāngkāśya (in Pali, Sankassa). It is the Sankasa of some, the Sakaspura of Spence Hardy, and the modern Sankisā.[2] The name Sankāśya or a variety of it seems to have been generally employed by the Buddhist writers of India, and the translators into Chinese and Tibetan usually centented themselves with transcriptions of the original. Another name for the place of the Buddha's Descent is that used in the Itinerary of Wu-k'ung. There it is designated *Ni-fo-wa-to* (泥嚩韈多), a puzzling word which the translators have taken to stand for the Sanskrit Devāvatāra.[3] This is doubtless correct, and the district obtained the name Devāvatāra or Devatāvataraṇam, in Chinese *T'ien-hsia-ch'ü* (天下處)[4], "Place of Devas' Descent", because Brahma, Indra, and hosts of inferior devas here appeared descending to earth with the Buddha. But as this name was not Buddhistic in appearance, the Deva

---

1 Fo-shuo-yi-tsu-ching, *ch.* 2 (No. 674). But the *Kah-pi-t'a* of our text may be the Kapisṭhala of the Brihat sañhita which the author of that work places in Madhyadeśa-see Ind. Ant. Vol. XXII p. 180 and Alberuni I. p. 300.

2 For Sakaspura and the Cingalese version of the visit to Heaven and descent therefrom see M. B. p. 308. For Sankisa see A. G. I. p. 368.

3 Shih-li-ching: J. A. T. VI. p. 358.

4 Divyāv. p. 150: Tsa-a-han-ching, *ch.* 19.

or Devatā was probably dropt in popular use, and the name Avataraṇam employed to denote the Buddha's Descent. Mr Rockhill's Tibetan text in his Life of Buddha relates that Buddha descended to "the foot of the Udumbara tree of the Avadjaravana (sic) of the town of Sāmkaśya".[1] Here the Tibetan probably wrote Avajaravana by a slip for Avatāravana or Avataraṇam.

From a curions little sūtra[2] we learn that there had once been at the place afterwards called Sankāśya an old chaitya (or tope), built in honour of Kāśyapa Buddha by his father, and called *Sêng-ka-shih* (Sankāśya). Before the time of Gautama Buddha, however, this chaitya had sunk down until it was all underground. When the Buddha descended from Heaven at this place, he caused the Chaitya to emerge above ground as a memorial of his return to earth. Afterwards it was found that the chaitya as it stood interfered with the traffic of the city, and so the king ordered it to be demolished. But during the night the chaitya left its site to the north of the city, and passed over the city to a spot in a wood about twenty *li* south of it. The chaitya of this sūtra is elsewhere a temple; and is described as the model for the one which five kings on Buddha's suggestion erected near its site.[3] This temple, called the Gods' or Kings' Temple, was erected as a memorial of the Buddha's Descent, and was probably the temple of our pilgrim's description. In the old sūtra, it will be observed, the chaitya of Kāśyapa Buddha is called Sankāśya, and this name is transferred to the city. As such the name is interpreted in another work as meaning *kuang-ming* (光 明) or "brightness", "clearness",[4] and this may indicate a reference to the legend of the chaitya of Kāśyapa Buddha.

The story of Gautama Buddha leaving Jetavana for the

---

1 Rockhill Life p. 81.
2 Fo-shuo-ku-shu-ching (佛 說 枯 樹 經).
3 Tsêng-yi-a-han-ching, *ch.* 28.
4 A-yü-wang-ching, *ch.* 3.

Trayastriṃśa Heaven, spending there the three months of Retreat expounding his religion to his mother and the devas, and of his glorious descent to earth again, is referred to in many Chinese Buddhist books, and with only few serious variations of detail. In some works the place of descent is near a sand, or a large tank, outside of Sankāśya city[1], and here the "tank" of the translation may represent *avatāra* in the original, this word having also the meaning of *tank* or *pond*. In some treatises the scene of the Descent is at Kanyākubja, which is placed in the Sankāśya country by one authority, and in the Andhra country by another[2]. The Tope of the Descent was the fifth of the Eight Great Topes connected with the Buddha's career, and it was at Kanyākubja. Wu-K'ung went to Devāvatāra to see this tope, but neither Fa-hsien[3] nor our pilgrim makes any mention of a great tope in their descriptions of the sights of the place, although Yuan-chuang, as we have seen, incidentally mentions a "great tope" afterwards.

The legend of the bhikshuṇī Utpalavarṇā making herself a magic Chakravartī, or Universal Sovereign, by which to be the first to greet Buddha on his descent; and her rebuke by the latter, who told her that Subhūti, seeing the spiritual body of Buddha, had been before her, is in several Buddhist works. But it is not in the account of the Descent given in the Tsa-a-han-ching, and in another treatise we have the bhikshuṇī, but Subhūti is not mentioned by name. The words "transformed herself" in the statement that the nun "transformed herself into a Chakravarti" are for the terms *hua-tso* (化作) and *hua-wei* (化爲) of the text. But the former, which is apparently taken from the Fo-kuo-chi or some other work, means *create* or *produce the appearance of by magic*. Utpalavarṇā was an

---

[1] A-yü-wang-chuan, *ch.* 2; Tsêng-yi-a-han-ching, l. c.

[2] Ta-shêng-pên-shêng-hsin-ti-kuan-ching, *ch.* 1 (No. 955); Pa-ta-ling-t'a-ming-hao-ching (No. 898).

[3] See Fo-kuo-chi, *ch.* 17.

arhat, and so had supernormal powers. She thus, according to various accounts, produced the appearance of a chakravarti with his seven treasures, 1000 sons, and fourfold army, and transferring herself into her own magic Chakravarti, obtained the foremost place in front of the actual kings and all the crowd assembled to welcome Buddha.[1] Subhūti at this time was sitting, according to Yuan-chuang, in a cave (that is, on the Gridhrakūṭa mountain near Rājagaha), but another version makes him to be in his own house. Knowing that the Buddha was coming down from Heaven he reflected on the vanity of phenomena, and realizing in himself the nature of phenomena, he beheld, by the vision of spiritual wisdom, the spiritual body of Buddha, that is, the transcendental philosophy of Prajñāpāramitā.

The Utpalavarṇā (in Pali, Uppalavaṇṇā) of this passage was one of the greatest and most noted of the bhikshuṇīs ordained by the Buddha. Her life as a laywoman had been extremely unhappy and, according to some legends, very immoral. She had two experiences which were especially distressing and produced on her a profound effect leading her, according to one account, to renounce the world. While living with her first husband she found him living in adultery with her mother, and her second husband brought home, as his concubine, her daughter by her first husband. Each of these experiences pierced her with sharp agony; and she left her home for ever.[2] When she became converted, and was admitted into the Buddhist church as a bhikshuṇī, she devoted herself to religion with enthusiasm, and attained arhatship. But

---

1 Ta-chih-tu-lun, *ch.* 10, Ta-shêng-tsao-hsiang-kung-tê-ching, *ch.* 1 (No. 288).

2 Mi-sa-sai-lü, *ch.* 4 (No. 1122); Tib. Tales p. 206. A very different account of this lady's admission into his church by the Buddha is given in the Fa-chü-pi-yü-ching, *ch.* 1 (No. 1353) where she is called simply *Lien-hua* or Utpala. For the previous existences of Uppalavaṇṇā see Dr Bode's "Woman Leaders of the Buddhist Reformation" in J. R. A. S. for 1893 p. 532. For her misfortunes see also Therī-Gāthā p. 144 and p. 198 (P. T. S.).

even as a nun she was put to shame and had trouble. And her death was sad, for she was brutally attacked by Devadatta and died from the injuries inflicted by him.[1] Her name "Blue lotus colour" may have been given to her, as some suppose, because she had eyes like the blue lotus; but it is also said to have been indicative of her great personal beauty, or of the sweet perfume which her body exhaled.

Subhūti is interpreted as meaning "Excellent Manifestation" which is Yuan-chuang's translation, or "Excellent good auspices", and is rendered in several other ways. It was the name of the Disciple who is sometimes mentioned along with Mahākāśyapa, Aniruddha and other great disciples of the Buddha.[2] But he is best known as the exponent and defender of the doctrines of Prajñāpāramitā. He was a son of a learned brahmin of Śrāvasti, and was educated in the orthodox learning. Afterwards he became a hermit, and then was converted to Buddhism and ordained.[3]

---

[1] Sar. Vin. P'o-sêng-shih, *ch.* 10 (No. 1123).
[2] Divyāv. p. 361; Saddharmapuṇḍarīkā, *chs.* 1 and 4.
[3] Bud. Lit. Nep. p. 296; Ching-lü-yi-hsiang, *ch.* 13 (No. 1473).

# CHAPTER XI.

## CHUAN V.

## KANYĀKUBJA TO VIŚOKA.

**From the neighbourhood of Sankāśya the pilgrim went north-west for nearly 200 *li* to the *Ka-no-kü-she* (Kanyākubja) country. This he describes as being above 4000 *li* in circuit. The capital, which had the Ganges on its west side, was above twenty *li* in length by four or five *li* in breadth; it was very strongly defended and had lofty structures everywhere; there were beautiful gardens and tanks of clear water, and in it rarities from strange lands were collected. The inhabitants were well off and there were families with great wealth; fruit and flowers were abundant, and sowing and reaping had their seasons. The people had a refined appearance and dressed in glossy silk attire; they were given to learning and the arts, and were clear and suggestive in discourse; they were equally divided between orthodoxy and heterodoxy. There were above 100 Buddhist monasteries with more than 10,000 Brethren who were students of both the "Vehicles". There were more than 200 Deva-Temples and the non-Buddhists were several thousands in number.**

The reading "north-west" at the beginning of this passage is that of the Common texts of the Records and Life; but the D text of the Records has "south-east". This agrees with Fa-hsien's narrative[1], confirms the correction proposed by Cunningham[2], and, as Kanauj is to the south-east of Sankassa, is evidently the proper reading. Moreover in the itinerary of the Sung pilgrim Kanyākubja is two stages (*ch'êng* 程) to the east of Sankāśya[3]. Fa-hsien

---

1 Fo-kuo-chi, *ch.* 18.
2 Anc. Geog. Ind. p. 376.
3 Ma T. l. *ch.* 338.

makes the distance between these two places to be seven yojanas or above 40 miles and this agrees roughly with Yuan-chuang's 200 *li.*

Yuan-chuang here gives to the capital and extends also to the country the correct name *Ka-no-kü-she* (羯若鞠闍) that is, Kanyākubja, while Fa-hsien, like some other writers, gives the name which was probably in use among the natives, viz. *Ka-nao-yi* or Kanoyi, that is, the modern Kanauj (or Kanoj). Another transcription of the classical name is *Kan-na-ku-po-she* (犍拏究撥闍) which is wrongly translated by *êrh-ch'u* (耳出) or "Ear-emanation". In a note to our text the name is properly rendered by "Hunch-backed maidens", the translation which the pilgrim uses, and the story of the origin of the name is related by the pilgrim.

According to this story long ages ago when Brahmadatta was king, and men lived very many years the name of the city was Kusumapura (that is, Flower-Palace or city). King Brahmadatta was a mighty sovereign and a great warrior; he had also the full number of 1000 sons wise and valorous and 100 fair and virtuous daughters. On the bank of the Ganges there lived at this time a rishi the years of whose life were to be counted by myriads; he was popularly called the "Great-Tree-Rishi", because he had a banyan tree growing from his shoulders; the seed of the tree had been dropt on him by a bird, had taken root and grown to be a huge tree in which birds had been building their nests while the rishi remained unconscious in a trance of prolonged absorbed meditation (samādhi). When he had emerged from the trance, and moved about, he had glimpses of the king's daughters as they chased each other in the wood near the river. Then carnal affection laid hold on him, and he demanded of the king one of his daughters in marriage. But all the princesses refused to wed "Great-Tree-Rishi", and the king was in great fear and distress. In this extremity, however, the youngest daughter made a sacrifice of herself by offering to marry the rishi in order to save her father and country from the effects of his displeasure. But when the circumstances were told to him the old rishi was very much enraged at the other princesses for not appreciating him properly, and he cursed them with immediate crookedness. In consequence of this the ninety nine princesses all became bowed in body, and the capital of the country was henceforth known as the city of the Hunch-backed Maidens.

This is a very silly story which probably has a good moral. The brahmins, it will be remembered, have a similar story to account for the name of the city of Kanauj. They relate that Vāyu, the Wind-god, also called a rishi, became enamoured of the 100 daughters of Kuśanābha, king of this country. The princesses refused to comply with the god's lustful desires, and he in his ire made them all back-bowed, and from this circumstance the city got its name Kanyākubja.[1] Another name for the district or country is *Mahodayā*, explained as meaning "the land of great prosperity". It is sometimes described as being in the Andhra country, as we have seen, and it is also said to be in the middle of India, in Madhyadeśa.

It will be seen that in the description which Yuan-chuang gives of Kanyākubja in the above passage he represents the Ganges as being on its west side. Cunningham makes him place that river on the east side, but this is a mistake. Other old authorities place the Ganges on the east side of Kanauj, where it still is. The city is also described as being on the Kāli-nadi an affluent of the Ganges on its west side. Fa-hsien merely describes the capital as reaching to the Ganges; but this evidently was not on the west side, as he tells of a tope on the north bank of the river about six *li* to the west of the capital.

Our pilgrim here gives the number of Buddhist establishments in and about the capital as 100. This number seems to point to a great increase of Buddhism in the district from the time of Fa-hsien, as when that pilgrim visited the Kanauj country there were apparently only two Buddhist monasteries at the capital. The "non-Buddhists", or *yi-tao* (異道), of our pilgrim who meet us so often in the Records, were evidently the priests or other professed ministers of the various non-Buddhist systems of religion. These must have increased and Buddhists decreased at Kanyākubja after our pilgrim's time, as when the Sung

---

[1] Dowson's Cl. Dict. Ind. Myth. s. v. Vāyu.

pilgrim visited the district he found topes and temples numerous but there were no monks or nuns.

We have next an account of the sovereign ruling at Kanauj and his origin.

> This sovereign was of the Vaiśya caste, his personal name was Harshavardhana, and he was the younger son of the great king whose name was Prabhākaravardhana. When the latter died he was succeeded on the throne by his elder son named Rāja-(or Rājya) vardhana. The latter soon after his accession was treacherously murdered by Śasañgka, the wicked king of Karṇasuvarṇa in East India, a persecutor of Buddhism. Hereupon the statesmen of Kanauj, on the advice of their leading man Bāni (or Vāni), invited Harshavardhana, the younger brother of the murdered king, to become their sovereign. The prince modestly made excuses, and seemed unwilling to comply with their request.

When the ministers of state pressed Harshavardhana to succeed his brother and avenge his murder, the narrative goes on to relate, the prince determined to take the advice of the Bodhisattva Avalokiteśvara (whose name is here given correctly in translation *Kuan-tzŭ-tsai*, the "Beholding Lord"). An image of this Bodhisattva, which had made many spiritual manifestations, stood in a grove of this district near the Ganges. To this he repaired; and after due fasting and prayer, he stated his case to the Bodhisattva. An answer was graciously given which told the prince that it was his good karma to become king, and that he should, accordingly, accept the offered sovereignty and then raise Buddhism from the ruin into which it had been brought by the king of Karṇasuvarṇa, and afterwards make himself a great kingdom. The Bodhisattva promised him secret help, but warned him not to occupy the actual throne, and not to use the title *Mahārāja*. Thereupon Harshavardhana became king of Kanauj with the title Rājaputra and the style Śīlāditya.

Continuing his narrative the pilgrim goes on to state that as soon as Śīlāditya became ruler he got together a great army, and set out to avenge his brother's murder and to reduce the neighbouring countries to subjection. Proceeding eastwards he invaded the states which had refused allegiance, and waged incessant warfare until in six years he had *fought* the Five Indias (reading *chü* 拒. According to the other reading *ch'ên* 臣, had brought the Five Indias under allegiance). Then having enlarged his territory he increased his army, bringing the elephant corps up to 60,000 and the cavalry to 100,000, and reigned in peace for thirty years without raising a weapon. He was just in his administration, and punctilious in the discharge of his duties. He forgot sleep and food in his devotion to good works. He caused the use of animal food to cease throughout the Five Indias, and he prohibited the taking of life under severe penalties. He erected thousands of topes on the banks of the Ganges, established Travellers Rests through all his dominions, and erected Buddhist monasteries at sacred places of the Buddhists. He regularly held the Quinquennial Convocation; and gave away in religious alms everything except the material of war. Once a year he summoned all the Buddhist monks together, and for twenty one days supplied them with the regulation requisites. He furnished the chapels and liberally adorned the common halls of the monasteries. He brought the Brethren together for examination and discussion, giving rewards and punishments according to merit and demerit. Those Brethren who kept the rules of their Order strictly and were thoroughly sound in theory and practice he "advanced to the Lion's Throne" (that is, promoted to the highest place) and from these he received religious instruction; those who, though perfect in the observance of the ceremonial code, were not learned in the past he merely honoured with formal reverence; those who neglected the ceremonial observances of the Order, and whose immoral conduct was notorious, were banished from his presence and from the country. The neighbouring princes, and the statesmen, who were zealous in good works, and unwearied in the search for moral excellence, he led to his own seat, and called "good friends", and he would not converse with those who were of a different character. The king also made visits of inspection throughout his dominion, not residing long at any place but having temporary buildings erected for his residence at each place of sojourn, and he did not go abroad during the three months of the Rain-season Retreat. At the royal lodges every day viands were provided for 1000 Buddhist monks and 500 Brahmins. The king's day was divided into three periods, of which one was given up to affairs of government, and two were devoted to religious works. He was indefatigable, and the day was too short for him.

Before proceeding to the next part of our pilgrim's narrative we may add a few notes to his very interesting account of the great Harshavardhana. At the beginning of the above passage we are told that this king was of the *Fei-she* (吠奢) or Vaiśya caste (or stock). This statement Cunningham thinks is a mistake, the pilgrim confounding the Vaisa or Bais Rajputs with the Vaiśya caste. Cunningham may be right. But we must remember that Yuan-chuang had ample opportunities for learning the antecedents of the royal family, and he must have had some ground for his assertion. Harshavardhana's father, Prabhākaravardhana, a descendant of Puṣpabhūti king of Sthāṇeśvara in Śrīkantha, "was famed far and wide under a second name Pratāpaśīla". To him were born two sons Rājyavardhana and Harshavardhana and a daughter Rājyaśrī, and he had also an adopted son Bhaṇḍi the son of his queen's brother[1]. The princess Rājyaśrī was evidently, as the "Harṣa-carita" represents her, an intelligent, accomplished lady, and she was apparently interested in Buddhism. She was present as a listener seated behind Harshavardhana when the Chinese pilgrim gave the latter a lecture on Buddhism. It may be noted here also that the Fang-chih represents Harshavardhana as "administering the government in conjunction with his widowed sister", a statement which is not, I think, either in the Life or the Records. Very soon after Rājyavardhana succeeded his father on the throne he had to go away to avenge the murder of his brother-in-law, and to rescue his sister imprisoned in Kanyākubja. He was successful in battle, but he fell into a snare laid for him by the Gauḍa king, according to the "Harṣa-carita", and was treacherously murdered. Hereupon Harshavardhana became king, and at once proceeded to rescue his sister, take revenge, and make great conquests. This is the Śīlāditya of our pilgrim's narrative and of the Life, a very interesting and remarkable personage.

With Yuan-chuang's story of Harshavardhana going to consult Avalokiteśvara we may compare the statement in the "Harṣa-carita" that he "was embraced by the goddess of the Royal Prosperity, who took him in her arms and, seizing him by all the royal marks on all his limbs, forced him, however reluctant, to mount the throne, — and this though he had taken a vow of austerity and did not swerve from his vow, hard like grasping the edge of a

---

[1] Harṣa-carita, *ch.* IV. (Cowell and Thomas tr.)

sword".[1] It seems probable that Harshavardhana in the early part of his life had joined the Buddhist church and perhaps taken the vows of a bhikshu, or at least of a lay member of the Communion. His sister, we learn from the Life, had become an adherent of the Sammatiya school of Buddhism.[2] Our pilgrim's sympathetic and generous praise of king Harshavardhana may be compared with the pompous, fulsome, and feigned panegyric of the king by Bāṇa.

In the above transcript from the Records the words rendered "reigned in peace for thirty years without raising a weapon" are in Julien's translation— "Au bout de trente ans, les armes se reposèrent". The text is *Ch'ui-san-shih-nien-ping-ko-pu-ch'i* (垂三十年兵戈不起). Here the word *ch'ui* is employed, as frequently, to denote "don the imperial robe", that is, to reign gently and happily. Thus the pilgrim tells us that there were thirty years of Śīlāditya's reign in which there were peace and good government. Our pilgrim has expressly stated that the king's conquests were completed within six years, and it is against text and context to make him represent the king as fighting continuously for thirty or thirty-six years. When his wars were over Śīlāditya (the style of Harshavardhana as king) proceeded to put his army on a peace footing, that is, to raise it to such a force that he could overawe any of the neighbouring states disposed to be contumacious. We shall presently see how a word from him was enough for the king of one of those states. Having thus made himself strong and powerful Śīlāditya was able to live in peace, and devote himself to the duties and functions of a pious but magnificent sovereign. He was now as fond of the solemn pomps and grand processions of religion as he had been of the marshalling of vast hosts, the "magnificently stern array" of battle, and the glories of a great victory.

We find two dates given for the death of king Śīlāditya,

[1] Harṣa-carita, *ch.* IV. (Cowell and Thomas tr.) p. 57.

[2] Life, *ch.* 5.

Chinese history placing it in the year A. D. 648 and the Life in 655[1]. Taking thirty-six years as the duration of his reign we thus have 612 or 619 as the date of his accession. The latter date agrees with a Chinese statement that the troubles in India which led to Śīlāditya's reign took place in the reign of T'ang Kao Tsu (A. D. 618 to 627). But the date 648, or rather 647, is perhaps the correct one. It must have been in 641 or 642 that, in conversation with our pilgrim, Śīlāditya stated that he had then been sovereign for above thirty years. This also gives 612 for the year of his accession, and the addition of six years to the thirty gives 648 as the date of his death. But the Chinese envoy despatched in the early part of that year found, on his arrival in the country, the king dead, and a usurper on the throne. Moreover it was in 648 that Yuan-chuang submitted his Records to T'ai Tsung, and Śīlāditya must have been dead before this work was drawn up in its present form.

For the words rendered in the above passage by "advanced to the Lion's Throne" that is, promoted to be chief bhikshus, the Chinese is *t'ui-shêng-shi-tzŭ-chih-tso* (推昇師子之座). This Julien understood to mean "caused them to go up on the throne". The words might probably have this meaning in other places, but no good bhikshu would mount a rāja's throne, and it seems better to take *shi-tzŭ-chih-tso* here in its Buddhist sense as the throne of the head of the Order. The term, we know, does mean *a king's throne*, but Śīlāditya did not use a throne; and the other use of the term seems to be here more correct and suitable. The Lion's Throne of the Buddhists was originally the seat reserved for the Buddha, as leader of the congregation, in the chapels and Halls of the Monasteries; and afterwards it became the throne or seat of the chief bhikshu of a place. Promotion to the Lion's Throne was given locally by pious kings, and did not inter-

---

[1] See Ma T. l., *ch.* 338; T'ung-chien-kang-mu, *ch.* 40 (T'ang T'ai Tsung Chên-kuan 22 y.); Life, *ch.* 5.

fere with precedence among the Brethren. Here Sīlāditya promotes the most deserving bhikshus at his court, and makes them his private chaplains, personally receiving from them religious instruction.[1]

By the term "good friend" *shan-yu* (善友), which the pilgrim here tells us was applied by the king to devout princes and statesmen, we are to understand the *kalyāna-mitra* of Buddhist use. This term means *good* or *auspicious friend*, and it is also employed in the sense of *spiritual adviser*, or *good counseller in matters of religion*.

Returning again to our text we have now an episode which belongs to a date five or six years later than the visit of which the pilgrim is here telling. To be understood properly the narrative must be read in connection with the account of Kāmarūpa in *Chuan* 10 and with the story given in the corresponding passage of the Life.

The pilgrim, we learn from these texts, was on his way hack to China, and had gone again to the great monastery of Nālandā in Magadha. Here he wished to remain for some time continuing his studies in Buddhist philosophy which had been begun there some years before. But Bāskaravarma, styled Kumāra, the king of Kāmarūpa (that is, Assam), had heard of him and longed to see him. So he sent messengers to Nālandā to invite and urge the pilgrim to pay him a visit. Yuan-chuang at first declined and pleaded his duty to China, but his old Buddhist teacher Śīlabhadra convinced him that it was also his duty to go to Kāmarūpa on the invitation of its king who was not a Buddhist. The pilgrim at length yielded, travelled to that country, and was received by the king with great honour. In the course of a conversation His Majesty said to Yuan-chuang.— "At present in various states of India a song has been heard for some time called the "Music of the conquests of Ch'in (Tsin) wang" of Mahāchina—this refers to Your Reverence's native country I presume". The pilgrim replied— "Yes, this song praises my sovereign's excellences".

At this time king Śīlāditya was in a district the name of which is transcribed in our Chinese texts in several ways. Julien calls it "Kadjoughira", and Cunningham identifies it with the

[1] A special seat or pulpit, called a "Lion's Throne", was sometimes given by a king to the Brother whom he chose to be Court preacher.

modern Kānkjol). He had been on an expedition to a country called *Kung-yü-ta*, and was on his way back to Kanauj to hold a great Buddhist assembly there. Hearing of the arrival of the Chinese pilgrim at the court of king Kumāra he sent a summons to the latter to repair to him with his foreign guest. Kumāra replied with a refusal, saying that the king could have his head but not his guest. "I trouble you for your head", came the prompt reply. Thereupon Kumāra became submissive, and proceeded with the pilgrim and a grand retinue to join Śīlāditya.

When this sovereign met Yuan-chuang, our text here relates, having made a polite apology to the pilgrim (literally, having said— I have fatigued you) he made enquiry as to Yuan-chuang's native land, and the object of his travelling. Yuan-chuang answered that he was a native of the great T'ang country, and that he was travelling to learn Buddhism. The king then asked about this great T'ang country, in what direction it lay, and how far it was distant. Yuan-chuang replied that his country was the Mahāchina of the Indians and that it was situated some myriads of *li* to the north-east of India. The king then relates how he had heard of the *Ch'in(Tsin)-wang-T'ien-tzŭ* (秦王天子), that is, the Deva-putra Prince Ch'in, of Mahāchina, who had brought that country out of anarchy and ruin into order and prosperity, and made it supreme over distant regions to which his good influences extended. All his subjects, the king continues, having their moral and material wants cared for by this ruler, sing the "song of *Ch'in-wang*'s conquests", and this fine song has long been known here. The king then asks the pilgrim whether this was all true, and whether his Great T'ang country was the country of the song.

In reply the pilgrim states that *Chi-na* (至那) that is, Chin was the designation of a former dynasty in his native land, and that Ta T'ang denoted the present dynasty; that the sovereign then reigning, T'ai Tsung, had been styled Ch'in-wang before he came to the throne, the title Emperor (*T'ien-tzŭ*) having been given to him on his accession. He then adds a compendious description of Ch'in-wang as Prince and Emperor.

The musical composition about which our pilgrim here represents the two Indian rulers as enquiring was known in China as the *Ch'in-wang-p'o-ch'ên-yao* (秦王破陣樂) or the "Music of Ch'in-wang's victory". Its history is briefly as follows.[1] In the year A. D. 619 T'ang Kao Tsu's

[1] See T'ung-chien-kang-mu, *ch.* 39 (T'ang T'ai Tsung 1st y.); T'ang-Shu, *ch.* 2 and 21; Ma T. l., *ch.* 129.

second son Ch'in-wang, or Prince of Ch'in, by name Shih-min succeeded in suppressing the serious rebellion of Liu wu-chow (劉武周) who ultimately fell into the hands of the Turks and was killed by them. In commemoration of Ch'in-wang's military achievments in suppressing this rebellion his soldiers got up a musical performance with song and dance. This musical composition was entitled "*Ch'in-wang-p'o-ch'ên-yao*" and also "*Shên-kung* (神功) *-p'o-ch'ên -yao*", but it came to be generally known by its short name "P'o-ch'ên-yao". The dancing or posture-making performance was called Ch'i-tê-wu (七德舞) or "Dance of the Seven Virtues", the name containing a classical allusion. The dancing was performed by a company of 128 men in silver hauberks and armed with spears. The emperor Kao Tsu ordered that the "P'o-ch'ên-yao" should be given when a victorious general returning from a successful campaign entered the capital. At the banquet which T'ai-Tsung, formerly Ch'in-wang, gave on his accession to the throne the dance and music were both performed. It is interesting to find that the fame of T'ang T'ai-Tsung's glory and achievments had reached the two Indian rulers if we can rely on our pilgrim's statements. It is also very remarkable that neither of Yuan-chuang's translators had read of Ch'in-wang, and it is pitiful to find Beal telling his readers that the Ch'in-wang of this passage is Ch'in-Shi-Huang-ti of B. C. 221.

The Records and the Life next go on to relate how the kings Śīlāditya and Kumāra, with their distinguished Chinese guest, proceeded by land and river in grand procession to the city of Kanyākubja where Śīlāditya had convoked a great Buddhist assembly. From this city, when the functions were over, the kings, we learn from the Life, with their Chinese guest, and attended by magnificent retinues, went on to Prayāga for the great periodical distribution of religious gifts and alms which was to be made there by Śīlāditya; and at that place our pilgrim bade his hosts farewell.

Before we take up again the thread of our pilgrim's

account of Kanyākubja we may add a few words about the great king who treated him with such marked distinction and kindness. This king, Śīlāditya or Śrī-Harshadeva or Harsha, "the Akbar of the 'Hindu period' of Indian history", was not only a great and successful warrior and wise and benevolent ruler: he was also an intelligent devoted patron of religion and literature, and he was apparently an author himself. His father had been a sun-worshipper; but he himself, while retaining publicly the religion of his father, and tolerant and liberal to other sects, was evidently strongly attached to Buddhism. As to his literary tastes we learn from I-ching that the king once called for a collection of the best poems written: of the compositions sent in to him 500 were found to be strings of jātakas (Jātakamālā). According to this author also Śīlāditya put together the incidents of the Cloud-riding (Jimūta-vāhana) Bodhisattva giving himself up for a nāga, into a poem to be sung, that is, he composed the "Nāgānanda". An accompaniment of instrumental music was added, and the king had the whole performed in public, and so it became popular.[1] The king was also a great traveller, and a seeker after knowledge of various kinds. His information about the martial fame and exploits of the Chinese emperor T'ai-Tsung may have been acquired on one of his expeditions to distant provinces. In the year 641 he sent an envoy to the Chinese Court, and apparently he sent another soon after. His title in the documents connected with the former embassy seems to have been "king of Magadha".

We return now to the pilgrim's description of Kanyākubja, and an abridgment of his account of the Buddhist memorials of the neighbourhood is all that is given in these pages.

To the north-west of the capital was an Asoka tope where the Buddha had preached excellent doctrines for seven days; beside it was a tope where the Four Past Buddhas had sat and walked for exercise; and there was a small tope over hair- and nail-relics

[1] Nan-hai-ch'i-kuei, sec. 32 and Takakusu p. 163.

of the Buddha. South of the Preaching Tope and close to the Ganges were three Buddhist monasteries enclosed by a common wall but each having its own gate. These vihāras had beautiful images, the Brethren were grave and reverend, and there were thousands of lay Buddhists to serve them. The shrine or temple (*ching-she*) of the three-fold vihāra had a casket containing a wonder-working tooth of the Buddha an inch and a half long, which was exhibited to crowds of visitors for a charge of one gold coin each. There were other sacred Buddhist buildings near the city, and there were also splendid temples to the Sun-god and to Maheśvara respectively.

From Kanyākubja, the pilgrim tells us, a journey of above 100 *li* south-east brought him to the city *na-fo-t'i-p'o-ku-lo* (Navadevakula). This city which was on the east bank of the Ganges, was above twenty *li* in circuit, with flowery groves and clear ponds giving interchange of sunshine and shadow. To the north-west of it, and also on the east bank of the Ganges, was a magnificent Deva-Temple. Five *li* to the east of the city were three Buddhist monasteries enclosed within one wall but with separate gates: in these monasteries were above 500 Brethren all Sarvāstivādins. Near the monasteries were the remains of an Asoka tope where the Buddha had preached for seven days. Three or four *li* north of the monasteries was another Asoka tope. This marked the spot at which 500 hungry demons, having come to the Buddha and attained an understanding of his teaching, exchanged the demon state for that of devas.

The *Na-fo-t'i-p'o-ku-lo* of this passage, restored as Navadevakula, means "New Deva-Temple", and the site of the city so called is supposed to be represented by the present Nohbatgang.[1] This city has also been identified with or declared to be near the village (in one text, but in the other texts, wood) of *A* (or *Ho*)-*li* (阿 or 呵 梨) which Fa-hsien places three yojanas south of Kanauj and on the other side of the Ganges. Our pilgrim's *city* may have been in the district of the wood (or village) but it cannot be identified with the latter. In the Life this city is not mentioned, and the Fang-chih calls it "Navadeva city". It is not unlikely that it was from the splendid Deva-temple which Yuan-chuang here describes very briefly that the city obtained its name. This temple, which

1 See Julien III. p. 350; A. G. I. p. 382.

was evidently of recent date, may have been devoted to the worship of Vishnu whose name Hari may be the word transribed by Fa-hsien's *A* (or *Ho*)-*li*.

Instead of "500 Hungry (餓) Demons" in this passage, the reading of the D text and the Fang-chih, the common texts have "more than (餘) 500 Demons". This latter is doubtless a copyist's error and the D reading is the correct one. From another source we learn that the Five Hundred Hungry Demons came to the Buddha and implored his pity: he thereupon requested Maudgalyayana to feed them. The Buddha had to enlarge their needle-throats to enable them to swallow the food: having eaten they burst, died, and went to Heaven. The Buddha explained that these creatures had once been so many lay Buddhists, and in that capacity had spoken rudely to bhikshus, calling them "Hungry Demons" when the bhikshus called on their morning rounds begging their daily food. The karma of this sin produced the rebirth of the upāsakas 500 times as Hungry Demons, and their faith in the Buddha, and prayer to him, obtained their release from misery and their birth in Heaven.[1]

The pilgrim, as we learn from the Life, remained at Kanyākubja three months, being lodged in the Bhadra-vihāra. Here he studied with the learned Buddhist monk *P'i-li-ye-se-na* (Vīryasena) the vibhāshā (or expository) treatise by *Fo-shih* (佛 使), "Buddha's Servant" or Buddhadāsa, called the *Chou* (胄)- or "Varma-vibhāshā." Julien, who apparently had a different text here, represents the pilgrim as reading the vibhāshā of Buddhadāsa "et le mémoire du maitre *ching-tcheou* (Ārya-varma) sur le *Pi-p'o-cha* (le vibhāchā)". A Buddhadāsa will be found mentioned in Yuan-chuang's account of "Hayamukha" as the author of a mahā-vibhāshā-śāstra. As this work was a book of the Sarvāstivādin school of the Hīnayāna its author cannot have been the Buddhadāsa who was a contemporary of Vasubandhu and a disciple of his brother Asanga.

1 Sar. Vin. Yao-shih, *ch.* 2.

Very little seems to be known about any śāstra-writer with the name Buddhadāsa, and there is no author with this name in the catalogues of Buddhist books as known in China and Japan.

## A-YÜ-T'Ê (AYODHYĀ).

**From the neighbourhood of Navadevakula city, according to the Records, the pilgrim continued his journey, going south-east; and after travelling above 600 *li*, and crossing the Ganges to the south, he reached the *A-yü-t'ê* (Ayudha or Ayodhyā) country.**

According to the account in the Life it was from Kanauj that Yuan-chuang went 600 *li* south-east to Ayudha. The capital of this country, which was about a mile to the south of the river, has been identified with the Ayodhyā of other writers, the old capital of Oudh. On account of difficulties of direction and distance Cunningham proposes a different site for Yuan-chuang's Ayudha[1]. But it seems to be better to adhere to Ayodhyā, and to regard Yuan-chuang's *Ganges* here as a mistake for a large affluent of the great river. The city was on the south bank of the river, and about 120 miles east-south-east from Kanauj. Its name is found written in full *A-yü-t'ê-ye* (阿喩駄也), Ayudhya (Ayodhyā), and the city is said to have been the seat of government of a line of kings more or less mythical.[2] We know also that to the Hindus Ayodhyā was the old capital of Rāma and the Solar race. It is possible that an old or dialectic form of the name was Ayuddha, and the Chinese translation of the Sanskrit word, which suits either form, means *invincible* or *irresistable*. Moreover we find that Yuan-chuang makes his Ayudha the temporary residence of Asanga and Vasubandhu, and other authorities represent Ayodhyā as a place of sojourn for these two illustrious brothers. Then the Ayudha of Yuan-

---

[1] A. G. I. p. 385. As will be seen there are serious difficulties in the identification of Yuan-chuang's Ayudha with the Sha-ki of Fa-hsien and with the Ayodhyā of other writers.

[2] Chung-hsü-ching, *ch.* 1 (No. 859).

chuang is apparently the *Sha-ki* or Saket, that is Ayodhyā, of Fa-hsien; this was ten yojanas south-east from the Ho-li village which was three yojanas south from Kanauj. Alberuni makes Ayodhyā to have been about 150 miles south-east from Kanauj, being 25 farsakhs down the Ganges from Bāri, which was 20 farsakhs east from Kanauj.[1] It is the Sāketā or Oudh of the Brihat-sanhitā which merely places it in the "Middle country".[2] It may be mentioned in passing that there is no reference to Ayudha in the account of king Śīlāditya's progress from Kanauj by land and river to Prayāga.

The Ayudha country, the Records proceeds to tell us, was above 5000 *li* in circuit, and the capital was above twenty *li* in circuit. The country yielded good crops, was luxuriant in fruit and flower, and had a genial climate. The people had agreeable ways, were fond of good works, and devoted to practical learning. There were above 100 Buddhist monasteries, and more than 3000 Brethren who were students of both "Vehicles". There were ten Deva-Temples, and the non-Buddhists were few in number.

Within the capital, the author continues, was the old monastery in which Vasubandhu P'usa in the course of some scores of years composed various śāstras Mahāyānist and Hinayānist. Beside this monastery were the remains of the Hall in which Vasubandhu had expounded Buddhism to princes and illustrious monks and brahmins from other countries. Four or five *li* north from the capital, and close to the Ganges, was a large Buddhist monastery, with an Asoka tope to mark a place at which the Buddha had preached to devas and men for three months on the excellent doctrines of his religion. Four or five *li* west from this monastery was a Buddha-relic tope, and to the north of the tope were the remains of an old monastery. Here *Shih-li-lo-to* (restored by Julien as Śrīlabdha), a śāstra-master of the Sautrantika School, composed a sautrantika vibhāshā-śāstra.

In a mango plantation five or six *li* to the south-west of the city was the old monastery in which Asanga P'usa had learned and taught. By night the P'usa went up to the Tushita Heaven, and there received from Maitreya the materials of three treatises which he taught by day to his disciples. These treatises, Yuan-chuang tells us, were the "*Yü-ka-shih-ti-lun*" (瑜伽師地論),

---

1 Alberuni Vol. I. p. 200.
2 Ind. Ant. Vol. XXII. p. 174, 189.

the "*Chuang-yen-ta-shêng-ching-lun*" (莊嚴大乘經論), and the "*Chung-pien-fên-pie-lun*" (中邊分別論).

The large Buddhist Monastery and tope, which in this passage are placed four or five to the *north* of the capital, are described in the Life as being to the *north-west* of the city, the distance being the same.

Our pilgrim's Śrīlabdha, whose name is translated by Shêng-shou (勝受) "Received from the Victorious", may perhaps be Tāranātha's "Sūtra-āchārya-Bhadanta Srīlābha", a Kashmirian and the founder of a School[1].

The three Buddhist treatises which Yuan-chuang here states were communicated to Asanga by Maitreya require a short notice. The name *Yü-ka-shih-ti-lun* most likely stands for "Yogāchārya-bhūmi-śāstra", as in Julien's re-translation, but it is possible that this was not the original name of the Sanskrit treatise. We have the work in Yuan-chuang's translation, made with the help of several Brethren, and with an interesting introduction by the pilgrim's friend, the distinguished scholar and official Hsü Ching-tsung (許敬宗), whose name has a bad mark against it in history. The treatise, which is a very long one, was *uttered*, we are told, by Maitreya. It is a metaphysical religious work on the basis of Buddhism, but it is not a *yoga* treatise as the term *yoga* came to be understood, nor is the word *shih* to be taken here in its ordinary sense of "master". The *yoga-shih* is merely a disciple who devotes himself to profound continued meditation in the seventeen *ti* (bhūmi) or provinces of faith and knowledge. It is not unlikely that the name which Mr. Bunyiu Nanjio gives as the second name of this treatise, viz. "Saptadasa-bhūmi-(or bhūmika)-śāstra-yogāchāryabhūmi", is the correct or original title.[2]

The "Chuang-yen-ta-shêng-ching-lun" is evidently, as Julien restores the name, the "Sūtrālaṅkāra-ṭīkā", the word *Mahāyāna,* which is required by the Chinese trans-

---

[1] Tār. S. 4, 67.
[2] Bun. No. 1170.

lation, being omitted from the title. We find the name also given as "Ta-shêng-chuang-yen-ching-lun", and a treatise so designated composed by Asañga was translated by Prabhāmitra, a kshatriya of Magadha and a contemporary of our pilgrim. This translation is evidently a work of great merit, and the treatise is interesting as giving Asanga's exposition and defence of Mahāyānism. It is a work in verse with a prose commentary throughout, but there is no reference to Maitreya as author or inspirer either of verses or commentary.[1]

The third treatise here said to have been communicated by Maitreya to Asanga is called by our pilgrim "Chung-pien-fên-pie-lun", the Sanskrit original name being "Madhyānta-vibhāga-śāstra". But this treatise, of which there are two Chinese translations, is represented as the work of Vasubandhu. The Chinese name which Yuan-chuang here uses for it is that given to Paramārtha's translation, his own translation having a name slightly different. The treatise in both translations gives the "Pien-chung-pien-lun-sung" by Maitreya, with a running commentary on it by Vasubandhu. Maitreya's work is a very short one in seven poems on seven subjects; and it was this work apparently which Maitreya, according to Yuan-chuang in this passage, communicated to Asanga. The term Madhyānta-vibhāga seems to mean, as translated into Chinese, "distinguishing between the mean and the extremes", that is, holding the mean between the negation and the assertion of existence.[2]

Above 100 paces to the north-west of the Mango Grove was a Buddha-relic tope, and beside it were old foundations at the place where Vasubandhu P'usa descended from Tushita Paradise to have an interview with his elder brother Asanga P'usa. Our pilgrim here represents these two brothers as natives of Gandhāra, and as having lived in the millenium succeeding the Buddha's decease (that is, according to the Chinese reckoning, before the third century of our era). Asanga, he tells us, began his Buddhist religious career as a Mahīśāsika and afterwards became a Mahāyānist: and Vasubandhu began his religious career in

---

1 No. 1190.

2 Nos. 1244, 1245, and 1248.

the school of the Sarvāstivādins. Yuan-chuang here tells a curious story about the two brothers and a great scholar who was a friend and disciple of Asanga, by name *Fo-t'ê-sêng-ha,* translated by *Shih-tzŭ-chiao* or "Lion-intelligence", the Sanskrit original being Buddha-siṁha. These three Brethren made an agreement that when one of them died and went to Heaven he should come back to earth at the first opportunity to enlighten the survivors as to his circumstances. The first to die was the disciple Buddhasiṁha, but in Heaven he forgot his promise. Then three years afterwards Vasubandhu died and went to Tushita Heaven. He had been dead six months, and no message had come from him, so the heretics declared that he and Buddhasiṁha had gone to a bad place. But at length Vasubandhu remembering his agreement found it in his power to keep it. So in the form of a Deva-rishi he descended to earth and visited his brother, telling him how he and Buddha-siṁha had fared in Maitreya's Paradise.

The story here given about the death of Vasubandhu is at variance with the accounts of the brothers given in the Life of Vasubandhu, and other works, according to which the elder brother dies first, leaving the younger brother still living and writing.

The pilgrim next tells of an old monastery 40 *li* north-west from Asanga's chapel, and having its north side close to the Ganges. Within this a brick tope marked the place at which the conversion of Vasubandhu to Mahāyānism began. According to the version of the story here given Vasubandhu, having come from North India to Ayudha, heard a portion of the Mahāyāna treatise *Shih-ti-ching* (十地論) recited by a disciple of Asanga, and was thereby led to reflect. He became convinced that he had been wrong as a Hīnayānist opponent of Mahāyānism, and was ready to cut out his tongue as the offending member which had reviled the "Great Vehicle". But his elder brother, who had wished to bring about Vasubandhu's conversion, interfered and taught him to use his tongue in the praise and preaching of his new creed.

In other works Asanga uses the pretext of fatal sickness to bring his brother from Ayodhyā to visit him at Purushapura, and there reasons with him and converts him to Mahāyānism. After the death of Asanga, his brother composed several treatises all expounding and defending Mahāyānism; and he died in Ayodhyā at the age of eighty years.[1] The Shih-ti-ching or "Sūtra of the Ten Lands" of this passage is doubtless the work called Shih-chu-ching (No. 105), the Daśabhūmika-sūtra. One of Vasubandhu's numerous treatises is a commentary on this sūtra entitled *Shih-ti-ching-lun* (No. 1194).

## A-YE-MU-K'A.

From Ayudha the pilgrim travelled east, he writes, above 300 *li*, and crossing the Ganges to the north, arrived in the *A-ye-mu-k'a* country. This country he describes as being 2400 or 2500 *li* in circuit with its capital, situated on the Ganges, above 20 *li* in circuit. In climate and natural products the country resembled Ayudha: the character of the people was good, they were studious and given to good works. There were five Buddhist monasteries with above 1000 Brethren who were adherents of the Sammatiya School, and there were more than ten Deva-Temples. Not far from the capital on the south-east side, and close to the Ganges, were an Asoka tope at a place where the Buddha had preached for three months, traces of a sitting and walking place of the Four Past Buddhas, and a dark-blue-stone tope with Buddha-relics. Beside this last was a monastery with above 200 Brethren, and in it was a beautiful life-like image of the Buddha: its halls and chambers rose high, and were of exquisite workmanship. It was in this monastery that the Śāstra-Master Buddhadāsa composed his great vibhāshā treatise of the Sarvāstivādin School.

The name of the country here transcribed *A-ye-mu-k'a* was restored by Julien in his translation of the Life as *Ayamukha*, but in the present passage he makes these syllables stand for Hayamukha. This latter restoration seems to be inadmissible; and as *A-* is the first syllable of the name in all the texts of the Life and Records, and in the Fang-chih, we must regard Ayamukha as the name which the pilgrim transcribed. It is not impossible that the correct form may have been Hayamukha or Āyamukha, the former word meaning "Horse-face" and the latter meaning a *creek* or *channel*. Cunningham, who finds Yuan-

---

[1] Vasubandhu-chuan (No. 1463).

chuang's Ayudha in the present Kākāpur, thinks that Ayamukha may be represented by "Daunḍia-khera on the northern bank of the Ganges". But these identifications are mere conjectures and are of little use.[1]

In the corresponding passage of the Life we are informed that the pilgrim left Ayudha in a boat along with a party and proceeded east down the Ganges towards Ayamukha. When about 100 *li* on the way, in a wood of asoka trees, the boat was attacked by Thugs who robbed the party. When these Thugs saw that the Chinese pilgrim was an uncommonly fine-looking man they decided to sacrifice him to their cruel deity Durgā. From this terrible fate the pilgrim was preserved by a providential hurricane which put the wicked Thugs in fear, and made them release their doomed victim, treat him with awe and reverence, and under his teaching give up their wicked profession, and take the vows of lay-Buddhists. After recording this episode the Life goes on to state that the pilgrim "from this went above 300 *li* east and crossed to the north of the Ganges into the Ayamukha country". The "this" here may be taken to mean the place of the encounter with the Thugs, and the distance from Ayudha to Ayamukha would then be 400 *li*. But the words "from this" in the above extract from the Life should perhaps be treated, in accordance with the text of the Records, as indicating Ayudha city as the point of departure. The pilgrim apparently travelled by land eastwards from the place where the boat was seized by the Thugs, and he crossed to the north side of the river near Ayamukha city. This river cannot have been the Ganges and it may have been the Sai. We may even doubt whether the river in the Asoka wood on which the Thugs had their piratical boats was the Ganges proper.

The great vibhāshā treatise, which Yuan-chuang here tells us was composed by Buddhadaśa in a monastery of this country, is probably the "Varma-vibhāshā" already

---

[1] A. G. I. p. 387.

mentioned, above p. 353, in connection with the pilgrim's account of Kanauj.

## PRAYĀGA.

From Ayamukha the pilgrim went south-east, he tells us, and after a journey of more than 700 *li*, crossing to the south of the Ganges and the north of the Jumna he came to the *Po-lo-ya-ka* (Prayāga) country.

There is evidently something wrong in the accounts which our pilgrim has given of his journeys in these districts. He applies the name "Ganges", apparently to more than one river, and it seems probable that his Ayudha and Ayamukha were on an affluent or affluents of the Ganges proper. From Kanauj he may have made an excursion to these two cities. From Ayamukha he apparently returned to the Ganges somewhere near Navadevakula, which was 20 miles to the south-east of Kanauj. From the neighbourhood of this place to Prayāga, going south-east, is about 140 miles or 700 *li*. Cunningham seems to take no notice of the statements in the Records and Life that Ayamukha was to the east of Ayudha. Moreover he wrongly represents Yuan-chuang as going by boat all the way down the Ganges south-east from the latter city to Ayamukha. So we cannot wonder that he finds it impossible to make distances agree.[1]

The pilgrim goes on to state that the Prayāga country was above 5000 *li* in circuit, and the capital above 20 *li* in circuit. This city, which apparently had the same name, he places at the junction of two rivers (viz. the Ganges and the Jumna). He praises the country, the climate, and the people. He tells us there were only two Buddhist establishments and very few Brethren all Hīnayānists. There were some hundreds of Deva-Temples and the majority of the inhabitants were non-Buddhists.

In a champaka grove to the south-west of the capital was an old Asoka tope to mark the spot at which the Buddha once overcame his religious opponents (that is, in controversy). Beside it were a Buddha-hair-and-nail relic tope and an Exercise ground. Near the relic tope was an old monastery in which Deva P'usa

---

[1] A. G. I. p. 388.

composed the "Kuang-pai-lun" for the refutation of the Hīnayānists and the conquest of the Tīrthikas.

Prayāga, the capital of this country, corresponds, as has been shown by others, to the modern Allahabad. The word *Prayāga* means *sacrifice*, or a *holy ground set apart for sacrifices.*

The Deva P'usa of this passage has been already met with at the Sources of the Ganges. His treatise here mentioned, the "Kuang-pai-lun", which we have in Yuan-chuang's translation, is a very short one in verse arranged under eight headings. It denounces the belief in individual permanence and argues against brahmins and others.[1]

In the capital, the pilgrim goes on to relate, was a celebrated Deva-Temple in front of which was a great wide-spreading umbrageous tree. In this tree once lodged a cannibal demon, hence the presence of numerous bones near the tree. Visitors to the temple, under the influence of bad teaching and supernatural beings, had continuously from old times all lightly committed suicide here. Lately, however, a very wise and learned brahmin of good family had tried to convert the people from their evil belief and stop the practice of suicide. He accordingly went up to the temple and in the presence of friends proceeded to kill himself in the usual way by mounting the tree to throw himself down from it. When up the tree, addressing the spectators he said — "I am dying (lit. have death); formerly I spoke of the matter as an illusion, now I have proof that it is real; the devas with their aerial music are coming to meet me, and I am about to give up my vile body from this meritorious spot." As the Brahmin was about to throw himself down from the tree to be killed his friends tried to dissuade him from the act, but their counsels were in vain. They then spread their garments below the tree; and when the Brahmin fell he was unhurt, but was in a swoon. When he recovered he said to the by-standers—"What is seen as the devas in the air summoning one is the leading of evil spirits, not the acquisition of heavenly joy".

The story here told leaves somewhat to be supplied in order to make it as intelligible to us as it was to Yuan-chuang's Chinese readers. For some reason not explained in the story it had long been an article of popular belief

---

[1] Bun. No. 1189.

that suicide at this Deva-Temple led to birth in Heaven. Then those who "threw away their lives" here were evidently left unburied and were supposed to be devoured by the man-eating demon who lived in the great tree. This tree was undoubtedly a banyan, and Cunningham thinks that "there can be little doubt that the famous tree here described by the pilgrim is the well-known *Akshay-Bat*, or "undecaying Banian tree", which is still an object of worship at Allahabad".

Not long before the time of Yuan-chuang's visit, he tells us, a brahmin "of good family" had tried to convert the people from their folly in committing suicide here. The Chinese rendered by "of good family" is *tsu-hsing-tzŭ* (族姓子) lit. "Son of a clan". This expression is one of very common use in Buddhist books and means simply "a gentleman". Yet Julien here translates it by "dont le nom de famille était *Fils* (Pouttra)".[1]

This brahmin gentleman, when up in the banyan tree, hears music and sees beings; and he thinks (or pretends to think) that these are the harbingers of a happy death giving an entrance into Heaven. But when he recovers from his swoon he recognizes, and declares, that he only saw in the air devas summoning him, that these were evil deities coming to meet him, and that there was no heavenly joy. The language here used belongs partly to a popular Chinese belief or fancy. The Chinese generally believe that dying persons often receive intimation or indication of what is to be their lot after they depart this life, and the information is supposed to be often conveyed by the appearance of a certain kind of emissary from the other world. These messengers from the world beyond are said to *chie-yin* (接引) or to *yin* the dying individual, that is to *welcome* or *introduce* him. It is these terms which are

[1] The phrase *tsu-hsing-tzŭ* is the equivalent of the Indian term *kulaputra*, "son of a family", that is, clansman, and the clansmen were regarded as well-born. In the Buddhist books *tsu-hsing-tzŭ* is applied to eminent laymen, and also to bhikshus, who moreover use it in speaking of themselves.

here translated by "coming to meet" and "leading". The Brahmin mistook the character of the *welcome* to be given. We are probably to understand that he taught his friends, and the people generally, that the music and angels of the suicides were in all cases harbingers of posthumous misery, not of bliss in Heaven.

On the east side of the capital and at the confluence of the rivers, the pilgrim proceeds, was a sunny down about ten *li* wide covered with a white sand. This down was called in the popular language "The Grand Arena of Largesse". It was the place to which from ancient times princes, and other liberal benefactors, had come to make their offerings and gifts. Yuan-chuang then proceeds to describe how king Śīlāditya acted on the occasion to which reference has already been made. The king, as we have seen, went in state from Kanauj to this place for his customary quinquennial great distribution of gifts, and alms, and offerings. He had come prepared, and he gave away all the public money, and all his own valuables. Beginning with offerings to the Buddhist images on the first day, Yuan-chuang here tells us, the king went on to bestow gifts on the resident Buddhist Brethren, next on the assembled congregation, next on those who were conspicuous for great abilities and extensive learning, next on retired scholars and recluses of other religions, and lastly on the kinless poor. This lavish distribution in a few (according to the Life in 75) days exhausted all the public and private wealth of the country, but in ten days after the Treasury was emptied it was again filled.

At the junction of the rivers and to the east of the Arena of Largesse, Yuan-chuang continues, every day numbers of people arrived to die in the sacred water, hoping to be thereby reborn in Heaven. Even the monkeys and other wild creatures came to this place, some bathed and then went back, others fasted here until they died. In connection with this statement Yuan-chuang tells a story of a monkey which lived under a tree close to the river, and starved himself to death at the time of Śīlāditya's visit. He adds that this occurrence led to the following curious and trying austerity-performance on the part of the local devotees given to austerities. High poles were erected in the Ganges at this place, each with a projecting peg near the top; at sunrise a devotee mounted a pole; holding on to the top with one hand and one foot, and supported by the peg, he stretched out his other arm and leg at full length. In this posture he followed keenly with his eyes the sun's progress to the right; when the sun set the devotee came down from his perch to resume it next morning. This painful austerity was practised with the view of obtaining release from mortal life, and it was carried on for several tens of years without relaxation.

This story of our pilgrim seems to be rather silly and not very intelligible. One cannot see the connection between the monkey's suicide and the devotees' practice on the poles. But if we regard the date given for the monkey's death, viz. the time of Śīlāditya's visit, as an accidental mistake (which the context seems to show it must be) then we probably have here a fragment of some old story told to account for absurd austerities still practised at the time of Yuan-chuang's visit. According to the Fang-chih the monkey of the pilgrim's story was a husband, and his wife was attacked and killed by a dog. The husband found the dead body of his wife, and with pious care carried it to the Ganges, and consigned it to that sacred river; then he gave himself up to grief, would not take any food, and after a few days died. It is probable that the original story also told how the bereaved monkey every morning went to the top of one of the poles at the bank of the river, and sat there gazing intently at the sky; that he came down at evening, and spent the night in his lonely home, and that when he died he rejoined his wife in Heaven. When the history of this pious uxorious monkey became generally known, seekers after Heaven were moved to adopt the means which they had seen the monkey use. So they set up poles in the river, and sat perched on these after the manner of monkeys, as the pilgrim describes, craning their necks to watch the sun through all his course from east to west. This is what they thought the pious intelligent monkey had been doing.

## KOŚĀMBI.

From Prayāga the pilgrim went, he tells us, south-west through a forest infested by wild elephants and other fierce animals, and after a journey of above 500 *li* (about 100 miles) he reached the *Kiao-shang-mi* (that is Kauśāmbī or Kosambī) country. This is described by the pilgrim as being above 6000 *li* in circuit, and its capital (evidently named Kośāmbī) as being above 30 *li* in circuit. It was a fertile country with a hot climate: it yielded much upland rice and sugar-cane; its people were enterprising, fond of the arts, and cultivators of religious merit. There were more than ten Buddhist monasteries, but all in utter ruin; and the Brethren, who were above 300 in number, were adherents of the Hīnayāna system. There were more than fifty Deva-Temples and the non-Buddhists were very numerous.[1]

In the corresponding part of the Life distance and direction of Kosambī from Prayāga are also given as above 500 *li* to the south-west. This agrees with the statement, in a subsequent part of the Life, that the pilgrim on leaving Prayāga journeyed south-west through a jungle for seven days to Kosambī. Cunningham, (who was misled by Julien's slip in writing 50 *li*, instead of 500, in his translation of the Life) identifies the city of Kosambī here described with the modern Kosam, which is only 38 miles by road south-west from Allahabad.[2] M. Saint-Martin could not offer any identification for our pilgrim's Kosambī, and seems to think that it lay to the north-west not south-west of Prayāga.[3] Cunningham's identification has been conclusively shown to be untenable by Mr Vincent A. Smith, whose studies on the subject have led him to the conclusion that "the Kauśāmbī twice visited by Hiuen Tsiang is to be looked for, and, when looked for, will be found, in one of the Native States of the Baghelkhaṇḍ Agency, in the valley of the Tons River, and not very far from the East Indian Railway, which connects Allahabad with Jabalpur. In short, the Satnā (Sutna) railway station marks the *approximate* position of Kauśāmbī".[4] But this identifica-

1 There is reason for suspecting the genuiness of the passage in the 5th *chuan* of the Life which seems to be a remembrance of the passage in the 3rd *chuan*. In transcribing the name Ghoshila the author uses characters different from those in the 3rd *chuan* and from those in the Records. This passage also makes the pilgrim go back from Prayāga to Kośambi south-west, and continue his journey from the latter going north-west.

2 A. G. I. p. 391.

3 J. III. p. 352 and see Map in J. II.

4 J. R. A. S. for 1898. [See now Dr Yost's article, ibid. 1904.]

tion also is beset with difficulties which seem to me insurmountable. For the pilgrim to go south-west from Prayāga was to go out of his line of travel, and although this detour might be necessary for one visit it would be unnecessary on the return journey. Mr Smith has noticed the discrepancy between Yuan-chuang's location of Kosambī and that given by Fa-hsien, and he thinks the latter's *north-west* is a clerical mistake for *south-west*, but, on the other hand, Yuan-chuang's *south-west* may be an error for *north-east*. Mr Smith, moreover, has not noticed the important difference between the Life and the Records as to the distance and direction of Viśākhā from Kosambī, and this difference increases the difficulty of identification.

Now our pilgrim's statements here, as to the bearing and distance of Kosambī from Prayāga and other places, are not in agreement with other accounts of the situation and bearings of Kosambī. Thus the Life, which in one place reproduces the words of the Records, in another passage makes *Pi-so-ka* (Viśoka), on the way to Śrāvasti, to be 500 *li* east of Kosambī, while the Records, as we shall see presently, puts it about 880 *li* to the north-north-east of the city. Again, Fa-hsien places the Kosambī country thirteen yojanas (about 90 miles) to the north-west of the Deer Park to the north of Benares.[1] This would make the city of Kosambī lie to the north of Prayāga. Then in the Vinaya we find that in going from Rajagriha to Kosambī one went by boat up the river, that is, the Ganges.[2] Further we read of the Buddha on his way from Śrāvasti to Kosambī passing through the town of Bhaddavatikā, and this was the name of the swift elephant of the king of Kosambī.[3] In some books the Kosambī and Kosala countries are adjacent, and the bhikshus of Sravasti and Kosambi keep Retreat at the same town in

---

[1] Fo-kuo-chi, *ch.* 34.
[2] Vin. Chul. XI. 1.
[3] Jātaka Vol. I. p. 206 (Chalmers tr.)

the Kosambī country.[1] So also when a hermit's life is threatened by the king of Kosambī in the Udayana Park the hermit flies to Śrāvasti.[2] Further in the Sutta Nipāta the deputation from the Brahmin Bāvari going to visit the Buddha at Śrāvasti proceed to "Kosambī and Sāketa and Srāvasti".[3] From all these it would seem that Kosambī, instead of being 500 *li* to the south-west of Prayāga, was rather to the north of that place, and it evidently was not very far from Śrāvasti. It was the capital of the Vatsa (in Chinese *Tu-tzŭ* 犢子 "Calf") country, and the land of of the Vatsas was in the Middle Region of the Brihat Samhitā.[4]

Within the old royal inclosure (*kung*) of the capital, the pilgrim relates, was a large Buddhist temple (*ching-shê*) over sixty feet high in which was a carved sandal-wood image of the Buddha with a stone canopy suspended over it. This image made miraculous manifestations, and no power could move it from its place: so paintings made of it were worshipped, and all true likenesses of the Buddha have been taken from this image. It was the one made for king Udayana by the artist conveyed to the Trayastriṃśa Heaven by Mudgalaputra at the king's request. When the Buddha descended to earth near Sankāsya the image went out to meet him and the Buddha put it at ease saying—"What I want of you is that you convert those distressed by error and and that you teach posterity".

The Udayana of this passage was the prince born to the king of Kosambī on the day on which the Buddha was born. His name (in Pali books Udena) is translated into Chinese in a note here by *ch'u-ai* (出愛), "yielding affection"; but it is also rendered by *ch'u-kuang* (光), "yielding brightness", by *jih-tzŭ* (日子) "the Sun", by *jih-chu* (初) or *jih-ch'u* both meaning "Sunrise". He is represented as originally a cruel wicked king with a very bad temper, and as an enemy to the Buddhists. But he took

---

[1] Sêng-ki-lü, *ch.* 28.

[2] Sar. Vin. Tsa-shih, *ch.* 3.

[3] Sutta Nipāta p. 185 (P. T. S.).

[4] Divyāv. p. 528: Yin-kuo-ching, *ch.* 1 (No. 666); Ind. Ant. Vol. XXII. pp. 170. 181.

by our pilgrim in the year 661.[1] The treatise has another title— "*P'o-sê-hsin-lun* (破色心論)", that is, "the sāstra which refutes matter and mind". The book is a small philosophical poem with an explanatory commentary on the relations of mind and matter. It teaches the unreality of phenomena, and consequently of our sense-perceptions apart from the thinking principle, the eternal mind unmoved by change and unsoiled by error. This work was regarded by its author as an exposition of the Buddha's views and teaching on the relation of mind to matter. It quotes and refutes tenets of the non-Buddhist Vaiseshikas and of the Buddhist "Vibhāshā masters of Kashmir". Some of the author's tenets are to be found in the "Lankāvatāra sūtra", but we cannot properly describe the Wei-shih-lun as a commentary on that sūtra.

> In a mango wood east of the Ghosilārāma were the old foundations of the house in which Asanga P'usa composed the "Hsien-yang-shêng-chiao-lun".

The translation of the title of Asañga's work here given means "the śāstra which developes Buddhism" that is, developes Buddha's teaching. The treatise, which we have in Yuan-chuang's translation[2], is an exposition and development of the "Yogāchāryabhūmi śāstra" already mentioned.

> At a distance of eight or nine *li* south-west from the capital, Yuan-chuang proceeds, was a venomous dragon's cave in which the Buddha had left his shadow after subduing the venomous dragon. This was a matter of record, but the shadow was no longer visible. Beside the Dragon's Cave was an Asoka-built tope, and at the side of it were the traces of the Buddha's exercise-ground, and a hair-and-nail-relic tope at which in many cases the ailments of devotees were cured in answer to prayer. This Kosambī country is to be the last place in which the Śakya-[muni] religion will cease to exist; hence all, from king to peasant, who visit this land feel deeply moved, and return weeping sadly.

---

[1] No. 1240.
[2] No. 1177.

According to the Mahāsañgika Vinaya the malicious dragon of Kosambī, An-p'o-lo (菴婆羅) by name, was subdued by the bhikshu *Shan-lai* (善來) or Svāgata.[1] Mr Cockburn, who does not accept the situation of the Dragon's cave given by our pilgrim, is disposed to identify the cave with one now called "Sītā's Window". This is "an ancient Buddhist Hermit's cave, cut into the vertical face of a precipice 50 feet high. This precipice forms the scarp of the classic hill of Prabhāsa, Allahabad District".[2] But this description, it will be observed, does not suit the pilgrim's account of the neighbourhood of the cave.

Our pilgrim here, it will be noticed, speaks of the *Shih-ka-fa* or Sakya dharma, that is, the dispensation of Sakyamuni, the system of belief and conduct which he established. The final extinction of this system which was to take place in Kosambī is predicted by the Buddha in the "Mahāmāyā sūtra". At the end of 1500 years from the Buddha's decease a great bhikshu at this city was to kill an arhat: the disciples of the latter would avenge the murder of their master by the slaughter of the bhikshu. The troubles caused by these crimes would lead to the destruction of topes and viharas, and finally to the complete extinction of Buddhism.[3] As the 1500 years were at the time of the pilgrim's visit about at an end, pious Buddhists were distressed at the signs of the near fulfilment of the prophecy.

From the Dragon's cave, the pilgrim tells us, he proceeded in a north-east direction through a great wood and, after a journey of above 700 *li*, he crossed the Ganges to the north, to the city of *Ka-she-pu-lo* (that is, Kāśapura or Kājapura). This was above ten *li* in circuit, and its inhabitants were in good circumstances. Close to the city were the ruins of an old monastery where Dharmapāla had once gained a great victory over the non-Buddhists in a public discussion. The discussion had been brought about by a former king who wished to destroy Buddhism in the

---

1 Sêng-ki-lü, *ch.* 20.
2 J. Ben. A. S. Vol. LVI. p. 31.
3 Mo-ha-mo-ya-ching, *ch.* 2 (No. 382).

country. Beside these ruins was an Asoka tope, of which 200 feet still remained above ground, to mark the place at which the Buddha had once preached for six months, and near this were traces of the Buddha's exercise ground and a tope with his hair-and-nail relics.

The name of this city, which is not mentioned in the Life, is restored by Julien as Kāśapura.

## P'I-SHO-KA.

From Kāśapura, the pilgrim narrates, he went north 170 or 180 *li* to the country which he calls *Pi* (or *Ping*, or *P'i* or *Fi*)-*sho-ka* (that is, perhaps, Viśoka). This country was above 4000 *li* in circuit and its chief city was sixteen *li* in circuit. The grain crops of the country were very plentiful, fruit and flowers abounded, it had a genial climate, and the people had good ways, were studious and given to good works. It had above twenty Buddhist monasteries and 3000 Brethren who were all adherents of the Sammatiya School. There were above 50 Deva-Temples and the non-Buddhists were very numerous.

On the east side of the road south of the capital was a large monastery. In it the arhat Devaśarman composed his "Shih-shên-lun" in which he denied the Ego and the non-Ego. At this place there had also been another arhat by name Gopa, who wrote the treatise "Shêng-chiao-yao-shih-lun" (or "Śāstra on the essential realities of Buddhism"), affirming the existence of the Ego and the non-Ego. The opposite doctrines of these two great religious philosophers led to serious controversies in the church.

The Life, which as we have seen makes Viśoka to be 500 *li* to the east of Kosambī, places the large monastery of this passage on "the left side (east) of the south-east road", but *tung*, "east" is possibly a clerical error for *ch'êng*, "city". The Life also gives the name of Devaśarman's treatise as "Shih-shên-tsu-lun (識身足論)", "the sāstra of the Foot of the Perception Body". We have the work in Yuan-chuang's translation, the title being as in the Life with the word Abhidharma prefixed.[1] Its Sanskrit title has been restored as "Abhidharma Vijñānakāyapāda

---

[1] No. 1281. See Bur. Int. p. 448: Tār. S. 56 and 296.

śāstra", but its short title, is "Vijñānakāya śāstra" as in our pilgrim's translation here. The treatise is one of the Six Pāda (*Tsu*) called Abhidharma sūtra of the Sarvāstivādin School, and it was considered by the Vaibhāshikas as canonical, but by the Sautrantikas as only the work of a bhikshu. Yuan-chuang, it will be noticed, calls the author an arhat, but in other places he is merely a bhikshu or sthavira. The work is a tedious argumentative treatise combating the views of a Moginlin who denied the reality of the Past and the Future, and arguing against other tenets apparently held by other early Buddhists. Our pilgrim's statement that it denied the Ego and the non-Ego, or "I and men", is a very unsatisfactory one.

The treatise by Gopa mentioned in the present passage does not seem to be in the Chinese collections of Buddhist works, and nothing is known apparently about the author or his work. As Devaśarman is supposed to have lived about 400, or, according to some, about 100 years after the Buddha's decease Gopa must have lived about the same time.

At this large monastery also, Yuan-chuang proceeds to narrate, *Hu-fa* (Dharmapāla) P'usa once held a discussion for seven days with 100 Hīnayāna śāstra-masters and utterly defeated them. In this district, moreover, the Buddha lived for six years preaching and teaching. Near the tope which commemorated his stay and work and which stood near the large monastery was a marvellous tree; it was six or seven feet high. This tree had been developed from a tooth-stick which the Buddha after using it had cast down. The tooth-stick took root and grew and flourished, and it still remained a tree in spite of the persistent efforts of heretics to cut it down and destroy it.

The Tooth-stick tree of this passage was above 70 feet high according to the Life and the Fang-chih. Fa-hsien, it will be remembered, has a similar story about his city of Sha-ki, and there the tree, as in our text, was only seven feet high.

Cunningham thinks he proves that the *Pi-sho-ka* or Viśoka (?) of Yuan-chuang is the Sha-ki (or Sha-ti) of

Fa-hsien, and the Saketā or Ayodhyā of Indian literature.[1] But in his arguments he seems to quite ignore the fact that Fa-hsien places Shaki thirteen (not as Legge has by a slip, three) yojanas or nearly 100 miles in a south-east direction from Kanauj and so either at or near Yuan-chuang's Ayudha which was 100 miles south-east from Kanauj. Then Cunningham makes the name of this city to be the same as that of the lady Visākhā: but Yuan-chuang, like others, transcribes the lady's name by three characters different from those which he uses for writing the name of this city. Further, from Shaki to Śrāvasti the direction was south and the distance eight yojanas or less than 50 miles, while from Viśoka to Śrāvasti it was 500 *li* or about 100 miles in a north-east direction. Moreover the Life, as has been stated, places Viśoka 500 *li* to the east of Kosambī. So, unless we agree with Mr V. Smith in treating Fa-hsien's distances and directions as mistakes, we cannot make Yuan-chuang's Viśoka to be Fa-hsien's Shaki, but the former may perhaps be taken to represent the Sāketa of the Buddhist scriptures.

The precisely similar stories about the Buddha's tooth-stick becoming and remaining a miraculous tree are in favour of the identification of Sha-ki and Viśoka. But they are not enough to prove that the two names denoted one city, as such stories were probably invented for several places. We have already met with a tooth-stick tree in the early part of the Records, and we are to meet with a third in a future chapter.

It is not impossible that Yuan-chuang made an excursion from Kosambī to Kaśapura, returned to Kosambī, and from the latter continued his journey going east to Viśoka. This would agree with the account in the Life which does not mention Kaśapura. Mr V. Smith thinks that Yuan-chuang's Kaśapura "may very plausibly be identified with the group of ruins centreing round Mohanlālganj" fourteen miles south of Lucknow. He adds— "Kursī, in the Bāra-

---

[1] A. G. I. p. 401.

bankī District, about 27 miles in a direct line from Mohanlālganj, corresponds admirably in position with Viśākhā [that is Viśoka] which was 170 or 180 *li* (less than 30 miles) from Kāśapura".[1] But these proposed identifications are not given as strictly accurate, and, as Mr Smith admits, the identifications must await further researches.

[1] op. c. p. 523.

# CHAPTER XII.

### CHUAN VI.

## ŚRĀVASTI TO KUSINĀRĀ.

From the Viśoka district the pilgrim travelled, he tells us, above 500 *li* (about 100 miles) north-east to the *Shih-lo-fa-si-ti* (Śrāvasti) country. This country was above 6000 *li* in circuit: its "capital" was a wild ruin without anything to define its areas; the old foundations of the "Palace city" were above twenty *li* in circuit, and although it was mostly a ruinous waste yet there were inhabitants. The country had good crops, and an equable climate: and the people had honest ways and were given to learning and fond of good works. There were some hundreds of Buddhist monasteries of which the most were in ruins: the Brethren, who were very few, were Sammatiyas. There were 100 Deva-Temples and the non-Buddhists were very numerous. This city was in the Buddha's time the seat of government of king Prasenajit and the foundations of this king's old palace remained in the old "Palace city". Not far east of these was an old foundation on which a small tope had been built: this was the site of the large chapel (Preaching Hall) which king Prasenajit built for the Buddha. Near the site of the chapel was another tope on old foundations: this marked the site of the nunnery (*ching-shê*) of the Buddha's foster-mother, the bhikshunī Prājapatī, erected for her by king Prasenajit. A tope to the east of this marked the site of the house of Sudatta the Elder (chief of the non-official laymen). At the side of this was a tope on the spot where Angulimāla gave up his heresy. This Angulimāla, whose name denotes Finger-garland, was a wicked man of Śrāvasti who harried the city and country, killing people and cutting a finger off each person killed, in order to make himself a garland. He was about to kill his own mother in order to make up the required number of fingers, when the Buddha in compassion proceeded to convert him. Finger-garland on seeing the Buddha was delighted, as his Brahmin teacher had told him that by killing the Buddha and his own mother he would obtain birth in Heaven. So he left his mother for the moment, and made a motion to kill the Buddha. But the latter kept moving out of reach, and by admonishing the murderer led him to repentance and conversion. Finger-garland then was admitted into the Order, and by zealous perseverance he attained arhatship.

In this passage the pilgrim, according to his usual practice, gives the Sanskrit form of the name of the country he describes, viz—Śrāvasti. This was properly not the name of the country, which was Kosala, but of the capital of that country. Fa-hsien uses the old and generally accepted transcription *She-wei* (舍 衛), perhaps for Sevat or Sāvatthi, and he makes the city so called the Capital of Kosala, and eight yojanas south from his *Sha-k'i*[1]. This last name, which may have been Sha-k'i, or Sha-ch'i, or Sha-ti, is supposed to represent Sāketa, but the restoration of the name and the identification of the place are uncertain. Mr V. Smith would change Fa-hsien's *south* here to *north-east* and his *eight* yojanas to *eighteen* or *nineteen* yojanas, changes which seem to be quite inadmissible as the pilgrim evidently made the journey.[2] In the Vinaya we find the city of Śrāvastī stated to be six yojanas from Sāket, and the former is apparently to the east of the latter.[3]

The site of the Śrāvasti of the present passage was long ago confidently identified by Cunningham with that of "the great ruined city on the south bank of the Rapti, called *Sahet-Mahet*" in which he discovered a colossal statue of the Buddha with an inscription containing the name "Śravasti". This identification has been accepted and defended by other investigators, but there are several strong reasons for setting it aside.[4] These are set forth

[1] Fo-kuo-chi, *ch.* 20.

[2] J. R. A. S. 1898. p. 523.

[3] Vin. Mah. VII. In another Vinaya treatise (Sêng-ki-lü, *ch.* 11) from Śrāvasti to *Sha-ki* is a two days' journey for Upali.

[4] Arch. Sur. India Vol. I. p. 330, XI. p. 78: A. G. I. p. 409. Set Mahet by W. Hoey, J. A. S. Bengal Vol. LXI (Extra number): An an-

by Mr V. Smith who, after careful study and personal examination of the districts, has come to the conclusion that the site of Śrāvasti is in the district of Khajūrā in Nepāl, a short distance to the north of Bālāpur and not far from Nepālganj in a north-north-east direction.[1] But this proposed identification also has its difficulties, and must await further developments. No discoveries have been made to support the identification, but there seems to be the usual supply of mounds and ruins.

The terms rendered in this passage by "capital" and "palace-city" are respectively *tu-ch'êng* (都 城) and *kung-ch'êng* (宮 城). But by the term *tu-ch'êng* here we are to understand "the district of the capital", what is called in other books "the Śrāvasti country" as distinguished from "the Kosala country". *Kung-ch'êng* here is taken by Julien to mean "the palace", and by Beal to mean "the walls enclosing the royal precincts". But we must take the term in this passage to denote "the walled city of Śrāvasti". That this is its meaning in our text is clear from what follows, and from the corresponding passages in the Life and the Fang-chih, and the description in the Fo-kuo-chi. In these treatises the words *tu*, *tu-ch'êng*, and *ch'êng*, all used in the sense of *capital*, are the equivalents of our pilgrim's *kung-ch'êng*. His usual term for the chief city of a country is *ta-tu-ch'êng*, and he seems to use *tu-ch'êng* here in a peculiar sense. It has been suggested by a learned and intelligent native scholar that the *tu-ch'êng* of this passage denotes the towns and cities of Kosala which were inferior and subordinate to the capital, the *kung-ch'êng*. The *tu-ch'êng* of ancient China were the cities which were the official residences of the subordinate feudal chiefs whose sovereign reigned at the royal capital. According to this interpretation the pilgrim states that the other cities of the country were in such utter de-

---

cient inscribed statue from Srāvasti, by Th. Bloch Ph.D. (J.A.S. Bengal Vol. LXVII. p. 274.)

[1] op. c. p. 527, and J. R. A. S. 1900 Art. I.

solation that their boundaries could not be defined; but the capital, though also in ruins, had old foundations by which its area could be ascertained. But it is perhaps better to take *tu-ch'êng* here as meaning "the Śrāvasti district".

The pilgrim here tells us that Śrāvasti had some hundreds of Buddhist monasteries, very many of which were in ruins. This statement as to the number of Buddhist monasteries in the district is not in agreement with other accounts which represent Śrāvasti as having only two or three Buddhist establishments. It will be noticed that Yuan-chuang mentions by name only one monastery, viz— the great one of the Jetavana. Fa-hsien, however, tells of 98 (in some texts 18) monasteries, all except one occupied, being round the Jetavana vihāra. The translation which our pilgrim gives for the name Prasenajit (in Pali, Pasenadi) is *Shêng-chün* (勝 軍) or "Overcoming army". I-ching, who transcribes the king's name as in the text and also by *P'o-se-ni* (波 斯 匿), gives our pilgrim's translation and another rendering, *shêng-kuang* (勝 光).[1] The latter means "Excelling brightness", and the name is said to have been given to the son born to Brahmadatta king of Kosala on the morning of the birth of the Buddha, on account of the supernatural brightness which then appeared. Another rendering for the name transcribed *P'o-se-ni* is *Ho-yue* (和 悅) which means *cheerful, happy-looking.*[2] The two latter translations seem to require as their original a derivative from *prasad* (the Pali pasidati), and the transcription *P'o-se-ni*, which is the one in general use, seems to point to a dialectic variety like *Pasenid.*

Of the old sites in Śrāvasti of which our pilgrim here tells us, the nunnery, the house of Sudatta, and the place of Añgulimāla's conversion are mentioned by Fa-hsien. But the earlier pilgrim does not seem to have known of

---

1 Sar. Vin. Tsa-shih, *ch.* 20; Rockhill's Life p. 16.

2 Shih-êrh-yu-ching (No. 1374)

or seen the remains of the king's palace or those of the chapel built by the king for the Buddha.

In Julien's translation of the last paragraph in the above account of the ancient sites of Śrāvasti city we have one of his mischievous glosses, which has been, as usual, followed and adopted by others. He translates— "Ce fut en cet endroit qu'[un des sectaires appelés] *Yang-kiu-li-mo-lo* (Añgouli-mālyas), abjura ses erreurs". There is nothing in the text to warrant the words which I have put within square brackets. If Julien had known the story he would not have written thus, nor of "les Añgoulimālyas", and "des scélérats du royaume de Çrāvasti" in the continuation. The pilgrim's narrative tells of only one man who had obtained the ill-sounding nick-name Angulimāla or Finger-garland. As the pilgrim knew the story this man was only a cruel murderer of Śrāvasti who cut off a finger from each person he killed, and strung the fingers into a garland. He also wanted to kill his own mother and the Buddha to secure him rebirth in Heaven.

The story of this terrible murderer is told more fully and with several variations of detail in other books. In some versions of the story the original name of the man was Ahiṃsaka or Innocent, in Chinese *Wu-nao* (無惱) or Inoffensive. He was at first a brahmin student of marvellous bodily and mental powers, and he was the disciple of a celebrated master. This master had a wife fair and frail, and Ahiṃsaka was falsely accused by her of having made an attack on her virtue. Fearing to lay violent hands on the troublesome clever disciple the jealous master thought to get rid of him by a terrible task. So he enjoined on Ahiṃsaka the necessity of attaining to immortality by abstinence from all food for a week, and within that period collecting 1000 fingers from as many human beings, whom he was to slay with a certain sword. The disciple very reluctantly undertook the task, and went about killing people and cutting off a finger from each person he killed, until he had obtained 999 fingers. At this stage his mother having come to him with food he was about to kill her, in order to complete his tale, when the Buddha appeared on the scene. The misguided youth soon yielded to Buddha's power, was converted and ordained, and rapidly attained arhatship.[1] In some of the Buddhist Scriptures Finger-garland is merely a cruel highwayman robbing and murdering, and rendering the roads impassable. The Buddha goes to the district infested by the murderer, and he goes unattended moved by great compassion: he meets with the murderer, calls on him to stay in his evil course and give way to his good karma.[2]

Our pilgrim and Fa-hsien, we have seen, found within Śrāvasti city a memorial of the place where this Finger-garland had been converted, and sanctified, and beatified. But this is against the general testimony of the Buddhist writings. According to these the murders were committed and the sudden conversion effected in the country beyond Śrāvasti[3], or at a place very nearly ten yojanas from that city[4], or in the Angutala country[5], or in the land of Magadha.[6]

The pilgrim proceeding with his description relates as follows—

> "Five or six *li* south of the city is the *She-to* wood (Jetavana) which is the *kei-ku-tu-yuan* (Anāthapiṇḍadārāma) the temple which king Prasenajit's great Minister Sudatta erected for the Buddha: formerly it was a saṅghārāma (monastery), now it is in desolate ruin."

According to Fa-hsien the Jetavana vihāra was 1200 *pu* (paces) outside the south gate of Śrāvasti, on the west side of the road, with a gate opening to the east, that is,

---

[1] M. B. p. 257. Hsien-yü-ching, *ch.* 11, and Der Weise u. d. T. S. 300: Ang-ku-mo-ching (No. 621) where the student has to collect 100 fingers: Tsêng-yi-a-han-ching, *ch.* 31.

[2] Rhys Davids Questions of Milinda in S. B. E. Vol. XXXVI, p. 355: J. P. T. S. for 1888 p. 2: Fo-shuo-Ang-ku-chi-ching (No. 622).

[3] Fo-shuo-ang-ku-chi-ching.

[4] Ang-ku-mo-lo-ching (No. 434).

[5] Tsa-a-han-ching, *ch.* 38 (Ang-ku-to-lo 央瞿多羅).

[6] Pie-yi-tsa-a-han-ching, *ch.* 1.

toward the highway. The 1200 *pu* of this account made above 5000 feet, and so the two pilgrims are in substantial agreement as to the situation of the Jetavana monastery. In other accounts this establishment is represented as being at a convenient distance from the city of Śrāvasti[1], but Nāgārjuna seems to describe it as having been within the city.[2] The term here, as before, rendered "temple" is *ching-shê,* and Yuan-chuang seems to use it in this passage in the sense of "vihāra". This is the sense in which the term is commonly used by the early Chinese Buddhist writers and translators. Thus Fa-hsien calls the great establishment now under notice the *C'hi-huan* (for Jetavana)-*ching-shê.* In our text this term is evidently used as the equivalent of *ārāma,* in the sense of *monastery*, and covers all the buildings of the great establishment.

The name "Sudatta" is translated by our pilgrim *Shan-shih* (善施) or "Well-bestowed" (also interpreted as "Good-giver"), and his *kei-ku-tu* is the old and common rendering for Anāthapiṇḍada. Yuan-chuang here calls Sudatta a "high official" (ta-ch'ên 大臣), and this title is applied to the man by other writers[3], but he was only a seṭṭhi or Householder. He had been engaged in trade, and had enormous wealth; he is said to have been a butcher, but this is probably a late invention.

> At the east gate of the Jetavana monastery were two stone pillars, one on each side of the entrance: these, which were 70 feet high, had been erected by king Asoka; the pillar on the left side was surmounted by a sculptured wheel and that on the right side by an ox.

The statement in this paragraph agrees precisely with Fa-hsien's account of the two pillars. Julien's rendering of it is inexplicable and Beal's is not correct.

---

1 See the She-wei-kuo-Ch'i-huan-ssŭ-t'u-ching (舍衛國祇洹寺圖經); Ssŭ-fên-lü, *ch.* 50; Sêng-ki-lü, *ch.* 23.

2 Fu-kai-chêng-hsing-so-chi-ching, *ch.* 4: Tsêng-yi-a-han-ching, *ch.* 33.

3 e. g. in Hsien-yü-ching, *ch.* 10.

On the site of the Jetavana monastery the pilgrim found only one building standing in solitary loneliness. This building was the brick shrine which contained the image of the Buddha made for king Prasenajit. This image, which was five feet high, was a copy of that made for king Udayana of Kosambī already mentioned.

This shrine was also the only building which Fa-hsien found in the Jetavana, and according to him it was the image in it which came from its pedestal to meet the Buddha on his return from the Trayastriṃśa Heaven, and which was to serve as a model for all future images of the Buddha.

We have next Yuan-chuang's version of the oft-told story how the Jetavana, and the Anāthapiṇḍada ārāma came into the possession of the Buddhists.

The seṭṭhi Sudatta, noted for his munificent charity, wished to build a vihāra for the Buddha whom he invited to visit him at his home in Śrāvasti. Buddha sent Śāriputra as an expert to act as manager in the matter for Sudatta. The only suitable site that could be found near Śrāvasti was the Park of Prince Jeta. When the Elder asked the prince to sell his park the prince said joking— "Yes, for as many gold coins as will cover it". This answer delighted Sudatta, and he at once proceeded to cover the ground with gold coins from his treasury (not as Julien has it, from the *trésor royal*). When all the ground except a small piece was covered the prince "asked Sudatta to desist, saying— "The Buddha truly is an excellent field, it is meet I sow good seed": so on the uncovered ground he erected a temple". Then the Buddha said to Ananda that as the ground of the park had been bought by Sudatta, and the trees had been given by Prince Jeta, the two men having like intentions, their merits should be respected and the place spoken of as "Jeta's trees Anāthapiṇḍada's ārāma".

In Julien's rendering of this passage he makes the pilgrim represent Sudatta as *unable* to cover all the Park with gold, but this is not in the text. Then Julien translates the words *Fo-ch'êng-liang-t'ien* (佛誠良田) by— "C'est, en vérité, l'excellent champ du *Bouddha*", but this is not at all the meaning of the expression. The words state plainly that the Buddha is an "excellent field" or generous soil, and this sort of expression is of very common occurrence in the Buddhist Scriptures. To give alms of food or clothing, or do any service to Buddhas, P'usas, or eminent monks or nuns, was to sow good seed in good ground, the crop to be reaped either in this life or in one to come. Hence the beings to whom such meritorious services are rendered are called "excellent fields", and of these the most "excellent field" always is the Buddha. In the present case the Prince wished to share in the reward which Sudatta would have, and in order to secure this result he remitted a portion of the price for the ground and built a "temple" (*ching-shê*) for the Buddha on the space unoccupied by gold coins. Some other accounts represent Jeta as refusing to sell even for as many gold coins as would cover the park; and when Sudatta claims that the mention of a sum makes a bargain, and Jeta maintains it does not, the Judges to whom the matter is referred decide against the Prince. This last is also represented as contributing a porch or vestibule to Sudatta's vihāra, and in no case is he described as building the whole monastery.[1] The statement which Yuan-chuang here makes the Buddha address to Ananda about the trees having been given by the Prince, and the ground purchased by Sudatta, is a stupid invention to account for the common way of designating the vihāra in Chinese translations. It was not the pilgrim, however, who invented the story, as it is found in other accounts of the transaction.[2]

The original Jetavana monastery, which was probably neither very large nor substantial and was not well protected, was destroyed by fire in the Buddha's lifetime.[3] After the death of Sudatta the place was neglected as there was no one to look after the grounds and buildings. A new vihāra was afterwards built on a greater scale but this also was burnt to the ground. At one time, we read,

---

1 Ssŭ-fên-lü l. c.; Chung-hsü-ching, *ch.* 11 (No. 859).
2 e. g. in Fo-shuo-Po-ching-ch'ao (No. 379).
3 Shih-sung-lü, *ch.* 61.

the place was utterly abandoned by the Buddhist Brethren and was used as the king's stables, but the buildings were again rebuilt and reoccupied by Buddhist monks. In its palmy days, before its final destruction and abandonment, the Jetavana monastery must have been a very large and magnificent establishment. We may believe this without accepting all the rather legendary descriptions of it still extant. Some authorities give the extent of the Park as 80 *ching* or about 130 square acres.[1] Others tell us that the grounds were about ten *li* (or two miles) in length by above 700 *pu* (paces) in with, and that they contained 120 buildings, or even several hundred houses of various kinds.[2] There were chapels for preaching and halls for meditation, messrooms and chambers for the monks, bathhouses, a hospital, libraries and reading-rooms, with pleasant shady tanks, and a great wall encompassing all. The Libraries were richly furnished, not only with orthodox literature but also with Vedic and other non-Buddhistic works, and with treatises on the arts and sciences taught in India at the time. The monastery was also well situated, being conveniently near the city, and yet away from the distracting sights and noises of the streets. Moreover the Park afforded a perfect shade, and was a delightful place for walking in during the heat and glare of the day; it had streams and tanks of clear cool water; it was also free from noxious stinging creatures; and it was a favourite resort of the good and devotional people of all religions. The native beauties and advantages of the place had been greatly improved by its first Buddhist occupants, for the Buddha directed his disciples to plant trees in the grounds and by the roadside. He also caused the grounds to be protected from goats and cattle, and had a supply of water brought in by artificial means.[3]

---

[1] Fo-shuo-Poh-ching-ch'ao.

[2] Shê-wei-kuo-Ch'i-huan-ssŭ-t'u-ching: Shih-êrh-yu-ching (No. 1374 tr. A. D. 392).

[3] Ssŭ-fên-lü, *ch* 50.

Continuing his description Yuan-chuang tells us that at the north-east of the Anāthapiṇḍadārāma was a tope to mark the spot at which the Buddha washed a sick bhikshu. This was a Brother who was suffering pain and living in isolation. The Master seeing him asked him what was his malady and why he was living alone. The Brother replied— I am of an indolent disposition and intolerant of medical treatment, so I am now very ill and have no one to attend on me. Then the Buddha was moved with pity and said to him— Good sir, I am now your medical attendant. Thereupon he stroked the patient with his hand, and all the man's ailments were cured. The Buddha then bore him outside the chamber, changed his bed, washed him and dressed him in clean clothes, and told him to be zealous and energetic. Hearing this the Brother felt grateful and became happy in mind and comfortable in body.

This story is related in several of the Buddhist Scriptures with some variations of detail. According to the Vinaya, and some other authorities, the Buddha and Ānanda one day going the rounds of the Jetavana establishment found a Brother lying in a chamber apart from all the others, and suffering from a troublesome and unpleasant malady. The sick man, who was apparently quite helpless, explained to Buddha that the Brethren left him to himself because he had been useless to them. This means that he had been a selfish lazy man refusing to help others or do his proper share of work. In the Vinaya the incident is made the occasion of the Buddha drawing up rules for the care to be taken of a sick bhikhshu by the Brethren.[1] In one book the Buddha is represented as telling the neglected sick Brother that his present misfortunes were the result of ill conduct in a previous existence.[2] In two treatises the scene of the incident is laid at Rājagaha, and these have other differences of detail.[3]

To the north-west of the ārāma, we are next told, was a small tope which marked the spot at which Maudgala-putra (Maud-

---

[1] Vin. Mah. VIII. 26: Sêng-ki-lü, *ch.* 28. See also the story in Vibhāshā-lun, *ch.* 11 (scene not given).

[2] Fo-shuo-shêng-ching, *ch.* 3 (No. 669 tr. A. D. 285).

[3] Tsêng-yi-a-han-ching, *ch.* 40; P'u-sa-pên-shêng-man-lun, *ch.* 4 (No. 1312 tr. cir. A. D. 970).

galyāyana or Moggallāno) made an ineffectual attempt to raise the girdle (or belt) of Śāriputra against the will of the latter. Once, the pilgrim relates, when the Buddha was at the Anavatapta Lake with a congregation of men and devas he discovered that Śāriputra was absent, and he sent Maudgalaputra through the air to summon him to the meeting. In a trice Maudgalaputra was in the Jetavana Vihāra where he found Śāriputra mending his canonical robes. When the Master's request was communicated to him Śāriputra said he would go as soon as his mending was finished, but Maudgalaputra threatened to carry him off by his supernormal powers. Śāriputra then cast his girdle on the floor and challenged his friend to lift it. Maudgalaputra tried all his magical powers; but although he produced an earthquake he could not move the girdle. So he went back alone through the air to Buddha, and on his arrival found Śāriputra already seated in the congregation. Thereupon Maudgalaputra declared that he had learned from this occurrence that the potency of *ṛiddhi* (possession of supernormal physical powers) was inferior to that of *prajñā* (spiritual intuition or transcendental wisdom).

This little story is told in several Buddhist treatises with considerable additions. In the "Tsêng-yi-a-han-ching"[1] it is the Dragon-king of the Anavatapta Lake who misses Śāriputra from the congregation, and asks Buddha to send for him. Here the legend is given with ridiculous wild exaggerations and, as in Yuan-chuang's version, there is the presence of an unfriendly feeling between the two great disciples. In the "Ta-chih-tu-lun"[2] the Buddha and his arhats are assembled at the Anavatapta Lake for the purpose of hearing jātakas told, and Śāriputra is missed. Maudgalyāyana is sent to bring him, and in order to hasten matters he finishes the mending of Śāriputra's garment by magic, a procedure which suggests to Śāriputra the idea of the trial of prajñā against ṛiddhi. When Maudgalyāyana saw that he could not even lift his friend's girdle from the ground against the owner's will, he knew it was useless to think of taking the man himself by the ear, or the shoulder, through the air to the Anavatapta

[1] *Ch.* 29.

[2] *Ch.* 45.

Lake. The Buddha used this incident, as he used certain other events, to teach the superiority of high spiritual attainments over the possession of great magical powers.

Near the "Raising-the girdle Tope", the pilgrim proceeds, was a well from which water had been drawn for the use of the Buddha. Close to it was an Asoka tope containing a relic of the Buddha, and there were in the vicinity, at places where he took exercise and preached, memorial topes at which there were miraculous manifestations with divine music and frågrance. At a short distance behind the Jetavana monastery was the place at which certain non-Buddhist Brāhmachārins slew a harlot in order to bring reproach on the Buddha. These men, as Yuan-chuang's story goes, hired this harlot to attend the Buddha's discourses and thus become known to all. Then they secretly killed her and buried her body in the Park. Having done this they proceeded to appeal to the king for redress, and he ordered investigation to be made. When the body was discovered at the monastery the heretics exclaimed that the great Śramana Gautama, who was always talking of morality and gentleness, after having had illicit intercourse with the woman had murdered her to prevent her from talking. But thereupon the devas in the air cried out that this was a slander of the heretics.

Fa-hsien and other authorities give the name of the unfortunate harlot of this story as Sundarī. This, it will be remembered, was the name of the fair charmer who once led astray a wise and holy ascetic. The word means *beautiful woman*, and it is rendered in some Chinese translations by *Hao-shou* or "Good-Head".[1] The woman of our story is also called Sundaranandī,[2] which is the name of a nun in the primitive Buddhist church. She is represented as the disciple (and apparently, the mistress) of one of the old non-Buddhist teachers of Kosala (or of another district). Seeing these teachers distressed at the growing preeminence of Gautama Buddha, she suggested to them the expedient here described for ruining Gautama and restoring her master and the other teachers to their former position of influence. But some authorities like Yuan-chuang and Fa-hsien represent the harlot as having

---

1 Fo-shuo-yi-tsu-ching, *ch.* 1 (No. 674).

2 P'u-sa-ch'u-t'ai-ching, *ch.* 7 (No. 433).

been forced by the Brahmins to attend the Buddha's sermons, and afterwards submit to be murdered. According to one account the Buddha had in ages before been an actor, and the woman a harlot at the same time and in the same place: the actor had then killed the harlot for her ornaments, and buried her body at the hermitage of a Pratyeka Buddha.[1] In another old story this Sundarī had been in a former birth a wicked queen, and the Buddha had been the wise and faithful servant of the king her husband.[2]

Continuing his narrative the pilgrim states that above 100 *paces* to the east of the Jetavana monastery was a deep pit through which Devadatta, for having sought to kill the Buddha by poison, went down alive into Hell. Devadatta, the son of *Hu-fan-wang* ("Peck-food-king"), had in the course of twelve years by zealous perseverance acquired the 80,000 compendia of doctrine; and afterwards, for the sake of its material advantages, he had sought to attain supernormal power. He associated with the irreligious (lit. wicked friends) and reasoned with them thus— "I have all the outward signs of the Buddha except two, a great Congregation attends me, and I am as good as the Ju-lai". Putting these thoughts in practice he broke up the Brotherhood (that is, by alluring disciples from the Buddha to himself). But Maudgalyaputra and Śāriputra, under Buddha's instructions and by his power, won the strayed Brethren back. Devadatta, however, kept his evil mind, put poison in his finger-nails with a view to kill Buddha in the act of doing him reverence, and fared as in the story.

The temporary "breaking up" of the Brotherhood instituted by Gautama Buddha by the schism caused by his cousin Devadatta is a famous incident in the history of the primitive Buddhist Church. The story of the schism is narrated in several books at greater or less length and with a few variations of detail.[3] According to some accounts there were 500 weak young Brethren seduced from the Buddha by Devadatta, and after a short time

---

1 Hsing-ch'i-hsing-ching (No. 733).

2 Fo-shuo-Poh-ching-ch'ao.

3 Vin. Chul. VII. 3; Rockhill Life p. 94; Dh. p. 145; Ssŭ-fên-lü, *ch* 46.

brought back again by Śāriputra and Maudgalyāyana. These 500 men then misled by the great schismatic had been his dupes many ages before. In one of their former births they had all been monkeys forming a band of 500 with a chief who was Devadatta in his monkey existence. On the advice of their chief these simple monkeys set themselves to draw the moon out of a well, and were all drowned in the attempt by the breaking of the branch by which they were swinging.[1]

It is worthy of note in connection with Yuan-chuang's description that Fa-hsien did not see any *pit* here. The latter describes the spots at which the wicked woman and Devadatta went down into Hell as having marks of identification given to them by men of subsequent times. The design and attempt to murder the Buddha by poison here described by Yuan-chuang are mentioned also by Fa-hsien, and they are found in the Tibetan texts translated by Mr Rockhill,[2] but they are not in all the accounts of Devadatta's proceedings. The great learning and possession of magical powers here ascribed to Devadatta are mentioned in some of the canonical works, and his claim to be the equal of his cousin in social and religious qualifications is also given.[3] But his abrupt bodily descent into Hell is generally ascribed to other causes than merely the abortive attempt to poison the Buddha.

Our pilgrim here, as we have seen, calls Devadatta's father *Hu-fan-wang* which is a literal rendering of Dronodanarāja. This Droṇodanarāja was a brother of king Suddhodana the father of Gautama Buddha. By a strange slip of the pen Julien makes the pilgrim here describe Devadatta as "le fils du roi *Ho-wang*", and the mistake is of course repeated by others. We are to meet with this troublesome man Devadatta again in the Records.

---

1 Sêng-ki-lü, *ch.* 7.

2 Rockhill Life p. 107.

3 Shih-sung-lü, *ch.* 36; Tsêng-yi-a-han-ching, *ch.* 47; Abhi-ta-vib., *ch.* 116.

To the south of Devadatta's fosse, Yuan-chuang continues, was another pit through which the bhikshu *Ku-ka-li* (Kokālika) having slandered the Buddha went down alive into Hell.

This man Kokālika is better known as a partisan of Devadatta than as an enemy of the Buddha. He was, we learn from other sources, an unscrupulous friend and follower of Devadatta, always praising his master and calling right wrong and wrong right in agreement with him. They had met in a former state of existence when Kokālika was a crow and Devadatta a jackal. The latter had scented the corpse of an unburied eunuch, and had nearly devoured its flesh, when the hungry crow, eager to get bones to pick, praised and flattered the jackal in fulsome lying phrases. To these the latter replied in a similar strain, and their feigning language brought on them a rebuke from a rishi who was the P'usa.[1]

Still farther south above 800 *paces*, the pilgrim proceeds, was a third deep pit or trench. By this *Chan-che*, the Brahmin woman, for having calumniated the Buddha, passed alive into Hell. Yuan-chuang then tells his version of the story of Chan-che whom he calls a disciple of the Non-Buddhists. In order to disgrace and ruin Gautama, and bring her masters into repute and popularity, she fastened a wooden basin under her clothes in front. Then she went to the Jetavana monastery and openly declared that she was with child, illicitly, to the preacher, and that the child in her womb was a Sakya. She was believed by all the heretics; but the orthodox knew she was speaking slander. Then Indra, as a rat, exposed the wicked trick, and the woman went down to "Unremitting Hell" to bear her retribution.

The loyal bad woman of this story, called by the pilgrim "Chan-che the Brahmin woman", is the *Chincha-mānavikā* of the Pali Scriptures[2]. This Pali name may also be the original for the *Chan-che-mo-na* of Fa-hsien and others, another form of transcription of the name being *Chan-che-mo-na-k'i* with *nü*, "woman", added.[3] But we find the original name translated by *Pao-chih* (暴志) or

---

[1] Fo-shuo-shêng-ching, *ch.* 3; Sar. Vin. P'o-sêng-shih, *ch.* 18.
[2] Dh.p. 338; Jat. 3.298; 4.187. Chinchī in Hardy M. B. p. 284.
[3] P'u-sa-ch'ü-t'ai-ching, *ch.* 7.

"Fierce-minded", that is, Chaṇḍamanā, which was apparently the early form of the name.[1] In a Chinese translation of a Buddhist work the woman is designated simply the "Many-tongued Woman".[2] According to one authority she was a disciple of the Tirthika teacher Keśakambala, and it was at the instigation of this teacher that she pretended to be with child to the Buddha in the manner here described. Another version of the story, and perhaps the earliest one, makes Chan-che (or Chaṇḍā) a Buddhist nun led astray by evil influences. When her trick with the basin is discovered she is sentenced to be buried alive, but the Buddha intercedes for her, and she is only banished. Then the Buddha gives a very satisfactory explanation of the woman's conduct. She had come in contact with him long ago in his existence as a dealer in pearls, and he had then incurred her resentment. They had also met in another stage of their previous lives when the P'usa was a monkey, and *Chanche* was the relentless wife of the Turtle (or the Crocodile) and wanted to eat the monkey's liver. So her desire to inflict injury on the Buddha was a survival from a very old enmity.[3] The Pali accounts and Fa-hsien agree with Yuan-chuang in representing Chan-che as going down alive into Hell, but, as has been stated, Fa-hsien differs from Yuan-chuang in not making mention of the pit by which she was said to have passed down.[4]

The narrative next tells us that 60 or 70 *paces* to the east of the Jetavana Monastery was a temple (*ching-shê*) above sixty feet high which contained a sitting image of the Buddha with his face to the east. At this place the Julai had held discussion with the Tirthikas (*wai-tao*). To the east of this *ching-shê* was a Deva-Temple of the same dimensions which was shut out from the western sun in the evening by the Buddhist temple, while

---

[1] Fo-shuo-shêng-ching, *ch.* 1 (Here *Chan-che* is a nun).

[2] Hsing-ch'i-hsing-ching, *ch.* 1.

[3] Fo-shuo-shêng-ching, *ch.* 1: Jātaka (tr. Chalmers) Vol. I. p. 142.

[4] In some of the books e. g. in the Ch'ü-t'ai-ching and the Fo-shuo-shêng-ching the woman does not undergo any punishment; in the former treatise moreover the occurrence takes place at Vesāli.

the latter in the morning was not deprived of the rays of the sun by the Deva-Temple.

Fa-hsien also saw these two temples, and he has given a similar account of them. But he applies the name *Ying-fu* (影 覆) or "Shadow Cover" to the Deva-temple while Yuan-chuang gives it to the Buddha-temple: in the former case the term means *Overshadowed* and in the latter it means *Overshadowing*.

Three or four *li* east from the Overshadowing Temple, Yuan-chuang continues, was a tope at the place where Sāriputta had discussed with the Tīrthikas. When Sāriputta came to Śrāvasti to help Sudatta in founding his monastery the six non-Buddhist teachers challenged him to a contest as to magical powers and Sāriputta excelled his competitors.

The contest of this passage took place while Sāriputta was at Śrāvasti assisting Sudatta in the construction of the great monastery. But the competition was not with the "six great teachers": it was with the chiefs of the local sects, who wished to have the young and successful rival in religion excluded from the district. In our passage it will be noted that the pilgrim writes of Sāriputta discussing with the non-Buddhists, and this seems to be explained as meaning that he fought them on the point of magical powers. This is in agreement with the story as told in some of the Buddhist books. All the leading opponents of the Buddha were invited to meet Sāriputta at an open discussion: they came and when all were seated the spokesman of the Brahmins, Red-eye by name, was invited to state the subject of discussion.[1] He thereupon intimated that he wished to compete with Sāriputta in the exhibition of magical powers: this was allowed and the result was that Sāriputta came off conqueror.

Beside the Śāriputra Tope was a temple (*ching-she*) in front of which was a tope to the Buddha. It was here that the Buddha

[1] Chung-hsü-ching, *ch.* 12; Rockhill Life p. 48. This tope to Śāriputra is not mentioned by Fa-hsien; it is perhaps the tope to Śāriputra in the Jetavana pointed out to Asoka in the Divyāv. p. 394; A-yü-wang-chuan, *ch.* 2.

worsted his religious opponents in argument, and received Mother Visākhā's invitation.

The spot at which the Buddha silenced his proud and learned opponents at Śrāvasti was supposed to have been marked by a special tope. This was one of the Eight Great Topes, already referred to, associated with the Buddha's career. We cannot regard the tope of this paragraph, or the temple of a previous passage, as the celebrated Great Tope of Śrāvasti.[1]

Of the lady here called "Mother Visākhā" we have to make mention presently. The *invitation* or request here mentioned was probably connected with the Hall she made for the Buddha and his disciples.[2]

To the south of the Accepting-invitation Tope, the pilgrim proceeds, was the place at which king Virūḍhaka, on his way to destroy the Sakyas, saw the Buddha, and turned back with his army. When Virūḍhaka ascended the throne, Yuan-chuang relates, he raised a great army and set out on the march [from Śrāvasti to Kapilavastu] to avenge a former insult. A bhikshu reported the circumstance to the Buddha; who thereupon left Śrāvasti, and took his seat under a dead tree by the roadside. When the king came up he recognized Buddha, dismounted, and paid him lowly reverence. He then asked the Buddha why he did not go for shade to a tree with leaves and branches. "My clan are my branches and leaves", replied Buddha, "and as they are in danger what shelter can I have?" The king said to himself— "The Lord is taking the side of his relatives — let me return". So he looked on Buddha moved with compassion, and called his army home.

Near this place, the pilgrim goes on, was a tope to mark the spot at which 500 Sakya maidens were dismembered by this same king's orders. When Virūḍhaka had taken his revenge on the Sakyas he selected 500 of their maidens for his harem. But

---

1 Dr. Hoey proposes to identify the *ching-shê* with its tope of this passage with "the ruins named Baghaha Bári" near Sahet Mahet, and he thinks that this may be the site of "Viśákha's Pūrvaráma". But this is quite impossible, and the pilgrim does not note, as Dr. Hoey says he does, that the *ching-shê* was "in strict dependence on the Saṅghārāma (of the Jetavana)", op. c. p. 38.

2 Or the request which the Buddha accepted may have been Mother Visākhā's petition to be allowed to present robes to the Brethren.

these young ladies were haughty, and refused to go, "abusing the king as the son of a slave" (*li-ch'i-wang-chia-jen-chih-tzŭ* 詈其王家人之子). When the king learned what they had done, he was wroth, and ordered that them aidens should be killed by mutilation. So their hands and feet were cut off, and their bodies were thrown into a pit. While the maidens were in the agonies of dying they called on the Buddha, and he heard them. Telling his disciples to bring garments (that is, for the naked maidens) he went to the place of execution. Here he preached to the dying girls on the mysteries of his religion, on the binding action of the five desires, the three ways of transmigration, the separation from the loved, and the long course of births and deaths. The maidens were purified and enlightened by the Buddha's teaching, and they all died at the same time and were reborn in Heaven. Indra in the guise of a Brahmin had their bodies and members collected and cremated, and men afterwards erected the tope at the place.

Not far from this tope, the pilgrim tells us, was a large dried-up pond, the scene of Virūḍhaka's extinction. The Buddha had predicted that at the end of seven days from the time of the prophecy the king would perish by fire. When it came to the seventh day the king made up a pleasure party by water and remained in his barge with the ladies of his harem on the water in order to escape the predicted fate. But his precautions were in vain, and on that day a fierce fire broke out on his barge, and the king went alive through blazes into the Hell of unintermitting torture.

We are to meet with this king Virūḍhaka again presently in connection with his sack of Kapilavastu. Fa-hsien, without mentioning the dead tree, makes the place at which the Buddha waited for Virūḍhaka to have been four *li* to the south-east of Śrāvasti city and he says there was a tope at the spot. In Buddha's reply to the king about his kindred being branches and leaves there was probably in the original a pun on the words śākkhā, *a branch*, and Śākya. By the answer of the Buddha the king knew that he was speaking from an affectionate interest in his relatives, and the king was accordingly moved to recall his army. The Buddha repeated the interview with the king twice and then left the Sākyas to the consequences of their karma.

The number of Sākya maidens carried off by Virūḍhaka

is reduced to six in the Vibhāshā-lun[1], but some other treatises have the 500 of our text.[2] In one treatise the number of the maidens is raised to 12 000, and they are all made whole by Buddha, and become bhikshuṇīs.[3]

The Chinese words here rendered "abusing the king as a son of a slave" are translated by Julien— "accablèrent d'injures les fils de la famille royale". But this cannot be accepted; and the meaning seems clearly to be that the young ladies called their king insultingly "son of a slave", that is, of a slave mother. Virūḍhaka's mother, we know, had actually been a household slave, but "son of a female slave" seems to have been among the Sakyas a favourite term of abuse for the king of Kosala.

By the "three ways of transmigration" of Buddha's address to the maidens the pilgrim probably meant us to understand the way of pain, the way of perplexity, and the way of moral action. These three "ways" are the agents which by their constant interaction produce the ceaseless revolutions of life and death.[4] But the term *san-t'u* (or its equivalent *san-tao*) is also used by the Buddhists in several other senses.

Continuing his narrative the pilgrim relates that three or four *li* to the north-west of the Jetavana Vihāra was the "Wood of obtained eyes (*Tê-yen-lin* 得眼林) in which were traces of an exercise-place of the Buddha, and scenes of arhats' samādhi, all marked by memorial topes. The story was that once 500 brigands had harried this country. When these criminals were arrested king Prasenajit caused their eyes to be torn out, and the men to be abandoned in a deep wood. Here they cried in their sufferings on the Buddha who, in the Jetavana monastery, heard their cry, and was moved with pity. A genial breeze blew healing from the Snow-Mountains, and the men regained eyes and sight. When they saw the Buddha before them they became converted, paid joyful homage to the Buddha, and went away leaving their sticks which took root.

---

[1] *Ch.* 11.

[2] Tsêng-yi-a-han-ching, *ch.* 26; Sar. Vin. Tsa-shih, *ch.* 9; Rockhill Life p. 121.

[3] Ta-pan-nie-p'an-ching, *ch.* 14 (No. 114).

[4] Ta-ming-san-tsang-fa-shu, *ch.* 12 (No. 1621).

Fa-hsien, who also places the "Wood of obtained eyes" four *li* to the north-west of the Jetavana Vihāra, does not know of brigands, and the 500 who receive their sight and plant their sticks were blind men resident at the monastery. Julien suggests "Āptanetravana" as possibly the Sanskrit original for "Wood of obtained eyes", but we know that the name was Andhavana. This means the *dark* or *blind wood*, and it was translated by *An-lin* (闇林) with the same meaning, or by *Chou*(晝)-*an-lin*, the "Wood of day-darkness". "Obtained Eyes" and "Opened Eyes" (*k'ai-yen*) are names which must have been given long after the Buddha's time, and it is possible that they exist only in translations. The Andhavana, as we learn from the pilgrims and the Buddhist scriptures, was a favourite resort of the Buddhist Brethren for meditation and other spiritual exercises. Here the early bhikshus and bhikshunīs spent a large portion of their time in the afternoons sitting under the trees on the mats which they had carried on their shoulders for the purpose. The Wood was very cool and quiet, impervious to the sun's rays, and free from mosquitoes and other stinging torments.[1]

Before we pass on to the next city in our pilgrim's narrative we may notice some of the more important omissions from his list of the interesting sights of the Srāvasti district. There were two mountains in this district, one called the *T'a-shan* or Pagoda Hill, that is perhaps, Chaityagiri, and the other called the *Sa* (in some texts P'o)-*lo-lo* or Salar (?) mountain, and of neither of these have we any mention.[2] Some of the serious Brethren in the early church resorted to these mountains, and lived on them for several months. Then our pilgrim does not notice the *A-chi-lo* (阿脂 (or 耆) 羅) or Aciravatī River

[1] See Sêng-ki-lü, *ch.* 9; Tsêng-yi-a-han-ching, *ch.* 33; Vibhāshā-lun, *ch.* 13; Sam. Nik. Vol. I. p. 128, 135 (P. T. S.). In the Sêng-ki-lü (*ch.* 29) we find the rendering "opening eyes wood", and so in other places.

[2] Sêng-ki-lü, *ch.* 32 (*T'a-shan*); Chung-a-han-ching, *ch.* 8 (*So* or *P'o -lo-lo shan*).

which flowed south-eastwards past the Śrāvasti city: nor does he mention the Sundara (or *Sun-t'ê-li*) or Sundarīkā River.[1] We read in other books also of the "Pond of Dismemberment", and this is not mentioned by the pilgrim. It was the basin of water near which the Sakya maidens were mutilated and left to perish. This is apparently the *Pu-to-li*, the "celebrated water of Śrāvasti", also called Patali and Paṭala. The Tibetan translators apparently had Pātali which they reproduce literally by "red-coloured". But the original was perhaps Pātala which is the name of a Hell, and it will be remembered that Yuan-chuang places the pond or lake through which Virūḍhaka went down into Hell close to the spot at which the maidens were mutilated. Then the lake is said to have received a name from this dismemberment. In the Avadāna Kalpalatā it is called the Hastagarbha or "Hand-containing" Lake, and this is apparently the meaning of the Tibetan name which Rockhill seems to translate "the pool of the severed hand".[2] Then that one of the Eight Great Topes of the Buddha which was at Śrāvasti is not mentioned, unless we are to regard it as the tope at Buddha's shrine already noticed. But the strangest and most unaccountable omission is that of the Pūrvārāma or East monastery. This great and famous establishment was erected by Visākhā known in religion as "Mrigāra's Mother". She was actually the daughter-in-law of Mrigāra; but after she converted that man, and made him a devout Buddhist, she was called his mother. In Pali her monastery is called Pubbārāma Migāramātu Pāsāda, that is, the East Monastery the Palace of Migāra's mother. This name is translated literally into Chinese, but the translators also render Migāramātu by *Lu-mu* or "Deer-mother", and Migāra is "Deer-son". This monastery which was

---

[1] Sêng-ki-lü, *ch.* 15 et al. (*A-chi-fo* river); Chung-a-han-ching, *ch.* 29; Tsêng-yi-a-han-ching, *ch.* 6; Tsa-a-han-ching, *ch.* 47; Sam. Nik. Vol. I. p. 167; Fa-chü-pi-yü-ching, *ch.* 1.

[2] Sêng-ki-lü, *ch.* 3; Shih-sung-lü, *ch.* 46; Rockhill Life p. 121.

second only to the Jetavana Vihāra was in a disused royal park. There were buildings at it for the residence of the bhikshus and bhikshuṇīs, and there were quiet halls for meditation and for religious discourse. Fa-hsien makes mention of this famous establishment and places its site six or seven *li* to the north-east of the Jetavana Vihāra. This agrees with references to the monastery in other books which place it to the east (or in the east part) of the city, and not far from the Jetavana.[1]

> Above sixty *li* to the north-west of Śrāvasti, the pilgrim narrates, was an old city, the home of Kāśyapa the previous Buddha. To the south of this old city was a tope where this Buddha after attaining bodhi met his father, and to the north of the city was a tope with his bodily relics: these two topes had been erected by king Asoka.

Fa-hsien, who places Kāśyapa Buddha's natal city 50 *li* to the west of Śrāvasti, calls the city *Tu-wei* (都維). These characters probably represent a sound like Topi, and the city is perhaps that called *Tu-yi* in a Vinaya treatise.[2] Fa-hsien also mentions topes at the places where Kāśyapa Buddha met his father, where he died, and where his body was preserved, but he does not ascribe any of these topes to Asoka. Hardy's authority makes Benares to have been the city of this Buddha and this agrees with several sūtras in Chinese translations. In a Vinaya treatise Benares is the city, and the king *Ki-li-ki* (吉栗枳) erects a grand tope at the place of Kassapa Buddha's cremation.[3]

---

[1] M. B. p. 233; Angut. Nik. Vol. III. p. 344 (P. T. S.); Tsa-a-han-ching, *ch.* 36; Chung-a-han-ching, *ch.* 29; Ta-chih-tu-lun, *ch.* 3. The term Pūrvārāma (or Pubbārāma) is sometimes interpreted as meaning "what was formerly an ārāma", or "a former ārāma", but this does not seem so suitable as "East ārāma". In the Sar. Vin. Tsa-shih, *ch.* 11, I-ching has Lu-tzŭ-mu-chiu-yuan (鹿子母蕉園) or "the old ārāma of Migaramāta".

[2] *Tu-yi* (都夷) is called a *chü-lao* of the Śrāvasti country in Sêng-ki-lü, *ch.* 23.

[3] M. B. p. 99: Ch'i-Fo-fu-mu-hsing-tzŭ-ching (No. 626); Fo-shuo-ch'i-Fo-ching (No. 860); Fo-shuo-Fo-ming-ching, *ch.* 9 (No. 404) where the name of the city *chih-shih* (知使) is said to be an old name

There were some other places of interest to Buddhists which are described in Buddhist books as being in this Kosala country. One of these was the *Ka-li-lo* (迦利囉) Hall which was at a large *cave* not far from the capital.[1] This transcription is perhaps for Kaṭīra which means a *cave*, and may have been the name of a hill; or it may be for Kareru, a place often mentioned in the Pali books. It was in the Kalilo Hall that the Buddha delivered the very interesting cosmological sūtra entitled "Ch'i-shih-yin-pên-ching". Then near the capital was the *So-lo-lo* (娑羅邏), that is, Sālāra hill, with steep sides, in the caves of which Aniruddha and some hundreds of other bhikshus lodged.[2] Farther away and about three yojanas from Śrāvasti was the Śākya village called *Lu-t'ang* (鹿堂) or Deer-Hall. Here the Buddha had an establishment in which he lodged and preached, and in which he was visited by the king of Kosala.[3]

---

for Benares: Sar. Vin. Tsa-shih, *ch.* 25, where *Ki-li-ki* king of Benares erects a grand tope to this Buddha.

[1] Ch'i-shih-yin-pên-ching (No. 549).

[2] Chung-a-han-ching, *ch.* 19.

[3] Tsêng-yi-a-han-ching, *ch.* 32.